THE MANNER OF MAN THAT KILLS

THE HISTORICAL FOUNDATIONS OF FORENSIC PSYCHIATRY AND PSYCHOLOGY

A DACAPO PRESS REPRINT SERIES

THE MANNER OF MAN THAT KILLS

BY
L. VERNON BRIGGS

DA CAPO PRESS • NEW YORK • 1983

Library of Congress Cataloging in Publication Data
Briggs, L. Vernon (Lloyd Vernon), 1863–1941.
The manner of man that kills.

(The Historical foundations of forensic psychiatry and psychology)
Repinrt. Originally published: Boston: R. G. Badger, Gorham Press, c1921.
Includes index.
1. Spencer, Bertram Gager, 1881–1912. 2. Czolgosz, Leon F., 1873?–1901. 3. Richeson, Clarence Virgil Thompson, 1876–1912. 4. Criminal psychology. 5. Murder–United States. I. Title. II. Series.
HV6112.B7 1983 364.1′523′0922 [B] 82-072287
ISBN 0-306-76182-3

This Da Capo Press reprint edition of *The Manner of Man That Kills* is an unabridged republication of the edition published in Boston in 1921.

Published by Da Capo Press, Inc.
A Subsidiary of Plenum Publishing Corporation
233 Spring Street, New York, N.Y. 10013

Manufactured in the United States of America

BERTRAM G. SPENCER

Springfield's mysterious burglar in 1910, aged 28, the year he shot Miss Blackstone.

THE MANNER OF MAN THAT KILLS

Spencer—Czolgosz—Richeson

BY

L. VERNON BRIGGS, M.D.

Director of the Massachusetts Society for Mental Hygiene, Member of the American Institute of Criminal Law and Criminology, Société Medico-Psychologique of Paris, France; New England Society of Psychiatry, American Medico-Psychological Association

BOSTON

RICHARD G. BADGER

THE GORHAM PRESS

Made in the United States of America

The Gorham Press, Boston, U. S. A.

TO

JUDGE JOHN Z. LOWE
for his inspiration and legal counsel

DOUGLAS A. THOM, M.D.
for his valuable suggestions
and

HELEN B. HOPKINS
for her research work

in its preparation
I dedicate this volume
as a mark of my
appreciation and esteem

INTRODUCTION

The time has come when we must more seriously consider means for the prevention of mental disease and of such crime as is a product of the brain incapable of normal functioning. Our Governor, Channing H. Cox, in his Inaugural Address in January, 1921, said:

"Last year Massachusetts expended $11,887,108 for the maintenance and improvement of the institutions conducted by the Departments of Mental Diseases, Corrections, Public Welfare and Public Health. This represents a large proportion of our public expenditures. Massachusetts has been a pioneer in the work of caring for the unfortunate and the afflicted and is today doing much in this direction which has not been attempted by other States. The policy in this regard has met with the general approval of our citizens and they insist not only upon a continuance of this work but that the work be better done. Our citizens must recognize the immense cost of it all and they must be prepared to pay for it. They must remember that some of this work has been made necessary because individuals are not doing things for afflicted members of their own families which they did in former generations, and because parents are not exercising the same degree of control and correction of their own children that they did in earlier times. Our only hope of remedy from this constantly increasing public expense lies in finding measures of preventing diseases of the mind and the body and preventing the degradation of morals. We are now trying some preventive measures that have done a great deal in checking the spread of tuberculosis and preventing the spread of other diseases. I recommend appropriations for further research in the endeavor to check the increase of the feeble-minded and to reduce, if possible, the number who are sent to correctional institutions."

Hon. B. Loring Young, now Speaker of the Massachusetts House of Representatives, in addressing the General Court at its opening, in 1921, stated that support of the institutions for the insane and feeble-minded would cost this year $8,400,000; payments for the Department of Public Welfare will cost $4,500,000; for Department of Health $1,500,000, and Department of Corrections $1,400,000; making a total of approximately $16,000,000, or 40% of our total expenditures.

"For the care of the defective, dependent and delinquent classes," he said, "the enormous expenditures which Massachusetts now makes, 40% of our total, should make us eager to find remedies for the distressing social conditions which these necessary expenditures prove to exist. We might well consider what measures of preventive health and social work would lessen this ever-growing burden for future generations."

I feel that all communities must support such a far-sighted policy as that expressed by Governor Cox and Mr. Young for the prevention of mental disease and crime. We are not today using the knowledge we possess, or the means we have at our command to stop the swelling of this stream of defectiveness and mental illness. With the exception of the important work that is being done by our out-patient departments or dispensaries, what are we doing to prevent the increase in the number of our mentally sick, with the consequent suffering and expense, not to speak of the loss to our community of their intelligence? Why are not more individuals saved? What are we doing to prevent crime which is so rampant now in our midst, resulting in the loss of lives and property and the increase of our dependents? It is to bring the above conditions to the attention of the public, it is to make communities realize that crimes, including murder, may often be prevented if the people are once awakened, that I have written the history of three crimes which might have been prevented, crimes which were inexcusable and a disgrace to our country. Society here punished the person it created. The original fault was the fault of society. Society, upon whom rests the responsibility, should be arraigned at the bar of Justice and put on trial and convicted instead of its product.

There is no excuse for any community not taking measures to recognize mental disease during its earliest manifestations. We should recognize the defectives not only in the schools but earlier, and then apply the remedy and not cease diligently to use all scientific means to cure mental illness before the disease becomes chronic, and so to direct and train the mind of the defective that at least he will become if not a useful, then a harmless member of society. In either case we must protect these individuals and the community from any harm consequent on their defectiveness or disease by directing their lives, if necessary, in hospitals or in schools.

Glueck says: "The management of the social problems created and kept alive by this huge army of failures in the business of living imposes a staggering burden upon the nation. It is an army responsible for more misery and sorrow than is even a world war, for death and bereavement are preferable to the lives that many of these unfortunates are obliged to live, and it carries with it a very serious menace to the future of the human race. . . . Education has something to do with preparation for life, and upon a personal conviction gained after a great deal of experience in the management and treatment of human failures, that no educator can successfully fulfill this important phase of his task unless he is concerned with the total individual, with his reactions as a social being, called upon to adjust and adapt continuously to the demands of life, and not merely with his receptacles of information."

Invariably an early study of the personality of these individuals will reveal certain character traits such as jealousy, cruelty, suspicion, egotism, negative self feelings, false pride, etc., which unless recognized and corrected while their minds are still plastic will eventually lead to paths which will prevent them from making the proper adaptation to their environment, the results being crime, pauperism, mental and physical disease.

On the other hand if these same instinctive forces be guided and directed and perhaps the environmental factors altered, and mental and physical occupation selected to suit each case, an avenue would be established which would take that individual out of chaos into a useful and happy life.

They cannot compete with normal people either socially or economically and they are knocked from pillar to post and often shut up without any intelligent effort being made to direct their energies. They are punished in their homes, in the schools and in prisons because they are incapable of adjusting themselves to that which is unsuited to them.

Some have undoubtedly been born without any sense of moral responsibility in their make-up, and a very large number have been warped by environment. Is it right to punish these individuals? It may be necessary to give them custodial care but our responsibility does not end there. To be sure, we should thus protect the public; but in making a man do a certain stunt or piece of work daily in an institution, we make him into a producing machine, we may not have done anything for him individually. Surely, in this enlightened age, these handicapped individuals are entitled to as much of our time and effort as is necessary to develop their capacities to the highest possible degree.

A plan for the defectives should, I believe, eventually be carried out along the following lines:

A building, or number of buildings, should be erected where this group may be individually studied according to their various medical, educational or re-educational requirements. It should not have any title suggesting hospital or custodial treatment, but might be called a school or training school. It should, however, be under expert medical supervision. The organization should also include one or more psychological and vocational experts and social workers, and a pathologist. There should be well equipped laboratories, a department where the three R's, ethics and hygiene would be taught, with classes for languages, music, etc.; departments of trades, craftsmanship and domestic arts, where instruction might be given in carpentry, cabinet work, carving, masonry, brickmaking, tile and cement work, plumbing, electrical work, shoemaking, tailoring, printing, farming, dressmaking, cooking, canning, preserving, laundry work, etc.; a department of occupational therapy, where a certain small group, incapable of continuous effort in any one direction, should be employed in various handicrafts, according to their therapeutic needs, such as basketry, weaving, lace-making, rug braiding and hooking, pottery, etc.

A school of this kind should be able to graduate into the community a number of its pupils each year, who should then be under the supervision of the social worker. There will be many who might never graduate, but every one of these defectives, however anti-social, should be given an opportunity to prepare himself to go out into the world and make good. It is by such methods together with the supervision he exercises over the patients who leave his school that Dr. Walter E. Fernald develops hundreds of feeble-minded individuals to safely take their places among normal people and guides them in the life he has found suitable for them in the community. Ninety-three of his former patients earned over $102,000 in 1920, and sixty-three served with honor in the World War; of these two were killed and several wounded.

A great assistance in the preventive work, especially in the early discovery of defectiveness, are and will be the laboratories and the consultations with specialists in the training schools. The laboratories will first scientifically examine the body at large, note the stigmata, and the variations in the relative size of the organs, look for syphilis, tuberculosis, and especially congenital syphilis, which often can be shown by an x-ray of the bones when other tests are negative. A study of the glands and their secretions is a most fertile field. Careful bacteriological and serological examinations should be made, and psychometric and psychonosological examinations and psychological studies, including studies of the emotion and will.

Every State should provide special units for the care and treatment, both educational and medical, of this so-called "defective delinquent" group. Their crimes and the burden of their support handicap our civilization whereas none need be harmful and many might be useful.

There are a great many who, in the light of present knowledge, may never be able to take any place in the community, but this does not mean that there is not perhaps a larger group who are capable of good work, showing marked ability in one direction or another, though this ability is sometimes misapplied.

To illustrate the deplorable results of neglect by society of mentally ill and defective individuals, I have written the life history of three cases where failure to appreciate the seriousness of their mental condition resulted in the death of six persons and involved untold suffering. In any of these three men, defectiveness or mental disease could easily have been recognized early in their lives. Their condition was actually recognized long before their crimes were committed, but when recognized nothing was done to help them owing to the neglect of society and to the short-sighted policies of our government as at present organized and administered.

Had our medical universities properly educated the physicians who saw these men; had our government, state and local, provided and carried out a systematic and fairly frequent examination of the school children in the several cities and towns; had they organized and carried on mental dispensaries and clinics conducted by highly trained specialists which were within the reach of every physician and in connection with clinics of other branches of medicine, and, lastly, had psychopathic hospitals been established for the earliest or acute cases of mental disease and schools for the education and training of defectives, the lives of these three men would probably have been saved, some use made of the faculties with which God had endowed them, and their three victims might still be living.

Again look at this question from a scientific point of view. What efforts tending to prevention are the scientists making with these cases? When we find a germ that kills people we do not annihilate it so that it is impossible to learn more about it. No, we put it under glass, nurse and study it under different conditions, find out its characteristics, its source and how it develops, so that we may be able to combat other germs of the same kind and render them at least harmless.

There is a question whether with a scientific examination into the minds, natures, environments and development of men who commit crimes of violence we should not find the cause and a means of prevention. At present our knowledge of their impulses is usually based on evidence in court and the statements of these individuals themselves. We know now that their minds are often of such a calibre that the fear of punishment does not deter them. With minds so primitive that they do not understand or fear death, or so diseased that they do not appreciate the consequences of their acts, these people go on unmolested until often they commit some deed which is followed by disaster and suffering. The fear of death did not deter men who were bent upon stealing sheep when they were hanged for it. Many and many other examples could we cite. Did the fear of death ever deter a person who was capable of becoming, as the expression goes, "blind with rage" from violence, or does a person who plots for revenge, which he believes he is entitled to, stop because of consequences, stop because of law? No, and no more does the regicide hesitate to give up his life to some great, though imaginary, cause which often results in the death of his victim. Would any person of low mental calibre, carried away by sufficiently strong emotion, be deterred by law from committing crime?

Does not this all tend to prove that we have not the remedy in law? I believe we have it in scientific study and investigation, in psychopathic hospitals and dispensaries properly supported by government and community, both financially and morally, and by proper rules and regulations of society which will protect the community.

The alleged excuse for law is that it will act as a deterrent. It does not so act with the classes we have under discussion. It did not so act with these three individuals whose histories I have written. Therefore, we must apply medical science. We must not wait for the law with its inexact science to act. We must take these individuals long before they get into the grasp of the courts. We must begin with them when they are children. We must watch over them, study them, change their environment, if necessary, guide and instruct them, and thus protect them and the community.

The real offender is society and not the children in the form of men, nor the mentally diseased. Due to the lack of proper laws or rules protecting people of this kind, the opportunity was afforded to commit these crimes. If society took enough interest to enforce proper regulations, these people would have been under intelligent supervision and, if need be, confinement. Medical colleges and Universities teaching medicine should make compulsory a course in psychiatry and neurology.

Miss Blackstone was shot by Bertram G. Spencer, a young man whom all the alienists who examined him pronounced a defective, a defective from birth, whose earlier life had demonstrated that he was not a safe individual to live unguided in the community, but he was allowed to go on in his wild career until in a crucial moment he lost control of himself and by an impulsive act destroyed the life of a useful member of society.

President McKinley was killed by a diseased man, a man who had been suffering from some form of mental disease for years. He was not medically responsible and in the light of present-day psychiatry and of modern surgical procedure, there is a great question whether he was even legally responsible for the death of our President.

Clarence V. T. Richeson was, I think, the only man ever executed in Massachusetts without a trial. He was a victim of hysteria with delusions, hallucinations, amnesic periods and delirium. He had exhibited signs and had had attacks of this disease for years, had been recognized as mentally unsound by several physicians who advised specialists in mental diseases to attend him. Still, he was allowed to "carry on" until his acts resulted in the death of a young girl of this State.

After making an earnest effort to obtain the results of the histological examinations of the brains of Spencer and Richeson which the late scientist Dr. E. E. Southard said he had been permitted to make and having failed one cannot help interpreting the secrecy regarding these results as indicating a possibility that the opinion of those who felt one or both of these condemned men were of unsound mind was substantiated by the microscopical examination of these brains after death. It is regrettable that such valuable information as would result from a careful microscopic examination of the brains in question should be withheld by the Medical Examiner even a day, information which might prove of inestimable aid to the medical profession for whose perusal and reference this book is written and many of whom have to do with similar cases.

The public who are really responsible for the death of these men should also be informed what the final analysis revealed, that they may know if these executions were justified and be better prepared to pass judgment on future occasions.

I would suggest that several new laws be enacted which will again advance Massachusetts another step beyond her sister States in the care of mental disease and defect. First, that Massachusetts shall grant licenses to practice medicine only to applicants who have complied with all existing requirements and in addition shall have passed an examination in psychiatry. Now that Harvard Medical School has a Chair of Psychiatry there is no excuse for her graduates not being prepared in this important branch of medicine. Other universities teaching medicine and medical colleges recognized by the Mass. State Board of Registration in Medicine must make compulsory a course in psychiatry if their graduates intend practicing in Massachusetts.

I would further suggest a law which will compel physicians in Massachusetts to report to the Department of Mental Diseases in accordance with rules and regulations to be prescribed by the said Department every known or doubtful case of mental defect or dangerous form of mental disease within twenty-four hours after becoming cognizant thereof, and that these reports should be kept on file at the said Department but shall not be open for public inspection. If after receiving the report of any particular case the Department of Mental Diseases believes that the said case is not receiving proper care and treatment, it may make such recommendations to the attending physician or other persons in interest as the welfare and safety of the person afflicted and of the public may require. Any physician who neglects or refuses to comply with the provisions of this act, or who violates any rule or regulation of the Department of Mental Diseases made under authority hereof, shall forfeit a sum not exceeding fifty dollars for each offence.

Again I would suggest that a law be passed which would abolish the distinction between medical and legal insanity in chronic cases, if not in all cases, and at the same time prevent the deplorable condition which now exists whereby the mentally defective and diseased are returned to our prisons again and again. The law I would suggest is as follows: Whenever a person is indicted by a grand jury or bound over for trial in the Superior Court who has previously been convicted of crime or who has previously been indicted, the clerk of the court in which the indictment is returned or the clerk of the district court or the trial justice, as the case may be, shall give notice to the Department of Mental Diseases and the Department shall cause such person to be examined with a view to determining his mental condition and the existence of any mental disease or defect. The Department shall file a report of its investigation with the clerk of the court in which the trial is to be held and the same shall be presented to the court or jury as evidence of the mental condition of the accused. This would in no way interfere with the rights of the individual to employ experts but it would tend to settle all questions so far as the State is concerned and prevent the deplorable condition which now exists in so many cases when our medical men are apparently pitted against each other and are held up to ridicule.

I believe that such a law, with its results, would soon discourage the plea of insanity in all cases found sane and responsible by a Department of Mental Disease, and that juries would invariably accept as final the report of such a Department who would be unbiased, unpaid by either side and whose experience is worthy of serious consideration. This would also leave the responsibility of a medical case with medical men. Is there a judge or attorney within this Commonwealth who would take a member of his family with two disagreeing physicians to a jury of laymen to make a correct diagnosis of the mental disease or defect from which he or she was suffering or to determine the extent of the disease? Still that is what the juries of this Commonwealth are determining every day. No more would a judge or an attorney go to a body of medical men to determine the intricacies of law. The law completely disregards medical opinion, still it asks physicians to pass upon *legal* responsibility. Psychiatrists should not be asked to pass upon questions of law any more than lawyers should be called in as experts upon questions of medicine. The cases to which alienists are called are medical cases and are either responsible or irresponsible medically, and that determination should be left to medical men.

As a result of our policies in this State we had in 1918, according to the census obtained by the "Special Commission Relative to the Control, Custody and Treatment of Defectives, Criminals and Misdemeanants," 11,495 persons committed to our penal institutions in that year, of which 6,733 or 58.5% were repeaters. It further appears from the same tabulation that they averaged 6.8 former commitments each. In the 21 county jails and houses of correction 5,727 of the 9,719 inmates entering these county institutions during 1918 were known to have served time before and the number of sentences served by these repeaters totalled 40,228. The records of these repeaters in county jails showed that 25 or more previous commitments was not uncommon, while some institutions housed men with as many as 100 terms of confinement recorded against them.

CONTENTS

PART I: SPENCER

PART II: CZOLGOSZ

LIST OF ILLUSTRATIONS

PART I

SPENCER

THE MANNER OF MAN THAT KILLS

CHAPTER I

HISTORY OF SPENCER'S CRIMES TO TIME OF ARREST, APRIL 5TH, 1910

Beginning in June, 1908, and continuing for nearly two years, a series of sensational crimes occurred in Springfield, Massachusetts, which completely baffled the police and so terrorized the inhabitants that when these crimes finally culminated, on March 31st, 1910, in the murder of Miss Blackstone, a young woman much beloved and respected in the community, public indignation and excitement reached a fever heat and the city was in a condition little short of panic. There was not very much doubt in anyone's mind but that these crimes had all been committed by the same person. Although they alike exhibited an almost unparalleled daring and bravado, they were evidently not the work of a professional burglar. In all there seemed a singular lack of motive; although houses were entered, lives threatened and property stolen, the actual gain was trifling and, in most instances, the risk taken was out of all proportion to the possibility of gain. Indeed this burglar frequently passed by valuable articles and took pretty trinkets of lesser value; the hours chosen for his entries were generally early in the evening when there was every risk of his being detected; when confronted, as he frequently was, by members of the family whom he was robbing, he seemed quite fearless so long as no noise was made; but a scream or any other loud noise excited him and frequently led to some demonstration of violence. He was known even to go out of his way while robbing a house to encounter the inmates, and on several occasions had conversation with them.

Of course there were many theories as to the perpetrator of these burglaries, but in spite of unceasing efforts on the part of the police, no clue of any importance fell into their hands up to the first week in April, 1910.

Miss Martha B. Blackstone, the woman who was murdered on the last day of March, 1910, was the daughter of Charles J. Blackstone, a well-known hardware man in Springfield. She was an only daughter, thirty-nine years old, and lived with her parents. She graduated from Smith College in the Class of 1893, and for the last two years had been teaching the first grade of the Jefferson Avenue School in Springfield. She was said to be a woman of high intellect and culture, and was respected and beloved by her pupils and associates. While teaching at the Jefferson Avenue School, she had made the acquaintance of the Misses Harriet and Lucy Dow, the former of whom was also a teacher there, and Miss Blackstone frequently visited them at Round Hill, where they lived with their mother Mrs. Sarah J. Dow.

Round Hill is an attractive neighborhood in the North End of Springfield. It is skirted by Plainfield Street on the south, by the tracks of the Boston &

Maine Railroad on the west, and Arch Street runs along its northerly base to Main Street. The early builders had had the taste to spare the fine trees, with which nature had endowed the Hill, and a number of attractive houses had been built in their shaded seclusion. The driveway ascends from Plainfield Street near the crossing of the Boston and Maine tracks, and curves downward to Arch Street on the north. Some houses face this driveway and others stand back among the trees, connected by a private avenue with the hill road and other streets. On the crest of Round Hill, to the right, perhaps a hundred feet from the driveway, stands the two-story frame dwelling in which Mrs. Dow and her daughters lived. It is a plain, but comfortable, modern two-family house. The Dows occupied the lower apartment, and a family by the name of Dwight the upper floor. The Dows' apartment consisted of six rooms: two parlors, connected by an archway, a dining room, kitchen, two bedrooms, a hall and a bathroom.

On the evening of Thursday, March 31st, 1910, Miss Martha Blackstone, as was her frequent habit, went to dine and spend the evening with her friends on Round Hill, accompanying Miss Harriet Dow home after school. The hours until dinner were spent in pleasant chat about the school work and other matters. Dinner was served at six, and afterwards Miss Harriet and her mother washed the dishes and tidied the house. Then all four women gathered about a table in the back parlor to amuse themselves with one of the puzzle pictures which were all the rage at that time. Miss Harriet Dow and her mother were sitting on a couch with the table drawn up in front of them, and Miss Lucy

Dow and Miss Blackstone were sitting opposite them.

They were pleasantly immersed in this game until the clock struck eight, when Miss Blackstone remarked that she must soon be returning home. About five minutes later Miss Harriet Dow *uttered a shriek*, and the others looked up to see a man standing in the doorway of the dining room. He wore a dark slouched hat pulled well down over his large, staring eyes. These were the only features clearly visible, as the lower part of his face was concealed by a black silk handkerchief. Afterwards they described him as a tall man, wearing a dark suit of clothes. He had a belt around his waist, from which was suspended a revolver-holster, but this they did not at first notice.

The man approached them, motioning with his hands and arms, making an inarticulate, guttural noise and demanding money. Mrs. Dow told him that they had no money; and all the women sprang to their feet and *screamed. On hearing the scream,* the intruder darted across the room and, taking up his position in the archway between that room and the front parlor, drew his revolver and demanded *quiet.* Miss Blackstone rushed screaming past him into the front parlor; instantly the man fired at her and she fell against the couch in a kneeling position, shot through the heart.

In the meantime Miss Lucy Dow had hastened to the telephone on the desk in the room where they had been sitting, but dropped the receiver at the sound of the shot and rushed into the front room in time to see Miss Blackstone fall. Her sister, *screaming all the while,* had also started to follow Miss Blackstone into the front parlor, but had slipped on a small rug in the archway and fallen. Her mother assisted her to her feet, urging her to be calm. Mrs. Dow then started to leave the room by the hall door to call for help; Miss Harriet saw the man approach the window, apparently to draw the shade. She moved toward where he was standing and *began to scream again;* he swore at her, and *told her to keep quiet*, and she then saw him raise his revolver and point it at her mother as she was leaving the room. She seized a chair and hurled it at him, hitting the arm which held the revolver. Turning upon her, he said, "Do you want to die? Well, die then!" and discharged the revolver at her. She fell to the floor and lost consciousness, the bullet having grazed her head.

Mrs. Dow appears to have been the only one of the four women who did not scream. She was an elderly woman in appearance, but young and alert in mind and action. After helping her daughter to regain her feet, she hurried upstairs in search of assistance, but found none of the Dwights at home. She escaped to the hall, opened the door and called loudly for their next door neighbor, Mr. Burnham. She heard a second shot fired and hurried back to the parlor, where she saw her daughter Harriet on the floor and Lucy at the telephone. The man was gone, and the front door was open as she had left it. She saw Miss Blackstone still kneeling beside the sofa with her face in her hands, and went at once to her; she drew the young woman's head into her lap and spoke to her; then she discovered that Miss Blackstone was dead, and she laid the body on the floor in front of the sofa.

The burglar had evidently escaped by way of the front door, and there was nothing to be seen of him a few minutes later when their neighbor, Mr. Burnham, and his son reached the Dow house in response to Mrs. Dow's summons for help.

Mr. Burnham immediately telephoned to Police Headquarters, and at 8.14 o'clock Inspector Costello reached the scene of the tragedy. The patrol wagon, on the way to Round Hill, bearing the detective, picked up Sergeant Littlefield and two other officers. Inspector Costello and Sergeant Littlefield entered the house, where they found Miss Blackstone's body on the floor. Miss Lucy Dow and her mother asked the detective to ascertain if Miss Blackstone was still alive. He found no signs of life from the pulse; Miss Harriet Dow he found apparently living.

Mr. Burnham sent in a trained nurse, Miss Ellison, who was at the time caring for a member of his family. She had heard the revolver shots soon after eight o'clock, and had looked out of the window from her patient's room where she was on duty, but had seen no sign of the tragedy until Mr. Burnham asked her to go over to the Dow house. She found Miss Dow lying on the floor, but conscious, and placed a sofa pillow under her bleeding head, and was about to give her a hypodermic when the physicians arrived.

Dr. W. H. Wilcox was the first physician to reach the house. He sent for Medical Examiner Bates and Dr. Sweet, the family physician, and Dr. Bacon was summoned by telephone a little later. Miss Dow was taken in an ambulance to the Springfield Hospital, where she ultimately recovered from what was said to be a fractured skull.

Miss Ellison said she went into the back room to prepare a bed for Miss Dow and while there locked the window through which the burglar had evidently entered. Apparently he had ransacked this room and then passed through the dining-room into the parlor. The Dows said later that there were articles of jewelry, including gold beads and pins, in a bureau which the burglar had rifled, two solid gold watches on a bureau in the other bedroom, a little old silver in a drawer beneath the china closet in the dining-room, none of which he took.

Of the crimes committed in Springfield during the two years prior to this affair, the following were attributed to the one "burglar," and were afterwards proved to have been committed by the same man:

On June 24th, 1908, while the family were sitting on the piazza, the house of Dr. Robert P. M. Ames, of 26 Seventh Street, was entered by way of the cellar, the burglar cutting a screen door, so that he could reach through and open it from the inside. While he was ransacking the house, as was afterwards learned, the family came in and went to bed. The burglar had concealed himself beneath the bed of Mrs. Ames, where he remained until they went to sleep. Then he continued his search and escaped with his booty, without giving any alarm. The articles taken from this house were later recovered from beneath a shed in the Boston & Maine freight yard, and included jewelry, silverware, and one shoe of a pair—the other he had left, as also articles of considerable value.

A month later, on July 25th, a man entered the house of George A. Luddington, at 29 Avon Place, through a back pantry window. He passed through the kitchen while Mr. and Mrs. Luddington were talking in the next room, entered a ground floor bedroom, and being disturbed, concealed himself beneath Mrs. Luddington's bed. He waited there until he thought she was asleep, and then attempted to escape. She woke when he moved and as she sat up and screamed, he demanded money and jewelry and forced her to give him her rings and two dollars in money. She later let him out by the back door.

The following night, July 26th, 1908, at the house of Fred D. Parsons in Union Street, a party were playing cards in a lighted room with unshuttered windows, and were held up by a masked man with a revolver, standing in the dark outside. The party screamed and scattered—the threat to shoot was not carried out, and the incident was dismissed as of little importance—probably a bad joke or the freak of a crank.

A few days later, July 30th, 1908, entrance was gained to the house of Hartley P. Buxton, 93 Garfield Street, through a rear door that had been left unlocked while the family were on the porch. The burglar was interrupted and concealed himself when Mr. Buxton came in and entered the bathroom. He then continued his search and escaped before the family retired, taking his booty with him.

On August 6th, 1908, a highwayman with a mask and revolver held up Michael J. Gilhooley, a motorman on the King Street car line at about half-past eight in the evening, at a lonely spot at the end of the route. O. D. Attwood, the conductor, saw the hold-up and escaped, but when Gilhooley also tried to escape the highwayman shot him through the leg, the bullet entering between the knee and the thigh. The robber rifled his pockets and took his pocketbook, containing ninety-three cents. He seemed content with this small sum.

On September 27th, 1908, the house of H. L. Miller of 32 Bradford Street was burglarized, and on November 30th the house of Mrs. Frances E. Page at 17 Sheldon Street was entered by way of a back bedroom window while the family were talking in the adjoining room. The burglar concealed himself in a clothes press and later under the bed. Mrs. Page and her daughter came into the room where the man was hiding, and the former went to bed; but before she fell asleep he made some slight noise which attracted her attention. She at once recalled her daughter, who lighted the lamp, placed it on the floor and discovered a man lying under the bed close to the wall. She had no view of his face, but said afterwards that he was "long." He had on no coat nor vest, but she observed he wore moccasins. The two women held a considerable conversation about the intruder, but he did not budge. They then left the room to call for help, and when they returned a few minutes later, found that the burglar had scrambled out, opened a bureau drawer and helped himself to a bag containing forty dollars, besides other belongings which were of little value, and had escaped through an open window. When the police arrived they could find no trace of him.

On Christmas Eve, 1908, Mrs. Helene J. Fiske was arranging Christmas gifts for her children on her bed in her home at 86 Calhoun Street, when she was confronted by a masked burglar who pointed a revolver at her. He started to pick up some of the more valuable presents, but Mrs. Fiske said "For God's sake don't take those—they are my children's!" "All right; I won't," said the polite burglar. She gave him two dollars and he also took some orange spoons and a napkin ring.

Nelson R. Hosley's house, at 22 Brookline Avenue, was entered in the early evening of March 12th, 1909, while the family were out. They returned at half-past ten and observed that a light had been made in the dining-room during their absence. Investigating, they found that miscellaneous articles were missing from the dining-room, chamber and closets. Miss Flora Sweetland, who lived with the Hosleys, said later that the burglar had take about a hundred different articles of little or no value, such as handkerchiefs, ribbons, etc. She said: "He took a number of little things that were on my bureau in my room that were practically valueless, and left my gold watch and other valuables that were right there in sight."

On the evening of April 8th, 1909, a party were playing cards in a brightly lighted room in the house of Mr. and Mrs. W. M. Swan, at 50 Bellevue Avenue. At half-past nine, Mr. Swan was upstairs putting his little boy to bed, and the guests rose to take their leave. As they opened the front door a man thrust his way past them into the house and held up the group at the point of his revolver, demanding money. One of the ladies attempted to grab his arm and he fired several times, embedding two bullets in the woodwork. Mrs. Swan called to her husband not to come downstairs, and the burglar emphasized her warning by firing up the stairway and shattering an electric chandelier, leaving them in partial darkness. He grabbed one of the guests, a Mrs. Tapley, and demanded her rings. At this moment, however, Mr. Swan threw down a pocketbook containing some new bills, shouting to the burglar as he did so to get out. The burglar forced Mrs. Tapley to pick up the purse and then grabbed it and backed out of the house without waiting for the rings or counting the money.

On April 10th, 1909, the house of Ex-Alderman Arthur H. Rogers was entered by way of a side kitchen window. His daughter, Miss Dell Rogers, was confronted in her room by a masked man. He flashed a searchlight on her as she stood by the window and demanded money and jewelry. She attempted to *scream* for help, but the robber frightened her into silence with a curse, saying she had got to keep still "or I will blow your head off." He then said, "That was just the trouble at the other house—*there was too —— much noise—that spoiled everything.*" Miss Rogers gave him a trinket and told him she thought there was no money in the house, but was finally forced at the point of a revolver to lead him downstairs to her mother's purse, which contained only two dollars. On the way downstairs the man entered the room of Miss Burt, Miss Rogers' aunt, an elderly lady; he did not disturb her beyond asking if she had any money and went away when she said she had none. He seemed perfectly fearless and even asked Miss Rogers where the men of the house were. The latter, fearing for her father's safety, declared they were not at home. After giving the man the money Miss Rogers started to pick up the telephone, but he made her put it down and grabbed the wire and snapped it out. He then took Miss Rogers into the kitchen, bound and gagged her and proceeded to rifle the sideboard of silverware, etc., after which he unbound Miss Rogers and made his escape, dropping the silverware outside when a call was made for help.

The next burglary reported in Springfield which was attributed to the mysterious "burglar" was on July 21st, 1909. Mr. Lewis J. Powers lived at 116 Pearl Street, only a few minutes' walk from the center of the city. His house was entered about 9.15 P. M. through a bathroom window. The lights were all burning, but the man proceeded fearlessly through the parlor, up the stairs, and searched several drawers and boxes in the rooms, but apparently did not find anything to his taste. Continuing through the brightly-lighted hall and up another flight of stairs to the third story, where the lights were also burning, he entered the room of one of the two maids, at the end of a long hall. She was sitting in her nightdress, reading a magazine, and looked up speechless when he asked, "Are you the hired girl here?" "Yes," she answered; and he looked through the open door into the next room, where a second maid was in bed. He told her to keep quiet and not say anything—that everything would be all right. She asked if she might get up and get into the other girl's bed. "Certainly," said the burglar. She came in and commenced to cry with fright, but the man said, "Don't cry. I wouldn't harm a hair of your head. Just keep quiet and tell me all you know—where do they keep the jewelry, etc.?" She told him that no one was home except Mr. Powers. All the rest of the family had gone away, adding, "What there is is downstairs." "Where?" said the burglar; and she replied, "I don't know as to that." He then inquired if there was any jewelry in the house and she said she did not think there was and that she knew of no money except what she had. He refused to take her money; then hearing a noise he inquired, "What is that noise?" and she said Mr. Powers had been downstairs a little while before. "There was nobody there when I came up," said the burglar. "He must have come back, then," said the girl. She asked permission to lock the door when he left, and he said, "Yes, you can lock it, but don't make a sound." She promised silence, and he said, "All right; I will take your word for it," and departed. He proceeded directly downstairs to Mr. Powers' room. Mr. Powers was packing his valise for a journey. The burglar commanded him to throw up his hands, pointing a large revolver at him and saying, "I want your money." Mr. Powers denied that he had any money, but offered the man a little change—less than $5 in all. He then inquired if there was any jewelry in the house, but upon being answered in the negative, he said, "All right," and started out by the front way. Shortly afterwards he returned and demanded to be let out the back way. Finding the door locked, Mr. Powers let him out of a window onto the back porch, whence he safely made his escape.

This crime had all the hall-marks of the others:—the early hour, the fearless masked man with a revolver and the lack of sufficient motive for even the apparently casual intrusion. It gave a fresh panic to the public, who had fancied the strange burglar already arrested or scared away.

Two weeks later, on August 6th, Mr. and Mrs. H. M. Ripley, of 266 Union Street, were encountered in their bedroom at eleven o'clock as they were about to retire by a masked man who was afterwards found to have entered the house by a ladder, which had been left against a near-by tree and which he had used to effect an entrance through a second story window. Mrs. Ripley saw him first and he cautioned her to be quiet. He then held them up, demanding money, but is said to have refused Mr. Ripley's watch which was all he had in his possession. The man returned a $2.50 gold piece which Mrs. Ripley offered him, on being told it was a "pocket piece." He made no further demands, but stopped and chatted pleasantly with Mr. and Mrs. Ripley for more than half an hour, discussing himself and his "profession," and then went off as he had come, removing the ladder after he had descended. Here was material for a very fair idea of the personality of the man, though it proved no clue to his identity.

It was a month before he ventured another burglary, which proved, financially, the most successful of the series. On September the fourth he entered an apartment at 6 Salem Street, belonging to Miss Eva D. Tessier, again through a bathroom window. Miss Tessier was out at the time, but encountered him on her return. A tussle ensued, but he finally subdued her by threatening her with his revolver, and forced her to give him all the money she had in the house, sixty dollars, and departed by the window through which he had entered. A week later, Miss Tessier thought she saw the same man on Main Street, but before she could give the alarm he had disappeared.

This was the last break generally attributed to the mysterious man, previous to the murder; though on September 23rd a man was discovered attempting to enter the home of Atkins E. Blair, at 66 School Street, by a ladder placed against the roof of a bay window.

He escaped before the alarm could be given. As will be seen later, this flight led to his undoing.

Not only the city of Springfield and the State of Massachusetts, but the entire country, were stirred by the accounts of the mysterious and apparently motiveless crime at the Dow house. The papers for days after the murder of Miss Blackstone contained mainly leading articles and editorials describing the crime in its minutest details and expressing the terror of the people of Springfield.

The Springfield Republican of April 2nd, 1910, voiced the feeling of the community in the following editorial:

MUST SPRINGFIELD HOMES BE ARMED?

The fearful tragedy in the Dow house on Round Hill has stirred the city mightily. Nothing has happened among us in years so terribly upsetting of the feeling of all security for life in the one place where it is to be expected—in the quiet and protection of one's habitation. Its effect is to create a reign of terrorism, particularly among the women, which is worse, in a way, than any that might have affected the early settlers of this region in relation to the Indians. They had the advantage of living all the time in full recognition of danger from a known and clearly designated source and of being individually prepared to keep themselves on guard to meet it. But not so with us and our civilization; we have thrown down all individual guard, and committed our security for life and property to constituted community agents. Such few enemies as we have walk unknown in our midst. Our homes are no longer castles of stockaded groups to ward off exterior dangers. Any of them can be entered with little difficulty, and in spite of all ordinary precautions; and it must be so. Our reliance for protection is and must be upon those especially appointed for the purpose.

If this dreadful murder and attempted robbery were an isolated happening—one of those chance occurrences against which no amount of care and preparation and police efficiency could guard, it would be of little use to do more than shudder and comfort the afflicted and go about our business. But unfortunately such is evidently not the case. This bloody event follows in a long series of terrorizing invasions of homes. Robberies and masked hold-ups within the home, any one of which might have ended in bloodshed and murder, had there been the slightest disposition manifested to resist the invasion or scare off the intruder. There is good reason to believe that the miserable imp of Hell who, in unspeakable cowardice, attacked these defenceless women and shot them down, is the same person who for more than a year has been creeping into other houses in the city, masked and armed, and demanding money of men and women at the point of a revolver. *He is clearly a man who makes robbery and possible murder a diversion rather than an occupation, for his gains of money are small, while his activities stretch over a long period.* He is doubtless regularly employed at a legitimate occupation. He may even be known as a faithful workman and law-abiding citizen. He may, in this case, have only just left his place of employment to give puzzling and terrorizing variety to his hours of toil by indulging his devilish propensity, which has thus far spared no part of the city or no time of twilight or darkness, no home on any account either of the defenceless character of the occupants or otherwise. And he still continues at large, as for a year or more past, ready to pounce in upon some cther home with evil purposes and a bloody determination. This man must be found and put out of the way. He has been suffered to roam about altogether too long. The police are doubtless doing their best to apprehend him. We may not lightly throw the blame all on them. They can not be expected to master every mysterious development of crime at the wave of the hand. They would be less open to unwarranted public criticism were it not that the administration of the service had been overturned in the name of needed reform for greater efficiency in the suppression of crime—and overturned for such an end, which is not now for the first time brought to public ridicule. But here is a case of crime whose safe persistence would under any circumstances call loudly for explanation in harmony with an efficient police establishment. It is bringing into all our homes a terrorism that is not to be endured forever in any constituency with the prosperity and growth of this city. If the word is not to go forth to every householder, "Arm yourself and stand guard through the night," this case must be hunted down to an ending.

In the same issue of the Republican, the leading article, four columns long, describes the public excitement, and says:

Not within memory have the people of Springfield been so profoundly shocked as they were yesterday by the wanton murder of

Miss Martha B. Blackstone . . . by a burglar or *crack-brained degenerate*. . . . Miss Harriet P. Dow, a teacher in the same school, whose skull was fractured by a bullet from the burglar's revolver, will probably recover, but her condition is critical and there is no certainty of a favorable outcome. The murderer is still at large and the police have so little to work upon that not much confidence is felt by the public that the capture will be made. Meanwhile the citizens are in such a frame of mind, of mingled horror and indignation, that they are disposed to hold the police department strictly accountable for results, for they feel that this tragedy is the culmination of a long series of outrages which the police have shown inability to deal with. Rightly or wrongly, the citizens are blaming the police for failure to capture the man who has committed the preceding atrocities. Public feeling was boiling yesterday, and resulted in a movement for a mass meeting for the purpose of seeing what the citizens want done about it. Business men yesterday requested the Board of Trade to arrange for such a meeting. All citizens are requested to be present and express their views. . . .

The state of the public imagination is well typified in the following extract from the same paper:

Members of the detective bureau are convinced that the murder of Miss Blackstone and the attack on Miss Dow were committed by the same man who perpetrated the half dozen robberies last year. This man lives in Springfield and was brought to Police Headquarters for purposes of identification following each of last year's hold-ups. He was seen by Capt. Boyle yesterday, but was not taken into custody for the simple reason that the detectives have always met with the same result in questioning him. He is described as about five feet ten inches tall, of medium build, smooth face and good looking. Furthermore he is about 32 years old, a college graduate, and a man who appears to have plenty of money, because he does not work for a living. He has among his possessions a black slouch hat, a black handkerchief mask, a blue steel 38-caliber revolver and holster. His eyes and presence are said to resemble those of the man who has been terrifying the city. Every time the police have questioned him, he has answered questions with few words, nearly always giving the information asked for and nothing more. The police say that he volunteers nothing and when cornered simply says he does not care to answer.

It will be remembered that most of those whose houses were entered by the burglar last year said that he was good looking, had the soft hands of a man of leisure and spoke like one who had received the benefits of an education. *His coolness in every case was equalled by his fearlessness and his utter disregard of consequences was always apparent.*

Several other cases were cited which show the state of strain under which both police and citizens were laboring. The history of the public excitement and futile search are well summed up in the headlines of the two most prominent columns of the Springfield Republican of April 3rd. This paper is so seldom given to sensationalism that the prominence it gives to this affair is very significant of the importance the search for this criminal had even in conservative circles at that time.

HUNT FOR BURGLAR
WHOLE CITY AROUSED

LARGE REWARD IS OFFERED

Mass Meeting of Citizens

STATE POLICE TAKE A HAND

Meeting of Board of Aldermen

City to Offer $500 and Gov. Draper Offers $500 of State's Money — Large Subscription from Citizens — No Definite Clew to the Murderer Except that Given by the Bloodhounds —Sensational Developments of the Day Cause a High Pitch of Excitement.

DOGS ON THE SCENT
MURDERER IS TRACKED

LENGTH OF MAIN STREET

Trail Lost at Longmeadow

AT STREET RAILWAY WHITE POST

Further Efforts Prove Futile

Marvellous Display of Bloodhounds' Powers in Crowded Thoroughfares — Scent is Picked up Outside of Window Where Murderer of Miss Blackstone Entered Dow House on Round Hill—Dogs are Tried at Thompsonville and Warehouse Point.

At the mass meeting $1,500 was raised in five minutes and confidence was expressed that the subscriptions started at the public mass meeting would reach $5,000, all but $1,500 of which was to be used as financial aid to the police authorities. A committee of citizens was appointed with absolute authority to spend this money as they might see fit. They immediately engaged Pinkerton detectives and set them to work on the case. "The three rewards offered," says the Republican, "aggregate $2500, and if a reward should be any inducement, this amount should at least serve to uncover some clew that will lead to some definite knowledge of the murderer's whereabouts."

Many columns of the papers of that day are given to the description of the dramatic attempt to follow the murderer with bloodhounds. A fine pair of these animals had been brought all the way from Poughkeepsie, New York, and they were immediately taken to the scene of the accident, and every effort made to put them on the right scent.

> Somewhat to the surprise of the police and public, who did not expect much from the man-hunters, owing to the time that had elapsed since the tragedy, says the Republican, the dogs took up a scent which the police believe was that of the murderer himself, and they followed it from the piazza of the Dow house on Round Hill, straight through the city, past Pecowsic to Longmeadow, where it was lost at a white trolley post. This gave birth to the theory that the murderer had there boarded a car and proceeded still southerly. Not satisfied that this performance of the bloodhounds could be depended upon, the dogs were brought again to the Dow house, and once more went out on the scent, this time picked out in a different way. The big, muscular animals could not be deceived, however, and, noses pointed to the earth, they began the journey over again. This time they travelled the same route, and at the same corner of Main Street were pulled off to await further developments.

As the coming of the hounds had been well advertised in the newspapers of the day before, great crowds were gathered along their route, and they caused much sensation as they passed through the city. Later, when the actual criminal had been discovered, he confessed to having patted these animals in the street! At 7.30 that evening the hounds made a third trial, repeating the same course as that of the morning, but in the end these efforts led to no clue.

There were so few clues to work upon that many persons, some of them of wealth and position, were under suspicion, and these suspicions are somewhat freely referred to in the papers, indicating that the police recognized that these crimes were not the work of a professional burglar. At the request of the local authorities, District Attorney Stephen H. Taft summoned two State detectives, Thomas E. Bligh from Pittsfield and James McKay from Northampton, both of whom went directly to work, after taking up the several phases of the case with Police Captain Boyle and the local detectives. To continue quoting from the Republican of April 3rd:

> Not in a generation has public sentiment been so thoroughly aroused. Members of the police department who have been longest in the service say that never have they seen Springfield so demonstrative. Yesterday was sensational enough in the murder case developments. . . . The inability of the police to effect the capture of the murderer, the picturesque appearance of the bloodhounds following the supposed trail down through the main street of the city, the mass meeting, the announcement by bulletins that thousands of dollars had been raised by the State, the city government and the business men of the municipality, for the purpose of bringing to justice *a degenerate who kills without provocation,* have served to create a feeling that is new to Springfield and appalling. It may have reached its crisis yesterday, but it is hardly likely the strain will relax until the murderer is caught.

The following proclamation was issued by the Governor of Massachusetts:

REWARD FOR APPREHENDING THE MURDERER OF MARTHA B. BLACKSTONE

Being of opinion that the public good so requires, the Commonwealth will pay the sum of $500 to any person who, in consequence of this offer, apprehends and secures the person who murdered

Martha B. Blackstone at the home of Mrs. Sarah J. Dow in Springfield, on Thursday evening, March 31st. This offer is made because, in my opinion, the person can not be arrested and secured in the common course of proceeding.

EBEN S. DRAPER.

Executive Chamber, April 2nd, 1910.

The Mayor and Board of Aldermen of the City of Springfield also passed an order, offering a reward of $500 for information that would lead to the arrest and conviction of the murderer.

During all this time of uncertainty, it will be observed that public opinion attributed the murder to the same man who had perpetrated the burglaries and other mysterious crimes of the preceding two years, and that in most surmises as to his identity the theory that these crimes could not have been committed by a normal man was clearly stated. The following analysis from the same issue of the Springfield Republican is significant, in the light of subsequent events:

A question that is being asked everywhere is "What kind of man is the burglar and murderer?" It is of great importance in the efforts to find him to know the answer, for in the absence of anything like a definite clew, it is about all the police have to work upon. The nature of the young man's crimes indicates clearly that he is not a professional burglar. His methods, while spectacular, are crude. Moreover, as has been clearly shown by the record of the burglaries and hold-ups charged to this man, booty has not been the chief consideration. Most of those who have studied the case believe that *the man is animated by a mania or craving for sensationalism. It is generally believed that he is a degenerate, but of an unusual sort,* for in all cases where women have been terrorized and held helpless no personal indignities have been offered them,* and the police have been obliged to look for *a moral pervert* of another sort. This man has seemed contented with the mere terrorizing of women.

The police are able to classify most professional burglars, but the work of this man does not come within the range of their experience.

* Later it was stated that there were one or two exceptions to this latter assertion.

He enters houses and reveals himself at hours when an ordinary burglar would not be seen, and his readiness to fire at Miss Blackstone is, in itself, evidence that he is not a professional, for a professional never fires unless he thinks it absolutely necessary for his safety. It is necessary, then, to consider the Springfield burglar as an amateur—a fool who is hungering for notoriety, *an insane person with a periodic mania for desperate deeds, or a degenerate of some sort.*

It is held that the man is either a degenerate or is subject to a mania. It is not believed that he is an ordinary street loafer, for if he had been it is thought that before now he would have given himself away. It is more probable that he is a young man regularly employed in the city, or a member of some family of means who is not dependent upon the proceeds of his robberies. This theory is strongly held by the police, who have had under suspicion from time to time men who are employed regularly and others who are ne'er-do-well sons of families who are in comfortable circumstances. The meager descriptions from the various houses, which tally very well as far as they go, point to a person of this sort. There are, of course, thousands of young men who answer the description. The burglar has evidently been close-mouthed about all his exploits.

We shall see how nearly true these surmises were, and how reluctant these clever analysts were to continue their argument as to the criminal's irresponsibility, after the actual culprit was found and their prophecies had been proven correct. The popular clamor for vengeance was too strong.

On the evening of September 23rd, 1909, it will be remembered, an attempt had been made to enter the house of Mr. Atkins E. Blair at 66 School Street. A man was dimly seen attempting to reach a second story window by way of a ladder placed against the side of the house—first by Mr. Blair's father-in-law, Mr. Simons. This old gentleman, being apparently of a cautious and somewhat secretive disposition, did not immediately give the alarm. A few minutes later, Mr. Blair himself saw the would-be intruder, who instantly retreated. Blair tried to follow him in the darkness, but the man escaped by running across the garden, through some tall dahlia stalks and over a bed of asters, over a fence and into the rear of the barn of the next neighbor, Mr. Packard, from whom he had borrowed the ladder, and thence probably into High Street, where he could easily escape detection among other pedestrians.

Mr. Simons was something of a horticulturist. The very next morning he went into his flower garden to work, and in the midst of a bed of asters he found a tiny gold locket, inscribed with the initials "B.G.S." in interlocking monogram on one side, and a little brilliant on the other. He picked it up and found within the pictures of an elderly woman and a younger one. He put the locket in his pocket and later showed it to the rest of the family.

The burglaries in this immediate neighborhood had become so frequent that several of the householders concerned got together to discuss the situation. These were Mr. Simons and his son-in-law Mr. Blair, Ex-Alderman Arthur H. Rogers, whose house on Temple Street had been entered the previous spring, and Mr. Robert A. Knight who lived next to Mr. Rogers. Mr. Simons showed these men the locket, and they procured directories, telephone lists and poll lists, and all the names beginning with "S" in these and every other available list were searched to find the owner of the initials "B.G.S." To their surprise, only one person was found whose name corresponded to these initials, Bertram G. Spencer, whose address was given as 53 Greenwich Street. As this man was listed as a brakeman in the employ of the Boston & Maine R. R., and as his residence was in a quiet, respectable neighborhood, no suspicion was attached to him at that time, and little more was done about the matter. Mr. Simons put the locket back into his pocket and refused to allow it to be given to the police, as he said he had little faith in their efficiency, and he probably feared to be the means of getting an innocent man under suspicion. He refused to permit his friends to tell the story of the finding of the locket. Mr. Knight, however, went to Chief Quilty, and advised him when searching for the burglar to look out for a man whose initials were "B.G.S.," whose mother was a rather stout woman and who had either a young wife or a sister. As he did not feel at liberty to give his reason for making this suggestion, Chief Quilty paid little attention to it, though when Mr. Knight telephoned later he was informed that the Chief had turned the matter over to Inspector Boyle, and that it had been looked into but that nothing had come of it. Mr. Knight heard no more from the police, and let the matter drop. The detective fund was not raised at that time, as a report had been spread that a certain person who had information was waiting for a reward to be offered.

But when the Pinkerton detectives were called in after the Blackstone murder, Mr. Simons finally consented to give up the locket, and it was placed in the detectives' hands on the Saturday evening preceding the arrest. A search of the directories led them to the same Bertram G. Spencer, whose address was given as 53 Greenwich Street, where it was found he had formerly boarded with a Mrs. Edgar C. Pierce. Mrs. Pierce, on being shown the enlarged photographs which had been made from the portraits in the locket, immediately said they were Spencer's mother and sister. Proceeding on her information, the detectives traced Spencer to his new address at 45 Porter Avenue, West Springfield, near the Old Toll Bridge, where he was living with his wife and son; and they found that he was working for H. L. Handy & Co. They kept him under surveillance for several days before arresting him. Porter Avenue is a thoroughfare that turns down to the left just beyond the Springfield Glazed Paper Factory at the end of the Old Toll Bridge. It is about a hundred yards long, and runs parallel to the Connecticut River. No. 45, where Spencer lived, was described as being one of fifteen houses, all built flush with the street and without any front lawns. It was a two and a half story detached house, with dormer windows and a roofed porch extending across the front of the house. A few straggling vines made a half-hearted attempt to climb up the pillars of the porch. The house was owned by a German, a cousin of Spencer's wife. The other residents of the street were all foreigners, for the most part Italians.

The account given by the Springfield Republican of the details of Spencer's arrest shows the extraordinary precautions of the police. It is too long to be quoted here in full, but according to this account Spencer was arrested on Tuesday, April 5th. He had been under suspicion since the previous Saturday, and his house had been watched by Detective Leith, one of the Pinkerton men employed by the Citizens' Committee. At 2.30 A. M. Captain Boyle was notified that the police were sure of their man and were only waiting for daylight to come before arresting him. The Republican continues the account:

Fearing the publication of such a report, Capt. Boyle got together the local and state detectives and the three Pinkerton men, and started out at once to bring in the man who later proved to be Spencer. All of the officers, including Capt. Boyle, Inspectors Raiche and St. Ledger, State Detectives Thomas E. Bligh, James McKay and Fred Flynn and the Pinkerton men, Harry A. Naughton and H. J. Murray, started across the Old Toll Bridge for Spencer's house on Porter Avenue, where Leith had been on guard. They remained in the vicinity of the house until about daylight (nine men in all!). Then with Bligh, Leith and Flynn, Capt. Boyle came back to the city to await near the Handy plant the arrival of Spencer, who would come to work at seven in the morning. Naughton, Murray, McKay, Raiche and St. Ledger remained near the Spencer house, concealed in the office of the Springfield Glazed Paper Company nearby. About 6:30 Spencer came out of the house and started for work across the toll bridge. Naughton and Murray shadowed Spencer clear to the Handy factory, where he was met by Capt. Boyle, Leith, Flynn and Bligh, who immediately placed him under arrest. Beyond appearing surprised and apparently confused at this turn of affairs, Spencer was little disturbed, and accompanied the officers to Police Headquarters without protest. The early reports of resistance were unfounded. Before leaving the Handy Plant, however, Capt. Boyle telephoned to the office of the Glazed Paper Company and had McKay, Raiche and St. Ledger search the house and bring in whatever might be found there that was of an incriminating nature.

Surely this demonstration of the majesty of the law was as melodramatic as even the "romantic vanity fed on penny dreadfuls" could desire!

Spencer willingly acknowledged that the locket was his, but explained that he had lost it some time ago—he did not know just when—running across lots to follow the patrol wagon.

In the itemized list of jewelry found in Spencer's house were included 105 pieces of varying value. The first seven items are watches, valued at from $3 to $25, No. 8 is "part of a brooch, pansy shape, with small diamond;" No. 9 "Emblem pin, D. A. R., engraved 'Esther Julia Pratt No. 24121,'" identified as taken from the house of Dr. C. S. Pratt of Brattleboro. There were rings, brooches, bracelets, etc., more than half of them plated and only one or two valued as high as $10

or $15. Many of them were practically worthless, as the D. A. R. pin. The list included, for instance:

19—Plated hoop bracelet	Value	$0.50
28—1 pr. plated nut link buttons	"	none
33—Gold scarf pin, four small pearls, center stone cut	"	1.00
34—Plated nut scarf pin	"	.25
35—Plated scarf pin with imitation jade	"	.25
36—Plated scarf pin with ruby doublet, bonnet effect	"	.50
39—Plated three-heart brooch, twined	"	.50
40—Small plated charm with Lord's Prayer	"	none
41—Plated clasp pin	"	"
43—Chatelaine pin, lady's face with wings	"	.50
44—Small medallion brooch—plated	"	.50
53—1 hoop silver signet top, old English "L"	"	"
47—Plated old-style oval locket, fancy front, plain back	"	none
54—1 signet plated hat pin	"	.50
55—Ivory carved charm, bull's head	"	.50
56—Porcelain brooch—lady's face and bust—plated back	"	.25
57—Plated scarf pin—imitation pearl	"	none
58—Plated ring with imitation pearl	"	.50
61—Plated ring with ruby doublet	"	none
64—Pair of porcelain brooches, flower pattern	"	.25
65—Small class pin, "B.B.S. '07" on it	"	none
66—Plated bar pin, engraved front	"	"
67—3 mother of pearl brooches, safety pin backs	"	"
70—Old collar supporter, imitation pearls	"	"
71—Plated guard chain, fox-tail pattern, with beads	"	"
72—Piece of plated rope chain	"	"
73—Silver brooch, imitation amethyst	"	"
75—Silver key ring	"	.25
77—Top of black comb with white stones	"	none
78—Silver, diamond shaped class pin, blue enamel "V.S."	"	"
80—Three small charms hung together—plated meat cleaver, carver and sharpener	"	"
81—Single stone, plated ring, imitation turquoise	"	"
82—Plated five-stone ring, imitation turquoise, 1 stone missing	"	"
83—String of red glass beads	"	"
84—Plated back collar button	"	"
87—Plated scarf pin, leaf	"	"
88—Pair of dumb-bell cuff buttons	"	"
89—½ pr. link cuff buttons, plated	"	"
90—" " " " " "	"	"

91—Plated fleur-de-lys watch pin.................	Value	none
92—Flat sterling hoop "Mizpah" bracelet.........	"	.25
94—Pin, triangle, Y.M.C.A. style................	"	none
95—Key ring	"	"
98—1 cameo spiral stud..........................	"	.50
99—Old style shirt button.......................	"	none
100—1 plated stud button........................	"	"
101—½ pr. cuff links............................	"	"
102—1 collar button, pearl back.................	"	"
103—1 " " silver back	"	"
105—Indian bead belt............................	"	"

The Springfield Republican on April 6th, the day after Spencer's arrest, was evidently still of the opinion that he was not a normal man. It comments on the arrest as follows:

Nothing is more difficult for the police to deal with than a casual murder when the criminal has once made his escape. If hate or love or jealousy or envy is at the bottom of the crime, there is usually a palpable clew, leading straight to the guilty man. . . . Or, if professional criminals are concerned, there is usually someone waiting hungrily for the blood money. A crime committed at random, on the contrary, upon a stranger, by a single person with no accomplices and no motives peculiar to himself, is a very different matter. . . . The burglary that ended in murder was the eighth offence which general opinion ascribed to one criminal or *monomaniac,* and however possible it may be for a miscreant to hide after a single offence, a series of similar crimes is a different matter. Their effect is cumulative. Each adds a little to the picture of the guilty man. . . . Clews? How could there not be, when at least eight people had seen the marauder clearly enough to swear to his identity—when several had had long conversations with him, when police and public alike had a true notion of his appearance and personality. Once he was seen and recognized in daylight by one of his victims, but made good his escape before a policeman could be called to the spot. In short, all the materials for detection, perhaps for conviction were in existence. . . . How many crimes went before the one that ended in murder can not be definitely said. Perhaps only their perpetrator has a complete list, but enough are known to give him as definite a stamp as any Claude Duval or Dick Turpin. *In each was a kind of wantonness, a daredevil bravado, a love of the spectacular and a lack of pecuniary calculation which strongly suggested either the monomania of an unbalanced mind* or a romantic vanity fed on penny dreadfuls, excited to the point of imitating Raffles, the Amateur Cracksman. . . . The house seemingly was taken at random. . . . He seemed to care little about money, demanding it, apparently, as a part of the rôle he was playing. It is not altogether surprising that crime of so queer and melodramatic a sort should not at first have been taken altogether seriously by the public. . . .

The Republican here chronicles at length various crimes attributed to this burglar, all of which were typical of the man's work. When the Round Hill murder occurred the circumstances were so clearly stamped with his methods that few people doubted that it belonged to the same series of outrages.

"All the circumstances were the same," says the Republican, "the tactics of the robber, his appearance, his eccentricities, correspond exactly. But for Miss Blackstone's demonstration, which upset his plans and prevented him from holding the family terrorized under his pistol in the fashion which he had seemingly enjoyed in previous raids, it is likely that the case would have ended like the others, with a flourish of a long pistol, a modest levy of ready money and a polite burglar backing off into the night. Evidently the burglar lost his head."

Continuing, the Republican suggests that *perhaps a nervous spasm plunged him into this new infamy.*

Upon his arrest Spencer was taken to police headquarters. He was compelled all that day to pass through the terrible ordeal of being subjected to attempts at identification by his supposed victims. He denied any connection with the burglaries or with the murder, but many of those who had been burglarized within the last two years were able to recognize him, so as to leave no doubt as to his identity, and they found among the articles taken from his room various trinkets which they recognized as theirs—some of them of so little value that they had not previously missed them.

Late in the day Mrs. Dow and her daughter came

to identify him, and they also found, with his other booty, the pearl pin which had been taken from their home on the night of the murder of Miss Blackstone, and Miss Dow was surprised to find an Indian bead belt which a friend had made for her and which she had not previously missed from among her possessions.

All day Spencer continued to protest his innocence and told various stories to account for his having the stolen trinkets in his possession. He said he had purchased the bead belt from an Indian woman at the station at Albuquerque, New Mexico, on his way home from California, and that he had paid fifty cents for it. But that night his rest was disturbed by the cries of a supposed drunken prisoner in a near-by cell, who kept accusing him of the murder of Miss Blackstone and repeated that Mrs. Dow and her daughter had identified him as the murderer. Was it possible that the accusations were made by imaginary "voices" which Bertram alone heard?

In the middle of the night State Detective Flynn was sent for and came to the cell where Spencer was confined. Spencer had complained of headache all day, and the city physician, Dr. Boyer, had prescribed bromides for him, to be administered every two hours. Flynn said that at this time Spencer seemed very tired and complained of a violent headache—"a tired headache." Flynn advised him to put his wrists under water and bathe his head, which he did, and then said he felt better. Spencer said to him, "Mr. Flynn, is it true—what this drunken fellow in one of the cells has been crying out—that Mrs. Dow has identified me as the murderer of Miss Blackstone?" Flynn replied, "I can't answer that question, Mr. Spencer."

Captain Boyle came to Spencer's cell the next morning at eight o'clock. Spencer said, "I want to talk with you, and talk with you alone." Boyle took him to the detention room, closed the steel door, and at Spencer's request, also closed the transom. Spencer then said that he wanted to tell Mr. Boyle his whole life story, saying: "If your conscience troubled you as much as mine did all night, you would want to tell your story to somebody. You can tell who you wish, or testify at any time you wish." He then began and told Capt. Boyle that when he was a small boy his father used to beat him severely and on one occasion had struck him with the butt end of a whip over the head, broken the whip stock and left him lying in his own blood. He said his mother found him there and supposed that he was dead. He told of stealing a jackknife when a little boy, and said that since that time he had stolen from every place he had been in all over the country. He then made a full confession of the Blackstone murder, which he repeated two days later to a stenographer.

In answer to Captain Boyle's questions he said that on Thursday, March 31st, he had left home about seven; he took the West Springfield trolley car and got off at Round Hill Bridge, near the watering tank, and he went directly to the Dow House. (In talking to the detectives he said he had not had any particular place in view when he started out.)

"I had on my everyday pants and my best coat and vest, an overcoat and my derby hat. I went to the windows first to see if they were open." Finding one of them unlocked, he then went around back of the shed and removed his overcoat, hat and inside coat and took off his shoes. "I put on my mask, my black handkerchief and my black felt hat, and went into the house through the window in the rear bedroom. I opened the door—I didn't know what it was—whether it went into the kitchen or where it went. I see it went into a closet —there were clothes hanging there. I had my search-light. Then I went to the drawer, opened it and looked for jewelry, and found a pin brooch, and there was a little blue stone and a bead belt. I went right through into the dining-room, and from the dining-room into the parlor. There were four women there. As I went into the door I stopped and looked around, and as I was looking around one of them saw me and screamed and jumped to her feet, and at that they all jumped to their feet. I says—I think I said, 'I want your money,' and at that *they all screamed.* I hadn't touched my gun even then—I hadn't thought of my gun. My revolver was in my holster at my left side. I advanced toward them open-handed, and they commenced to scream and one started toward the door and two, I think, came toward me; one grabbed me; the other lady took a chair—raised a chair over her head, and *they were all screaming at the same time, and something—kind of a blank—appeared to me there, the same as if I could hear voices in every direction,* and I was so excited that the only thing I could think of was to shoot to scare somebody—to get out. I grabbed my gun and—bang! bang!—like that—and started toward the door, and there was a woman right there near the door and she was screaming, and I pushed her aside and the door was open and I run out to the stoop—the front piazza—and over the railing and around the building to where my coat and hat was, and my shoes. I took them and ran down through the woods until I got to a big chestnut tree on the side of the hill. I sat down and put my shoes on and my coat and hat, and went down over a fence, through a yard and out onto Main Street, opposite Bancroft. From there I went down Main Street to Church, where I saw Jim . . . Dowling, I think his name is, standing at the telephone box. He is an officer. I went down Church Street as far as Chestnut, up north to Carew, Carew to Chestnut, Chestnut to Bridge and Bridge home. I arrived between a quarter past eight and a quarter to nine—I think that was the time. I went into my room, took my things off, got out my gun and started to clean it. I found two empty shells, cleaned the gun and reloaded it and placed it under the head of my bed—under the pillow—I always keep it there. After my wife had gone to bed, I put the black hat in the stove—I think I left the black handkerchief out in the hall." Spencer continued that he had gone to bed somewhere around 9.30 and had slept with his wife—had slept soundly. He said he had taken the pearl pin and the belt from the Dow house, and he also described "a little mottled stone—a mixed colored stone," which he had found there and which Miss Dow had not missed, though it was later found among his things and identified by her. He said he had never known the Dows and did not know that he had once boarded under the same roof with them.

One can hardly believe that a normal man, sufficiently frightened, under such circumstances, to fire into a group of helpless women, could be so relieved by the explosion that he could collect himself sufficiently to remember to get his clothing and cover his tracks—and certainly no one, however hardened to crime, could have been so free from fear of consequences as to sleep soundly after committing such an act, if he had any real comprehension of the seriousness of his offence.

Spencer then confessed to the fifteen burglaries in Springfield which we have previously described. In recounting the affair at the Swan house he said, "I tried to get in the windows at that house, and there was every one of them locked, so I went around and saw some people sitting in the parlor. . . . As I stood there on the porch meditating—thinking what I would do—I see someone come toward the door, and they had hats on—I forget whether it was one or two or three women and some children, and it come to me in a flash that when they opened the door I would go in, make them all stand back and get what I could. As they opened the door I walked right in on them. I don't remember what I said, but I know one of the women started to grab me—I guess I pulled the gun up, demanding money, and one woman grabbed my hand and shoved it down, and as she did that—an impulse, I suppose—I pulled the trigger and the gun went off right beside her. *They all started to scream and holler.* While they were screaming I shot out the lights and I grabbed one woman and told her if she didn't give me some money I would kill her—trying to make her give me some money. And a man hollered downstairs, 'Here it is! Here it is!' and he dropped some down. I told her to go and pick it up and she gave it to me and I left the house."

Spencer's accounts of the other breaks correspond with those of the persons whose houses had been entered, and all show the same casual method, reckless of consequences. He seems to have been equally pleased with his plunder, so long as he got something, whether it consisted of money or jewelry of some value, or whether he took mere bright, tawdry trinkets such as might have attracted the eye of a child.

On Thursday, April 7th, the papers all over the country were full of Spencer's confession. Again we quote the Springfield Republican:

> It is an extraordinary story of crime that Spencer tells, not the story of a professional criminal, but that of *an amateur hungering for sensational experience, or perhaps it might be said, of a degenerate,* for it developed yesterday that Spencer had, from his youth up, engaged in practices destructive to uprightness, and it was suspected that he was the victim of a drug habit, from characteristic marks on his arm and the possession of a hypodermic syringe. [This story was afterward disproven and the syringe found to have been stolen from the home of Dr. Daly at White River Junction.] These facts may explain the strange character of the young man who has entered so many Springfield houses in a seemingly aimless way, and finally, without need or provocation, wantonly murdered a fine woman, beloved because of her qualities, by a large circle of friends. . . . Two days ago it was possible to conceive of a lynching party, because of the great grief and indignation; yesterday there were even those who expressed sympathy for the young man who now finds himself in so desperate a plight—but not many, for though a relentless doom, such as Spencer faces, is a horrible thing to contemplate, there are not many but feel that it has been abundantly earned by the *young pervert, by his reckless sensationalism and wanton cruelty.* . . .
>
> . . . There are rarely more pathetic scenes than that yesterday when the grief-stricken mother went to see her guilty son, and he wept in her embrace, his reserve entirely gone, his defiance and indifference finally swept away by the realization that all hope was gone, and that his refuge, as in his babyhood, was in the arms of the mother who loved him best. So at the last, softened human nature had its way, even with one who had been able, after a murder of extraordinary atrocity, to sleep peacefully, perhaps, at night, to go regularly to work and laugh and joke with his mates, to wager that the murderer would never be caught, and to show a bold front to the police even after it seemed hopeless. At many points Spencer's spectacular career of crime has touched varying phases of human nature, but nothing has been more affecting than the complete crumbling of his hardened shell yesterday and the resolution of the desperate criminal into the young man with ordinary feelings and affections. . . . In spite of his confession . . . the Commonwealth

will accept no plea of guilty. This might be done under the law, but it has not been done in a capital case for 50 years, so that Spencer will have a trial as full and fair as may be, before he is sent to death.* This, owing to various complications, may not come until next fall. Nobody doubts that Spencer told the truth yesterday. His words relating to his early life and the more recent spectacular crimes, were mingled with tears, and the evidences of grief were so abundant that it was difficult to believe that this was the young man who had terrorized citizens in their homes with so much nonchalance, and had finally, with the utmost brutality, shot down two defenceless women. . . . He confessed to all the breaks attributed to the "burglar," and said that *he took great pleasure in reading about them in the papers.*

On the same day a ring, marked "W. H. Childs" was identified as having been taken from the house of Dr. C. S. Pratt, in Brattleboro, Vermont, on the night of July 23rd, 1908. This was one of the boldest of a series of ten robberies that took place in Brattleboro within a space of two months. Spencer was at that time brakeman on a freight train running into Brattleboro, and he spent his nights in that town in the caboose, hanging about the streets part of the evening. The break at Dr. Pratt's occurred during the evening, while the bailiffs and selectmen were holding a conference as to what should be done to apprehend the burglar who had been terrifying the town. In the meantime, the burglar was ransacking the Pratt house at his leisure, Dr. Pratt and his family being absent. No trace of the burglar was found and the police gave up the search, after notifying the police departments far and wide to be on the watch for the stolen jewelry. Several hundred dollars' worth of jewelry, etc., were claimed to have been stolen, but among other and more valuable things missing were a glove buttoner and an emblem "D. A. R." pin.

Spencer confessed to this burglary in Brattleboro,

* Compare with Richeson case.

and also to other breaks in White River Junction, including the house of Dr. W. O. Daly. From Dr. Daly's house he took a lot of odds and ends, which included beside the hypodermic syringe, already mentioned, "a grip, a medicine case, a cigar case, brush and comb, surgeon's scissors, two shirt-waist pins, collar case, silver ash tray, leather fob, two bottles of tablets and a jar of ointment—*a sort of collection,"* says the Springfield Republican, *"that seems to have been characteristic of Spencer, who stole whatever came handy, whether he wanted it or not."*

Mr. L. D. Wheeler of White River Junction he held up in his barn, forced him to hand over his watch and a sparkling scarf-pin. "He handed it out," said Spencer in his confession, "just handed it out to me. I says: 'You stay here and don't make a noise—you stay here ten minutes,' and I went out and put on my coat and hat—I could see him through the barn window; he just kind of walked around leisurely and stood there, and I went away; he was staying there when I went out of sight."

In a like manner, during his railroad experience, he had robbed five houses in Greenfield, including those of former Sheriff Wilson L. Smead, Frederick L. Green and W. S. Hutchins; and he admitted having entered a hotel in Northfield and stolen $5 from a guest.

The Springfield Republican of April 8th, 1910, has a long editorial on the dangers of sensational literature of the "Raffles" variety. It says, in part:

Whether he had read the "Raffles" stories is not known, but his performances might well have followed such readings and have been the direct product of them. The description of an attractive personality, engaged in outwitting the officers of the law, and particularly the casting about such affairs the pleasant atmosphere of romantic adventure, may and does *exert a powerful influence of suggestion on minds not positively resistant to such influences. Upon such a nature as that of our criminal, already advanced along the road of wanton lawlessness, the charm of Raffles fiction would be great and even commanding. Spencer fairly revelled in the excitement which he caused in defeating police guardianship.* Nevertheless, it must be recognized that he was but a clumsy operator, and as such ought to have been caught long before murder was done. *But he was a type;* there was cause and effect in his work; and Switzerland does well to interdict "Raffles" stories. . . .

It was apparent from his methods, his behavior and the character of the loot that he gathered that he was after excitement and sensations more than loot—*he was a burglar for the fun of the thing. In other respects he seems to have been normal,* or so nearly so that he was never suspected of any crime, and *his peculiarities* were thought of only after he had proved to be guilty of an almost unheard-of series of criminal acts. He was said to be a good companion, though hasty in temper. Women spoke of him as a gentleman, and mentioned his kindliness. And yet this young man had been a thief pretty much all his life, had stolen, according to his own admission, from nearly everybody he came in contact with, even his closest friends. *Apparently his conscience from early boyhood had been stunted, else how could he have gone about his daily work, cheerful and undisturbed, knowing that he was causing terror, distress, and finally death?*

As a craftsman, his methods were of an unheard-of crudity, and the fact that he was not caught earlier is due to his perfect assurance and freedom from worry—or at least to the ability to conceal it—and even more to a fool's luck. Imagine a professional burglar leaving part of his clothing outside of a house he was about to enter. In case of accident it might either delay his retreat or he would have to leave it as a tell-tale, and parade the streets in his burglar's get-up. Or suppose . . . Spencer had been casually held up by an officer and found to have the big revolver strapped to his person! . . . Even after the murder, Spencer dwelt calmly in the midst of damning evidence, such as common sense would have at once destroyed. Such are the methods that have baffled the police for two years. They are baffling for the precise reason that they are so different from what might have been expected.

One might continue to quote volumes from the newspapers of that time to prove that popular opinion before the arrest held the burglar and murderer to have been abnormal, degenerate or insane. These deductions were made from the evidence of the crimes themselves: their lack of adequate motive, their sensationalism and the reckless daring of the unknown criminal. And after the arrest and even after Spencer's confession, in spite of the popular clamor for a victim, the papers all over the country continued to argue on the same grounds from the full evidence then before them.

H. J. Murray, one of the Pinkerton detectives on the case, is quoted as having said, "There is no case in the files of the Pinkerton Detective Agency which is in any way paralleled by that which has been enacted in this city." . . . Mr. Murray said that among the unusual points of the Spencer case were the succession of events following the murder and the character of the murderer himself. . . . He pointed out that Spencer was a kindly man about the house, careful and considerate of his wife, doing many little things to assist her in the household. The fact that he was not addicted to the use of liquor, drugs of any kind or tobacco was regarded as significant in making his case unusual. . . . Spencer's long, uninterrupted career of crime was due, the detective said, not so much to cleverness on his part as to luck. Murray said that Spencer did not choose the house he was about to enter with any relation to the probable amount of valuables to be found therein. He just strolled about the streets and selected any house which happened to appeal to his fancy.

CHAPTER II

HISTORY OF SPENCER'S LIFE—EXAMINATION OF SPENCER IMMEDIATELY AFTER HIS ARREST BY THE COMMONWEALTH'S ALIENISTS — SPENCER'S TRANSFER TO BRIDGEWATER STATE HOSPITAL, SEPTEMBER 17TH, 1910.

History of Spencer's Life

Bertram Gager Spencer was born in Lebanon, Connecticut, on June 9th, 1881. He came from what is called good American stock on both sides of his family. The Spencers were well known and respected in the community, the father, Wilbur L. L. Spencer, having for years kept one of the two village stores; more recently he had given up the store and confined himself to managing his farm and dealing in farm machinery. He was known as a stern, upright man, deeply religious, and had been superintendent of the Sunday school in Lebanon for eighteen years. Mrs. Spencer was a devoted wife and mother, popular among her neighbors and interested in church work. There were three children, of whom Bertram was the oldest.

So much for a superficial glance at the family as they were known in the community; but on inquiry we find that there were eccentricities in all the members of this village family, and that there was a long history of mental disease and nervous instability on both sides for four generations back—soil for the development of the constitutional psychopath.

Bertram Spencer's *father* had all his life been subject to fits of uncontrollable temper. The history of Bertram's childhood is a series of episodes, showing his father's extreme irritability and excitability, and the inconsistency of a nature deeply pious and with a stern sense of duty at the same time with so little self-control that he was capable of acts of inhuman cruelty to a helpless child and abuse of a devoted wife. Mrs. Spencer at the trial testified that her husband had slept very little for the past twenty years; he always had a light in the next room, with the door open so that it would shine into his room. She said he was extremely jealous and suspicious that people were trying to torment him or to conspire against him, doing things to annoy him without cause; he always slept with a revolver under his pillow; he had been subject to "nervous attacks" for at least twenty-five years; in May, 1911, she found him sitting up in bed, groaning and saying that he didn't know what was going to happen to him—"He was afraid he was going insane, and wanted me to promise that I wouldn't have him sent to an institution if he did. He said there were all sorts of things going through his head—bad things." Such attacks she said were of frequent occurrence.

As our history will show, Mr. Spencer could not brook opposition in the family, and was in the habit of using a revolver to maintain family discipline. Aside from possible injuries from repeated cruelties, the mental impression made upon a sensitive child by such example and such treatment played an important part in his future development.

The *paternal grandfather,* William L. Spencer, died in the Hospital for the Insane at Middletown, Connecticut, on September 15th, 1899, of senile dementia.

A neighbor, Robert B. Gordon, said that William L. Spencer was always threatening to go to law—"He would get into a rage if anybody crossed him and talk law." Mrs. W. L. L. Spencer also testified at the trial as to her father-in-law's having been insane. He had lived with them before he was committed to the State Hospital at Middletown.

Paternal Grandmother. William L. Spencer married a Mary Hughes, who had previously been married to a man named Date. According to her son, "She was silly at times and cunning at times in her latter days." She died in Franklin, Conn., according to the records, of "softening of the brain." This grandmother had two children by her previous marriage whose history is significant.

Paternal Aunt. Helen Date Tiffany, the half-sister of Bertram's father, died in the Worcester State Hospital for the Insane, on April 22nd, 1911, at the age of 56. She had been four years in the hospital. The Superintendent, Dr. Hosea M. Quinby, testified that she was insane: "She had delusions of hearing, delusions of wealth, mistaken identity, and various delusions along that line."

Paternal Uncle. David B. Date was brother of this woman and half-brother of Spencer's father, who said of him, "He was very erratic in many ways and always scheming."

Paternal Great-grandfather. The father of William L. Spencer, Ambrose Spencer, according to the testimony adduced at the trial, was a neurotic and had outbreaks of violent temper. His grandson, William K. Spencer, said that he had been to see him in his last illness, and that "his mind was all gone"—"He didn't talk as though he knew me." Wilbur L. L. Spencer said that his father had told him that Ambrose Spencer had "insane spells—fits, he called them."

So much for the history on the father's side. The history of Bertram's mother and her family is as follows:

Mother. Kate E. Spencer is of a neurotic temperament and inclined to fits of melancholy. On two occasions, when depressed, she tried to take her life: in 1894 she confessed that she attempted suicide by taking laudanum—"but I should have taken anything else, had it been in reach," she says in a letter, dated February 14th, 1912. Dr. N. L. Drake, for some years the family physician in Lebanon, deposed that in 1896 Mrs. Spencer had been treated by him for an injury to her wrists. "She said that in a sudden fit of despondency and anger she had tried to end her life by cutting both wrists, adding that if the knife had been sharp enough she would have accomplished it. She realized that she had done a foolish and rash act on impulse." Mrs. Spencer is a highly-strung, over-conscientious woman, whose life seems to have been one continual sacrifice to the peculiarities of her husband and children, with the idea of family insanity never far from her mind. In her family there have been three generations afflicted with mental disease.

Maternal Grandfather. Judson A. Gager, father of Mrs. Spencer, was an irritable, quick-tempered man, according to the testimony of his neighbors, very nervous and addicted to drink. Of Bertram's four grandparents, he was the most nearly normal.

Maternal Grandfather's Aunt. Eliza Gager died in

1906 at the Spencer's home in Lebanon of "softening of the brain." She was feeble-minded and had been insane all her life, as both Mr. and Mrs. Spencer, their family physician and various family friends testified. She had delusions of hearing for a great many years—imagined she heard people talking to her, and that a boy and girl were hiding behind the door trying to annoy her, and that Indians were attacking the house.

Maternal Grandmother. Mrs. W. L. L. Spencer's mother, Mary Davis, wife of Judson A. Gager, died in June, 1866, at the age of 37. She had "hysterical fits" throughout her life and was mentally deranged a long time before she died.

Maternal Great-grandfather. Mary Davis Gager's father, Nathaniel Davis, the husband of Hannah, died of "softening of the brain" at Newport, Rhode Island, in 1872, at the age of 78. "He was deranged for several years before he died."

Mother's Uncle. William H. Davis, the son of Nathaniel Davis, was mentally unsound and died of "cerebral congestion," at the age of 60 years and 6 months.

Mother's Cousin. This William H. Davis had a son of the same name who died of "inflammation of the brain," at the age of 40 years and 10 months. Thus for three generations in Mrs. Spencer's mother's family there had been insanity.

I could furnish much data to show that the other children of Mr. and Mrs. W. L. L. Spencer were neurotic, if not psychopathic. Indeed, from a medical point of view, their symptoms would be considered quite as abnormal as those of their father and of Spencer himself.

The story of Spencer's childhood is one continuous tale of insubordination and severe punishments. The child seems to have had a lovable side to his nature and his relation with his mother was always most affectionate and happy. She understood the boy, and did not attempt to cross him or to *force* obedience, but patiently guided him along the lines of the least resistance. But with his father, almost from infancy, there was a conflict of wills followed by the application of physical force. The father being the stronger, he won out physically, but he never gained a moral victory, nor is there anything to show that the child profited by experience, or that fear of punishment acted in any way as a deterrent to his impulsive wrong-doing a second time. Indeed there is good reason to believe that, in this instance, had the rod been spared the child might not have been spoiled; though nothing could have made Bertram Spencer a normal man. He might have been protected from unnecessary strain and excitement, and by constant example and kindly understanding, trained to habits of self-control, which would have enabled him to be a useful worker and a harmless member of society.

The following history is made up largely from his mother's account of his childhood and early youth, given at his trial and in letters, confirmed in almost every detail by the father himself and by numerous friends and neighbors. Among these latter it is interesting to note that those who knew Bertram but slightly, or with whom there had been no conflict of interests—who had never had occasion to "cross him" in any way—considered him a normal boy; many found him socially attractive, gentle and polite. But everyone who had had an opportunity to observe him closely, at home and abroad, at work and at play, or who had disagreed with him ever so slightly, testified to his sudden fits of temper, his utter lack of self-control and the peculiar symptoms which he manifested from time to time after one of his outbreaks.

Bertram seems to have been a healthy infant, but he did not walk or talk until he was over two years old. When the child was only nine months old he was sitting at the table in his little high chair while the family were eating, and was attracted by the bright color of a dish of radishes; he reached for them and his father whipped his hands with the side of a silver knife; when he cried, he was taken from the table and severely punished for crying. "After this he exhibited extreme nervousness while sleeping," says his mother; "he would start and cry out in his sleep."

Again, in the winter following his third birthday, he was taken by his parents to a church "social" in the evening, and the child was told not to touch the books. "He had a fondness for looking at pictures and books," said his mother. "But the child escaped my attention and during the evening I found him on the floor with a book, looking it through." When they reached home, his father punished him severely, and the child wriggled out of his father's hands and fell, striking the back of his head on an old-fashioned, air-tight stove, and cutting quite a gash at the base of the skull.

Another pathetic tale is told by his mother of her attempt to teach him to say "Now I lay me." "I taught him a little prayer, and there were certain parts of the prayer the child couldn't commit to memory. His father whipped him with a stick for not being able to

BERTRAM G. SPENCER
1882
Aged 7 mos. 2 days.

BERTRAM'S FATHER, MOTHER AND SON

BERTRAM G. SPENCER
1886
Aged 5 years.

He thought it was just because the child was contrary—or obstinate."

At the age of seven Bertram had another very severe punishment. He had raked up some leaves in the back yard and set fire to them. To punish him for this childish offence, his father took him into the woodshed, tied his hands behind him, put his head on the chopping block and threatened to cut it off if he ever repeated the offence. His mother said that when he came in from the woodshed there was blood on him and he was very much excited, crying and screaming. This was soon after one of Mrs. Spencer's other children had been born, and the nurse, Mrs. Henrietta Post, who was then present, confirms this statement. Mrs. Post said that Spencer, as a little child, was "queer, odd and strange—wanted his own way—very excitable."

In 1890, when Bertram was nine years old, he was permitted to sell papers after school, but his father told him that he must be home by five o'clock. One day he stopped on the way home to play with a schoolmate and did not return until about six. Again his father whipped him severely and took him to the door and pushed him out, saying, "Never show your face here again."

In addition to his other shortcomings, Bert frequently ran away from home and had to be brought back by the "hired man" or one of the neighbors, and was severely punished on such occasions; but his father said that there was very little, if any, improvement after these punishments. "He wouldn't do the same thing immediately afterwards, but soon afterwards he would perhaps do the same thing and even worse."

Bertram was incapable of learning by experience,

and his father, in spite of his religious principles, apparently made little effort to control his own violent, cruel temper, but gave way to his rage whenever the child's backslidings were brought to his notice, even using a revolver to force the boy when he resisted punishment. It would appear that even in his early surroundings, Bertram was very suggestible, and did learn from example; his outbreaks of temper, as he grew older, were very similar to those of his father. Had he been brought up in different environment, and had his father been a wise, self-controlled man who understood his son's limitations and did not ask too much of him, it is possible that Bertram might have developed into a more nearly normal man. But with continual friction and frequent exhibitions of unreasoning rage from his father, the boy's defective nature made the development of self-control an impossibility and fostered a tendency to secretive habits, which made fertile soil for the growth of criminal traits.

When he was eleven years old, the boy stole a jackknife from the village store. On discovering this, his father took him into the horse barn and whipped him severely with a horsewhip, striking him on the head—and then left him. In testifying about this occasion at the trial, Mr. Spencer said he did not know which end of the whip he had used—"In my excitement, he might have been hit in any part of the body." Mrs. Spencer said: "I heard the boy's screams and went to him and took him in and cared for him—put him to bed. He said his head was hurt, and I saw that it was hurt. *He said that it had been done with the butt of a whip. Ever since that time he has made complaints of his head.*" In various other statements, both Mrs. Spencer and Bertram himself have attributed some permanent injury to this punishment, Mrs. Spencer also claiming that some serious brain injury had been sustained at the time when, at the age of three, he had fallen from his father's hands against the stove.

During the summer following his thirteenth birthday, Bertram was accused of not having fastened the barn door securely, so that the cow got away during the night and did some damage. His father punished him by taking him into the woods, where he tied him to a tree, whipped him, and left him "for the wolves to devour." He then went to the mill, some two or three miles beyond, and did not return for an hour or so, when he untied the boy and brought him home.

One day in the same summer, 1892, Mrs. Spencer was entertaining two friends who had driven from an adjoining town to visit her. Bertram had been told to harness a horse and buggy, which had been ordered by the minister to take a drive. His mother asked him to put up the guest's horse first, saying that a few minutes' delay would not make any difference. For not returning promptly to the store, where the minister was waiting for the horse and buggy, his father punished him severely. Bertram escaped from him, and ran, very much excited, crying and screaming, from the store to the house, followed by his father, who completed the punishment in the kitchen in the presence of Mrs. Spencer and her guests. According to Mrs. Spencer, he used his fists and kicked the child, and told him to leave home. She sent Bertram away to Troy after that, but later he came back and went to school in Lebanon.

His teacher, George E. Briggs, testified that "he did

not seem a normal child—was different from the others. He would fly into paroxysms of anger without very much cause. He could not grasp mathematics—it was difficult for him to learn." Mr. Briggs' efforts to explain Bertram's lessons to him were without practical result; he found him unable to concentrate. "On one occasion, during the noon intermission," said Mr. Briggs, "he was playing a game with another boy and at the same time two little girls were playing a game; as one girl pursued the other, she crossed his path as he was pursuing the boy, and he flew into a paroxysm of rage over it; his face changed color and he stopped, rushed up to her, and struck her in the eye. He seemed to have no power to control himself." Mr. Briggs thus described another incident: "I heard a boy taunt him for being kept away from school—several boys seemed to be taunting him—and he drew a knife and rushed at the nearest boy and tried to stab him in the back. He seemed to have no control of himself. I remember punishing him once with a strap, but the punishment had no effect upon his course of conduct." Mr. Briggs said that the work he was giving Spencer at this time—in his fourteenth year—was not much more than third or fourth grade.

When Bertram was fourteen, his mother took him to Boston, and he enlisted at Charlestown on the receiving ship "Wabash," but remained in the Navy at this time only a few weeks, being discharged on August 14th, 1895, for disability. Dr. Henry LaMotte, at that time Assistant-Surgeon in the U. S. Navy, who signed the report of Medical survey on which Spencer was discharged, and which declared him "unfit for service" on account of "eneuresis," testified at the trial as follows:

"He had three varieties of imperative impulses. He, on two or three occasions, when talking to me and other men in the hospital, suddenly stopped talking, and jumped on the bed, or on a chair. He also, on several occasions, took down his trousers and showed his parts to other boys. He urinated in his hammock, but not in his bed. Every time he slept in his hammock while he was in the hospital he urinated in the hammock. He was quiet, reserved, somewhat depressed; but he would suddenly have a flash of apparent merriment; a foolish smile would come over his face, and he would lapse into the same stupid, apathetic attitude which he had before. I was ordered to report on this man by the Board of Investigation." Dr. LaMotte added that he thought he had had Spencer under observation for about a month; he said he had passed urethral sounds two or three times. He was not allowed by the Court to testify as to his opinion of Spencer's mental condition, not being able to qualify as an expert, though he had had considerable experience with mental cases. The report did not state all the symptoms and conditions for which Bertram was discharged.

We may here quote the opinion of a neighbor, Joe Stedman, who had known Bertram from his birth, seeing him constantly until he was ten, when Stedman had left Lebanon; but who came back at intervals to visit and saw a good deal of Bertram. He spoke of Bertram's conduct as showing "impaired mentality." "I saw him do things I didn't consider exactly right—that an ordinary mind would not do." Spencer had attacked Stedman many times when they were children. Stedman told of seeing Spencer throw a 1 or 2 lb. weight at one of his father's clerks. "At that time he looked wild—a characteristic look—I would explain it as crazy—sort of wild, infuriated and uncontrollable." There were many such spells, too numerous for Stedman to remember, covering at least twenty years, he said. Comparing Bertram's anger with that of an ordinary man, Stedman said there was "a difference in facial expression, a violent rage—peculiar appearance of his eyes, which I couldn't exactly describe intelligently."

In 1896, when Bertram was sixteen, his mother heard an explosion, and rushing out, found Bertram unconscious on the ground, with a gun blown to pieces near him. He had been firing it by holding it directly over his head, and he received a deep wound on the head from the exploded gun, as both parents testified.

In the same year, to punish him for running away from home, he was taken by his father to the woods and ordered to cut some hickory sticks. He was then compelled to remove part of his clothing and the father took off his own coat and gave the boy a severe whipping. In describing this, Mr. Spencer said that he had a revolver, which he laid on his coat near by, and told Bert to make no outcry—that he was going to give him the severest punishment of his life and that "if he made too much fuss, I would shoot him." A Mr. Lattimer, who was working for Mr. Spencer at this time and who lived at their house, testified, "There were several marks on the defendant's body, which covered most of the body from the head to the heels. He had the appearance of having been severely beaten."

A friend of the family, Horace B. Bailey, of Gill,

Conn., whom Bertram visited about this time and on various other occasions for as much as a week or so at a time, said: "If you approached or spoke to him on any subject, quick, he would give a wild, indifferent look; if you agreed with him, everything seemed to be all right, but if you didn't agree, it seemed to disturb him."

Mr. Spencer described an occasion when he and Bertram had started for a drive together, and Bertram had put his arm on the back of the seat of the buggy. "We were riding out of the yard, and he was at my side and he put his hand in the hollow of my back, like that—and it seemed to me intentional, and I turned around and gave him a cuff on the side of the head, asked him what he was doing it for, and he jumped from the wagon and left me. I immediately followed him and called to him. He swore at me and continued to run. I went into the house and got the revolver and fired in his direction as he was running through the pastures."

In the spring of the following year, 1897, Bertram went fishing one Saturday night, and as the outbuildings were closed when he returned, he left his fish-pole standing by the back door. His father came in and stumbled over it and caught the fish-hook in his leg. He said: "It aggravated me—excited me, and I took it immediately, without thought, and broke it into several pieces." When Bertram saw his rod broken, he came rushing into the house in terrible excitement. His mother said he was in a nervous frenzy—acted like a crazy man—went into hysterics, cried and screamed.

The same year he ran away from home and came back during his father's absence to get his clothes. His mother persuaded him to go upstairs to bed. When

Mr. Spencer returned he suspected Bertram was in the house—like the ogre in the fairy tale—and went upstairs in search of him, followed by his wife. According to Mr. Spencer, Bertram drew a revolver when his father approached him and attempted to fire at him; the latter jumped on the bed and grabbed it, and a tussle ensued, during which the lamp was upset and the bedding caught fire. Mrs. Spencer screamed, and the father let go his hold upon Bertram after taking the revolver from him, and the boy jumped up and ran downstairs, followed by his father, after the latter had first hastily extinguished the fire. Mrs. Spencer continued her testimony by saying, "Taking a pair of overalls he (Bertram) went out into the cold night, barefooted, and ran to the home of a neighbor about a mile away, his father firing five shots from the back door as he ran through the yard and down towards the road." The neighbor, Mr. Clark H. Standish, who had known Bertram from birth, confirmed Mrs. Spencer's statement as to her son's condition. Mr. Standish had heard the firing, and said Bertram had shown him an injury in the fleshy part of the thumb that night after he got into the house, which he said was caused by one of his father's shots. The next morning Mr. Standish lent him some clothes, and in the afternoon his mother and sister came to see him and found him very excited and nervous. Mr. Standish said: "I heard him sobbing and crying from the barn to the house, though the windows were closed. It was a hysterical sob. When I went in he was in a hysterical shape and all of a-tremble." Mr. Standish said he had seen Bertram on another occasion at his house when he was very melancholy and had not much to say to anybody. "I have seen him at school get mad at the other scholars—when I worked in the store and post-office, which is close by the school. He would fly into a rage on small provocation—did not appear to have control of himself at those times. When anybody crossed or opposed him he would fly at them in a rage—strike at them. I have seen him pound smaller boys beside the schoolhouse, when I have stood on the store stoop."

Mr. Standish also told of an occurrence when he and another man were digging a ditch for Mr. Spencer: "Bert wanted the best shovel, and the other fellow and I were paid wages, and the other fellow wanted the best shovel and Spencer took it." This man, Sweet, took the shovel away from the boy and threw down the old shovel he had been using. Spencer grabbed this shovel and was about to attack Sweet with it when Standish interfered and took it away from him. Then, according to Standish, "He commenced to cry and make motions, crying and heaving and sighing—seemed to be very excited and hysterical because we took the shovel away from him, and he went off a little way and put his hands to his face and commenced to go off into hysterical shapes."

Shortly after the fish-pole episode, Mrs. Spencer sent Bertram away to her cousin's in Providence, where he stayed for about three months. A very sympathetic letter to Mrs. Spencer from this cousin, Mr. Tilley, speaks of Bert's having been cut in the wrist with a razor, with which he had been "fooling" in the barber shop on his way back from work, "which necessitated taking four stitches, and came very near being a serious affair, and will probably lay him up for a week or two. The doctor says he thinks it will not result in permanent injury, but was an extremely close shave." Mr. Tilley continues, "Somehow I have had a feeling since Bert came that it was all a mistake for him to leave home at his age, and that somehow father and son should be able to help each other better than any stranger could help him; and I have had a serious talk with Bert this afternoon and I know he would be glad to come home, and do the best he can to fill the place he ought to occupy." He then goes on to speak of Bertram's health:

> Bertram has not been well since he came. He had one quite sick turn and was threatened with typhoid fever and had a doctor, and he has had quite a cough hanging over him since, though he has been doctoring for it. The city does not agree with him. You probably remember, Will, when you was a boy, and probably you made some slips and was something of a trial to your friends, and you know that *you* are liable to make mistakes, and so ought to have charity for your boy. I think it would be a mistake for Bert to confine himself to any factory or any other place where he could not use his natural gifts for trading. . . . I feel that Bertram needs his home and you need him, and if I can pave the way to a reconciliation, I shall be pleased. The doctor thinks he can remove the stitches Monday, and that the wound will heal quite rapidly, as Bert *has good habits* and probably has good blood.

Bert did not come home at this time, however, but went to Norwich, Conn., to work for a carpenter named Calvin Briggs, with whom he lived for some time. Mr. Briggs testified at the trial that he had noticed Bertram's peculiarities in some ways: "At times he seemed jolly and jovial, and at other times he would perhaps sit back in a corner and whistle and put his hands up to his face, or something of that kind." At one time his mother was sent for, as Bert had been arrested for drunkenness. When she reached Norwich, Mrs. Briggs told her that they had had some young people spending the evening; they were playing and singing. Bertram was sitting with his head in his hands, and suddenly jumped up and rushed out of the door, and that was the last she saw of him until the next morning. He had been despondent, she said, all day. He told his mother that he had gone out into the street in a fit of despondency and was later found in a dazed condition and taken to the court house. If, as the story would indicate, Bertram had been drinking at this time, it was an unusual event, the only mention of such a happening in all his history. His mother declared that she had never known of his drinking on any other occasion.

From Norwich Bertram went to New Haven, where he stayed for about two months, and from there to a cousin's in Portland. Later he went to Hartford, being at this time about eighteen years old. He remained in Hartford about three months, working in a department store and there is much testimony of his peculiar temper from his associates there. His fellow clerks, Richards, Killian, Hunter and Tedworth told of his springing over a counter and attacking a cash boy who had been annoying him with a hammer, colliding with a customer on the way. They all seem to have been impressed with the peculiar quality of his anger. Richards said, "At times he would have a vacant stare, as though he lost himself. If anybody crossed him, he seemed to get into an uncontrollable rage; he seemed to lose complete control of himself." At the time of the attack upon the cash boy Richards said, "He seemed like a wild beast—he didn't seem to have any control over himself. After colliding with the lady he kept on going until he was stopped by some of the other clerks." Hunter said, "He looked wild; he became very nervous, turned, twisted all around, and then he made a leap on top of the counter and straight over. He was a very nervous boy at that time in his actions. We took a little interest in him, and he stated that he had been used bad at home, and gave that as the reason why he had left." Tedworth also told of this incident, and of another, when Spencer had thrown a hammer at a boy, saying: "At that time he looked very much as though he was not quite right. He threw it hard enough to kill the boy if it had hit him." He said that Spencer manifested his excitement by "wild actions, the expression of his eyes, the way he rushed around—acted. He acted a good deal like a bull that is mad—wild—a wild expression. The wild expression of the eyes I noticed more than anything. At the time he threw the hammer he said he wished that he had killed the boy—or something to that effect." Mr. Killian, who was the head of the department in which Spencer worked, gave a still more detailed account of his peculiarities. Speaking of the time when Spencer had thrown the hammer at the boy, Killian said, "Spencer all of a sudden, with a rage, took a hammer and let it fly at the cash boy. I said, 'If you hit that boy, you will kill him right in his tracks.' He made the remark that he didn't care if he killed him—or something to that effect. I tried to tell him to be more quiet and not to do such a thing, but he raged right up and kept going—swearing just the same. . . . While he was waiting on customers he was inattentive and seemed to wander away from his business; his eyes looked at times kind of glaring, as if he wasn't all there at the time. When he threw the hammer at the cash boy his eyes looked glaring—a wild look in them. He appeared as if he couldn't control himself. I don't think he realized what he had done."

Killian said that when Spencer had been there a few days he received a small paper box through the mail. "I was standing near him when he got the mail, and he opened this package, and in the package were some sweet peas, and a pipe buried underneath. He looked in the box when it was opened and fussed over the sweet peas, and he took out the pipe and said, 'My mother sent that. My mother is good,' and then he started in and swore about his father. His manner and appearance seemed like a boy—he held his head as if in sorrow—more like a younger boy—he was so tickled to see that come from his mother." Killian added that he remembered Spencer because he was so different from the other young men that came in there. When Killian told this story in court, Bertram wept.

Dr. LaMotte, the Naval Surgeon who examined Bertram for the Board of Survey, afterwards looked up his record in Hartford, and he reported to Mr. Stapleton, Spencer's counsel, that "almost everybody with whom he came in contact recognized him as 'crazy,' as they put it."

After this, Bertram went home again to live. A friend of the family, Mrs. Euretta M. Watrous, of Portland, Conn., whom he used to visit often for several weeks at a time during this period of his life or earlier, said she had once seen him coming downstairs after some other boys with a revolver in his hand, and she had stopped him and demanded the revolver. "He seemed almost blind with rage. He said he was going out to fix a boy that had something against him. He appeared very wild and very angry. He had a habit of looking at you just an instant, and then casting his eyes down sideways in a kind of sly expression, I call it."

Bertram's mother said that "in February, 1900, he started to spend the evening with a young woman who lived down town. He was grabbed from behind, bound hand and foot and gagged, and left lying in the snow and slush from half-past seven until eleven in the evening. This was done by boys older than himself, because one of them was jealous of Bert's attentions to this girl. If anything happened it was always Bert who did everything, and the boys were always ready to give him a kick down hill. I know who four of the boys were who took part in tying him up. That was the beginning of his carrying a revolver. He was a martyr to the whipping post for all the deviltry committed by those eight or ten boys." This, and many other stories, show that, like most defective children, Bert was never popular with his companions. Like the others, he was "picked on" while he was little, and made a scapegoat when he grew older; his dangerous temper was fostered by continual persecution and lack of understanding at home and abroad, in spite of his mother's tender sympathy and repeated efforts to spare him.

A similar episode occurred one Sunday in May or June of the same year. He had left home to go to church in the evening, but returned in a very excited condition, complaining of pains in his head. He told his mother that he had left church early, as he could not sit still on account of a carbuncle on his neck. On the way home he had stopped to speak to a young man opposite the home of Mr. N. B. Williams; here he was accosted by another young man, who struck him several blows and knocked him down. Bertram said he had warned the fellow three times to let him alone, threatening him with his revolver, and had finally fired at him. From various things in the account, we gather that this quarrel was also about a young woman.

Bertram was inclined to fits of depression at this time, and in May, 1900, shortly before his nineteenth birthday, he attempted suicide by taking laudanum. His mother had been away on a visit with her daughter, and on her return at four o'clock in the afternoon she found him on the bed unconscious, with an empty 4 oz. bottle beside him, which had contained laudanum. Bertram afterwards said it had been half full. Drs. Drake and Danielson were summoned, and the former remained all night and, with Mrs. Spencer's assistance, kept Bertram moving around the room at intervals until morning. He told his mother afterwards that he had had a love affair, and that he had attempted to take his life because he did not wish to live any longer. Dr. Drake, who had treated Bertram for various illnesses, and had known him especially well from 1895 to 1901, said he formed the opinion that Spencer was depressed and despondent at the time—that it was one of those impulsive acts peculiar to youth of a strongly neurotic temperament. He was not allowed at the trial to express an opinion as to Spencer's mental condition, nor was Dr. Danielson.

After this attempt on his life, Bertram again enlisted in the Navy, and this time he remained in the service eight months and made one cruise. Dr. LaMotte made inquiries as to the cause of his discharge and wrote Mr. Stapleton (Oct. 19th, 1911), "I have received word from one of the doctors of the U. S. Board of Survey that at the time of his discharge from the Navy, the ground for which his discharge was given was 'enuresis,' and that he considered Spencer defective mentally, but it was thought better not so to label him, as he might outgrow the defect and become a useful citizen."

Bert was then sent to the Mount Hermon School, where he remained for two terms, during 1901 and 1902. The teachers in that school testified to his bad temper, insubordination, bad language and lack of self-control. The reports show failures in most of his studies. One of his teachers, Mr. Wellington E. Aiken, said that at one time he was summoned to the dormitory, where he found Spencer packing his trunk, talking loudly and making a great deal of noise. When told to be quiet he became violently angry, swore at the teacher and appeared to be regardless of consequences. The teacher left the dormitory for a short time, and on his return found Spencer smoking. As this was against the rules, Mr. Aiken requested him to desist, and as Spencer refused to obey, he gave him until seven o'clock in the evening to decide whether he would obey the rules or leave the premises. When he came back after supper, Spencer had packed his trunk and left. Later he returned to the school and came to Mr. Aiken's room and apologized.

Mr. Horace B. Bailey of Mt. Hermon said that Spencer visited his house at various times. Mr. Bailey had been formerly employed as an attendant for the insane for thirteen years, in an asylum in Poughkeepsie, and he had been observant of Spencer's behavior. He said that if you approached him suddenly or spoke to him unexpectedly he "would give a wild, indifferent

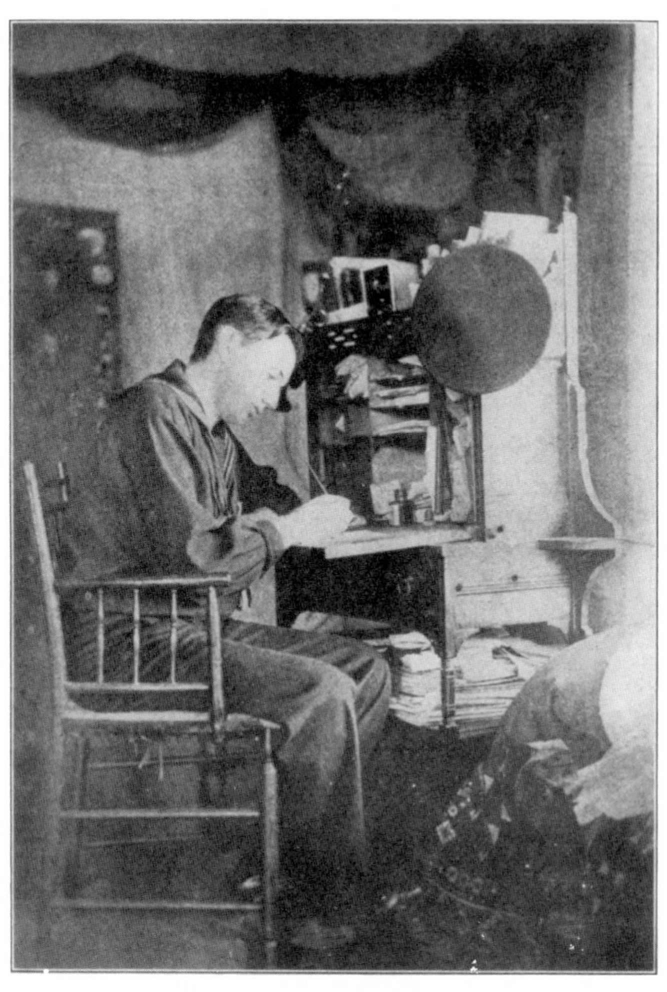

BERTRAM G. SPENCER

Second enlistment U. S. Navy 1898, aged 17 years.

look; if you agreed with him, everything would be right, but if you didn't agree, it seemed to disturb him." Bailey was not allowed to testify at the trial as to his own opinion of Spencer, nor to compare him with the patients previously under his charge in the insane asylum.

Probably it was after he left Mt. Hermon that Spencer worked for a few weeks for his board with Gardiner J. Oakes, of Bernardstown, Mass. Mr. Oakes said of him, "Once in awhile he would have a kind of poor spell, change color and clap his hands up this way. I says to him, 'What is the matter, Bert?' and he says, 'I will be over it in a minute.' There might have been half a dozen of these spells, more or less." He also spoke to Mr. Oakes of his headaches, and was melancholy and gloomy at times.

Spencer again returned home, and for awhile assisted with the work on the farm. One day about this time, he was working in a ditch with a neighbor, Benjamin Franklin Carpenter, with whom he was talking when his father came out and said, "Come, boys, more work and less play here." Carpenter said, "The boy immediately flew into a passion such as I have never seen, unless it was an insane person. . . . He jumped out of the ditch with the shovel, and immediately started for his father, and you don't know what kind of an expression was on this boy's countenance! It was wild and staring, and he uttered words that I can't repeat—I didn't understand them. He immediately hoarsed up, and kept on going for his father with the shovel as though he was to strike him." As Mr. Spencer described Bertram's appearance on this occasion, "His features were distorted, his eyes were bulging and he was in a very excited state. The saliva was running out of each corner of his mouth. . . . He was certainly ferocious looking. It was the only time in my life that I was ever afraid of him." Mr. Carpenter interfered, and Bertram ran into the house "cursing and throwing his hands." Mr. Spencer said, "I remained outside about my work, and could hear him cursing and swearing, and loud noises and pounding, and at times it seemed as though he was smashing things up there—I really didn't feel safe—I didn't think it was safe for me to go in at the time. The noises lasted for two or three hours, if not longer. He seemed to have no control of himself—I don't think he realized what he was doing." Mrs. Spencer said, "He came rushing in, screaming and crying in hysterics, and it seemed to me it was more than an hour before I could quiet him. Saliva ran from his mouth, and his eyes glared like a wild man, and he was all the time cursing and swearing in a frenzy—the worst attack I have ever seen him in. I noticed that he had a thick tightening in the throat—it was a hoarse sound. While in this frenzy his bowels moved and he soiled his clothes. He had the same symptoms other times when he had spells. He frequently wet the bed until fourteen or fifteen, also wet his clothes."

Mr. Carpenter told of Bert's flying into a passion when ploughing because his horse was "a little fractious" in going around the corner of the field. "He seemed to fly into a passion, you know, and grabbed the horse by the head and went to flogging it with his fists about the head."

The boy was often hysterical for no apparent cause. His mother had observed him to have melancholy spells when he would weep violently and sob, usually under excitement from some provocation. Sometimes, as often as once or twice a week, he would be melancholy without apparent provocation, and his mood was changeable in the extreme—first he would be melancholy and then would suddenly brighten up. His manner was hysterical in sobbing and crying, and sometimes in laughing, she said—you could hear him sobbing in another room, or from outside the house. There was a characteristic similarity in his spells, but some of them were more intense than others. His mother also said, "We would frequently be at table when he would say, 'Mother, did you speak to me?' and I would say, 'No, why?' He said, 'I thought I heard someone speak to me.' That was a common occurrence. He would look up and say, 'Mother, did you speak to me?' " Several other persons testified to this peculiarity of Bert's—the tendency to hear imaginary voices.

Spencer first went to Springfield about 1903, and worked for the Street Railway Company, serving at different times both as motorman and conductor, and he also served as brakeman on the Boston and Maine R. R. for a time. He probably did not remain in any of these positions very long, however, for in the same year, 1903, he went out to California. Here he boarded at intervals—as much as twelve months in all—with Mrs. Anita Martland, a family connection who seems to have taken considerable interest in Bertram. She said, in a written deposition, "When he first came from the East he worked in Hale Brothers' department store. When he left there he came to our house and stayed for awhile; then he went to Seattle. He went up on the ship 'Montera'—I believe he worked on the ship.

Then he came back and got work at the Oakland Traction Company, as conductor on the cars. He was living at my house at the time he worked for the Traction Company; then he went away—I don't remember exactly where he went to, but he came back and worked for the People's Express Company, as shipping clerk. . . . Well, the earthquake came, and I believe he got work as a carpenter, and then he left us."

Mrs. Martland said, "He acted very queer at times, and about every two weeks. Sometimes he was melancholy and would cry and cry by the hour. He was hit on the head by his father when a boy of about six years of age, and at certain times he would have these terrible pains in his head. For instance, he would get up in the morning complaining of his head, and I would bathe it for him. Then again he would curse and swear whenever he happened to have these pains. He was abused by his father when at home. He would indulge in a spell of swearing or cursing, and pace the floor at times for over half an hour; then I would get him to lie down and go to sleep, or he would amuse himself playing the piano, and I got his mind off it this way. I wrote and told his mother, and she said she had the same trouble with his father. He would swear when he had these pains; then he would go away in the evenings sometimes, about 8.20 o'clock, and did not show up until four o'clock the next morning. He had been with me two weeks when he did that. . . . I noticed that when he would have these spells there was a vein or artery under his right ear that pulsated so violently it was noticeable to anyone. His condition and appearance were entirely changeable at the times when he had these spells. He was a perfect gentleman out of these

BERTRAM G. SPENCER
1906
In California, aged 25 years.

spells; when in them he was like a raving fool. These changes took place about every two weeks. I bathed his head with various cooling lotions—I could not touch his head, as it was very tender and caused him great pain when there was any pressure. My judgment is it was on the right side" (referring to the artery).

Mrs. Lucy T. Lewis, a former resident of Lebanon and friend of the Spencer family, who was living in Oakland when Spencer was there, said that he had called upon her in Oakland and had behaved like an insane person, was excited, wild-eyed, nervous, wandered about the room, would not sit still. He was there between two and three hours, and during that time talked of scarcely anything but the abuse of his mother by his father, but he did not mention his father's abuse of himself. He sat first in one chair and then in another. "I didn't know what to do—I was afraid of him. I felt that no person in his right mind would talk that way. I simply asked him about his mother; he said that his father had struck her in the face and dragged her around by the hairs of her head. It was out of the ordinary anger. He didn't act like himself."

Spencer was during his stay in California a member of the National Guard. He confessed that he stole the revolver with which he later killed Miss Blackstone from the Armory of F Company, California National Guard, in Oakland. He remained in the West for about three years, returning East in 1906 and again went to Springfield, where he secured employment with the Street Railway Company as conductor. He boarded with Mrs. Bessie E. Walters, at 83 Carew Street, where he lived before he went West.

Mrs. Walters said at the trial that she had observed that Spencer was "rather a peculiar fellow" in several ways; that he was "kind of flighty like—hard to get along with in lots of ways. He would speak to me in the dining-room," she continued, "and probably there would be nobody in there but he and I, and I would be going round fixing my table and he would say, 'Did you speak to me?' 'No, I didn't speak to you.' 'Did anybody call me?'—I have heard him do this a good many times, I could not tell just how often; I didn't pay no attention to it, of course, but he often asked me the question." She said that she had seen him when he was melancholy: "You would speak to him, and he would not answer—kind of despondent lots of times." She also told of an occasion when Spencer had a scuffle with his room-mate, George Kenmouth. He was trying to pull Kenmouth out of bed. Kenmouth jumped up and made for him, and Spencer grabbed Kenmouth by the throat. "He looked terrible; he looked like a wild man or a crazy man or something. He looked certainly as if he was going to do some desperate deed. I spoke to him. . . . He dropped his hold he had on the boy and turned to me and says, 'It's a good thing you spoke—I would just as soon kill him this minute.' So he reached out his hand and they shook hands, and there was all there was of it—they were friends the next minute." Mrs. Walters said that Spencer had no provocation whatever to be angry while he was with them. "He was a man we all stood in fear of for that reason—to get him angry. He would get into a passion of temper, and this was the reason we avoided it as much as we could. *He had lots of stuff, lots of curious stuff, things that wasn't of no value to anybody, sticks and stones and such things.* He claimed they had a history—he had them for souvenirs—nothing of any value to anybody except himself—rather curious for a fellow to have. He used to wear badges and pins —I didn't examine what they were—I have often seen him have lots of those things."

Mrs. Gladys L. Wyman, a trained nurse who had previously had two years' experience in caring for the insane at Northampton, had boarded at Mrs. Walter's when Spencer was there before going to California, and had been there with her husband for two years after his return. She noticed that he acted queerly at times, and said he had one bad outbreak before he went West: "He wasn't pleased with his dinner at all, and the meat, especially, didn't suit him. He looked it all over and then threw it to one side of the table, exclaiming that the meat wasn't fit for a dog to eat. I myself and the rest of the boarders had eaten the same meat as he had to eat. His eyes stared—he had a glaring stare in his eyes—he was pale of face—his tightening of the lips and twitching of the face—that was all I noticed at the time. Previous to this his table manners were very polite. . . . He thought that people were trying to get the better of him—made remarks that people were trying to outdo him.

"After he came back from California I noticed a decided change in him. He was more impulsive in his manner, and got riled at very little things, and I noticed a very peculiar look in his eyes after he came from the West." She then described at some length a controversy at the table, when she asked him whether he had made a certain slurring remark about her husband. "He said, 'Mrs. Wyman, if I knew who had told you that, I would kill him'—and by the expression of his face and eyes, I think he would have—he completely lost control of himself—clenched his fists—he was very excited." Bertram had a hammock which he kept hung high to prevent others using it, and at times he would say that someone had interfered with the hammock, when there was no ground for such an accusation, and he would get excited and tremble. "Oftentimes," continued Mrs. Wyman, "he would be in the dining-room and no one there; I was in the kitchen, and he would call out and ask me if I was talking to him—when no one would be speaking. I would see him sit at the table or in a chair—he would sit in a moody condition, and then all of a sudden he would brace up and ask if anyone was talking. One time, especially after he came from the West, we had a phonograph, and Bert being fond of music, I invited him up to the room to hear the phonograph. He sat all the evening until it was time to go away, and the only word he spoke that evening was 'Good-night.' "

Mr. Willard L. Wyman, a brakeman on the Boston and Albany Road, had formerly been an attendant for two and a half years at the Northampton State Hospital for the Insane. He had worked with Spencer and boarded at Mrs. Walter's for some time while Spencer was there. Wyman said of Spencer, "He sat down in the house—in the kitchen; we would be talking. Perhaps he would sit there for twenty minutes and perhaps an hour, and he wouldn't say anything—then he would look up and say, 'Did you speak to me?' He would pick up his hat and go out—he wouldn't say anything. I have seen him act that way on several different occasions when we were all in the kitchen together."

Wyman told of one occasion when he was conductor on a car and Spencer was motorman on the same car. Spencer insisted that Wyman should come out front and sing with him. Wyman declared that he could not sing, but Spencer urged that he join in on the chorus. "When he got to the chorus, I come in with him; he told me it wasn't high enough. He started over again, and when he got to the chorus I come in again. He told me I couldn't sing any more than a damned hog—went to the back end of the car and didn't speak to me again all night. He spoke up kind of quick. He was kind of white when he pulled the curtain to go inside—I turned my head around and he looked as though he was going to fight in a minute. The next morning he come down to breakfast and says, 'Hello, Billy,' just the same as though nothing had happened."

Others of Spencer's companions of this period spoke of his peculiarities. Napoleon Bourque of West Springfield told of Spencer's peculiar paleness when angry about a baseball glove. He refused to speak to Bourque for over twenty-four hours after this quarrel. He had also noticed Spencer's sudden paleness on another occasion, when he had passed in the street a man who he thought had misused him. Robert E. Miles, who had been fireman on the Boston & Maine R. R. when Spencer was brakeman, told of Spencer's having threatened him with a revolver after a scuffle in which he had knocked Spencer down.

Spencer was married on March 18th, 1908. He had been for some time paying attentions to Miss Minnie

Amberg, a bookkeeper and stenographer, daughter of Herman L. Amberg, who was employed by the H. L. Handy Company. Mr. Amberg objected to the match, and he testified at the trial that after Bert had been calling on his daughter for about a year, he came one Sunday and wanted to take Miss Amberg out by force, her father having refused to let her go out with him that day. "He called me all the names you could think of," said Mr. Amberg, "and he threatened to kill me. He was going to knock my head off. The girl left my house and got married without my consent, and we had a falling out and I didn't see any of them for a year." Bertram and Miss Amberg took out a license in Springfield, and were married in Boston the same day. They lived for awhile at 53 Greenwich St., Springfield, and it is said that he lost his position on the Boston & Maine R. R., where he was employed as brakeman, through a row that he had with the engineer because he insisted on ringing the engine bell as a signal to his wife every time they passed Greenwich Street.

Bertram had many positions in Springfield, never remaining very long in the same place. He was not only, at various times, motorman and conductor on the street railway, fireman and brakeman on the railroad, but, according to the Springfield Republican, he was employed in the Stevens-Duryea Factory at Chicopee in the shipping room, afterwards by the Atlas Motor Car Company, and still later he went to work for the H. L. Handy Company, where his father-in-law also worked.

Several events are described as having taken place after his marriage which are particularly significant. At one time he started with his wife, his sister, Mrs.

Pulz, and her husband for a row on the river. The boat they intended to use belonged to his wife's grandfather, Mr. Krailing, a German who owned the house in which the Spencers lived on Porter Avenue, and who lived with his wife in the upper apartment. Spencer asked Krailing for the key to the place where the oar-locks were kept and Krailing said he didn't know just where it was, and had no time to hunt for it. Mrs. Pulz said at the trial, "My brother was very angry. He immediately started for Mr. Krailing and said he would throw him into the river. My husband, Mr. Spencer's wife and myself did as much as we could to hold Mr. Spencer—my husband had hold of his arm, and I had my arms around his neck. We pleaded with him not to touch Mr. Krailing, and it was with great effort that we restrained him. He was all the time, during this time, talking very loudly—screaming at the top of his voice, so that it could be heard, I should have said, a quarter of a mile away. A crowd collected from the houses near. He said, 'Let me get at him! I want to throw him in the river.' He had a very wild look in his eyes—there was a glassy look about them." Mrs. Pulz said she had seen him have such outbreaks a great many times—"As long ago as I can remember, he was never able to control himself if anyone crossed him." She had observed his tendency to melancholy moods, and said that one had only to point a finger at him with the suggestion of tickling to cause him to scream and laugh and run away.

All those present at the time of the attack upon Mr. Krailing seem to have been impressed by the violence of Bertram's outbreak. Mr. Norman Pulz, husband of Bertram's sister, said that "when Spencer got mad he was in a frenzy—he would shout as if he didn't know what he was saying—mixed his words all up. I always tried to get along with him the best I could—I knew his temper." Mr. Krailing, in confirming the story of the attack upon himself, spoke as if he were afraid of Spencer—"He looked so bad. . . . He looked all the time bad. He don't look good to me—I am afraid for him. He has a bad eye for me, and I think he was crazy." Mrs. Krailing, who was also a witness to this incident, said, "He looked just like a wild man. His eyes were sticking out. I was afraid, too!"

Speaking of his character as a neighbor, Mrs. Krailing said, "Oh, he was most all the time nervous—I saw him all the time"—meaning daily, as they lived under the same roof. . . . "He was sometimes all the time nervous and doing something that was not right. He killed his bird—his canary bird. I saw him standing there on the back piazza, and he was pale and his eyes sticking out—just kind of nervous, all worrying, and his mind—he looked so worried about it, so half-nervous—he looked half out of his mind; that is the reason I didn't ask nothing of him." In her broken English, she described another incident, when he killed a cat: "He come out of the cellar and got the cat and bumped it on the pieces and threw it on the river on the ice. I don't know what for—he was half crazy, too—he looked so."

On another occasion, Spencer's mother and sister were spending an evening with the young couple in their home. Bertram and his sister sang several songs together, and then Bertram complained of headache and lay down on the couch. His sister continued singing, and suddenly Bertram jumped up and asked her why she had not been over to see them in the last two weeks. She said she had been busy and unable to come, whereupon, as his mother put it, "he went into those frenzies and cursed and swore—called her names—he seemed much excited. It lasted all the rest of the evening. When he had one of these attacks he had a wild stare and looked more like a wild animal than a human being; he made a peculiar noise with the throat. He would hoarse right up as soon as he began to talk; he would raise his voice, which would become almost a scream."

After he returned to live in Springfield, Bertram went back to Lebanon occasionally to visit. Charles A. Gager testified at the trial that he had met him there at a dance, and that he had seen him draw a pistol during a heated argument with another man, who knocked it from his hand.

Mrs. Spencer had an idea that Bert's career as a burglar began in 1903—that it was suggested to him by the following occurrence:

Bert's mother was told by a neighbor that Bert had been arrested for burglary. A Hartford paper had published an account of the crime, and said that the criminal was named Bertram G. Spencer. Mrs. Spencer hurried to Springfield, and found Bertram in bed at his boarding place, 105 North Main Street. He had been working late the night before and had not yet risen. Mrs. Spencer said, "Bert started out the next day to follow up the story, and traced it to Philo Burgess, who lived near South Windham, whose son was determined to go with the girl I have referred to before. It seems two men, one a mulatto and the other a white man, had been arrested for entering houses with false keys and burglarizing. One gave his name as Bertram Spencer, and was possibly one of two boys who came from state homes to work for us, one of whom proved to be dishonest. What I am aiming at is this: after Bert went back to Springfield, in almost every letter he would sign his name 'Bert the Burglar' —ridiculing the idea of his ever doing such a thing." Bertram was of a suggestible nature, and it is possible that this episode and the repetition of the signature may have helped to urge him on to his career of crime.

Eight months before his arrest, Spencer went to work for H. L. Handy & Company. Mr. Horace H. Clement, a buyer for the H. L. Handy Company, testified as follows: "I spoke to him one day about a car that did not check out right and he lost his temper; he cried and swore, and there was a hatchet that was on an egg-case, and he reached for that. He was excited—he didn't appear to have much control of himself. He shut himself into the butter refrigerator." Mr. Handy, in telling of this incident, said, "I heard him talking to Mr. Clement, and Mr. Clement saw in what condition he was and decided he could do nothing with him. . . . He made actions as if to grab a hatchet, but didn't, and then turned and went into the butter box." Mr. Handy followed him, and saw him in one corner cf the refrigerator, crying. "He had his arms over his face, sobbing loudly."

Examination by Alienists

At the time of Spencer's arrest, Stephen S. Taft was District Attorney for Hampden County. Spencer's history may here be continued by a quotation from a speech which Mr. Taft made on October 31st, 1910, during his campaign for re-election for office. After referring to the semi-judicial nature of the office of District Attorney, Mr. Taft took up the Spencer case and said:

"In the latter part of April a most brutal homicide was committed in this city. People were nervous, excited, horrified, and it was felt by everyone that there was but one punishment which ought to be meted out to the perpetrator of the crime. Four days after the homicide, Spencer was arrested, and after the property stolen from the house in which the unfortunate woman was killed had been identified, confessed that he was the man. Under the law of the Commonwealth, the Attorney-General has direction of all capital cases, and the duty of preparing and presenting the case was placed upon me by the Attorney-General.

"The facts were presented to the next Grand Jury in May, and an indictment for murder in the first degree was found. At that sitting of the Court Spencer was arraigned and counsel were appointed by the Commonwealth to defend him. The senior counsel, appointed by the Court on May 16th, 1910, was excused from service because of ill health, and on August 3rd, 1910, other counsel was substituted for him by the Chief Justice. The case was set for trial at the earliest possible moment after such counsel had been appointed. Because of the repairs in the Court House, there was no court room in which a trial could have been had until one week before the time fixed, and during that week the Grand Jury was in session.

"A statute passed by the Legislature in 1909 provides:

If a person under complaint or indictment for any crime is, at the time appointed for the trial or sentence, or at any time prior thereto, found by the Court to be insane, or in such mental condition that his commitment to a hospital for the insane is necessary for the proper care and observation of such person, pending the determination of his insanity, the Court may commit him to a state hospital for the insane, under such limitations as it may order.

"The counsel for the defendant, taking advantage of this statute, asked the Court to determine whether Spencer was insane, or whether his commitment to a hospital was necessary for proper care and observation pending the determination of his sanity. The only question before the Court was whether such commitment was necessary. Spencer had been, at my request, examined by three alienists, and every one of them told me that in their judgment his commitment was necessary. A district attorney can not employ alienists without the consent of the Court. I understand that it has been suggested that, when it was found that the three alienists consulted would not declare Spencer to be sane, it was the duty of the District Attorney to have employed other experts. I did not so conceive my duty at that time, nor do I now. Three men, eminent in their profession, two of them in the employ of the State, had been consulted, and it seemed to me then and it seems to me now, that their statements should be taken as true. I understand that the other candidate for the office has said that I am capable, honest—but that in this case I showed a lack of discretion; that I ought not to have put the alienists upon the stand; and with this proposition I take issue. In my judgment, a district attorney, knowing that there was serious question concerning the mental condition of a defendant about to be brought to trial, who should conceal the information and proceed with the trial and perhaps obtain a verdict which should send the defendant to the electric chair, would be derelict in his duty and almost as culpable as many convicted defendants."

The above extract sums up the situation as to the experts' examination, but a few details are of interest. Mrs. Spencer wrote me that after Bertram's arrest she read an article written by Dr. Philip Kilroy, a nerve and brain specialist of Springfield, saying that Bertram was "no more responsible than a child for what he had done." The devoted mother immediately saw Dr. Kilroy and told him Bertram's history, and the doctor suggested that she see District Attorney Taft and tell him all. "Mr. Taft was a stern man," she writes, "but he seemed interested in what I told him, and assured me he would consider the matter, but of course would be obliged to do his duty. . . . By sending Bertram to Bridgewater and taking the attitude he did, Mr. Taft lost his office as District Attorney that fall."

The press generally having described the burglar as "a defective," "an abnormal person," "a pervert," "a maniac," etc., it was only natural that the District Attorney should take up the question of Spencer's sanity. Within forty-eight hours after his arrest, Dr. John A. Houston, Superintendent of the Northampton State Hospital, was called in to examine the prisoner. He expressed such doubts as to Spencer's mental condition that other experts were called in.

In May, 1910, Col. Charles L. Young had asked the Court to appoint himself and Christopher T. Callahan as Spencer's counsel. Mr. Callahan was ill at the time, but as soon as he was able to go to Springfield he protested against being connected with the defense of Spencer, and Judge Schofield excused him from service. Mr. Richard P. Stapleton was shortly afterwards appointed in his stead. The reason for the assignment of counsel at this time was that the trial of the case was set down for September, 1910.

On Saturday, September 17th, 1910, Chief Justice Aiken and Judge Sanderson held a hearing on the Spencer case, and four alienists appeared before them, representing the Commonwealth and the defense. These alienists, Drs. Courtney, Quinby, Houston and Tuttle, all agreed that Spencer's commitment to an asylum for observation was the proper procedure. Their testimony was as follows:

Dr. Houston testified that he had been connected with institutions for the insane for twenty-three years, and had been Superintendent of Northampton State Hospital for thirteen years. He said that he had examined Spencer three times, and had not been able to satisfy himself that Spencer was responsible; that he believed the man should be sent to a hospital for observation. Dr. Houston said that he considered Spencer insane—that is, that his was a defective mental state, if not degenerative, probably dating from puberty.

Dr. Tuttle testified that he had been connected with the McLean Hospital as physician or as Superintendent for thirty-one years; that he had seen Spencer at the request of the District Attorney, and that he believed that he was a proper person to be committed to an insane asylum for observation. Later he testified that Spencer "was a defective individual and had been so from birth," and said he was not certain whether the man could resist doing wrong.

Dr. Hosea M. Quinby testified that he had been Superintendent of Worcester State Hospital for over thirty years, and that he had examined Bertram G. Spencer twice at the request of the District Attorney. He said that these examinations, together with Spencer's heredity, the confession, the manner in which he conducted the burglaries, incidents connected with the burglaries and his impulsive outbreaks at other times during his life, indicated to him a person who was suffering from some mental aberration, and it was his opinion that it was a case which would at least eventuate in dementia precox. He said that he had examined Spencer first alone, and then in the presence of Dr. Houston and Dr. Courtney, and that he thought it very fitting that Spencer should be sent to Bridgewater where he could be further observed.

Dr. Joseph W. Courtney testified that he had made four examinations of Spencer—one in the presence of Drs. Houston and Quinby—that he felt there were grave doubts as to Spencer's responsibility, and suggested that he be put under observation in a proper institution for that purpose. Later he said that he considered Spencer "insane and irresponsible."

When these examinations were made there was no question in the minds of these experts of Spencer's malingering, and this array of experienced psychiatrists had no doubt as to his abnormality, and were unanimous in their opinion that he was a proper case for the Bridgewater State Hospital for further observation. Spencer at this time had had no opportunity to observe and imitate an insane person or a mental defective, and it would be an insult to one of these eminent experts to imagine that he could have been deceived by Spencer in examinations made immediately after his arrest—or indeed at any other time. The fact that the Commonwealth's experts were unanimous in their opinion certainly justifies the course pursued by District Attorney Taft.

After Spencer's arrest, his lawyers, Stapleton and Young, requested a change of venue, on the ground that there was so much popular feeling against the prisoner in and about Springfield that it would be impossible to get an unprejudiced jury in Hampden County. They asked for a hearing in Worcester County. It is said that a change of venue has never been granted in the State of Massachusetts, and with no precedent, Chief Justice Aiken refused their request.

With Spencer, locked in the jail, was Eugene Farrar of Springfield. He was supposed to keep continual watch over Spencer, so that he might do no harm to himself, and was with him eighteen days. He later testified that Spencer "acted queer" and that he "thought he was insane," that he spent much of his time catching flies on the wall, that in the midst of a game of cards, he threw the cards down and accused Farrar of cheating, grabbed the cards from the table, threw them on the floor, picked them up and began to tear them—and ended by sitting down on his bunk and crying.

Under date of April 27th, 1910, Spencer wrote to his mother from Hampden County Jail, Springfield. This is the first letter I have from Spencer to his mother:

BERTRAM G. SPENCER

Aged 29

1910, during his confinement in York Street Jail, Springfield, Mass.

My dear, dear Mother,

Your three loving, heartbroken letters are before me. I hardly know where to begin, as we are allowed only one sheet of paper and one envelope a day. . . . When I think of it, I almost go blind with grief—cry and think and think and cry, and when I get through am all at sea to know *why, oh Mother, why it ever happened or had to be.* God knows I always tried, oh so hard! to do right by everyone. This impulse has followed me from ten to twelve years old up to the Round Hill affair. Oh! to God! I could go to sleep and forget it all—but no; I dream about it, and when I awake there are the barred windows and doors to refresh my memory. Oh, dear! will this awful torture ever end! It has taken me over an hour to come this far, and I may have to finish in the morning as my head is bursting. Keep up, Mother dear! There is a crown of glory awaiting you on the other shore—and there I want to go, too. When we are laid to rest, may we lie side by side to all eternity.

In a later letter he writes:

Only yesterday someone put in the paper that I had my cell decorated with women's pictures and flowers, and all I have and want is Mother's, Minnie's, Colly's and Wilbur's—— These are the "vile pictures," etc., that the paper has got to talk about.

While Spencer was in jail, his behavior varied from day to day, and at times he became violent. Dr. Charles P. Hooker, the jail physician, said that he was called to the jail to see the prisoner on May 18th, 1910, and found the patient writhing about on the floor with his wrists in a muff, which the prison officials had put on to restrain him. Later Spencer accused Dr. Hooker of trying to poison him. Dr. Hooker testified that he threatened Spencer with the dungeon if he did not behave, "You are faking, Spencer. You have the choice of one of two things: either go into the dungeon on bread and water for ten days, or go back to your cell and behave yourself." The insane are often amenable to threats and punishment, so Spencer went back to his cell and was quiet for a time.

Transfer to Bridgewater

Immediately after the hearing, September 17th, 1910, at which the expert alienists gave their testimony, Chief Justice Aiken ordered Spencer to be removed to the Bridgewater State Hospital for the criminal insane for observation. In the order for his removal, the Chief Justice said, *"It appearing to the Court from the testimony of experts in insanity,* that Bertram G. Spencer, of Springfield, in said County, under an indictment for murder, is in such condition that his commitment to a hospital for the insane is necessary for his proper care and observation, pending the determination of his sanity. . . ."

CHAPTER III

HISTORY AT BRIDGEWATER

September 19th, 1910, to August 1st, 1911

Spencer was removed to the Bridgewater State Hospital on September 19th, and a month later the Superintendent, Dr. Elliott, made the following report to the Chief Justice, in accordance with the order of the Chief Justice that reports of Spencer's condition should be sent to him monthly.

Bridgewater State Hospital,
at Bridgewater, Mass.
Railroad Station: Titicut, (N. Y., N. H. & H. R. R.)
Alfred Elliott, M.D., Medical Director.

October 17th, 1910.

To the Honorable Chief Justice of the
Superior Court of Hampden,
Springfield, Mass.

Dear Sir:

In accordance with the order of the Honorable Court, I hereby report on the condition of Bertram G. Spencer, who was committed to this Hospital from the Superior Court at Springfield, September 19th last, for the purpose of determining his mental condition.

When Spencer was admitted he was somewhat depressed and emotional. He was coherent, however, and realized why he was sent here. Voluntary attention at this time was somewhat defective, and memory, especially for remote events, fragmentary and unreliable. Patient has not shown evidence of hallucinations at any time of our examinations, but has manifested some weak, ill-defined ideas, which may almost be classified as delusions of persecution. These ideas, however, are not firmly fixed, and do not influence his life or actions, and are evidently the result of faulty judgment and at present have no important relation to patient's mental condition.

Apparently patient's most prominent mental symptoms lie in the sphere of moral sense. Since early childhood he has followed perverted sexual acts, and even after his marriage, was addicted to masturbation. He is entirely without remorse for the many crimes of his past, without sorrow and without pity for the people he has wronged, and he relates them without the slightest evidence of mental anguish. The only sorrow expressed in connection with his past life is solely because his deeds have reacted to his personal disadvantage, and have resulted in depriving him of his liberty. He shows no true appreciation of the enormity of his crimes or the remote consequences of the same. His reasoning on all important subjects or events of his life is manifestly rudimentary and superficial.

In his daily hospital life he is imaginative, fault-finding, impulsive and very sensitive. At times he is childish, will sulk, refuse to talk and assume the attitude of a much injured person. At other times he is very emotional. Will talk about suiciding, and an hour later will be enjoying a game of ball or entertaining the other patients by singing. He often intimates that the officers are down on him and against him, but this idea apparently finds no permanent place in his mind. At times he manifests symptoms that suggest the beginning of a delusional and dementing process, but of this it is too soon to speak with any degree of certainty.

At the present time, it is my opinion that the degree of Spencer's mental deficiency and the obliquity of his moral nature is so great that it constitutes real insanity. Aside from this there are symptoms that call for further observation and study.

Very truly yours,

Alfred Elliott,
Medical Director.

After Spencer's transfer to the Bridgewater State Hospital, his suggestible nature soon showed the effect of what he saw, heard and felt at this institution. This is best told in his own words, in letters which he wrote from Bridgewater and in a diary which he kept during his residence there, from which I extract such parts as show the conditions under which this young man was placed for observation as to his sanity, and his reaction to the sort of hospital environment into which he was thrown, and to the unpleasant experiences to which he was subjected as a witness or which were related to him by his sane and insane criminal companions. Distressing as they were, many of the incidents here related were corroborated by other inmates and attendants, entirely without Spencer's knowledge, and some of them are cited to show what is evidently referred to in Dr. Elliott's reports as "almost delusions," "faulty judgment," "false conclusions," etc. There is a mixture in Spencer's letters and diary of what at times were evidently delusions, and of what at other times are undoubtedly facts. Some of these stories may have originated in the brain of some companion of a stronger mind, who wished to see Spencer get excited, or who desired to use him to further some plan or complaint of his own.

In one of the first letters Spencer wrote from Bridgewater State Hospital he describes conditions and says:

> . . . I hope and pray my trial comes right away and it is all over soon and I am sentenced to death, for then my troubles will soon be over; for this place is Hell, Hell, Hell on earth, and most everyone says it is growing worse every year. There is not one person up here in the Northeast who, when they ask a question can get a civil answer, and if things don't go just right they bang the door and rattle their keys in the lock, as if they were locking up beasts instead of human beings. . . . I am getting near the truth and they are trying to punish me in all sorts of ways, but I laugh Ha, ha, ha! A man referred to me as a witness about what the attendants and night watchmen were doing and Dr. Elliott says "You don't want to pay any attention to what he says—— He's not reliable." . . . If I can't get any more satisfaction in asking for what I want than I have in the past, what's the use of asking? It only keeps me all stirred up, and my head aches enough almost every day without being tantalized almost to death or otherwise irritated. There are over 25 murderers in the big court of about 300, and where I am only two—and why should they not let me in the other yard? . . . I get so wrought up I can't sleep half the night, and I get up and pace my room.

In a letter every line of which is underscored, dated from "State Tantalization, Titicut, Mass., Oct. 25th,

1910," he writes to his father and mother of the "hundred words from Doctors Elliott and Baker," and says:

You shall hear them and they shall be sown broadcast, no matter what I have to suffer. . . . Death ten thousand times—ten thousand times, than to be confined in a prison of Hell on earth because the ones at the head down to the stool pigeons are the cause. Only this last week the night watchman beat up another poor fellow, and every one is powerless to raise a finger, and his cries for help are heartrending. Why, in the name of humanity, aren't these things enacted when the public or the Union reporter is there???? No, it is done when everyone is supposed to be blind. Baker says to me, with his cunning smile, "Did you see all this with your own eye?" "No, I did not." He says, "Oh, then it's not so; for men can fall down," he says, "and get cut and bruised without being struck." How smart! There are two men I have become acquainted with since I came here that are not crazy by any means, and they saw it all with their own eyes, and heard what I heard with my own ears. . . . All last night and today I have had *one of my hard headaches* and in the next room there is a fellow was up half the night one night last week, and he asked the night watchman if he could call the doctor, as he had severe pains, and the watchman said "Why, he won't come tonight—— You's have to wait till morning." So he did, and when the physician came round next morning the fellow started in to tell him, and the physician shut the peep-hole, not even waiting for the poor fellow to finish. What's the use of asking for anything here?

In this same letter, after stating that he is confined in the "Northeast Violent Ward" on the top floor, and that the yard he is allowed to use is called the "Bull Pen" and contains seventeen persons, he writes:

One of the "patient-attendants," who is perfectly sane, told me he would ask Dr. Baker if he would let me go over in the other yard to play baseball and football. Baker says, "Why, he's up in the Northeast now, and if we let him go over there, we will have to let two or three others go." "Well," this fellow says, "He has never done anything you should use him that way. Those others you spoke of, two tried to get away, and the other kicked a fellow to death. You've got cause to keep them over there, but you haven't Spencer, for he has not done anything." "Well," Baker says, "as far as we're concerned, he should go over there, but the people outside would make a kick—see?" I am not here for kind treatment—it is only to make me suffer every way possible. . . . They set me at table where there were seemingly two nice fellows. The first day I sat there they offered me katsup, milk, doughnuts, etc., and I wondered how it was they were so well favored. . . . I went to supper one night out of the three first and I said something and they hung their heads. I repeated it twice, thinking they did not hear me, but they did and would not speak—— Why?—because they were ————'s and ————'s stool pigeons, and after trying to pump me about my case and find out nothing, then they were told to let me alone and not to speak—so the good little boys did just as they were told. Then after that, the one who sat opposite me every little while would carelessly drop his foot down on my foot. What was that for? Just to aggravate me into striking him, and then they would have an excuse for shutting me into my room. I get every kind of punishment that is given here but that and beating, so I can't suffer much worse. This morning an attendant came up and began, first one foot and then another, to wiggle my chair, which got me so worked up I could hardly contain myself. . . . I heard direct from an attendant that they were going to judge me sane and send me back to Springfield for trial within six months. They have made an awful breech between fathers, mothers, wife, sister and brother, by saying their loved ones was using other men and boys for immoral purposes, which such things are impossible, as no one is allowed alone together, but their nice, lying way turns the loved ones. They seem delighted if a patient is forsaken and hated by everyone and if they can make enemies among the patients.

In a letter of Nov. 20th, 1910, he writes:

I am going to sing "Beautiful Isle of Somewhere" today. Have been moved over in the big yard and another room since I was beaten, and am helping the boys in every way I can. . . . Love to my dear boy and you all. Write Minnie, and tell her how I am, and send her my deepest love and kisses.

Under date of December 31st, 1910, he writes:

Things have transpired that to anyone with a human mind seems impossible, and in the three months yesterday I have been here, I have heard from other mouths, heard with my own ears and seen with my own eyes that which, if before my arrest anyone had informed me of the same, I should have thought they were having the greatest of delusions, but it is all too true. . . . But when you told me at our interview yesterday, in Dr. Elliott's office, that my mother had requested you to call and talk with me, it was so unexpected that I could not say one half I could had we been alone, and not where I had to tell my affairs to the so-called "Devil's Angel." . . . I arrived at this place Monday, September 19th, and was put in the big yard for two days with 300 other unfortunates of from vagrants to the murderer, and dumb to the educated, and as the papers had predicted my coming, I was being anxiously awaited to pour their tales of woe in upon my own. As I listened, for awhile I forgot my own troubles, and wondered if what these fellows were saying were true. It all seemed like a dream, and I tried to drive such thoughts away. The first night I slept in what is called Corridor 3, in H. Building, with my window open all night, no pillow and only a thin blanket, with the night-watchman—nurse, Dr. Elliott calls them—looking in upon me every hour, with a bulls-eye light, which kept me restless. But my room was clean and my bed comfortable, and I was making up my mind to like my surroundings and make the most and do my best in everything. My mother and wife came the next day to see me, and I told of the room I had, and I thought by Dr. Elliott's and Baker's seemingly courteousness that I would be encouraged in many ways; but instead, the reverse, which I will state to the best of my education and ability, which is limited. In two days I was changed from this ward into what is known all over the buildings as the worst ward and yard in the place —the Northeast—and the yard is termed the "Bull Pen," where the very worst are considered to be. . . . We have not a truthful word to say or write about it, being intercepted by Dr. Elliott, Baker and Nugent, and branded as delusions or hallucinations. Different ones were speaking of the changes they were making me undergo, as I had done nothing that they should put me in the "Bull Pen," so I asked the doctors why they had put me over there, and they said "because it's quiet and no confusion"—and by far it was the noisiest.

He goes on to describe conditions in the Northeast and the "Bull Pen," and says that the bed to which he was transferred sagged in the middle, so that his back ached every morning; that he asked Dr. Baker to change the spring, but Dr. Baker answered, "I guess its good enough"; that his toothbrush, soap, towel, handkerchiefs and other little things were kept from him until his family interfered, although they were in the dress-suit case taken from him when he entered the hospital. He cites many instances of abuse. Among other things he writes:

There is an attendant here who is so ignorant that he has to have one of the patients make out his report, and I saw this same attendant, because he could not get a muff off a patient's hand quick enough, and because his fellow attendants were laughing at his clumsiness—he drew back and slapped his charge side of the face, and the poor fellow was standing there patiently waiting for the attendant to finish unbuckling. Another attendant by the name of ————, because a patient stopped in line to talk to an imaginary person, grabbed him by the collar, pulled him away, struck him an arm blow in the back of his neck, and kept kicking him in the backsides out of my sight. . . . An attendant by the name of ———— helped tie a sheet around an old man's neck of almost sixty years, gave him a beating and kept him in his room for three days.

On March 3rd, 1911, Spencer wrote:

I sent out something like fifteen or sixteen letters for you and others to read, and then go to the Governor, E. M. Foss, but through the advice of Mr. Thompson of Hartford, Mr. Smith of Lebanon was advised to send them all to Dr. Copp, and he in turn sent a Dr. Fuller here. As soon as he began to question us, everyone began to be skeptical and suspicious, for he began by saying "You sent out a letter to Dr. Briggs and others by Spencer, did you not?—I am from the Board of Insanity, representing Dr. Copp, and I am here in his interests." Well, that put a damper on everything, for some of these men knew of Dr. Copp . . . and as soon as they saw me after this interview, they told me of their fears, and it has all come true. They are trying to give everything a clean whitewash and protect Dr. Elliott and Dr. Baker, saying we are doing Dr. Elliott a great injustice.

On January 15th, 1911, the following letter was written by Dr. Owen Copp, Executive Officer of the State Board of Insanity, to the Rev. Eugene B. Smith, of Lebanon, Conn.:

Dear Sir:

The matters referred to in your letter, with enclosures, of Jan. 23rd, relative to the conditions at Bridgewater State Hospital, have been carefully inquired into, with the following result:

The authors of these letters are among the most desperate, dangerous and discontented men in this institution of imbecile and insane criminals. Unfortunately, they must be kept securely on one ward, where there is opportunity for exchange of ideas and experiences, and collusion in their determined purpose to get away. These men have formed many cunning and skillful plans for escape, which have fortunately been frustrated—oftentimes by the confession of one of the insane collaborators. *It is to be regretted that for a time Spencer was obliged to stay in this ward, and so was subjected to the worst influences of the institution.* He was found pliable in the hands of older criminals, who attempted, as they do on every occasion, to create a sensation and seek some possible means of escape. Spencer's complaints are found to be almost entirely from hearsay. Those which relate to his own maltreatment are confined to one instance, when he alleges he was struck by a blackjack by an attendant. Very careful inquiry into the matter shows that there was no witness to such an occurrence, that examination of Spencer presented no evidence of such violence, and that another patient voluntarily told the Superintendent that he was asked to say that he saw the assault, but that he did not, and that he did not see how another patient (who said he saw it) could possibly have seen it. Spencer is a weak character; he shows poor judgment, and is now easily influenced. Please do not infer that the authorities are not keenly aware of the possibilities and dangers of unkind and harsh treatment in the conditions which are bound to arise from time to time in such an institution. The opportunities for trouble are greater than in a jail, because of the greater freedom and closer association of the patients. As a result of our investigation, involving two visits to the hospital by a physician from this office, and conversations with authors of the letters which you sent us, as well as with the officers of the hospital, the conclusion has been reached that these complaints are in some instances gross exaggerations, and in others, fabrications. Some of the occasions mentioned have been subjects of the most thorough investigation. It is the impression at the hospital that Spencer himself has become wiser, and appreciates to some extent that he has been imposed upon. He has for some time been removed from the ward where these more troublesome patients are located, and is doing some better. We thank you for calling our attention to this matter, and will be glad to answer any further questions which you may ask.

Trusting that this may help to relieve your anxiety over the situation, I am

Very truly yours,
(Signed) Owen Copp, Exec. Officer.

In a letter written to his mother in February, 1911, Spencer says:

Who recommended Dr. Copp to Mr. Smith, and did he (Mr. Smith) go to see Dr. Briggs, or send those letters to him? It looks to all here that Dr. Elliott or Dr. Copp had influenced Mr. Smith. . . . Dr. Fuller asked me why I sent those letters to Dr. Briggs and by whom, and I said Mr. Smith.

On February 25th, 1911, he wrote to his wife a letter in which he said:

I am still living in the courage for the approaching day that I can crush the rascals that branded me as a lunatic and confined me in this murderous den—an innocent man of crime—and not only that, but robbed me of the support you deserved from me, my darling wife. . . . If I can, I will put a stop to this idea of keeping sane men confined in this department. . . . Doctors and attendants hate me as they hate the Devil—I have no doubt but that they will attempt to turn your kind affection from me, if you pay any attention to them. They have many poor fellows confined here for years for nothing but a simple offence of drunkenness. . . .

From Spencer's diary while he was at Bridgewater State Hospital, I extract the following:

Meals at Hotel Tantilization for a week, beginning Tuesday, Nov. 1st, 1910: Corn meal, molasses P. Rico, bread and oleo, tea and water; Wednesday A.M.: hash, bread and oleo, coffee and water; noon, pea soup, bread, coffee and water; night, apple sauce, bread and oleo, tea and water. Thursday A.M., rice and molasses, bread, oleo, tea and water; noon, stew, bread, coffee and water; night, bread, oleo, gingerbread, coffee and water. Friday A.M., oatmeal and molasses, bread, oleo, tea and water; noon, clam-chowder—tastes like a sewer smells—bread, coffee and water; night, bread, oleo, 2 doughnuts, tea and water. Saturday A.M., corncakes and molasses, bread, oleo, coffee and water; noon, meat, turnip, 2 potatoes, bread, coffee and water; night, gingerbread, 8 prunes, bread, oleo, tea and water. Sunday A.M., beans, bread and oleo, coffee and water; Sunday noon, Nov. 6th, 1910, meat, 2 potatoes, bread, rice pudding, coffee and water; night, mush and molasses, 2 doughnuts, bread and oleo, tea and water. Monday A.M., bologna, bread and oleo, coffee and water; noon, stew, bread, coffee and water; night, apple sauce, bread, coffee and water. Tuesday A.M., hash, bread, oleo, coffee and water. This ends the bill of fare for each week alike.

Treatment to patients at State Hospital, Titicut, Mass., beginning Wednesday night, Nov. 2nd, 1910. Had an awful pain at base of spine; asked for hot water bottle and doctor. Throbbed all night. None came, and at noon I was in pain, and Dr.—sent word by Supervisor—for him to tell me I would be better off out in the yard, so I had to go, much against my will, as it is so cold today. Tonight Dr. Nugent painted my back with iodine, Thursday night, Nov. 3rd. Saturday morning two attendants knocked down and beat with fists King, a stubborn patient, Nov. 5th, 1910. Saturday, Nov. 6th, Joe Patterson asked the night watchman for a drink three times, and as he, ———, came around, Joe asked him a fourth time, and ——— says "Shut your d——— mouth," and slammed the port. Sunday, 4 P.M. I asked Tom Pickles, Supervisor, if he would change my eating place so I could eat side of Mr. Childs, and buy and share eatables together. "No, oh no!" he said, "I can't do anything like that. You are not going to be here long anyway. It won't pay." It is getting so when I ask a favor of any kind the answer is always "We'll see," and that's the end of it. Over in the big yard they are out at play 20 minutes before we are, and stay there 15 to 20 minutes after we come in. Thursday, Nov. 10th, 9.30 A.M., as we were out in the hall, waiting to go down into the yard, a patient by the name of Mike Murphy began to complain of what the attendant had done to him, and the head attendant, ———, told him to "shut up his yap," or he, ——— would lock him up; but he kept right on talking, and ——— came down to the foot of the stairs and grabbed him by the throat, and attendants ——— and ——— dragged him up the stairs far as his room, and then ——— kicked him time and again, for all we stood in the door. I ran over to where the two were kicking him, and I says "———, for Heaven's sake, what are you doing? Don't kick a man like that when he's helpless!" And he glared at me, saying, "Shut your mouth, or I will lock you up!" I said "I shall not shut up, and I shall report this." And he says "Ha ha! Your reporting will amount to about as much as the wind's blowing." I says "You just wait and see!" With that, he says, "Pull off your rags!"—doubling up his fists—"and I'll teach you to interfere." I says, "I'm not looking for any trouble, or to interfere, but you have no right to kick one." He says, "Go to your room." I says, "All right; that suits me to a T." When I got to my door I took off my shoes, and as I went to go in, he, ———, *struck me an awful blow with his blackjack back of my ear, almost knocking me senseless.* He says, "You think you can come here and tell us how to run this place," shaking his fist at me. He said "We'll fix you before you've been here long," slammed the door and went away. Oh, people little realize what we're up against. They little realize. Tom Pickles has just been up and I told him the whole story. He says, "Don't say anything outside; they have no right to hit or kick either you or Mike Murphy and whenever you see or hear anything, just report it to me and I'll report it to the doctors." How was it he came up here so quick, if ——— had not told him to try and smooth it all over in this nice way? They all hang together, and nothing can be done in their minds. How confident ——— was my complaining would not amount to anything, and he was right, so far as anything coming from it in here.

Thursday, Nov. 10th, 1910.—I am afraid. My head has bled and ached all the morning and afternoon. I sent a letter to Mother this noon, Nov. 10th, 1910, asking for aid. Tom Pickles told me he would have the doctor call and give me something for the bruise and cut on my head. It ached and pained me so all night—I was walking most all night. I could eat no dinner yesterday—just a bite for supper, and no breakfast.

It is now 8.30 A.M. Friday, and no doctor yet—— Seems as if my head would burst at times. I sent a letter to Dr. Elliott at 5 P.M. last night, asking for an interview at his earliest. He has not come yet. Mr. Childs (a patient) told me yesterday he had had four or five attendants fired for brutality. . . . I wrote another letter to Dr. Elliott, and sent it by Mr. Childs direct, 12.30 Friday noon. Dr. Elliott sent for me at 5 P.M., and after telling him of the brute ———, he said he would make a thorough investigation.

Sun., Nov. 13th, 1910. Mr. Childs and I sang "Holy City" today. It was well-spoken of. Was introduced to Mr. Reuff, our regular and smart preacher. . . .

Nov. 24th. An attendant was discharged Nov. 22nd, Tuesday night, for giving Archie Mills alcohol. Two attendants are over here two years and are not naturalized citizens yet and both are hard-hearted. For dinner, Turkey, squash, 2 potatoes, celery, bread and coffee, mince pie and dressing.

Sunday night, ——— and ——— beat Joe Patterson again. Everything is cold on the table, coffee, tea and eatables. A new attendant every other thing, and almost every one has the picture of brute stamped all over him. The fellows gamble, to help pass away the day, with dice, cards and quates. The candy Mother sent two weeks before Thanksgiving never came. People have complained time and again of never receiving their goods, going or coming—— It's plain where they are held up. . . .

Friday, Dec. 2nd, 1910. This same date I saw a fellow have a fit, and this ——— (attendant) sat still and laughed at him. I have smelled liquor on their breath a number of times, and have heard Edward Holcroft often speak about same. There is a Post-Office on the prison side run by Horace Blackstone, and our mail is then brought over here and distributed by Charles Tibbitts, Clerk and Notary Public. Horace Blackstone is Superintendent. . . .

Dr. Elliott claims to thoroughly look into each man's character before hiring. The last one he discharged is in Boston, tending bar. He calls them nurses.

Sunday, Dec. 4th, 1910. An inmate they call Dave was talking to himself, and an attendant mocked him for fully five minutes, and not until Dave got up and walked away did he stop. The storekeeper, Kingsley, is a town constable, and he certainly knows how to keep his price up on everything. Down in the mess room, everything is cold at every meal and the dishes are covered in grease; bread smells and tastes musty half the time. Dr. Baker says they never saw anything of my candy. The drinking fountain in the Upper North is *filthy*. There is a fellow who sleeps on the bare floor and gets beat every other thing. If any patient gets obstinate, they put him in a room, open the window, and he suffers from cold and exposure—not a thing is allowed him. Out in the yard this cold weather, without woolen underwear, woolen socks, sweater, or even to be comfortable. About religion; Dr. —— has told patients religion was a farce, and Dr. Baker goes where there is a large crowd of woman singers. Dr. Elliott told my mother they were classifying the men fast as possible—— You ought to see what mingle together!—also that he was putting out every effort to broaden their minds and have the men have self-respect. Dr. Elliott says he looks into an attendant's character well before hiring him.

Friday, Dec. 9th, 1910. They think more of their wards than they do their dining rooms, and when people come they show them all the clean places and praise up the pomp and show. The library is positively no good—— All there is is in the double book-cases in the guard room. There is a Mr. Nolan who was knocked down, kicked and teeth knocked out, for asking an attendant to refrain from killing a patient, and his testicles were so injured that he urinated half a pint of blood, and he said a protestant brought him a rubber hot water bottle for relief. . . . Dr. L. Vernon Briggs of Boston never uttered a more true word than when he said these places hire brutes and ignorant people.

Friday, Dec. 16th, 1910. Harry Dale, who is an epileptic, falls down anywhere, and today he fell head first into a drift of snow, and two attendants stood by with their hands in their pockets, when three inmates ran up and straightened him up and took him to bare ground. That's a sample of ————'s so-called nurses! . . . Ask about what Mr. Benjamin Morris has to say about this place and the treatment towards patients. Faxon, a patient who tears his clothes to pieces, is put in a room with nothing on—no bed to sleep on—and is beat almost dead at times. . . . Nagle, a patient who tried to get away a year ago, died a few days ago, and he was kept in a cold room, nothing to eat and often beat something awful. A colored fellow by the name of George Washington was beat and almost kicked to death by attendants, and witnessed by George Green, colored. He was choked and kicked to death by an attendant who has since left. . . . The table is never cleaned off at night, and in warm weather cockroaches and flies are in and on everything. Ice water through the winter, and in summer none is to be had at times. . . .

Tuesday, Dec. 20th. Dr. L. Vernon Briggs of Boston was here and asked me to write him what I had seen first, what I had heard with my own ears at night, second, what has been told me by patients. I told him what Dr. Elliott had said about him.

Wednesday, 6 A.M., Mr. John Murphy was choked and struck in his room by Attendant ———, because he is all the time praying, and they say it is annoying to them.

Mr. Smith of Lebanon was here today, Tuesday, Dec. 20th, 1910, and talked with Mr. Joe Hastings, Mr. Jim Johnson and Mr. Mike Murphy about my being hit Thursday, Nov. 10th, 1910, by ———.

Thursday, Dec. 28th, 1910, ——— and ———, attendants, used the strong arm on a patient, bending the poor fellow's arm around up under his shoulder blade, and pulling and yanking him as if he were a bag of sawdust until his clothes were half off him. His name is Joseph F. Sullivan. He is a dope, and his hands are almost black at times from some cause I do not know.

Saturday, 9.50 A.M. Samuel Smith had a fit out in the yard and did not come out from it for ten minutes. Mr. Griffin and I held his head off the cold ground, as it was raw and cold out. I rubbed one hand and Martin Griffin the other, an attendant walking back and forth taking no notice of him. When he came to enough to walk, Griffin and I helped him across the yard to his ward. There we asked an attendant to let him lie down, because he could hardly stand. The attendant said no, it was against the rules—— He would have to go down to the smoking room, where there is nothing but hard wooden benches and no backs to sit on, or lie down on the cement floor. One of the new attendants, here only a few days, by the name of ———, yelled at a patient this noon, saying "Hurry up there you G—— D——— fool, or I will have to help you!"

Sunday night, January 1st, 1911, Nicholas di Flavio was beaten by two attendants, ——— and ———, unmercifully. When he started to tell the doctor, he kissed his hand. A patient who is directly opposite, by the name of Joseph Perry, heard the attendants choke and punch this Italian. His age is about 55 years old.

Monday afternoon, Jan. 2nd, 1911, we were turned out into a hard rain for half an hour before Pickles let us in. Mr. Morris, an attendant, stood just inside of the door out of the rain, and Pickles started to call him down, and Mr. Morris said, "You needn't think I'm going to stand out there in the rain for no dollar a day job." Nothing more was said. We all came in, but wet almost through—then the next day we have to put on our damp clothes or go without. This Nicholas di Flavio was taken up to the hospital. Sunday night, January 8th, 1911, a supervisor dragged Tom

Welch out of the dining-room by the throat—strong arm hold.

Dr. Elliott, on Monday Jan. 9th, 1911, because he saw Burnett Westhaven, Chern and I fooling, told the attendant, Mr. Fenton, always to stop anyone who was fooling. He didn't say anything about stopping the patients when they get to fighting until one or other are cut and bruised—all these he never sees. . . .

Monday. . . . I reported Attendant ——— for slapping Tom Welch, and today, Sunday, Jan. 15th, 1911, he is gone. Whether he left or was discharged I do not know, but he is gone and the boys are rejoicing. ——— has also been discharged. Why was it they kept ———?

Sunday, Jan. 22nd, 1911, Jerard told me that ——— said to an attendant that I was not sick—I was a big bluff so that I could stay in my room. "Why," says Morris, "He's a smart fellow!" "Smart fellow in what?—Killing a poor, innocent girl?" says ———. ——— and Dr. Elliott come from the same place Nova Scotia. . . .

Last night, Monday, Jan. 30th, 1911, I had some names and dates of beatings done by ——— and ——— on the Northeast, and had been given to Joe Hastings, and he put the paper in his pocket with his private letters sent by Jim Johnson, and Attendant ——— came down after Hastings had gone to bed, with two others, and took the piece of tissue paper out and destroyed it so I could not get it. Don't this go to show they are afraid it will get out? Swift is Attorney General. I see Mr. Dana Malone has no more to say.

Monday, Feb. 6th, 1911, at about 2:30 P. M., I was called out to the guard room in Pickles office to talk with Dr. Fuller, an agent of the State Board of Insanity, asking about what I wrote to Dr. Briggs for, also who I gave the letters to and if Mr. Smith took them, and why I had done this. I told him for the welfare of these poor unfortunates who had been so ill-used by doctors and attendants, and whenever I had reported the matter nothing was ever done. He asked me if I wrote to Mr. Faxon's father. I said yes, and told him I had seen him kicked, beat and made to go without his meals and bedding. Then he asked me about my trouble, and I told him about ——— beating Mike Murphy and myself. I asked him about writing to the people I had wronged, and he said "I advise you not to." George Green and Josiah Johnson were called out, but never saw the doctor. Green is one of the principal witnesses, as he was years up in the hospital and saw two men absolutely killed by attendants, and he is feared by the doctors and Mrs. ———, the Matron up there, as she has sanctioned it all, making a remark once that she did wish an old man would hurry up and die, so she could have his room, as they were short of rooms.

Friday, Feb. 10th, at noon, while eating sewer clam chowder, this same doctor came in through the mess room, with Dr. Elliott in the lead. I was told he stopped in the inner dining room and tasted of the bread, spitting it out on the floor, also looking into the chowder can and surveying the room in general, but he hurried right through where I eat, coming from the office direction. He talked with Houldcraft, Nichol, Westhaven, Allen, etc., but left out Green and Johnson again. . . .

Sunday, Feb. 26th, 1911, while eating my dinner of cold beef, I saw a funny piece of fat, and on looking closely discovered it to be a big abscess—I was about to eat it when I discovered it.

Thursday, March 2nd, 1911. While in the North this A. M., I heard of Thomas Hamburg being taken into his room and beat by Supervisor ——— and Head Attendant ———, for talking out loud. His face was covered in blood, and was witnessed by John Malvey and Lewis Rogers, Albert Russell, William Sullivan, and many others. At just before noon, an attendant by the name of ——— kicked a patient in the legs and body for not standing in line.

Same date, Friday, March 3rd, 1911, ——— and ———, both supervisors, took Miles O'Leary, by both strong-arming him, out through the dining room and away down through the corridor, out of sight of us all—and then, such screams of pain! Then one of the attendants shut the door so we could not hear the screams, but we did, and in about two minutes the two supervisors came back, both white as sheets, as if they were all out of breath. Witnessed by George Green, Edgar Houldcroft, G. List and many others. Mr. Cody would like an interview with Dr. Briggs. At Thanksgiving time, Dr. Baker told me they killed over 40 hogs that weighed over 250 pounds apiece, and the Boston paper said that 800 pounds of pork was to be eaten at Bridgewater on that day with proper fixings. There are over 100 cows, and we hardly ever get any milk—no butter, only oleomargarine; over 1000 hens, and never an egg do we or the attendants see, so one tells me. Dopes help out in the kitchen to do the cooking, string and toilet paper are often found in the soup and gingerbread; cups, spoons and plates of tin are sometimes filthy.

CHORUS

Beautiful Queen of Roses, kissed by the morning dew,
Each pretty flower discloses virtues I find in you.
White means your soul so pure, dear, red means your love
most true.
You are my garden of beautiful roses—My own rose,
my own rose, that's you.

MOTHER'S SONG

When I was but a boy, my mother's pride and joy,
I wandered far from that dear fireside place;
And the sorrow I have seen could not be placed upon a screen—
You'll never miss your mother till she's gone.

CHORUS

In fancy I see her there, seated in her old arm chair—
You'll never miss your mother till she's gone.

Wednesday, March 15th, 1911.—Assistant Supervisor ——— and Attendant ——— strong-armed and choked a Jew by the name of Attar Naman at about 2 P. M., because he did not want to put on his shoes and go out doors. Witnessed by Patient Jerard.

Monday, March 20th, 1911.—This morning a patient came up to my door saying, "Have you heard the good news?" I said "No, what is it?" "There's a long piece in the Post about Governor Foss going to investigate all insane hospitals, and helped by Dr. L. Vernon Briggs." I shouted for joy and it has been read by hundreds already. What a happy expression on the men's faces when they were talking about it in the yard! There are many Boston Posts subscribed for by patients, but only one found its way in. . . . This afternoon a patient by the name of Charles Murray, colored, fell on his knee, hurting it to that extent that he had to be carried up into the hospital. Upon arriving, Mrs. ——— met them in the doorway, saying, after she had been told what they had brought him up for—"Take him right down again. I have had no orders to receive him yet." What a thing for a so-called matron to say and do! It shows . . . that the so-called hospital is by name only. Everyone is watching the papers with longing eyes for Governor Foss' and Dr. Briggs' glorious work towards the uplift of poor unfortunates. God bless them both!

Tuesday, March 21st, 1911.—Attendant ———, the one who struck me in the head with a blackjack, remarked just outside my door to his chum and a man of his own stamp that Dr. Briggs was going to raise wages to $75 or $100 a month. He said it twice over, so I took it it was meant for my benefit. . . .

Thursday, April 6th, 1911.—A patient named Husler, one who is full of delusions, struck or kicked Attendant ———, and they put him in a room and Dr. ——— came, injecting some fluid by hypodermic syringe method, weakening and causing deathly sickness. If patients strike one another, seldom is there anything done about it, but let a dope or anyone strike an attendant, and they take him, beat or inject the needle so often that he is often taken to the "so-called" hospital, and he may recover after being subjected to all kinds of torture, and oftentimes they have died—giving them cold plunges, leaving their windows open all night through freezing weather, sometimes no bed and sometimes no clothes to cover even their bodies. . . . It is reported that patients who have been buried on the farm—their graves have been ploughed over and planted on.

Wednesday, April 12th, 1911.—John Kinney broke out 7 windows in the lower smoking room, and today, Thursday, April 13th, 1911, they put him in the Northeast. He is five years over his time here. Friday or Saturday a patient cut John Boynton in the legs with a piece of pipe made into a knife. Stockleburg is the patient's name. Wednesday and Thursday Dr. Elliott had one half of each afternoon out in the front ward or office, asking different questions relative to my case. "How much was the jewelry worth taken from the Dow home, and do you think it worth over $5?" I said I thought about that. *"Would you plead guilty in the second degree if the Court asked you to?"* I said "It's for my lawyers to decide, not me." He said, "In case they bring in First Degree, you know what that means?" I said, "I get so downhearted at times, I wish it would turn out that way." "In case you get Second Degree, would you prefer to go to Charlestown or to come down here?" I said, "If you had a son, which place would you like him to go?" He said, "There is not much difference in places, only I advise you in either case not to pay attention to patients, as you will find your best friends among the officials. You got in wrong to start with so if you go to Charlestown, don't go there thinking you can reform the place, because they have rules and regulations which they have to compel the prisoners to live up to. I do not believe in muck-raking. There is no good coming from it on either side," said he; "If you are here two years from now, you will say, I am sure, that the officials are your best friends. How are things going on now down in the dining room? Do you eat well?" . . .

When I remarked about the graveyard here for the poor unfortunates, I did not know that they planted over their graves, and that all that marks their resting place is a small pine board with numbers on. . . . They say there is lots of mounds that ought to show, but have been ploughed up. There are a few mounds only marked by just plain pegs. No respect for the dead at all. The old tomb is now used as a cook-house.

When Minnie comes Monday, I will send these notes by her, also a chain Jim Johnson made for Mr. Smith, with a letter written on tissue paper for him, too.

The remainder of the diary is copied directly from Spencer's manuscript, with occasional omissions, italics representing his underscoring the occasional errors and the peculiar punctuation being his own.

Tuesday, April 25th, 1911. . . . There is not an hour day or night that passes but that I suffer *unknown* to human eyes, but God knows just how much and how sorry and bewildered to know how *I ever came to such an ending,* also how all through my life it has been my aim to live an honest, clean life, and after I married my *"darling Wife,"* I always thought how happy I could make my home by being ever *truthful, faithful and a loving husband,* and *thoroughly clean* in my morals; *yet I failed.* Twice did I deceive my darling, and those two times were I unfaithful, but *always truthful, loving* and *attentive,* thank God, as any man could be. . . .

It's a *"big sacrilege"* to call this place a Hospital—anything but that. If the Christian people think we are all Insane and void of principle, and our word is not to be taken, then in *Humanity's name,* why don't they spend some of the donated money and hire men to come into these places and find that the truest facts have not even yet been mentioned regarding Brutality and the medical farce and general run of this Insane Prison, *"Not Hospital."* Then the public could be informed from a sane man and not a patient. I have told only the *God's truth,* and truth can never be stretched regarding what has gone on here in the past. Even the dead can not lay in peace. They allow an attendant or farm boss to breed foxes that were brought into the walled enclosure on the farm, and they have burrowed down under the dead bodies, where they make their homes. They have ploughed up and planted all over the dead graves the past two (2 years) I have seen it all with my own eyes. . . . There are six foxes now on the farm.

Monday, May 1st, 1911. In today's paper there's a picture supposed to be me, and a piece of *lies* that goes with all the other *lies* that have been printed about *this place and myself,* stating that I am *"enjoying myself"—What a lie, never suffered more in my life* than the *past year, day and night,* and I have asked these people to let me write a letter to each of the *"poor Blackstone" and Dow families,* telling them of my *sorrow and suffering,* and that *my last prayer* will be for forgiveness from *God* and *Them.* There are many here who say it sounds just like ———'s way of getting back at me in a quiet, off-hand way, because I have tried, "oh," so hard, in a *truthful and gentlemanly* way to expose the *low, contemptible actions* of *Drs.* ——— and ——— and *Attendants,* also *Supervisors* and *State Board,* and this is the weapon they are using to get back at *me* and excite the people on the outside to *frenzy heat.* How well they always guard themselves by speaking of this place as *"Pavillion"* and the back yard, when the wind blows, the fine sand dust sweeps across the yard to that extent you can not see at all. The drainage of this yard is down in the North end corner, and is fed by spit from 300 men daily, all the overflow of two toilets summer and winter, and when this receptacle at the North end of the yard gets full, they take off the cover and spread the contents out over the yard where the sun and wind dried it out and the wind blows it all over the yard, up into the highest and most far rooms surrounding it, where we have to sleep in it and everything covered with this same yard dust. . . .

Perhaps I can never prove, but God knows how much I have *suffered,* also those that have come to see me and have received letters from me. All the *real comfort* I have is in the reading of the *dear letters* of my *dear Mother and Wife,* and I often *yearn* for a *letter* every day when I seldom get but one a week from my *dear Wife*—Mother generally writes 3 times a week, and she does not *realize how much comfort they bring* to me, neither does my *Darling Wife.* It seems as though every day would be my last, as I am so "lonely," and death is far better than being away from her love and affection. *She alone knows how I love her, and will know it better as she grows older.*

Monday, May 9th, 1911. In yesterday's Sunday Boston American there was another heartrending piece about me that was all false and exaggerated to the fullest. Does anyone believe, I wonder, that I do not *suffer day and night* for the *sins* I have *committed?* Don't I suffer for the *hearts that have ached* and *those* that *will ache for years to come?* Do I play my mandolin because I am happy? *Far from it,* it's because it not only *soothes my aching heart,* but it *comforts other sorrowing hearts.* I have been *told time and again* that my *playing* for *others* has done more *good* than the *sermon preached* here. If so, why should I be *censured* for *trying* to do what is *right* and *bring cheer and comfort* to those who are *downtrodden, friendless* and *sick?* It's my duty, as a *Christ believing* man, to *pray to God* for *forgiveness* and *peace* of *mind,* and *try* to *be cheerful among* my *fellow unfortunates,* helping them in turn to be cheerful and to *do right* and *be cheerful.* And if the *Christian people* will not *encourage me,* I will do it alone, knowing that in *God's sight* I am doing his *teachings,* even though I *suffer* by it in the end. People who have these false reports published about me are trying to do me an injury, and I *pray to God* to *forgive them, for they know not what they say.* Neither do I know their motive, but *God does.*

Tuesday, May 9th, 1911. Had an interview with Dr. Elliott, but got no satisfaction other than that he said he told Dr. Tuttle I played the guitar, and I said no, it's a mandolin, and that I played ball and worked on the farm, and he said not to think Dr. Tuttle put any such piece in the paper. I said then, for the *respect* of *my people,* I wished him to *contradict those statements* made in the Boston Post of Monday, May 2nd, 1911, and the Sunday Boston American of May 7th, 1911. He said: "I will answer any questions your folks wish to ask and will deny anything that is wrong to them, but not the newspapers. Your folks can have published what I write if they wish, but I shall not," so that if the papers make a comeback he will not have to answer. . . .

Wednesday night, May 10th, 1911. A patient who is crazy as a lime, by the name of Joseph Frenette, a Frenchman, was beat and choked by Attendants ——— and ———, who is on my ward, upper North, Corridor 6. Two big lumps on the back of his head; Thursday morning he refused to go to bed the reason. Saturday night, May 6th, 1911, when Mrs. ——— got off the train in Boston, after spending the day here at Titicut with her husband, was accosted by an attendant, ———, who asked Mrs. ——— if she would go to supper with him. She refused, scared almost to move. He then asked her if she would stay all night with him at some hotel, saying she was foolish to stick by her husband. When she came to see her husband Saturday, May 13th, 1911, she told him the whole story, and they together wrote and signed their names, stating the facts to Dr. Elliott, asking him to do what was right in the matter or they should. . . . Last Sunday a patient who is in for burglary wrote his mother a long letter, and Dr. ——— would not send it, and told this patient that when he stopped "roasting" this place he or Dr. ——— would send his letters, and not before. So his last Sunday letter did not go. Mr. ——— and his wife have got Representative Quinn on their side and other influence, and perhaps your acquaintance with her will be a help and pleasure to you both. She is a woman who should be loved by all. She writes her husband every day, and comes to see him every Saturday, way from Salem, and arrives here every time at 8 A.M. . . . Alfred W. Gerard is the patient's name who tried to send his letter and the doctors stopped it. Last Friday, May 12th, 1911, Dr. ——— took the same two patients up to his wife's home to mow the lawn and clean up around that he did once before. One was a fire-bug who has been in here 8 years. The attendant who took them up is the one who insulted Mrs. ——— Saturday, May 6th, 1911. . . . In yesterday's letter, Mother dear, you ask me if I showed Dr. Tuttle the scar on the back of my neck. . . . He asked about the Pitcher affair and about my always carrying a revolver and wanted me to explain about the gun bursting, and I told him that I was just coming to you when you got to me from the house, and I was up in the lot just above where the machinery building is now and that Pitcher's striking me in the stomach first caused me to pull my gun and fire how many times I don't remember. He asked me why I always carried a light, mask and revolver, and I told him I had gone out a number of times without even a jack-knife in my pocket. He says

I suppose you took the light to see with and the mask to conceal your identity and the gun to scare whoever you came in contact with. I said I'm sure I don't know, yet it all seems feasible as I look at it now. He says "Would you like to go to trial?" I said "Sometimes I wish it all over." He says "Do you mean you feel like suicide?" I said "Yes, then it would all be over, and then I think of my mother, wife and child and I want to live." He said *"Would you plead to 2nd degree murder?"* I said "It's just as my lawyers say." He says "You know the meaning of First Degree?" I said "Death." Then he got up and excused himself for keeping me so long, and *saying that Mr. Callahan had sent him here to interview me;* saying goodbye and shaking my hand, he left for the front office where Dr. Elliott and he talked together. Dr. Elliott told me that Dr. Tuttle asked him if I played ball, etc., in the interview I had the other day. Dr. Baker hardly looks at me since he knows I was reported for trial, and I am just as well-pleased, for I never look at him but what I think what a ——— is behind those smiles and honeyed words, and Dr. ——— is the same, only he does not smile. I do not know Mr. Houldcroft's address, and I do not know whether he has gone west or where. This will be mailed Saturday night, May 20th, 1911.

It will be noted that he emphasized most of his words when he was excited over personal matters. In describing the real or imaginary wrongs of others he is apparently more calm, and these peculiarities are less frequent, or absent altogether. His handwriting was invariably clear and legible, except when he was excited or emotional.

H. J. McLean, who was an attendant at Bridgewater when Spencer was there, has written much about Spencer and events which took place in the institution at that time. His efforts to improve conditions while he was still employed as an attendant resulted in his dismissal.

CHAPTER IV

POLITICAL CAMPAIGN IN WESTERN MASSACHUSETTS, AS AFFECTING SPENCER. REPORTS OF BRIDGEWATER AUTHORITIES TO CHIEF JUSTICE AIKEN. REMOVAL OF SPENCER FROM BRIDGEWATER TO SPRINGFIELD FOR TRIAL, AUGUST 1ST, 1911.

Political Campaign

The sending of Spencer to Bridgewater had created another furore in Springfield and vicinity, and whether or not he was insane, public opinion resented any influences being brought to bear to keep him from being tried for his life. While it is wholly untrue that any such influence existed, the public was more or less incensed, and took revenge on the District Attorney, Mr. Taft, who came up for re-election in 1910. The hottest contest that ever was waged in western Massachusetts for this office took place that year, both Mr. Taft and his Democratic opponent, Christopher T. Callahan, taking the stump, and the Spencer incident was used as an issue in the campaign. Mr. Callahan defeated Mr. Taft by a big majority, and soon laid plans for bringing Spencer to trial. Mr. Callahan says that the trial was not the result of a "political issue" between himself and Mr. Taft; that his candidacy for the Democratic nomination for the District Attorneyship had been announced long before the September hearing. His actual nomination, however, did not take place until

October 9th, and the following extracts from the Springfield Republican point to the conclusion that the Spencer case was a not unimportant issue in the campaign.

Evidently Mr. Taft, though he had acted in accordance with his conscience and with his idea of the duties of his office, nevertheless realized that he was under a heavy fire of public criticism, whether or not Mr. Callahan had opened a direct attack upon his policy in the Spencer case; and he must have felt that his office, in spite of a large Republican majority in the district, was in jeopardy; for the Springfield Republican of Oct. 27th, 1910, says:

> District Attorney Stephen H. Taft, one of the speakers at a Republican rally last night in the Central Street Schoolhouse, strongly defended his action in the Spencer murder case, and made a forceful reply to the criticism of his failure to prevent Bertram G. Spencer, the self-confessed murderer of Miss Martha B. Blackstone, from being committed to the Bridgewater asylum for the criminal insane without demanding a formal trial. Mr. Taft declared that he was moved to allow Spencer's removal without a fight simply through the dictates of his own conscience, and that his ambition to be reelected was not a factor in the case. Mr. Taft said he did not care whether he was reelected or not, if the price of reelection had to be the consciousness that he had done wrong.

On October 28th, 1910, speaking of a Democratic rally in Pittsfield, this paper says:

> Christopher T. Callahan, candidate for District Attorney, was the second speaker. Mr. Callahan said that when he became candidate he hoped the contest for the District Attorneyship would be settled without a personal discussion between his opponent and himself of their respective qualifications for the place. Lawyers dislike to pronounce adverse judgment upon the professional work of their brethren, and he was reluctant now to say one word that might be construed as a reflection upon the legal ability of the District Attorney. That there might be no such misunderstanding, he would declare now that Mr. Taft was a very good lawyer with an excellent standing at the bar.

But criticisms had been passed by a large number on his method of handling several important cases, not necessarily involving any question of his legal ability, but going rather to the soundness of the discretion which attaches to the office of prosecutor. Among these cases was one which, on account of its horrifying character and the terror which the criminal had struck into the hearts of the people of the whole country, had caused more discussion than all the others. He was alluding to the case of the notorious burglar and murderer of the Springfield school teacher, Miss Blackstone, Spencer, who, he said, was now *luxuriating in the comforts and leisure of the insane* asylum at Bridgewater. For the reasons stated, he regretted that it had become necessary to discuss the matter.

"But," said Mr. Callahan, "the District Attorney himself has taken the public platform to defend his action, and is making an explanation of it, which, if taken to be accurate by the voters, not only justifies his course, but invests the prosecutor with a nobility of motive and capacity for skill in dealing with cold-blooded murderers which almost make me ashamed to dispute his claim to reelection. I do not agree that the District Attorney's action was for the good of the Commonwealth, and I can not appear to acquiesce in and endorse his explanation by further silence. Mr. Taft says he would rather go down in defeat than send an insane man to the electric chair. So would I, and so would every other lawyer with a spark of conscience in his soul. But that is not the issue. I do not understand that one voice has called for the execution of an insane man. The great complaint against Mr. Taft is that he did not meet the tactical motion of the murderer's lawyers for his commitment to an asylum with sufficient caution and energy. Everybody understands that Spencer's skillful counsel regarded it as the first great step to deliver him from the law's penalty to get him into an insane asylum by the order of the court, and thus forever after commit the Commonwealth to the theory that the man was insane.

"At Springfield and Holyoke Monday night I shall discuss Mr. Taft's method of meeting this strategy of the defendant's counsel in detail. It is enough to say now that it was imprudent, to say the least, to put the Commonwealth's own experts on the stand to support this request of Mr. Spencer that he be placed in an asylum for observation. It was more than imprudent that the District Attorney himself should elicit testimony from these experts that will make their testimony hereafter utterly valueless, if Spencer should finally be put upon trial. I say these things because it appears that these opinions were based, not upon observations of the prisoner solely, but upon observations taken in connection with the family history of the defendant and certain alleged facts in his career. How were these facts brought to the minds of the experts? As facts established by evidence from the witness stand? Not at all. They were furnished by the defendant's family and friends, and accepted by the experts without legal proof. These facts, in my opinion, should have been submitted under oath in open court, and should have been subjected to the test of careful cross-examination. Of course, if the Commonwealth could show that these facts should not be accepted as true, the experts very likely would not agree in the notion that the defendant was crazy."

Mr. Callahan continued at some length in this vein, arguing the evil results that might spring from such procedure, citing other cases and stating that "a chagrined and indignant public has raised its voice." The same issue of the Republican gives Mr. Taft's defense:

Speaking of the cases of Spencer, Mrs. Berquist and George Creley, all of whom were committed for insanity, Mr. Taft said that the Court had to decide the question of the sanity of a prisoner, and if it is found that he is insane at the time of the trial he is acquitted on the ground of insanity and committed, while if found sane he must stand trial. Mr. Taft said he fully realized the state of the public mind at the time of Spencer's arrest. Then he told how Drs. Houston, Quinby and Tuttle either found Spencer insane or would not pronounce him sane. He said, too, that if Spencer had been put on trial, the jury would have acquitted him on the ground of insanity. Mr. Taft stated that if, at any time, Spencer should be found to be sane again, he could be brought back and put on trial, and that no one would be more pleased than he to send him to the chair; but he said that he desired to be possessed of a clear conscience, rather than put on trial a man whom three experts had found to be insane. He said he was being criticized for not having secured other experts to say Spencer was sane, "but," declared Mr. Taft, "I am not in office to hire or buy witnesses." He said he had had and still had ambition to be reelected District Attorney, "but," said he, "I say to you and I'll say to the world, I don't care how it affects my chances for reëlection, if I know I did right."

Mr. Taft made another speech that evening in Holyoke (October 28th), and at a third Republican rally, held on the evening of October 31st, he continued in the same vein, answering Callahan's criticism of his use of the Commonwealth's alienists as follows, according to the Springfield Republican of November 1st:

"It has been said that the alienists testified not only from their examination, but from the history of the defendant, and that the District Attorney should have examined the witnesses who testified, or who might have testified, as to his history. My opponent has been kind enough to say that I am a good lawyer, but he belies his words when he suggests that I permitted this history to be used by the alienists without confirming its accuracy in every detail. A statement was submitted to the Attorney General, forwarded to me, which was seen by the alienists, and I verified or caused to be verified all the facts stated thereon. I should certainly have failed in my duty had I permitted the experts to take into consideration the past history of the man, unless I had become certain that the facts stated were true. I personally interviewed men and women in Connecticut who had known Spencer from childhood, and verified the facts stated in the history of Spencer and his family, and a district police officer, at my direction, was several days employed confirming these facts.

"Believing that the court, in passing on the motion that Spencer be committed for observation should have knowledge of all facts, and believing that it was my duty to disclose to the court all the facts within my knowledge, the alienists consulted by the Commonwealth were put upon the witness stand. The court found that it was necessary that he should be committed under the provisions of this act. I suspect that some of the persons who criticise my course did not appreciate just what would have been the outcome had any other course been taken.

"As the case now stands, Spencer is confined at the prison for insane criminals at Bridgewater for observation. If he is pronounced to be sane, he can be brought here and tried. It is not a case where there is any question about the ability of the Commonwealth to prove the facts concerning the commission of the offense. That evidence is plenary, and if he is pronounced sane, no man will be more ready to try the case against him and convict him of murder in the first degree than I will. There seems to be a feeling that there is a possibility that he may in some way again be at large. But that is impossible. If he appears to be sane he can be placed upon trial, and if convicted, be executed in the electric chair. If he is acquitted by reason of insanity, by law he must be committed to the prison for insane criminals at Bridgewater for life, and can only be discharged therefrom by order of the Governor and Council; and no one suspects or imagines that Massachusetts will ever have a Governor who will permit the man who has committed all the horrible offenses that Spencer has committed to be free again. So that, whatever may happen, if Spencer does escape the electric chair, he will be confined as long as he shall live."

After referring to the unjustifiableness of a District Attorney putting on trial for life a man who is insane or whom he believes to be insane, Mr. Taft said, "It might be that the alienists were mistaken in their opinion concerning the mental condition of the defendant, but the Medical Director of the prison for insane at Bridgewater, to which Spencer was committed by an order of the Court requiring a report to be made to the Chief Justice of the Superior Court monthly, in his report to the Chief Justice, said, 'At the present time it is my opinion that the degree of Spencer's mental deficiency and the obliquity of his moral nature is so great that it constitutes real insanity. Aside from this, there are symptoms that call for further observation.'

"It is easy, my friends, to be criticised for that which has been done, especially by persons who are not familiar with all the facts and conditions of this particular case. I had every incentive to try this man, and to ask for a verdict which should send him to the electric chair. The horrible crime which he committed warranted it. My own wish to see the proper punishment administered, my knowledge of the intense feeling throughout the community, my desire for the commendation of the people in my conduct of the office, everything prompted me to try this case; but however bitter might be my feelings toward the defendant, I could not, under my oath of office, performing its duties as I understood them to be, conceal from the court the evidence in my possession, and no court could, by any possibility, have escaped making the order which was made, if the evidence was fairly presented to it."

The same issue of the Republican (November 1st, 1910) quotes Mr. Callahan as saying, at a Democratic rally held in Springfield on the previous evening, at which Governor Foss was the chief speaker, that he regretted that a public controversy over the professional work of a brother lawyer had been injected into the campaign, but it was not his fault, he said; even in his speech accepting the nomination, he had deliberately refrained from making any reference to the Spencer case or to the other cases which have aroused more or less feeling on account of the way in which the interests of the Commonwealth have been dealt with. But Mr. Taft had taken the public platform for the purpose of defending himself. Mr. Callahan said that, inasmuch as he disagreed with the District Attorney's contentions, it would be foolish to permit the latter to coin votes on a combination of his eloquence and Mr. Callahan's silence. He then continued at some length, repeating much of what he had said in former speeches, and saying, among other things:

"In the fact of the overwhelming evidence of his guilt, there was but one way out. Nothing was more certain than that Spencer's defense would be insanity. It seems to me that in this awful case, Spencer ought not to be permitted to escape some penalty of the law, unless, under the finding of a jury, his insanity was established beyond a doubt."

Mr. Callahan continued at great length on this theme. From the reported speech we select the following paragraphs:

"I find, by reference to the reports of the hearings in the daily papers that the defendant's counsel were as familiar as the District Attorney with the doings and opinions of the Commonwealth's experts. I find that Mr. Stapleton used their testimony to his own great advantage. I am informed that every expert in the employ of the Commonwealth was called to the stand and committed to the theory either that Spencer was insane or that there was such doubt as to his sanity as to make further observation necessary. . . . I am here to say that it was very imprudent, to say the least, for the Commonwealth to put the defendant in possession of its evidence at that stage of the proceedings. Whatever might have been the duty of the Commonwealth at the trial itself, it is very questionable if proper considerations of the Commonwealth's interests can justify the proffer of the Commonwealth's evidence in a preliminary skirmish like this. Moreover, as I read the opinions of these experts, I find that they were based, not upon the observation of Spencer alone, but upon alleged facts furnished by himself, his friends and his family. Now it is common knowledge that before a fact can be considered in passing upon a question of the defendant's insanity, it must be testified to in open court and subjected to the test of direct and cross examinations. . . .

"My friend admits that he did not oppose Mr. Spencer's request for commitment to the bucolic pleasures of Bridgewater, and argues with some fervor that, if he is pronounced sane by the authorities there, he can be put on trial and convicted. How, I would like to know? Upon the testimony of the Commonwealth's experts, who have already under oath committed themselves to the theory of insanity? *It is possible, of course, that they may hereafter be persuaded to believe that Spencer is sane,* but of what value, in the average jury, would their testimony be? As I understand the situation, every expert in the employ of the Commonwealth has showed his hand.

"No, my friend, the great complaint made by the people is not that you refuse to send a crazy man to death, but that you are not sufficiently cautious in dealing with a claim of insanity by a man whose sanity had never been questioned up to the time of the murder, for nearly a week after it, and up to the moment when his confession excluded any other possible defense. They complain that the Commonwealth's case has been made practically valueless, and that because of this Spencer will escape the penalty of the law. They feel that if there is any reason why the extreme penalty of death should not be invoked, this man, instead of enjoying the comforts and attentions of an insane asylum, should at least have been sentenced to the toil and privation of imprisonment for the remainder of his natural life."

Mr. Callahan referred, continues the Republican, to the importance of keeping the office of District Attorney out of politics, and, in closing, said: "If I am elected, I shall deal mercifully with the first offender and with the erring boy or girl, when mercy will not make a farce of justice, but I pledge myself to deal so vigorously with the murderer, the burglar, the fire-fiend, the man who invades another's home to destroy it, and with those who terrorize the community in other ways, as to make this district unattractive to them."

In the same issue of the Republican, we read in the editorial column:

Lawyer Christopher T. Callahan, the Democratic candidate for District Attorney, is disposed to bear down heavily on the Spencer case, that most deplorable affair that needs no rehearsal in Springfield. The phenomenal meanness of the wretch who terrorized this community will not soon be forgotten, and popular indignation demanded that he be sternly dealt with. Such was the feeling with which District Attorney Taft approached his public duty. It seems to be a fact that the lawyers, who should be the best judges of his course under the extraordinary circumstances that confronted him, are practically agreed that the District Attorney ought not to be condemned for the course he pursued. They endorse it. Here, for instance, is a letter from a leading lawyer in a neighboring county—and a Democrat at that, who writes: "I think the course of District Attorney Taft in the Spencer case was most proper. Fortified as it was with the views of the alienists and endorsed by two judges of the superior court, including the Chief Justice, it does not seem to me he is open to attack."

But Mr. Callahan thought otherwise, and continued to attack him throughout the remainder of the campaign. The Springfield Republican of November 4th says that at a Democratic rally held at North Adams on November 3rd, Mr. Callahan referred to local cases as showing a lack of attention to duty on the part of District Attorney Taft. He again reviewed the Spencer case in detail and repeated at much length his attack on Mr. Taft's conduct of it.

Many local election forecasts about this time predict Taft's defeat, even in the Republican strongholds, on account of dissatisfaction with his record in the Spencer case. Mr. Callahan knew his public and his eloquence triumphed. On November 9th, in its account of the election returns, the Republican says:

Lawyer Christopher T. Callahan of Holyoke has defeated District Attorney Taft, with his own city going for him with a whoop. The reasons for that local favor were not far to seek. . . . The Spencer case played its part in Springfield and beyond, but it was by no means the sum of the opposition. . . . Who imagined that Mr. Taft could have been defeated by a plurality of 2662?

In the same issue, speaking of the local vote, the Republican says:

District Attorney Stephen S. Taft, defeated in the Western Massachusetts district for reelection, managed to run ahead of his opponent, Christopher T. Callahan, in this city, by 345 votes.

Thus we see that, though Mr. Taft was defeated in a strongly Republican district, with the Spencer case as one of the leading issues against him, in Springfield, the city most concerned in this case and in which Spencer was best known, Taft had a fair majority. Apparently the people of Springfield were not dissatisfied with Taft's manner of handling the case.

Reports of Bridgewater Authorities

We have already quoted Dr. Elliott's first report to Chief Justice Aiken, made after Spencer had been a month at Bridgewater. The second report was dated November 16th, 1910, and, omitting the printed heading, reads as follows:*

To the Honorable Chief Justice of the
Superior Court of Hampden,
Springfield, Mass.
Dear Sir:—

In compliance with the order of the Honorable Court, I hereby make my second monthly report upon the mental condition of Bertram G. Spencer.

During the greater part of the past month Spencer has refused to talk with the Medical Director or his assistants, and any attempt to draw him into conversation was met by an outburst of profanity. His reason for so doing appears to lie in a general dissatisfaction with his environments, and his inability to accommodate himself to the necessary rules and regulations of an insane hospital.

From his letters and his conversations with officers and other inmates, and from his general attitude towards the institution and the officials in charge, *it is evident that Spencer is suffering from general ideas of persecution. The underlying cause of these false*

* The italics are my own in these reports and elsewhere in the book, except where otherwise stated.

ideas or delusions appears to be the faulty reasoning and impaired judgment of an arrested or mal-developed brain.

Spencer's life is daily dominated by irresistible impulses, and his will-power is too weak to control them and his reasoning is so faulty that he seldom arrives at correct conclusions. The exalted ego, so characteristic of the imbecile, is very prominent in the patient's mental make-up, and while in many ways he appears to be rational, his utter disregard for truth, his lack of moral feeling, decency or remorse, together with general ideas of persecution and his inability to accommodate himself to his environments, especially when it is manifestly in his favor to do so, are strong arguments, to my mind, that *Spencer is insane.*

Very truly yours,

Alfred Elliott,
Medical Director.

The third report is dated December 17th, 1910:

To the Honorable Chief Justice of the
Superior Court of Hampden,
Springfield, Mass.

Dear Sir:—

I hereby make my third monthly report upon the mental condition of Bertram G. Spencer, committed to this hospital until further order of the Court. Spencer has been much more agreeable and reasonable during the past month. He has taken practically a normal interest in life and his environments and has joined in the different games and amusements of the hospital. He has not shown any new evidence pointing to delusions, and I can not see that there has been any signs of increasing dementia. *I do not think there is any chance to dispute the fact that Spencer is and always has been a moral imbecile of a rather low order.* It is still my opinion, however, that he knows right from wrong, at least in the abstract, but while knowing the right, *his mental defect is so great that he is unable to do the right or avoid the wrong.*

There is such mental impoverishment in his case, as in most borderline cases, that it is not strange that reasoning and judgments are at times so faulty as to constitute *weak, incoherent delusions.* His peculiar mental soil also favors the development of various psychoses and the gradual growth of any latent disease, together with the many weak delusions that are so often a transitory feature in patients with unstable nervous systems.

Very respectfully,

Alfred Elliott,
Medical Director.

The reports continued to be sent in to the Chief Justice monthly as follows:

Jan. 16th, 1911.

To the Honorable Chief Justice of the
Superior Court of Hampden,
Springfield, Mass.

Dear Sir:

In compliance with the order of the Honorable Court, I hereby make my monthly report upon the condition of Bertram G. Spencer.

There has been no material change in the mental condition of our patient since the report of Dec. 17th last. Spencer has made considerable gain in weight, is somewhat more contented and a little less fault-finding. He is much less emotional. His inability to concentrate his mind upon any line of thought or work is still marked, but evidently this is of long standing and dates back to his school days. His memory remains fragmentary and uncertain and his mind acts slowly and within narrow limits. His inability to reason clearly and to analyze events of everyday life leads to errors of judgment and false conclusions. There has been no evidence of homicidal or suicidal tendencies since received, and no hallucinations or delusions noted, except as facts improperly interpreted, the result of faulty reasoning, might be considered as such.

I am still of the opinion that *Spencer is a moral imbecile with strong and uncontrollable criminal tendencies and perverted moral instincts,* together with some minor symptoms which go with unstable mental make-up under the stress of confinement and the influence of asylum life.

Most respectfully yours,
Alfred Elliott,
Medical Director.

Feb. 17th, 1911.

To the Honorable Chief Justice of the
Superior Court of Hampden,
Springfield, Mass.

Dear Sir:

In accordance with the decree of the Honorable Court, I hereby make my monthly report on the condition of Bertram G. Spencer.

In this report I am unable to add anything of value to my former reports. Spencer has improved physically, is less emotional and somewhat better contented. *Prolonged observation, however, but strengthens our opinion that Spencer is deficient in moral understanding, as the result of mental defect of long standing.* I have not observed any well-defined symptoms pointing to any acute mental psychosis or rapidly dementing process.

Most respectfully,

Alfred Elliott,
Medical Director.

March 17th, 1911.

To the Honorable Chief Justice of the
Superior Court of Hampden,
Springfield, Mass.

Dear Sir:

The Medical Director being away on leave of absence, I hereby make the monthly report on the condition of Bertram G. Spencer.

During the past month patient has been quiet and has not at any time acted like a person dominated by active delusions or hallucinations. While in conversation with the Assistant Physician he is rather surly and fault-finding, but when talking with the patients he is just the reverse. When out of doors he takes active interest in the various sports and the remainder of the time spends in drawing and painting. I cannot see any change, either mentally or physically, since the last report.

Very respectfully,

L. A. Baker,
Acting Medical Director.

April 17th, 1911.

To the Honorable Chief Justice of the
Superior Court of Hampden,
Springfield, Mass.

Dear Sir:

I hereby make my monthly report as to the condition of Bertram G. Spencer, who was committed to this hospital for the purpose of determining his mental condition.

There has been no important change in this man's physical or mental condition since my last report to the Honorable Court. His daily life, conversation, actions and correspondence all point to a mental defect, but recently I have not observed anything that would lead me to believe he is suffering from any acute mental aberration, and I am of the opinion that his mental condition is of long duration, dating from early life or congenital in nature.

Very respectfully,

Alfred Elliott,
Medical Director.

The May report, which follows, is similar, continuing to affirm that there has been no change in Dr. Elliott's opinion, though he expresses it more briefly than at first:

May 17th, 1911.

To the Honorable Chief Justice of the
Superior Court of Hampden,
Springfield, Mass.

Dear Sir:

In compliance with the order of the Honorable Court, I hereby make my monthly report on the mental condition of Bertram G. Spencer.

I am unable at this time to add anything of importance to my former reports. Spencer takes what may be considered for him a normal interest in life. He plays ball and other games, sings, talks and laughs in a natural way and is not abnormally depressed or excited. There has been no mental deterioration noted since coming here and no evidence of delusions or hallucinations which modify his actions. His everyday life shows that *there is and probably always has been a deficiency of moral understanding which manifests itself in criminal acts.*

Very respectfully,

Alfred Elliott,
Medical Director.

June 19th, 1911.

To the Honorable Chief Justice of the
Superior Court of Hampden,
Springfield, Mass.

Dear Sir:

I am unable at this time to add anything new to my former reports on this case. Mr. Spencer is in splendid physical condition, eats and sleeps well, does some little work in our garden, and enters with zest into the usual amusements and sports of the Hospital. He has not at any time manifested delusions or hallucinations, and under the ordinary precaution and restraint of hospital life, has not shown suicidal or homicidal tendencies. During the nine months he has been under observation, I have not been able to find evidence that his crime was the result of an *acute* mental aberration, but *it is still my opinion that there exists in this man a defective mental state which dates from birth or early childhood and manifests itself in weakness of the moral rather than the intellectual sphere and is associated with strong criminal tendencies.*

Very respectfully,

Alfred Elliott,
Medical Director.*

* This report of June 19th proved at the trial to have been one of the most significant. Copies of all the other reports were furnished me, but by

This, to my mind, is rather a strong expression of Dr. Elliott's opinion that Spencer was not mentally responsible for his act, but if we examine the latter part of this report, we notice a departure from his usual form of phraseology. He does not say that Spencer had no mental aberration when he committed his crime, but that the crime "was not the *result* of an *acute* mental aberration." Although he still says that there exists in Spencer "a defective mental state," he no longer classifies him as "a moral imbecile."

Under date of June 30th, Dr. Elliott sent the following letter to his Superintendent and Trustees:

To the Superintendent and Trustees
of the State Farm.
Dear Sirs:—
After sufficient observation to enable me to determine concerning the sanity of Bertram G. Spencer, I have to report that in my opinion he is sane and never has been legally insane, and therefore advise that he be removed from the Bridgewater State Hospital.
Yours respectfully,
Alfred Elliott,
Medical Director.

The Trustees accordingly reported to the Court as follows:

State Farm, Mass., June 30th, 1911.
To the Honorable Chief Justice of the
Superior Court,
Springfield, Mass.
Dear Sir:
In accordance with the law, the Superintendent and Trustees of the Bridgewater State Hospital have voted that in their opinion

some strange oversight this one was not included among them, and I was for a long time at a loss how to procure a copy of it as these reports are not included among the other documents admitted at the trial in the official report of the case as published by the Commonwealth. I finally succeeded in getting a copy of the report of June 19th, through the courtesy of Dr. John H. Carlisle, the present Medical Director of the Bridgewater State Hospital.

Bertram G. Spencer is sane and should be removed from the insane hospital.

Very respectfully,
John B. Tivnan, Chairman,
Payson W. Lyman, Sec.
Hollis M. Blackstone, Supt.

Dr. Elliott's last report to Chief Justice Aiken follows:

July 17th, 1911.

Dear Sir:—

I hereby make my monthly report on the mental condition of Bertram G. Spencer.

After observing this man for ten months I have to report that in my opinion he is sane and has never been legally insane. The Superintendent and Trustees of this Hospital have also reported that in their opinion Spencer is sane and ought to be returned to the prison from which he was transferred.

In our interviews with the man from time to time he has never shown evidence of delusions or hallucinations and has never intimated the existence of irresistible impulses to injure any one, except at such times as his actions were dominated by anger. In considering our record of this case, which includes his previous history as given by himself and members of his family, I do not find that at any time in his life was he in mental conflict with the desire to do wrong, as he says that at no time did he feel anxious to lead a different life until he was arrested and confined in prison. We also note that he showed deliberation and planning in arranging for and carrying out his crimes. For instance, he used a black muffler instead of a mask, as the latter might be considered as evidence against him if found on his person. Says he never carried burglars' tools, and seldom used force to enter a building. He also wore his regular shoes, took them off before entering a house and replaced them after leaving. Such deliberate planning and execution, without remorse of conscience or a struggle to overcome his desire for crime leads me to believe that his crimes were not due to an irresistible impulse or obsession. Again, the variety of crimes he admits, to wit: robbery, murder, rape, shooting at a man, carrying concealed weapons, etc., do not, to my mind, point to mental obsession.

In connection with the crime for which he is at present held, it is of importance to note that on a previous occasion patient fired several shots at a man because the man said something that angered Spencer.

In considering the time he caused rape, or attempted rape, with robbery, we do not find that he showed remorse or a struggle against such deeds, as would be expected if he were under an obsession.

It seems to me his crimes have been for gain, revenge or to satisfy his passion, or to protect himself when overtaken in criminal deeds, and were not the result of an irresistible impulse or obsession or the reaction of a delusion or hallucination, or the result of some acute mental aberration.

Very respectfuly,

Alfred Elliott,
Medical Director.

The analysis of Dr. Elliott's last report is interesting and it is inconceivable that certain discrepancies should not have made a stronger impression upon the jury when Spencer was brought to trial. The very arguments which Dr. Elliott had previously used as evidence of Spencer's irresponsibility are, in this last report, brought forward to prove that he was not "legally insane."

In this report July 17th Dr. Elliott says that Spencer "has never intimated the existence of irresistible impulses to injure anyone except at such times as his actions were dominated by anger." Yet in his report of November 16th he had said, "Spencer's daily life is dominated by irresistible impulses and his will power is too weak to control them and his reasoning so faulty that he seldom arrives at correct conclusions."

Again, he says in the last report, "Such deliberate planning and execution, without remorse of conscience or a struggle to overcome his desire for crime, leads me to believe that his crimes were not due to an irresistible impulse or obsession." But if Spencer were, as Dr. Elliott had repeatedly stated in writing and verbally, a "moral imbecile of a rather low order" with "uncontrollable criminal tendencies and perverted moral instincts," why should he have had "remorse of conscience" or have struggled to overcome his desire for crime? And as to "deliberate planning and execution," that would hardly be proof of sanity in a man suffering from "false ideas or delusions," whose reasoning was "so faulty that he seldom arrived at correct conclusions," who had "general ideas of persecution," whose "inability to reason clearly and to analyse events of everyday life leads to errors of judgment and false conclusions," who had always had a "deficiency of moral understanding which manifests itself in criminal acts."

In the report of November 16th Dr. Elliott says: "His utter disregard for truth, his lack of moral feeling, decency or remorse, together with general ideas of persecution and his inability to accommodate himself to his environments, especially when it is manifestly in his favor to do so, are strong arguments, to my mind, that Spencer is insane." And in the last report this same lack of moral feeling, decency or remorse is used as an argument for his sanity—at least they convey the impression to the lay mind that Dr. Elliott so considers them. Dr. Elliott says: "The variety of crimes he admits . . . do not to my mind point to mental obsession," but he does not say that they do not point to mental disease or mental defect of some sort.

However, we make no plea for Dr. Elliott's conclusions at one time or the other, but merely quote from his reports to show their inconsistency, in spite of the fact that Dr. Elliott month after month repeats that there has been no change and that there has been nothing of value to add to his former reports, and that "prolonged observation strengthens our opinion that Spencer is deficient in moral understanding as a result of mental defect of long standing." In his reports of June 19th and

July 17th he denies none of the statements made in his previous reports, and yet he claims that a man is not "legally insane," though he is "a moral imbecile of rather a low order" with "strong and uncontrollable criminal tendencies"; that "while knowing the right his mental defect is so great that he is unable to do the right or avoid the wrong," and whose "reasoning and judgments are, at times, so faulty as to constitute weak, incoherent delusions."

Before any official order appeared for the return of Spencer to Springfield for trial, rumors that such action was being contemplated reached the ears of the inmates of the Bridgewater State Hospital. These rumors were some months in advance of the change in the reports from Bridgewater, and were probably based upon the fact that Mr. Callahan had been elected partly on the issue of the Spencer case; and though he may not have actually promised to bring Spencer to trial if elected, there is no doubt that he was elected with the expectation that he would do so. The regular term of the Superior Court in Hampden County is in May, and the May term for the year 1911 was the first term after the election of Mr. Callahan as District Attorney. Evidently Spencer's lawyers expected him to bring the case up at that time, for Mr. Stapleton wrote me on March 23rd that he had been appointed counsel for Spencer and that the case would be placed on trial some time in May. Dr. Elliott's reports by this time had become more stereotyped, which may have led Spencer's counsel to believe that he was changing his opinion in regard to the prisoner's sanity. At any rate, at some time in the spring of 1911 District Attorney Callahan requested

Attorney General Swift to assist him and appear with him in connection with the bringing to trial of Spencer, particularly with reference to the medical experts. After looking into the matter, the Attorney General called in conference with himself and Mr. Callahan the four experts, Drs. Elliott, Tuttle, Quinby and Fuller, shortly after June 19th, on which date Dr. Elliott had sent in his June report to the Court. At this conference the Attorney General brought out the significance of the legal definition of insanity, as applied by the courts in such cases, and *on the basis of this definition* the physicians agreed in their opinion that Spencer was not legally insane, as they later testified at the trial. That Dr. Elliott, after his years of experience with criminal insane cases, should have needed such instruction is strange. In his testimony at the trial he admits that it was the explanation of "what the law meant by legally insane—the definition of knowledge between right and wrong and uncontrollable impulse"—which caused him to declare Spencer sane, and that he had this definition in mind when he used the term "legally insane." He said that Spencer "knew the difference between right and wrong at the time the act was committed" and that "he was not controlled by an irresistible impulse." Dr. Elliott must have had the legal interpretation of these terms put before him on many previous occasions. He never gave any really satisfactory explanation of why he changed his mind in regard to Spencer, though he admitted on the stand that he had been annoyed by the letters Spencer had sent out from the hospital. If the accusations made in these letters were delusions, they should not have annoyed the Superintendent, who must have been accustomed to such symptoms among his patients; but if Spencer was sane, they were not delusions. If Spencer was sane and lying, why was no attempt made to disprove his statements? Dr. Elliott also admitted at the trial that arguments in his July report relating to the details of the crime—the use of a black muffler instead of a mask, etc., were used after he had a talk with an officer who visited Bridgewater from Hampden County. No amount of questioning changed the stand that he took that he could not recall the name of the officer or the date he visited the institution, but he did admit it was prior to his June report. What value could be attached to the opinion of the Trustees or of the Superintendent of the State Farm that Spencer was sane? I understood the Superintendent scarcely ever saw him, and I question if there were not some of the Trustees who never saw him. Dr. Elliott admitted on the stand that their opinion was not entitled to any weight. At the time of the trial, when Dr. Elliott was cross-examined regarding his sudden change of opinion he hung his head and did not reply to some questions; he became so agitated when the defendant's counsel was making it appear by his questions that Dr. Elliott had done a wrongful act in sending the man back for trial and that he knew he was insane, that he took a pointer which was near him, and after handling it excitedly for some time, broke it in his apparent embarrassment while testifying.

In returning Spencer to the Court for trial the Commonwealth was "treating the offense instead of the offender," as Dr. Guy Fernald said in one of his able articles on the treatment of defectives, in referring to the fact that neither psychiatrists nor institution heads are empowered to treat defectives as they should be treated.

Return of Spencer to Springfield from Bridgewater for Trial

The application for the return of Spencer from Bridgewater must have been made directly to the Chief Justice by the District Attorney, for there are no docket entries in the case from September 17th, 1910, to July 25th, 1911, when the following order was sent to Sheriff Embury P. Clark:

To the Sheriff of Hampden:
You will forthwith cause Bertram G. Spencer, now under care and observation pending the determination of his insanity, at the Bridgewater State Hospital, to be removed therefrom to the jail at Springfield, there to be held in custody in accordance with the process by which he was originally committed to the jail, and this shall be your authority therefor.

John A. Aiken,
Justice of the Superior Court.

On Tuesday, August 1st, 1911, Deputy Sheriff Studley arrived at Bridgewater at 9 A. M. with Chief Justice Aiken's order. Spencer was handcuffed and they left on the 10:15 A.M. train from Bridgewater, arriving at Springfield at 2:19 P.M. Deputy Studley is quoted as saying that Spencer had not been informed that he was to be brought back until he, the Deputy, arrived; that on the journey Spencer spoke very little, but that what he did say was on the general line of what he had said before. The attendants at the jail noticed that Spencer wore the same dark suit of clothes which he had worn when he was taken to Bridgewater. According to the report of the Springfield Republican of the following day, he had very little to say to the jail attendants on his return, and he appeared about the same as when he went away. In commenting on Spencer's return, the Republican said:

> In the public mind the fact that Spencer was allowed to go to the Hospital without a trial, either rightly or wrongly, was a very effective political argument against Mr. Taft.

As we have said before, to those who had to do with Spencer or were near him after his return to Springfield Jail, there seemed to be little change from his condition when he was sent from the jail to Bridgewater. John Joseph Landers, who was serving a term for vagrancy, at the Hampden County Jail from June to September, 1911, was set to watch Spencer for about a month after his return. He described one occasion upon which Spencer "acted quite wild." According to Landers, Spencer had previously been complaining of a headache; one of his fellow prisoners on the same corridor had attempted suicide by hanging, causing some commotion which had excited Spencer. Landers had assisted in taking the man down, and on his return he said he found Spencer in a state of great excitement. "He threw his hands down and said they were killing the man—that they were 'kneeing' him. He cried, 'Let me out—I'll take him off!' He run back and forth in his cell, picked up his spittoon and broke it, broke the stool that he sat on himself, threw the cups around, and the salt and pepper box, and he threw his bedclothes and his own clothes all around. He didn't pay no attention to me. He run from the front of his cell to the back of it, put out his hands and grasped the air, and kept looking at the floor." Spencer remained in this condition for about fifteen minutes, then went and lay on the bed and started crying. He cried all the rest of the day, at least until Landers went off duty at two o'clock. Before this episode, Spencer had been seated quietly at his table drawing.

Another prisoner, William McCart, who was serving a sentence for drunkenness at the Springfield Jail, was put to watch Spencer at night for about a month, from September 28th to October 24th, 1911. He said Spencer had a great deal of headache, and used to put cloths wet with cold water on his head; he had often seen him sit on the side of the bed and clasp his head with both hands. "He used to look up—like that [illustrating]—and he would call out as loud as ever he could call, 'Keep quiet up there!' He asked me if I heard anybody talking about him, and I said no, I didn't. So he said he had heard talking, and they were talking about him. He used to laugh sometimes, but he mostly sat across the bed with his back up against the wall, and I heard him sobbing sometimes—'H-a-a, H-a-a, H-a-a!' He used to have a gurgling in his throat like—as if something was in the throat, and he made a strange sound." McCart said that whenever the bar was thrown to open or close the door, it made a noise, and Spencer would jump up and look around "with a wild look." "He would shut his fist and . . . look as if he wanted to find out what the noise was." Spencer took a dislike to another attendant named Moody, and McCart said he would "go into a mad fit" whenever Moody passed. "He sometimes would throw himself around, on the bed you know, bumping his head against the wall. He told Moody one time he hated the look of him. I never seen Moody do anything to him. The only thing I ever see, he used to go forward and look through the bars and he didn't like that—he didn't like anybody to do that—but he hated Moody for doing it more so." McCart said Spencer made sounds in his sleep as if he were talking to someone, but McCart could not make out what he was saying.

CHAPTER V

THE TRIAL—INCLUDING PREVIOUS COURT PROCEEDINGS AND EFFORTS FOR A NEW TRIAL, TO TIME OF SENTENCE TO DEATH, JULY 2ND, 1912.

On March 23rd, 1911, I received a letter from R. P. Stapleton, Esq., Counsellor at Law, Holyoke, Mass., in which he told me of having been appointed by the court Senior Counsel for Spencer. He said that he had been informed that I had made an examination of Spencer while he was confined in Bridgewater, and that he desired my opinion. This letter resulted in an interview, in which Mr. Stapleton asked me to appear for the defense. Later I got the following letter from the District Attorney:

COMMONWEALTH OF MASSACHUSETTS

Office of

DISTRICT ATTORNEY, WESTERN DISTRICT

Holyoke.

August 16, 1911.

Dr. L. Vernon Briggs,
208 Beacon St.,
Boston, Mass.
My dear Sir:

Dr. Alfred Elliott, Medical Director of the Bridgewater State Hospital, informs me that you were among those who have visited Bertram G. Spencer, who was confined there for observation as to his sanity, and who has been removed to the Springfield Jail for trial, probably in November, upon the ground that he is not and never has been legally insane. Will you kindly inform me whether you made your visit in behalf of the defendant, and what your opinion is as to his mental condition?

Very truly yours,
(Signed) Christopher T. Callahan,
District Attorney.

In reply I wrote:

My dear Sir:
Your letter of August 16th is at hand and read today on my return from New Hampshire. May I ask if you wish my opinion as an expert?

I never received any answer to this letter.

On October 30th, 1911, Chief Justice Aiken authorized my employment as an expert in the Spencer case, at the request of Mr. Stapleton.

On August 23rd, Mr. Stapleton wrote me:

You have undoubtedly learned that Bertram G. Spencer, who was confined at Bridgewater, has been returned to the jail at Springfield, Mass. After Dr. Elliott and his assistant, Dr. Baker, had repeatedly for eight months, in written reports over their signatures, declared Spencer insane, through some ——— they suddenly took the other tack, in June of this year. The sequence of events is certainly significant.

On Monday morning, November 13th, 1911, Spencer was placed on trial. From the beginning, there was apparent a feeling of vindictiveness against the prisoner by many in the court room—a marked exception were the presiding judge and those who appeared for the defense. So lightly did some of those interested take the seriousness of the situation that facetious remarks and laughter were heard from time to time. It seems counsel for the defense thought the attitude of the Attorney General prejudicial to the rights of the defendant and remonstrated in open court against remarks made by the Attorney General and the District Attorney.

Motion to quash the indictment was overruled by Judge Crosby. Assistant Attorney General Greenhalge was brought into the case to assist Attorney General Swift.

On the second day of the trial, November 14th, District Attorney Callahan opened on behalf of the Commonwealth. He rehearsed details of the murder and the testimony he intended to bring out to establish them. In closing his opening address, he said:

> It is well to understand that in our Commonwealth simple insanity, a word which can be and is stretched to cover a multitude of mental imperfections, does not excuse a criminal. It is not sufficient for the defense to show that he is a moral pervert, or that he is mentally defective. There are few of us who are wholly free from these imperfections. It is not enough that the alienists may pronounce him insane. The evidence must go farther and show that he was so far insane that, at the time he committed the crime, he did not know the difference between right and wrong, or that, if he did know the difference, he had no control over his will, and did the criminal act under an irresistible impulse. If you are satisfied that he did know the difference between right and wrong and was not governed in his actions by an irresistible impulse, then you must find that he was not legally insane.

During the reading of the District Attorney's opening Spencer showed a good deal of emotion, and when the clerk read the indictment he wept convulsively. The following correct description of the defendant's appearance at the opening of the court on the 14th was given by the Boston American, which says:

> Spencer is a study. He sits well back in the steel cage and seems oblivious to the brass-buttoned jail turnkey, Nat P. Wade, seated in the cage by his side. His head is tilted back slightly and a pair of large eyes, almost round, stare fixedly and vacantly ahead. His receding forehead is furrowed with wrinkles, wrinkles that tremble

and quiver. His ears are set back deep in his head; his large eyes open and shut continuously; he trembles from head to toe; the furrows in his forehead keep up a continuous twitching; his hands, atremble, drum his chair at times, and then his knees and his feet, with legs generally crossed, shake as with palsy. His face is ashen. Seated in front of the cage and a little to one side were the most noted alienists in the state, headed by Dr. L. Vernon Briggs, of Boston. Dr. Briggs is supported in his view of Spencer's condition by Drs. J. W. Courtney and E. B. Lane of Boston, and Dr. J. A. Houston of Northampton State Hospital. Alienists for the state, headed by Dr. H. M. Quinby of Worcester, include Dr. George H. Tuttle of McLean and Dr. Daniel T. Fuller of Boston. Just outside his cage sat Spencer's mother and wife. The paper goes on to state that after the District Attorney began reading Spencer twisted and turned in his seat . . . grabbed the railing of the cage like an enraged animal, and called out at times.

When the District Attorney was making his opening, Spencer broke in with "My God, no, no!" The District Attorney at one time when Spencer was sobbing aloud, directed his eyes at the counsel for defense and said in a loud tone so the jury could hear, "Is this not a little premature?" Later this remark was stricken from the records. When the Attorney General quoted Spencer as saying to Miss Dow before shooting her, "If you want to die, die!" Spencer broke down and called out "No, I never said that!"

The details of the murder were established by various witnesses, including Mrs. Dow and both her daughters, the neighbors, the doctors who had been called in to attend the victims and the police who had traced Spencer; and on the third day, November 15th, the full confession of Spencer to Captain Boyle, made on April 6th, 1910, was read by the stenographer who took the notes, Miss Bessie C. Niles.

Later, when State Detective Bligh was testifying, Spencer's eyes were fixed on him, and finally, after one statement of Bligh's, Spencer leaped from his seat to the front of the cage, with a terrific yell that sounded like a shriek, and cried out, "Why don't you tell the truth!" Turnkey Wade and another court officer, who was five feet away, jumped on Spencer and bore him down, the prisoner continuing to shriek, "Why don't he tell the truth!" Reporters who were in the way of Spencer's plunge leaped aside and there was considerable confusion. Spencer's cries filled the court room after he had been overpowered, and Judge Crosby directed a recess, which lasted 25 minutes. Spencer, whose strength seemed all spent, was supported as he was led from the room, and was still shivering and shaking when they brought him back.

The New York World of November 16th gives a graphic description of this or another similar episode in court:

Spencer leaped to his feet and tried to burst out of his cage. He shook at the little gate until it looked as if he would tear the whole railing from its fastenings; his hair was flying, his big eyes wild with fury, his mouth dripping. He threw out his arms, his fists were clenched, and he yelled at the top of his big, strong voice, "Damn you! For God's sake, why don't you tell the truth—the truth—the truth!" His custodian, a fat slow turnkey, finally managed to grab him and yank him, writhing and struggling, to his seat. Rapidly came the sharp thwackings of Judge Crosby's gavel. They seemed to be beating on the prisoner's raw nerves. At every crack of the gavel he convulsively started. There came a silence. "Well, well, well," whined the prisoner, "Well, why don't he tell the truth?"

Significantly to those who think that Spencer is only acting, continues the *World,* despite that he has continually kept up his sudden glaring of the eyes, his jerks and twists of the body, his spasmodic movements of the neck, his ceaseless, crazily rapid tetering of the upper foot of his crossed legs, stood the fact that this great outburst of emotionalism on his part came at the time when the State was about to close its case and the opening of the defense to begin with an argument by white-haired, impressive Col. Charles L. Young. While his lawyer was making his opening plea, Spencer, who had staggered out at the recess, shaking his head, his hair in his eyes, his lips twisted and uttering a steady stream of groans, was no more quiescent than before. Twice, when a side door slammed, he leaped in the air; once, when his lawyer in great earnestness raised his voice to a high cry, the seemingly tortured man threw up his hands and cried, "Good God! Why does he yell that way?" When Mr. Young told of the time when Spencer had been tied to a tree, at the age of thirteen, and left "for wolves to devour," the prisoner cried tragically, "Ugh! the wolves, the wolves!"

The World article continues:

Finally and sweepingly, in his opening, Col. Young declared that there were well-defined and identified cases of insanity in both the maternal and paternal branches of the man's family, and concluding, he told the jury that Spencer did not ask to go free; he asked only to be judged by the prenatal facts in his life as the defense would produce them, and to be committed to an institution for the insane —"until such time," ended the lawyer, "as God, in His wisdom, shall call him to account from above." "Yes, that's right," moaned the "gentleman burglar," "that's right, that's right."

When court adjourned he was still writhing and weeping hysterically. He kissed two fingers that his wife thrust through a square of the cage. He tried to kiss his mother, through the slender bars, but their lips could not meet. He was led away, floundering in the legs, his head wagging, apparently in a complete state of prostration.

The opening statement in behalf of the defendant was made at the end of the afternoon session on the third day of the trial by Col. Young. In it he said:

We have but one defense and upon that our evidence will depend a mental defectiveness, mental incapacity, mental unsoundness, and as our brother said, that is a legal defense. . . . We will show you that this man is unable to distinguish right from wrong to the extent that the law requires in order to constitute capacity to commit crime, that he is a victim of impulses and desires which he is unable to control, and they are wholly uncontrollable; so that he is unable by reason of mental incapacity and mental unsoundness to do the right and avoid the wrong. We will point out to you injuries of various kinds. . . . Now we are not going to contend that these are the causes of his mental incapacity, but we are going to contend that they are causes which have a tendency to cripple largely his mental effectiveness; we will show that prior to his birth he was subjected to influences prenatal, which marked and consigned him to criminal acts of various kinds which it is alleged that he committed.

We will show you that he has the most violent outbreaks from the most trifling affairs even—not even so great as you noticed here a few moments ago, but from the most trifling causes an outbreak would come beyond his own control—that indicates, as will be told by those who know and have studied into these things, this man has the incapacity of mind and the unsoundness of mind which could not be normal under any circumstances, as you will see and as you will learn and know from the lips of those who have been with him by day and by night, by his side here and there, by laborers and fellow servants and by those who have carefully watched him for the purpose of trying to ascertain—and did ascertain. . . . Many of these outbreaks were characterized by the same symptoms he showed when he took the life of this young girl. We will show you that while in . . . Hartford, Connecticut, he made murderous assaults that showed his mental unsoundness. We will show you that he had these tendencies to commit these crimes, that came from a suggestion which he received about the year 1903. We will show you that when at school there was that incapacity to learn or study or to retain that which was taught him, failing in his studies as a boy, fearful outbreaks here and there at school, with the teachers and the scholars—all of this will be given to you by those who have had some interest in him and sympathized with him at the time. We will show you that . . . he had delusions that some one was talking—voices here and there and everywhere, around and about him—not knowing where they came from—yet no one spoke anywhere.

Col. Young continued to outline the plea of the experts, and then reviewed in detail the family history of the prisoner, and the significant events of his childhood, but he neglected to bring out in his address the peculiar features of Spencer's crimes in Springfield and elsewhere which had made the newspapers and the people at large decide, even before the criminal was discovered and his history known, that these crimes could have been committed by no one in his right mind. In reviewing the trial at this late date, it would almost seem that a great opportunity was lost by the defense in not dwelling more particularly upon these often motiveless, haphazard crimes, and especially in not bringing out more clearly the weakness of any motive for appearing in the midst of the group of women on the night he shot Miss Blackstone as against the risk incurred. This and a dozen similar events prove conclusively the lack of any design in Spencer's crimes, other than that of temporary relief from a compelling impulse.

Attorney General Swift interrupted Attorney Young several times while he was delivering his address to the jury, but Mr. Young appeared to have the better in the tilts, and succeeded in placing before the jury all that he had set out to present to them. District Attorney Callahan changed his attitude as Mr. Young proceeded with his speech from one of cold and almost contemptuous indifference to one of extreme earnestness and interest. Up to the time that Attorney Young began to speak, the attack upon Spencer had been powerful and relentless.

The first witness for the defense was called on the morning of the fourth day of the trial, Thursday, November 16th, Mrs. Kate E. Spencer, mother of the prisoner. She testified at length as to the family history and the events of her son's early life, which we have quoted elsewhere, and as to Bertram's more recent peculiarities of behavior. During Mrs. Spencer's testimony, Lawyer Stapleton, for the defense, administered a stinging rebuke to the Attorney General for smiling before the panel of jurors when Mrs. Spencer testified as to certain acts of her husband. Mr. Stapleton, in language in every way courteous, said: "I think the Attorney General might refrain from laughing at the testimony." Mr. Swift replied that he could not help it, to which Mr. Stapleton answered, "If you want to laugh, you might at least wait until you argue the evidence. At present the testimony is entitled to respect." It is evident Mr. Stapleton appreciated the importance of the effect that such an action as smiling at the evidence of the defense by one holding the highest legal position in Massachusetts might have upon the jury.

Mrs. Spencer was a very good witness and appeared to have an excellent memory, and her story alone was cumulative evidence, to us who have made a study of mental disease, that her son was far from being a normal individual. No doubt could have been left in any one's mind, after hearing her testimony, of her son's dangerously bad heredity, of his peculiar, unstable disposition, of the many abuses and the constant atmosphere of friction and misunderstanding to which he had been subjected as a child, to his moody disposition and frequent outbreaks of uncontrollable temper, to his habit of carrying a revolver and drawing it upon slight provocation, and to the fact that he frequently heard "voices" when no one was speaking. Her testimony lasted into the afternoon session, and Mr. Callahan's grilling cross-examination failed to weaken any of her statements. One after another, other witnesses were called, who confirmed her statements in almost every detail, and added others of the same character.

The second witness was Charles A. Gager, who testified as to Spencer's having drawn a revolver during an argument with another man at a dance; Dr. Danielson followed, confirming the story of the attempt at suicide by taking laudanum. An effort was made by the defense to get Dr. Danielson's opinion as to Bertram's mental condition before the jury, but he was not permitted to testify on this subject as he could not qualify as an expert; and Mr. Callahan brought out that Dr. Danielson had signed Bertram's certificate of health for admission to the Mt. Hermon School, stating that he had no "nervous" disease, such as chorea, epilepsy, etc. However, Mr. Stapleton brought out the statement that Dr. Danielson did not have in mind insanity or mental defect when he answered the printed question on the application blank with that statement.

The neighbors, Mr. Bailey and Mr. Carpenter, followed with their accounts of Bertram's peculiarities and events in his childhood, Mr. Bailey testifying that "if you approached him or spoke to him on any subject quick he would give you a wild, indifferent look. If you agreed with him everything seemed to be right. If you didn't agree he seemed disturbed." Mr. Carpenter testified to the ditch digging episode related on page 85, and also that while Spencer was at table eating and no conversation was going on he would start up suddenly and say "Mother, did you speak to me?" and that he was very nervous and had attacks of sobbing and crying.

Clark H. Standish, another neighbor, told of the episode of the digging of the ditch when Spencer went into hysterics and made an attack; also of an incident when he appeared in the night at Standish's barn barefooted with only short blue overalls and a night shirt on when it was raining hard and very cold. He asked for a blanket so that he might sleep in the barn and Mr. Standish gave him some horse blankets. Mr. Standish said there was an injury in the fleshy part of his right thumb which Bert told him had been caused by a shot from his father when he left the house. This shot Mr. Standish said he heard a little while before Spencer got to his barn.

He was followed by three teachers from the Mt. Hermon School, who testified as to Bertram's backwardness in his studies, his insubordination, bad language and violent temper. Bertram's uncle, William K. Spencer, next testified as to mental peculiarities in the family, and especially as to those of his own father, William L. Spencer, and of his grandfather, Ambrose Spencer. Mrs. Wattrous, of Portland, Conn., followed with her account of Bertram's strange outbreaks when he seemed to be blind with rage, but she could calm him down by coaxing and talking to him, and she also took a pistol away from him which she still has; and the first day of testimony for the defense was closed by that of Samuel N. Hyde who testified that Mr. Spencer's uncle David B. Date's mind was affected, that he was "off his base."

On the fifth day of the trial, Friday, November 17th, Spencer's sister, Mrs. Cornelia H. Pulz, told of the episode in Springfield when Spencer had had an altercation with Mr. and Mrs. Krailing, his wife's grandparents, as given on page 95. She also testified as to the wild and glassy look he had in his eyes at times when anyone crossed him and at those times he was never able to control himself; that if you pointed a finger at him with the idea of tickling him he would always run away and scream.

Gardiner J. Oakes, a former employer of Bertram's, testified to spells that Spencer had when he would change color and clap his hands. He remembered at least half a dozen of them, they would be over in a minute. He complained of his head and was "melancholy and gloomy" at times. The deposition of Henrietta Post, Mrs. Spencer's old nurse, was then read, further confirming Mrs. Spencer's story of the child's early life, his punishment by his father, as told on page 71, and his "queer, odd and strange" disposition. His father-in-law, Herman L. Amberg, next testified as to Spencer's behavior while courting his daughter and as to his exhibitions of violent temper while employed by the H. L. Handy Company. Among other things Mr. Amberg said "he was going to knock my head off." "He showed a very violent temper at times; with the least provocation he would fly off the handle and throw a hatchet at some of us, or anything he had in his hand; he locked himself up in the refrigerator, excited and trembling. I was almost frightened at his face, the way he looked, the peculiar look in his eyes. He changed from the action of a schoolboy in one minute to acting like a raving maniac."

Four of Spencer's fellow clerks in the Hartford department store testified as to his assault on the cash boy with a hammer because he had "evidently crossed his track" in some way, to his swearing about his father when he received a box of sweet peas from his mother, and other manifestations of dangerous temper. There next testified Mrs. Gladys May Wyman, a trained nurse who had known Spencer during his residence in Springfield and had boarded in the same house with him for about six years. We have already quoted from her testimony, on page 91, which was rather significant as she had had two years' experience in the care of the insane at the Northampton State Hospital. Her statements, as well as those of Mrs. Walters later in the day, established Spencer's mother's account of his apparently hearing "voices" on many occasions. Her husband, William L. Wyman, who had also been an attendant at the Northampton State Hospital, also testified as to Spencer's hearing voices, and as to Spencer's peculiar behavior and eccentricity at his boarding-house and when employed by the street railway company, as related on page 93.

Mr. Nelson R. Hosley, whose house was one of those entered by Spencer, was then put upon the stand. He testified as to the theft of a small notebook of no value to anyone, among other things taken from his house; and Robert E. Miles gave his evidence as to Spencer's having drawn a revolver and threatened his life after a simple quarrel over a seat when they were both employed on the Boston and Maine Railroad. Napoleon Bourque testified as to Spencer's unaccountable anger with him in a misunderstanding about a baseball glove. The last witness of the day was William McCart, a jail attendant, whose testimony has already been quoted on page 151.

In reporting the events of this day of the trial, the Springfield Republican of the following morning, November 18th, says:

> . . . Later in the day, it became necessary for Judge Crosby to admonish the spectators and all concerned for the first time since the trial opened. Willard L. Wyman of this city was on the stand, and had testified concerning the time when Spencer wanted him to sing and then chided him because he couldn't. He said that Spencer had told him that he "couldn't sing any better than a hog," or words to that effect. Under cross-examination, the District Attorney forced the witness to admit that this characterization of his vocal abilities was probably correct and warranted by the sample which Spencer heard. This brought considerable laughter, which rose above Sheriff

Clark's rappings for order. Judge Crosby then stated, so that everyone could hear, that he felt forced to remind all that the court room was not a place of amusement, and that the laughter was grievously out of place.

The Springfield Union of Saturday morning, November 18th, 1911, in commenting on parts of the testimony given the previous day, says:

> Another incident that brought relief from the monotony of testimony regarding the mentality of the prisoner and his ancestors occurred during the cross-examination of Frank G. Bedworth of Hartford, who had testified in direct examination that Spencer "looked like a bull" when he was pursuing the cash boy through the department in which he worked in the Brown, Thompson and Co. Store in Hartford. Mr. Callahan attempted to qualify the witness as an expert on bulls, and learned that he had once nearly been the victim of a bull that stood on the shore of a pond where Mr. Bedworth was fishing from a plank. Mr. Callahan then attempted to learn what the witness knew about bulldogs and afterwards tried him on his knowledge of angry cats.

The sixth day of the trial, Saturday, November 18th, commenced with testimony from Dr. Hosea M. Quinby, Superintendent of the Worcester State Hospital, who said that Helen Date Tiffany, a great-aunt of Spencer's, was admitted to his hospital November 14, 1907, and died there April 22, 1911, that she was insane and had false hearing, delusions of wealth and various other delusions. He was followed by a former neighbor of the Spencers in Lebanon, Joe Stedman, who testified that Bertram threw a one or two lb. weight at one of Mr. Spencer's clerks while in the store, that he would at times have a characteristic wild, glassy look, that when he was infuriated he was uncontrollable; that he had seen him in this condition at least twenty times, this during his school days. The Springfield Sunday Union of November 19th, after reporting the testimony of this man, Joe Stedman, says:

When Mr. Callahan was grilling Stedman a hunted, desperate look came into the prisoner's eyes, and he struggled in the cage. Turnkey Wade grasped him by the arm and shoulder and Spencer's wife put her hand through the bars to hold his other hand. "Now he makes me so mad," Spencer mumbled when Mr. Callahan was questioning Stedman about the youth of the prisoner, when the witness said he saw him playing in Lebanon. When his wife tried to hold his hand, he snatched it away from her and tried to put it against his face. "Let me alone!" he growled snappishly, and fell back, mumbling incoherently.

There was next called to the stand Harry L. Watts, a brakeman, who described a quarrel with Spencer over the respective merits of two local newspapers, from which the latter had not recovered for over a year. Then the defendant's father, Wilbur L. L. Spencer, testified at length concerning his own abuse of Bertram when a boy, saying that "at a very tender age I remember I punished him and he slipped out of my hands and fell on the stove; that in trying to correct him in his prayers I punished him with a curtain stick at his bedside;" that for "raking leaves in the back yard and setting them afire I tied his hands behind him and put his head on a chopping block and told him if he ever done it again I would sever his head from his body." That at about nine "I hit him on the head with a whip; I was so excited I might have hit him on any part of his body." That he remembered taking Bert to a place in Lebanon called "Mack's Woods" about two miles from his house and he said: "I tied him to a tree and told him I would leave him there for the wild animals to devour. I had business at a station, a grain station that was two miles beyond and I left him tied until I went there and returned. At another time we were riding out of the yard and he was at my side and put his hand in the hollow of my back. It seemed to me intentional. I cuffed him side of the head and he jumped from the wagon. I followed, went into the house, got a revolver, came out and fired in his direction as he was running down through the pastures." The father also testified to other incidents which are given more in detail on page 75.

The Springfield Daily News of that evening, in speaking of W. L. L. Spencer's testimony, says:

> The witness indicated no emotion when telling about tying his son to a tree in Mack's Woods and leaving him there "for wild beasts to devour," while he went to the grist mill about two miles distant. . . . He was as calm in telling about the heartrending scenes of the punishments in the early life of the prisoner as one would be in describing the happenings at a church social. He told about placing Bertram's head on the chopping block and threatening to cut it off, with as little apparent concern as one would have in placing the head of a chicken on the block for execution.

The next witness was John Joseph Landers, the prisoner-attendant at the Hampden County Jail, who testified as to Spencer's attacks of excitement in the jail when he broke his spittoon and threw cups, salts and peppers about, and other incidents given on page 150. The Court then adjourned until Monday, November 20th.

On the seventh day, November 20th, witnesses were called to testify to the many trivial and useless articles taken by Spencer in his burglaries. Dr. Ames told of his having taken one of a pair of lady's shoes. Spencer's mother was recalled to tell of a large bag she had found in Spencer's rooms and which she had turned over to the police, containing old badges and other valueless trinkets, which he had evidently collected with much care. More might have been said on this matter, for the list of articles stolen, as published by the police, consists largely of trinkets and bits of broken imitation jewelry in most cases of no value whatever, and in many others valued at as little as 25 cents.

Dr. LaMotte, the Naval Surgeon, testified on this day. The Boston American of November 22nd said:

> While Dr. LaMotte was testifying Spencer hung his head and wept quietly. He jerked with nervous excitement. His wife reached in through the iron lattice of the cage and patted him gently. He quieted, then they chatted together.

Spencer spent most of the time after his arrest in trying to catch flies in his cell in the Springfield Jail, according to the testimony of Eugene Farrell, the next witness, who had been his cell mate for eighteen days. He was followed on the stand by Mrs. Lucy T. Lewis, of Oakland, California, who testified to Spencer's strange behavior in her home in Oakland, describing him as at times greatly excited, very nervous and wild eyed, and Mrs. Anita Martland's deposition was also read. In a letter written to Mrs. Martland, put in by Mr. Callahan, Spencer says:

> I have fought this double self, as no one knows, and through pride I have kept my wrong doings within myself, whereas if I had told someone of my uncontrollable desires nineteen years ago, I could have been put away and this awful thing would never have occurred. This desire to steal began when I was but nine years old, and by degrees has led to my arrest, April 5th, 1910, and with my temper that has followed me always and at a flash notice has been the cause of many unhappy recollections that I have longed and wished were never so. . . . It is strange to me, Nettie, that so much money as I have been entrusted with and only once did I take from my employer, and hundreds and thousands of dollars have been entrusted to my care and I never thought of taking a penny. And to think that I should go out from all that was good and steal, here and in every place I have been, and end up by killing a poor defenseless woman at any other time I would protect with my life—but the awful screaming of four women I suppose unnerved me and here I am. . . .

No period of Spencer's life previous to his arrest was left uncovered by the defense; witnesses were produced to testify to his violent behavior and lack of self-control, as well as to other peculiarities of aspect and demeanor in every year of his life from early infancy. Dr. Drake confirmed the story of the laudanum poisoning as told by Mrs. Spencer and by Dr. Danielson, and added his own account of Mrs. Spencer's attempt at suicide by the same means. The last witness for this day was Dr. John A. Houston, Superintendent of the Northampton State Hospital.

Dr. Houston was examined and cross-examined at great length, and much time was taken in attempts to get him to define and classify Bertram's degree of mental defectiveness. The doctor stated definitely, however, that Spencer's was a "defective mental state, if not degenerative, probably dating from puberty." This, he said, had been his first opinion before Spencer was sent to Bridgewater, and he said he saw no reason for changing it. He stated that there were a great many cases of irresponsible mental deficiency that it was difficult to classify by name. He said that Spencer's impulses were in a large sense imperative and uncontrollable.

On the eighth day, November 21st, Dr. Elliott was put on the stand by the defense, and the greater part of the day was taken by his examination and that of Dr. Lane. The court ruled that Dr. Elliott's reports were not admissible as affirmative evidence, but that if the doctor testified on the stand to anything that was contrary to what he had stated in any report, that report would be admissible. Dr. Elliott was well known to be a hostile witness, in the legal if not in the social acceptance of the term, and there was much wrangling over his testimony; though, as we have said in presenting his reports, his opinion was not proved to have changed in regard to Spencer's mental condition, except in so far as its expression was restricted by the legal definition of insanity furnished him by the Attorney General previous to the trial. The reports were finally admitted as evidence, though as I have said elsewhere, they were never published with other documents admitted at the trial.

The prisoner was in a most excitable condition all the time Dr. Elliott was testifying, and broke in upon his testimony in a manner unprecedented in any court in the history of criminal jurisprudence. The following account, taken from the signed report of Edwin J. Park in the evening edition of the Boston Globe of the same day, is substantiated by verbatim records of the court stenographers:

> For the first time since the trial began the prisoner was looking at a witness direct, and he kept his unblinking eyes fastened on Dr. Elliott. As the doctor testified Spencer, who had been fidgeting about in his seat but not removing his eyes from the doctor's face, began muttering. Dr. Elliott paid no attention to him but continued with his testimony and said that after Bert had been in Ward E-2 for a month he was removed to what is commonly called at the State Farm the Northeast Ward which, he said, was "for conspirators who attempt to escape or show signs of violence." When Dr. Elliott gave this testimony, Spencer threw his right hand back to his hip pocket, his lips drew back from his teeth in a snarl, and he hissed out some words which were unintelligible to the reporters. Turnkey Wade, who was in the seat with Spencer, said something to him and placed a restraining hand on his right arm, while the prisoner's wife, who sat close to the cage on Bert's right side, also spoke to him and tried to reach through the bars and grasp his left hand, but he threw her hand aside. . . . Dr. Elliott said . . . "After I had kept Spencer in that ward for a month, I decided he could be removed to Building E. He wanted to go back to that building as there was a larger yard there, and he wanted to be where he could play ball,

and——" Dr. Elliott did not finish the sentence. With a wild cry that sounded like a combination of a shriek and a wail, the prisoner jumped from his seat to the front of the steel cage, with Turnkey Wade clinging to him, and yelled: "You lie. You are a liar, a contemptible liar, and I want the court to know he is lying."

Turnkey Wade is a big and powerful officer, but his efforts to drag Spencer away from the front railing of the cage, which is about three feet high, or to force him back into his seat, were unavailing, and Deputy Sheriffs Leyden and Malone, both big, husky men, jumped over the railing into the dock and fell upon the prisoner with Wade. Spencer fought all three of them with fists and feet, and a desperate battle, which lasted several minutes, ensued, before the three officers, after fighting all over the dock, succeeded in flooring the prisoner. Finally he went down, with the three officers piled on top of him, but he did not stop fighting and struggling and it was at least three or four minutes before the weight of the officers on his legs, arms and body squeezed enough of his strength out of him to cause him to let up in his impotent battle.

Meantime, while he was fighting with the officers, Spencer's voice was raised to a high pitch, and among the things he said was:

"Yes, I want the jury to hear me. I want every man and woman in this building to hear me. He's a liar—contemptible liar from start to finish! I won't let him lie. I begged and begged of him to let me out of that stinking, nasty yard that he put me in. It isn't fit for a dog to be in. No, I won't shut up!—I will let everybody know it. You can kill me this minute—I don't care—I won't shut up—I want everybody to hear me. He's a contemptible beast—a murderer. He murdered men out there by the thousands and buried them out in the fields. I won't let up—I want to tell of it. I want everybody to hear. He has brutal punishment. They kept punishing me there—they kicked me in the ribs! I have been to that man and begged and begged on my knees that he would protect me. He laughed at me—laughed at me! And he says 'We will investigate—we will investigate.' But when did he investigate? Oh, such men as you ought to be killed—killed to the last man!"

While the fight in the cage was going on between Spencer and the three officers, Bert's wife jumped from her seat and tried to get into the dock, but Court Officer Cummins grabbed her and held her back. Bert's mother and sister, who were behind the wife, also tried to get to the cage, but Cummins had caught the wife in a narrow place and they could not get by her. The tears coursed down the cheeks of the young wife and she wailed "O Bert! O Bert! O Bert! Oh, let me get to him! Oh, please let me get to his side!"

After the officers had held Bert down for a few minutes and his struggles had partially ceased, while his outcries had degenerated into a series of groans and squeals, Judge Crosby said calmly: "We will take a recess," and the jury was led out. Then Spencer, with the brawny hands of four court officers grasping him, was half led and half dragged from the court room and was removed to a remote anteroom.

As the jury was leaving the court room after the outbreak, the clerk said something to Attorney General James M. Swift about its having been an exciting incident, and Mr. Swift replied: "Yes, it was; but I was prepared for it; I had seen it coming all the morning." Lawyer Stapleton, who overheard the remark, spoke up promptly and said to the Attorney General: "You had no right to make such a remark in the presence of the jury—it was highly improper." Mr. Swift retorted that he had not made the remark within the hearing of the jury, as it had passed beyond the range of his voice.

Removed to a small room off the court, Spencer kept up his tirade against Dr. Elliott, and to the appeals of his counsel to control himself and not interrupt the proceedings of the court, he screamed out, "I won't keep quiet when they are trying to take my life away."

To Sheriff Clark, who also asked him to refrain from further outbreaks, the prisoner yelled, "I'll have my say. You've had your say, and it's my turn now—they can't keep me still."

Spencer cried and yelled and screamed for nearly half an hour after he was removed to the anteroom, and it was three minutes over an hour after the outbreak before the officers felt it safe to bring him back to the court room. Spencer's legs wabbled and he walked in between two supporting officers, and his legs and arms and hands twitched like those of a man suffering from St. Vitus' dance in acute form. Spencer's mother and sister were so overcome by the scene that they did not return for some time after the prisoner had been brought in, but his faithful wife followed him and whispered words of counsel through the steel cage.

After the recess the examination of Dr. Elliott was continued, and in the course of his examination and cross-examination, Dr. Elliott admitted in so many words that he still held all the opinions expressed in his reports, except as to possible delusions or hallucinations, but that *in view of the definition furnished him by the Attorney General,* he now held the opinion that Spencer was not "legally insane"—that he knew the difference between right and wrong. But we know that even the July report admitted the existence of "irresistible impulses" at such times as "his actions were dominated by anger." If he had any "irresistible impulses," it would seem that he should have been called "legally insane." Dr. Elliott also admitted, in answer to Mr. Stapleton's questioning, that he might have referred to "primary dementia, paranoid form," in discussing Spencer's condition with the Rev. Mr. Smith of Lebanon. During Dr. Elliott's testimony as to his defectiveness Spencer muttered, "Oh, that terrible voice!"—referring to the witness, who was talking in deep tones.

The Rev. Eugene B. Smith was the next witness called. He said he had visited Spencer in Bridgewater on the 22nd of December, and that Dr. Elliott had then told him in regard to Spencer's stories as to his treatment and the conditions in the institution that, while Spencer was sincere and honest in his belief that they were perfectly true, they were nevertheless all a delusion. He said he had asked Dr. Elliott whether Spencer was not suffering from a form of paranoia, and that the latter had replied, "Exactly," and had explained to him what that form of paranoia was; that when asked if it was incurable, Dr. Elliott had replied, "Absolutely." He also said that Dr. Elliott had told him that he would be very sorry to have to send Spencer back to Springfield to stand trial.

Dr. Edward B. Lane was the next witness sworn by the defense, and he testified that it was his opinion that Spencer was insane and that by reason of insanity he was unable to refrain from doing the act with which he stood charged, and that he did not understand the nature or consequences of his act.

Reference to the events in the Dow home seemed to

irritate Spencer. He had been quite composed before, but as the Attorney General's questions came to dwell on the details, he showed increasing signs of uneasiness and anger. Dr. Lane was finally asked to read from his notes of the testimony of the Dow women, and by this time Turnkey Wade and Spencer's wife were exerting all their efforts to restrain the prisoner. He threw off their restraint, and when Dr. Lane read the words which Spencer was alleged to have said when he shot Miss Dow—the same words which had excited Spencer the week before—Spencer shouted, "I'll give you something—I'll give you something! Yes, I mean you, you son of a bitch!" Wade was compelled to use considerable strength to hold him in the cage, and Deputies Malone and Leyden jumped in to help, and his voice finally became inaudible as he was pressed down on the bench. "From the bottom of this human pile," says the Springfield Union, in describing this scene, "came Spencer's muffled voice: 'Let me alone! I'm all right!' When he sat up, with his hair tousled and his frame shivering, his wife tried to soothe him by stretching her hand through the wire lattice in order to take hold of his hand. This seemed to direct his anger toward her, and he struck her hand and several times ordered her to let him alone. The man continued to mutter and curse under his breath, to cry and make inarticulate sounds, but did not again interrupt the proceedings until later, when Dr. Courtney was called to the stand. The outbreak had caused very little confusion within the bar of the court, but a number of spectators rose in their seats to get a better view of the scrimmage. Sheriff Clark immediately ordered all the men to sit down, and all the men immediately did so, but a large number of women paid no attention to the order and remained standing, whereupon Judge Crosby said, 'Let everyone who has remained standing be sent from the room.' So many of the women sat down immediately that it was impossible to distinguish those who had disobeyed the order of the judge, but two women were finally expelled in a state of great indignation."

A second outbreak occurred later, during Dr. Courtney's testimony (also in behalf of the defendant) when the prisoner became much excited again at a reference in the hypothetical question to the shades not having been drawn in the Dow house. Spencer muttered to his wife, and finally broke out, "Judge, I want to tell you something about the case. Those shades were drawn. I never went into a house where there were shades up. Don't let this man come here and tell you that there were no shades there—don't let him tell you that lie!" Again the prisoner was quieted by the officers.

Dr. Courtney testified that it was his opinion that the prisoner was irresponsible—that he was insane. He said that Spencer was unable at the time of the deed charged to distinguish between right and wrong—that he was dominated by an irresistible impulse, and the cross-examination failed in any way to shake or qualify his testimony.

I was the next witness, and I also testified that it was my opinion that the prisoner was insane at the time he committed the act with which he was charged; that I did not think it had been possible for the prisoner at that time to distinguish between right and wrong—that he was dominated by an irresistible impulse. During the cross-examination Attorney General Swift gave me an opportunity to present the following history which had not before been testified to: That Spencer found himself at the throat of his child twice and had been torn away by his wife before he realized what he was doing; that he remembered hearing the child scream and remembered nothing else until his wife took him away from the child; that he once found himself two blocks away from his house in his nightgown with a desire to visit houses before he realized what he was doing, then finding himself in his night clothes returned, disturbing the family. When his wife asked him what he was up for he said he was chasing a burglar away from the house, and he threw some matches outside of the window to corroborate his story, so that the burnt matches would be found in the morning. In the morning he took his wife and other members of the family to the open window, showed them the window and the burnt matches and an officer was passing by and he also showed the officer the open window and the matches. That twice at a theatre he had to leave in the middle of a play in response to a compelling impulse to enter houses and commit burglaries. That he walked to Longmeadow and back one night trying to resist the impulse of going into different houses and he said the Devil tempted him at every house and finally he saw a mop hanging on a pole just before he got at his own house and he took it home and gave it to his wife, being satisfied as long as he had got something. At another time he went out for one of his expeditions, struggled against it, went back to his house, then returned and after wandering around took a brake shoe from a house and lugged it home and thought it was still in his yard. That he told me that at times he was satisfied with a stickpin or any little fancy cup; at other times he felt he wanted to take everything in the house, in fact the whole house; that the thing that attracted him in the jackknife he stole when a boy was the little inset or inlay of brass; that he always took first stick-pins if he could find them, otherwise bright things that were shiny or attractive or pieces of china or ornaments. If he could not find these he would take anything.

On re-direct examination, I told of my conversation with Dr. Elliott on the occasion of my visit to Bridgewater, and said that Dr. Elliott had stated to me at that time that he considered Spencer a high-grade imbecile—that he had investigated the charges made in Spencer's letters to his mother and that they were all delusions. That Dr. Elliott had also told me on this occasion that Spencer was under delusions with regard to his father before he came to Bridgewater.

The defense rested with the conclusion of the testimony of the three experts, and the Commonwealth then called a number of the neighbors of the Spencer family in Lebanon to refute the testimony as to Bertram's peculiarities and the family history. Their testimony, however, did not disprove the main facts in the history of Spencer's life that had been offered by witnesses called for the defense. In substance, they merely stated that they had never known of Bertram's outbreaks, or that they had forgotten if such outbreaks had occurred. One of his former teachers, Miss Louise W. Cooley, testified that she had given Bertram a certificate recommending him for the Navy; under cross-examination, however, she admitted that he was "always in trouble," and told of one occasion when he had run home and got his father's revolver and strutted about the school yard with it; she also admitted that he had been accustomed to run home without permission when he wanted a pencil. Charles B. Noyes, Deputy Sheriff of Lebanon, although he testified that he had never seen anything peculiar about the prisoner, related how Bertram's father came to him on two different occasions and told him that the boy had run away and asked Noyes to go out and get him and bring him back. Charles L. Pitcher, one of Spencer's former companions in Lebanon, told of a fight he had had with Spencer: he had been walking home with two girls, with one of whom Spencer had formerly been intimate; he met Spencer with another young man and accused Spencer of following him about; Spencer had then attacked him and had directed the other fellow to get a stone and knock him on head. "I made him drop the stone," said Pitcher, "and when I turned around, there was Spencer with a pistol out about ten feet away from me. At once I saw what he would do, and as I had no desire to be shot in the back I turned him around. He fired three shots; I fended off the pistol hand after he fired the first shot; I was too close to him and he couldn't get his pistol between the two of us . . . *I don't know as I thought it was anything peculiar about him—seeing it was him.*"

Frederick A. Dean, a former dancing master, after testifying that he had never noticed anything peculiar about Bertram and that he considered him amiable, pleasant and agreeable, admitted that as a child he had caused disturbances in the dancing class, that when he was as young as five years of age he had been a little disorderly, that at home he did things that his parents disapproved of, and that on one occasion he had done some injury to the stove, so that the class had to be stopped until it could be repaired. Various former acquaintances of Spencer's in Springfield also testified that they had not noticed Bertram's peculiarities, likewise a number of fellow workmen in the street car company, the Boston and Maine Railroad and other places where Spencer had been employed, both in Hartford and Springfield. Although all these men testified that they had never seen anything peculiar, unusual or eccentric about Spencer, none of them claimed to have seen Spencer under conditions tending to excite him or to arouse his temper, and none had been witnesses of the events described as peculiar by the witnesses for the defense. Motorman Gilhooley testified as to having been held up and shot by Spencer. He was the last witness for the ninth day.

On the tenth day Mr. Callahan continued to examine former acquaintances of Spencer's in Springfield, especially among the railway employees and policemen. Many of them had known him but slightly, and it was natural that they should testify that they had not noticed anything unusual or eccentric about him. One of them told of Spencer's row with the engineer, Hathaway, because the former had insisted upon blowing the whistle of the locomotive as a signal to his wife, in spite of orders. He did not consider Spencer's behavior eccentric or unusual, he said, "no more than any other man that has a fiery temper."

The testimony of these witnesses bore out the fact that when Spencer was on the Boston and Maine Railroad he used to wear a revolver in a holster, with which it was his habit to shoot from the top of the freight cars. A number of the former railroad and street car employees who testified in behalf of the Commonwealth had since become members of the police force. The testimony of Harry J. Stone, the night guard at the Hampden County Jail as to Spencer's outbreak in the early morning of May 18th, 1910, has already been given in his history on page 105. The story of this pitiful event was corroborated by Turnkey Wade, including the account of the application of mechanical restraint and the prisoner's removal to "Chicopee House." Dr. Hooker was then put on the stand and gave his testimony as to what he believed to have been Spencer's "faking" on this occasion. At this point, his testimony was interrupted by an outbreak from the prisoner, who rose in his cage and shouted, "Faking, you son of a bitch! You are the one that tried to poison me. You are the one that put poison in my cup. I wasn't faking then, was I?" Turnkey Wade grabbed him and endeavored to force him back to the bench, and Spencer went on crying, after a struggle: "I was faking, was I? I was faking? No, I won't shut up! I won't shut up! I will let everybody know what he was doing: he was trying to put poison in my cup, in my water, one night. I caught him—another man saw me—saw him—saw him putting it in my cup—in my salt and pepper shaker. I was faking, was I?" Wade was helped by two deputies, but "the turnkey did not need much assistance," says the Springfield Union of November 23rd:

> He slammed Spencer down on the bench in the cage, and the prisoner grunted. He lay for a minute groaning and grunting, every once in a while muttering aloud "Faking, was I?"

Then, as Wade and his deputies stood about him, he said "Go away. No need of standing and holding me—I am all right, I am all right." He then resumed his seat and was given a glass of water.

Sheriff Clark was brought in to testify that Spencer had refused to talk to Col. Young when the latter had first been appointed his counsel, and upon cross-examination he corroborated other testimony as to Spencer's behavior in the jail. Mr. Charles L. Simonds, who had found Spencer's locket and kept it for six months, was the next to testify, and after him Captain Boyle was recalled and testified that both Kantor and Mrs. Walters had spoken of Spencer as a normal individual in previous interviews with him.

But Mr. Callahan's star witness in refutation of the defense of insanity was Horace M. St. John, alias Edwin R. Bell, an inmate of the Charlestown State Prison, who had previously been sent from the prison to Bridgewater because he was insane, and who had been one of Spencer's companions at the latter institution. Bell said that he had become rather intimate with Spencer. . . . "I was talking with Bertram G. Spencer a little while after he had been singing a song in the chapel. We were rehearsing for a show; and I spoke to Spencer and I said to him, 'Any man that can sing and draw and play around like you doesn't seem to be particularly insane.' He shook his head a good deal like that [illustrating]—and then he told me that as long as he did that he had an idea the doctors would think he was insane. At another time he told me that he thought if he invented a few lies about the institution, said that there was brutality and such things going on down there, that he thought that Dr. Elliott would think that he had delusions, and therefore keep him in there and declare him an insane man. At another time I asked him about this—about this killing affair—and I asked him, I says, 'Couldn't you have taken this woman and given her a good swift punch under the jaw and made your getaway?' . . . and he said 'Well, I could, but dead people tell no tales.' At another time I was speaking about it, and he told me that if this woman had been alive that she might have identified him a little later, and that he thought it was the best thing he could do for his own good to kill her. I informed Dr. Elliott about it."

Under cross-examination, Bell, or St. John, admitted that he had still five years and two months to serve in Charlestown for assault with intent to kill. Mr. Stapleton brought out that the conversation in which Bell asserted that Spencer had said that as long as he told stories about the institution he thought Dr. Elliott would think he had delusions had taken place about Thanksgiving time, and that he had reported to Dr. Elliott that the prisoner had practically told him that he had feigned insanity. He was somewhat confused about the date at which he had given this information, but thought it was not until August that he had written a letter to Dr. Elliott about it, and he said that Dr. Elliott had come to him in October, after the doctor had resigned as Superintendent at Bridgewater, and that he had questioned him about Spencer in Dr. Baker's presence, and that he, the witness, had been returned to Charlestown on the 27th of October. Bell said that Spencer had told him that the story about being hit with a ring was not true—that he had made the wound on his own head with a piece of glass; that he had not been hit by the Attendant LeMae—the witness said that he did not know whether Spencer had actually been hit. Bell admitted having sent out a letter from Bridgewater to the Boston American, admitting that he himself had feigned insanity and complaining that he was being held at Bridgewater after acknowledging that he had been feigning.

Now, admitting the very doubtful credibility of this witness, his evidence seems to us not to be worth considering as testimony as to Spencer's mental condition. If, as Bell said, Spencer actually did tell him that he was feigning insanity, this did not in any way prove that the prisoner was not actually insane. An insane person may be as capable of feigning as anyone else, nor would it have been strange for Spencer to claim to be feigning when he was not actually doing so. He might have made some such boast to a companion. Nor were the counts upon which Spencer was said to have been feigning recorded by Dr. Elliott nor anyone else as symptoms of his insanity.

Bell is said to have denied that he was transferred from Bridgewater back to the Charlestown State Prison after he had told his story in order that it might be used at the trial, which could not have been done if he was still under commitment as insane. Now he was insane in the eyes of the law when the conversation took place at Bridgewater, and Dr. Elliott must have thought so, else he was guilty of keeping a sane man in his institution for the insane. And if Bell was insane and did have delusions, what was his form of insanity? But in Dr. Elliott's opinion, he recovered his sanity about eight weeks after he voluntarily wrote a letter to Dr. Elliott with statements that he would help Elliott in his contention that Spencer was legally sane.

The District Attorney next read to the jury the report of the Medical Survey at the time Spencer was discharged from the Navy, giving the cause of his discharge as "enuresis"; and after considerable discussion between the lawyers and the Judge, two letters from Spencer to the principal of the Mt. Hermon School were admitted as evidence. In the first of these, he applies for admission to the school, stating that his education has been sadly neglected "since a young boy, and I realize more and more each day how poorly fitted I am to battle with the world." The letter is very well expressed, but though it was undoubtedly written by Spencer, it bears the hall marks of having been dictated by one of his elders—as such letters generally were, for youths of his age at that time. The second letter is more characteristic of Spencer, who was, as we know, an excellent letter-writer, in spite of some defects in his education. It was written soon after he had left the Mt. Hermon School:

Springfield, Mass., June 9, 1903.

Professor Cutler,

Dear Sir:

Hearing of your sad loss, let me, as a friend, express my sympathy. Your wife was a lovely woman, and I hope you both meet in the hereafter. I hold no ill-feeling towards you, Mr. Cutler, and I am trying to lead an honest, upright and God-fearing life. I have no bad habits, and what I done up at Mt. Hermon was done more to be smart. I ask your forgiveness for all my foolish actions, and may God be with you in all your afflictions and be a comfort to you in the end.

Yours most respectfully,

(Signed) B. G. Spencer.

105 Main Street.

The next witness called was Dr. Leonard A. Baker, Assistant Physician at Bridgewater, who said that in Spencer's case it was his opinion that there was a degree of mental defect, but that he was not insane, in spite of the fact that he wrote in his report to the Chief Justice under date of March 17, 1911, that he saw no change either mentally or physically since the previous report made by Dr. Elliott on April 17 in which Dr. Elliott said: "Prolonged observation, however, but strengthens our opinion that Spencer is deficient in moral understanding as the result of mental defect of long standing." Dr. Baker said that all of Spencer's complaints of abuses at Bridgewater had been investigated, and that in one instance they were proved to have been founded on fact.

Dr. Quinby was then called. The prosecution asked him a very long hypothetical question as follows:

Q. Assuming that on March 31, 1910, shortly before 8 o'clock in the evening, a man arrived at Round Hill in Springfield and tried the windows in the house occupied on the lower floor by the Dow family; that, having found the window there in the back bedroom of the house closed, but unlocked, the man went behind another building near by and there removed his shoes, stiff hat and coat, and put on a soft, dark hat and tied a black muffler or handkerchief over the lower part of his face and returned to the house and entered it, for the purpose of committing a burglary, being at the time armed with a revolver and carrying a flash light, through a window of the back bedroom, there taking a brooch pin, a bead belt and another stone or gem from the bureau drawer in that bedroom; that he then went through into the dining room of the house and came to the door leading from the dining room into the back parlor, as shown in evidence upon the plan before you; that in the back parlor were four women around a table over in the northwest corner, playing with a picture puzzle; that as the man advanced through the doorway from the dining room into the back parlor he made a guttural sound, not otherwise described, and a movement of his hands toward the women and advanced into the room toward them; that the four women stood up, screaming, and that the man demanded that they keep quiet; that the women made a concerted motion toward the front parlor and on toward the outer door; that the man drew his revolver, proceeded through the back parlor and through the archway, as shown on the plan, to the front parlor and demanded their money, saying "I want your money"; that one of the women replied, "We have no money in the house"; that one of the women, Miss Harriet Dow, slipped on a rug under the archway and fell; and one of the women, the mother, Mrs. Dow, came and helped her up, telling her to be calm; that another of the women, Miss Blackstone, had gone ahead and was near the door leading from the front parlor into the front hall, as shown in the plan, when the man took a quick stride and placed himself almost in front of her, near the door, and shot her, and she fell over upon the sofa; that Miss Harriet Dow went toward the man where he was standing, and commenced to scream again, when the man swore at her, asked her to be quiet, again demanded the money and then stepped toward the window leading from the front parlor out under the piazza,—the north window, as indicated on the plan,—the shade of which was halfway up, and made a motion towards it; that meanwhile another of the women, Miss Lucy Dow, had started for the telephone in the northeast corner of the back parlor, and another, the mother, Mrs. Dow, was escaping into the hall, and the man raised his arm with his pistol in his hand and pointed it towards her back; that Miss Harriet Dow took a chair that was there and hurled it at him, hitting his arm; that the man then turned from pointing towards Mrs. Dow in the hall and pointed the revolver at Miss Harriet Dow and said, "Do you want to die? Well, die then!" and fired at her, striking her in the head, and she fell; that meanwhile the mother, Mrs. Dow, had gone upstairs and the man, who had done the shooting, disappeared through the front door, out on to the front porch, jumped over the railing on to the ground and from there had gone back of the building, the other building, obtained his shoes and his clothing that he had discarded, ran down the hill through the woods until he came to a large chestnut tree; that he sat at the foot of that tree, put on his shoes and his clothing, took off his mask and hat, put them in his pocket, went down through and over a fence, and on to Main Street, almost opposite Bancroft Street; that he started to go along south on North Main Street, which would be towards the center of Springfield, until he saw a police officer, one James Dowling, whom he knew, standing at the police signal box; that he did not desire, did not wish to go by the policeman; that he turned and went up Arch Street to North; from North, southerly to Carew, on Carew to Chestnut Street, from Chestnut Street to Bridge Street; over the bridge to West Springfield, to his home on Porter Avenue in West Springfield; that he arrived home about quarter of 9; that he went into the house and into his bedroom, closed the door, took out his revolver, cleaned it and reloaded it, when he found there were two empty shells therein; that he placed the revolver under the pillow, and also the flash light which he had carried with him, and took the black soft hat and put it into the stove, where there was a coal fire—were you able to follow that hypothesis, Doctor? A. I think so, fairly well.

Q. Taking that assumption that I have just given you, whether or not it is consistent with the action of a sane man intent on committing burglary and seeking to escape capture; assuming that he feared that the screams of the women assumed in the question, or their escape while he was in the house, would lead to his apprehension and arrest; my question is, on that assumption, was the action of that man consistent with the action of a sane man? A. I think his act was consistent with that of a sane man at that time.

Q. Taking the same assumption, whether or not it is your opinion that the man assumed in the question knew the difference between right and wrong, and that he was liable to punishment therefor when he committed the crime described in my question? A. I think that he knew the difference between right and wrong.

Q. Whether or not, upon the same assumption, the same man was, in your opinion, at the time when he committed the crime described, acting under the compulsion of an irresistible impulse? A. He was not.

Q. Did you hear read in court the confession of the defendant here? A. I did.

Q. And have you since read it over, copies of it, so that you have it in mind pretty well? A. I have.

Q. Then, Doctor, in addition to the hypothesis which I first gave you, assuming that this same man had committed without detection a series of fourteen burglaries and one hold-up in about two years prior to September 23, 1909, as stated in that confession, that on the evening of said September 23, 1909, he placed a ladder against the roof of the piazza of a house, intending to enter the second-story window which he saw open, but was frightened away by some one appearing in the house and quickly slid down the ladder; that in doing so he lost a locket engraved with his initials and containing the pictures of his mother and sister, which he feared would lead to his detection, so much so that he returned the next night and endeavored to find it at the house where he thought he had lost it; that subsequently to that he refrained until March 31, 1910, for a period of over six months, from committing any other crime for fear that the locket might have been found and that it would lead to his detection and punishment, and that further, before he started to commit the crime which took place at the Dow house as already assumed, he had made up his mind that the locket had not been found and there was no longer fear of detection through that,—whether or not this hypothesis, in addition to the assumption already given, leads you to the opinion that the man at the time when he shot Miss Blackstone on the evening of March 31, 1910, knew right from wrong in the sense already given you, or was acting under the compulsion of an irresistible impulse? Do I make myself clear? A. I don't——

Q. Perhaps I will ask you those questions separately. Whether or not this additional—the second assumption that I have just given you—leads you to the same conclusion, that the man in the assumption knew the difference between right and wrong? A. From that incident I should draw a conclusion as to his condition at the time that he slid down the ladder, but I don't know how I can draw a conclusion in regard to that at the time of shooting.

Q. I fear I have not made my question plain to you. Does that assumption that I have given you lead you away from the conclusion that you have already expressed? A. It does not.

Q. Whether or not it would tend to confirm it? A. Yes, I think it would tend to confirm it.

Q. That is, whether or not the fact that for a period of over six months after attempting this September 23, 1909, crime, where he lost his locket, for fear that the locket might have been found and that it would lead to his detection and punishment, and further, before he started to commit the crime which took place at the Dow house as already assumed he had made up his mind that the locket had not been found and there was no longer fear of detection through that,—would that confirm your opinion that he knew the difference between right and wrong? A. It would confirm my opinion that he had self-control, certainly.

Q. Well, to answer the precise question, that he was not acting under the compulsion of an irresistible impulse on the night of the murder, if I understand you rightly? A. I can't see what that has to do with the night of the murder.

Q. Well, if it does not affect your judgment I won't dwell on it. The question in brief is, Doctor—I want to make myself plain, and it is a very long question and it is pretty difficult for you to keep in your mind, as it would be for me if I didn't have it here. Would the fact in connection with the other facts assumed here, that having lost the locket and fearing detection from the loss of that locket, and so refraining from committing any other crime for six months—would that fact strengthen your opinion that he was not, on the night of committing this crime as outlined in the question, acting under an irresistible impulse? Let me add to that that before starting out on this crime he had made up his mind that there was no danger of detection from the loss of that locket any longer. A. That incident conveys to my mind the impression that the man was able to control himself, and not, as he claimed, was driven by an irresistible impulse to commit burglaries.

Q. That answers the question precisely, Doctor, I think. Now, in addition to the hypotheses already given you, assume that the reason for the crimes which have been committed by the man in the assumed question was because he liked a nice home and nice things and was not earning money enough to support the kind of home that he wanted,—would that strengthen the opinion you have already expressed, or otherwise? A. It would strengthen it.

Q. Having in mind beside the hypotheses already given you, Doctor, I will ask you to assume that the man described to you is the defendant, and taking into consideration his age, appearance and physical characteristics as you have found them and seen them, his ancestry and history as testified to in court by the mother and father, his own statements so far as testified to, and taking into consideration the appearance and testimony of the father and mother as they appeared upon the witness stand, his history at Bridgewater as given in the reports in evidence,—whether or not you are of the opinion that this defendant on the night that he shot Miss Blackstone knew right from wrong, and that there was a punishment attached to the commission of the wrong? A. I do.

Q. And whether or not in your opinion at the time of the shooting of Miss Blackstone he was acting under the compulsion of an irresistible impulse? A. He was not.

The cross-examination of Dr. Quinby by Mr. Stapleton brought out the following questions and answers:

Q. Of course that is largely a question of the degree of the defect, is it, whether you would call him insane or not? A. Well, not all high-grade imbeciles are sufficiently defective to be insane.

Q. Some alienists would classify among the insane those who are suffering from any severe mental defect? A. No, I think there is a distinction there.

Q. I take it, Doctor, that the insane are to a certain extent amenable to discipline? A. Certainly.

Q. All but the most extreme cases are amenable to some discipline? A. Some of the extreme cases are amenable to discipline.

Q. And taking that evidence as a whole, excluding the father and mother of the defendant, you say that that might be—a heredity of that sort might be one of the predisposing causes to insanity? A. I think it might be, yes, sir.

Q. Well, of a man's four grandparents, if one died of senile dementia, and was eccentric for many years before his death; if another one died of softening of the brain at the age of forty-three;

if a third one has hysterics during the greater part of her life and was out of her mind for some months before her death, and if the fourth one was irritable, nervous and addicted to drink,—with the four grandparents as I have described and assuming that to be true, it would be a rather bad heredity for a grandchild, wouldn't it? A. Be a rather bad heredity for a grandchild.

Q. Is the fact that a child about the age of twelve is doing unsuccessfully third or fourth grade work, that at the age of nineteen or twenty is doing unsuccessfully elementary work, entitled to any consideration in arriving at the conclusion as to whether or not there is a mental defect? A. It is.

Q. Is the fact that at the age of fourteen years the child is afflicted with enuresis entitled to some consideration? A. I should think it might be.

Q. You examined this defendant over a year ago at the request of the district attorney? A. I did.

Q. And after those two examinations you, with Dr. Houston representing the State, held a conference in Worcester with Dr. Courtney representing the defense? A. Yes.

Q. As a result of that, Doctor, you testified before the hearing on motion to commit this defendant, held before Judge Aiken of this court and Judge Sanderson? A. I did.

Q. And you were asked the question: "In your opinion what was the nature of that mental aberration?" and the answer was, "When it comes to giving a name to it I shouldn't want to say positively. My impression was it was a case which would eventuate at least in dementia præcox. Still, I shouldn't want to be pinned to that opinion at the present time." A. That was my opinion at that time.

Q. Dementia præcox, I take it, is a broad term? A. Yes.

Q. Which is used in a somewhat different sense by different alienists? A. Yes.

Q. By some it includes cases of imbecility or degenerative types, and others would use it more strictly as you do? A. Yes.

Q. You were asked the question: "So far as you had any opinion, that was your diagnosis of the nature of it?" to which you said, "It seemed to me very probable?" A. That was my opinion.

Q. And you were asked the question further: "Whether or not what you say, Doctor,—I should like to know,—you say he is under some mental aberration,—but I should like to know whether or not in your judgment he is in such a case or frame of mind, or his mind is in such a condition, that you are able to form an opinion now whether he is or is not responsible or was or was not responsible for this offence?" And your answer was: "I am very much in doubt as to his responsibility—as to the degree of his responsibility." A. That was my opinion at that time, certainly.

Q. To allow you, Doctor, to state your whole opinion at that time, I will ask you, you were further asked the question: "What do you say, Doctor, as to whether in your judgment the statute of 1909 which allows him to be committed to an insane asylum for observation is one that would well be invoked in this case—that ought to be invoked in this case?" to which you answered: "I should think it is very fitting." A. That was my reply to the question.

Q. And you were asked by the Honorable Chief Justice Aiken of this court: "What is your answer to that?" and you repeated: "I think it is very fitting that it should be invoked in this case." Is that—— A. That is my answer.

Q. And you were also asked if you desired further time for observation, and you answered that you should. A. That was my answer.

The next witness sworn was Dr. Daniel H. Fuller of the State Board of Insanity. Dr. Fuller's answer to the hypothetical question: "Assuming these to be the facts and all the facts that I am permitted to consider, I think it is" (i. e. consistent with the action of a sane man). On the same assumption, he did not believe Spencer to have been acting under the compulsion of an irresistible impulse; and again under the same assumption he believed Spencer knew the difference between right and wrong, with reference to punishment for his act.

On cross-examination, Dr. Fuller said that there are a great many among the insane who have knowledge of right and wrong, and that in most of the insane institutions a large number of the inmates are amenable to discipline and that every institution has its rules for the discipline of the inmates. Also, he testified that in his opinion the average child of four or five years old has some idea of right and wrong; that such knowledge might or might not exist, and that the power which enables a man to resist an impulse is called his "power of inhibition," and that a high-grade imbecile, acting on these ideas which arise in his mind does so because his power of inhibition is lacking or defective, and that that deficiency in his inhibitory powers might be very little or very great; also that insane men play instruments very well. His testimony lasted over until the eleventh and last day of the trial, most of Mr. Stapleton's questions covered generalities as to the traits of mental defectives.

When the lawyers had finished with Dr. Fuller, Dr. George T. Tuttle was called. Dr. Tuttle stated that he had arrived at the conclusion after his first examination of Spencer that he was a defective individual—had been so from his birth—that he knew right from wrong; but Dr. Tuttle said that he had been unable at that time to decide whether the prisoner could resist doing wrong—whether he was not under the compulsion of an irresistible impulse. After his second examination and with the information put before him at the trial, Dr. Tuttle thought Spencer was not acting under such an impulse. He said, in answer to Mr. Stapleton's cross-questioning, that Spencer might at times have been unable to control himself.

Before the court adjourned for a recess, Mr. Stapleton asked Judge Crosby whether the court would follow the language of Chief Justice Shaw in the case of "Commonwealth v. Rogers, in 7 Metcalf," in regard to the standard of right and wrong, and Judge Crosby read the following quotation from Chief Justice Shaw in that case, saying that he intended to use it in his charge to the jury:

> A man is not to be excused from responsibility if he has capacity and reason sufficient to enable him to distinguish between right and wrong as to the particular act he is then doing; a knowledge and consciousness that the act he is doing is wrong and criminal, and will subject him to punishment. In order to be responsible, he must

have sufficient power of memory to recollect the relation in which he stands to others and in which others stand to him; that the act he is doing is contrary to the plain dictates of justice and right, injurious to others and a violation of the dictates of duty.

In his closing argument for the defense, Mr. Stapleton reviewed the facts, as proven by the witnesses, of Spencer's almost unbroken line of heredity of nervous or mental defect, of his undoubted peculiarities and the unusual outbreaks and punishments of his early life, calling the attention of the jury to the statements made by the doctors on both sides that an imbecile requires a very special sort of training for his own safety and the safety of the community, and emphasizing the fact that Spencer's early training was such as to warp and twist his mind and incline him toward criminal acts. He again recounted Spencer's outbreaks as testified to by his companions wherever he had been up to the time of his arrest, and called their attention to his peculiar suggestibility, citing the example of the false report of his arrest for burglary, saying:

What effect of suggestion will that have upon a diseased and disordered brain that has been defective from birth and twisted toward criminal life by impulse, training and treatment? All of the alienists have told you that an imbecile is peculiarly liable to suggestions, and I leave you to reason out what influence that suggestion had upon the mind of this defendant to lead him to take up a criminal career. . . . It is true he had always been addicted to stealing. He had always had that accursed desire to steal which he could never master and which dominated him, and through some method or other the suggestion came into this diseased brain to enter houses, and the entering of them took possession of him, and after awhile it dominated him. First it charmed him, it fascinated him, and then it took possession of him and drove him out to a life of crime. And it was progressive, in a degree, because first he merely entered houses and did not show himself. But after awhile, under the actuating intellect, he must have the dramatic setting. He might be able to escape detection easily if he would enter and go away—but no. In that enfeebled brain comes the idea that he must show himself—that he must be dramatic—that he must appear with a mask.

Mr. Stapleton then reviewed the experts' testimony, inquiring why it was that Dr. Houston had been summoned only a day after Spencer's arrest, if there were not something peculiar or unusual about his conduct, and if the police did not themselves believe there was something wrong with him. He made a very strong point of Dr. Elliott's change of front, imputing to him a motive in declaring Spencer sane after asserting to the contrary for eight months in his reports to the Chief Justice, and saying: "Gentlemen, I say to you in all seriousness, in all honesty, that when Dr. Elliott sent that man back here for trial, he committed a greater crime against the majesty of the law than ever Spencer committed."

In rehearsing Dr. Hooker's testimony that he believed Spencer to be shamming insanity in the jail, on the ground that his pulse was normal and that he had been amenable to discipline, Mr. Stapleton called attention to the fact that Dr. Hooker had arrived some hours after the outbreak had begun, and that the patient had probably calmed down by that time; and he cited the fact known to all who have had the care of the insane that most of them are amenable to discipline. He argued the inconsistency of Spencer's antagonizing the doctors by sending out a continuous flow of complaints from the hospital, if he were really sane and merely shamming insanity. Mr. Stapleton continued at length to argue the weakness of the Commonwealth's counter evidence of Spencer's sanity, saying very truly that a number of these witnesses, who had "noticed nothing peculiar" about Spencer, had nevertheless cited instances in his career which were distinctly abnormal. In reviewing the statements of the witness Bell from the Charlestown State Prison, who had said that Spencer had told him he was "faking" insanity, Mr. Stapleton said: "There isn't one scrap or particle of evidence in this case, by any man, that as they examined Spencer at the time he was in confinement since a year ago last April—that Spencer ever shook his head in that fashion" (illustrating). "Dr. Quinby examined him, Houston, Baker and Fuller, on behalf of the State. . . . He says (referring to Bell) Spencer told him the stories of complaints were fakes and that he saw a cut on the back of Spencer's head, and that after Spencer complained that he got hit with a blackjack, he says that Spencer confessed that he had made it himself with a piece of glass. And Dr. Baker, from that institution, who saw Spencer twice, and who says he examined Spencer's head at the time of the blackjack episode, says there wasn't any mark there. . . . And you have besides the fact that Dr. Elliott and Dr. Baker said that Spencer believed these complaints; so that you have got to take their word in perference to that of a confessed felon. . . . Now, gentlemen, if they thought this man was feigning, why couldn't they have produced an alienist to show that? . . ."

The point that Mr. Stapleton missed in regard to the charge of Spencer's having feigned insanity, is that whether or not he was feigning is of little importance and would have no significance as proof of his sanity or insanity. That he was very suggestible has already been shown, and in the environment of an insane hospital it is natural that he should have imitated the actions of his companions, especially as he had an abnormal love of sensational acting. This we see plainly proved by his fondness for dressing up and appearing in the guise of a desperado in his different burglaries.

Mr. Stapleton pleaded that he was not asking to have Spencer set free, but that he should be confined for life, by order of the court, in an institution for the insane; and in case they were still in any doubt as to the insanity of the defendant, he was at least entitled to the benefit of that doubt; that at any rate, even if Spencer were sane, he should not be convicted of more than a second degree offense.

Mr. Swift's able summing up for the Commonwealth left untouched no little point in the evidence which could be turned to the advantage of his argument that Spencer was sane and responsible, that his crimes were deliberately planned and that he should bear the full penalty for the crime of murder in the first degree. After summing up Bertram's crimes and their motives, as he interpreted them, he said:

> He has demonstrated in that dramatic way in which he committed his robberies, his burglaries, his hold-up—pulling down his hat over his face, pulling the black handkerchief over his face and about his nose, so that only about so much of his face was visible, that he liked to have things arranged in a theatrical manner. In all of that he was an actor—he was an actor when the police came in and arrested him. He was an actor every day of his life.

He then attributed Spencer's behavior at the time of his arrest and afterwards in the Springfield jail, to acting with the deliberate object of establishing the defense of insanity, and said that the District Attorney sent for Dr. Houston because he knew, even at that early date, that the defense would be insanity. He continued his argument on this line, stating that toward spring Spencer believed he had convinced the Bridgewater authorities and Dr. Briggs of his insanity, and that he relaxed his efforts that he might go out and play baseball and enjoy the "garden where the flowers were springing up"; and that his behavior at that time became so normal that Dr. Elliott changed his opinion as to his mental condition. Dr. Elliott is beginning to wake up—"no evidence of delusions or hallucinations which modify his actions." That is in May; now in June he says: "Spencer is in splendid physical condition, eats and sleeps well, does some little work in our garden, and enters with zest into the amusements and sports of the hospital." Mr. Swift continued: "The prisoner wants you to send him back to Bridgewater, to enter with zest into playing baseball and football." (Continuing to quote from Dr. Elliott's reports) "He has not at any time manifested delusions or hallucinations, and under the ordinary precaution and restraint of hospital life, has not shown suicidal tendencies. That is June 19th."*

Mr. Swift continued to quote Dr. Elliott's later opinions to prove that he was at last "waking up." How absurd it would be if a group of men, such as the various experts who had examined Spencer and including Dr. Elliott whose entire work was with the criminal insane, had been for eight months deceived by a mere malingerer—and a mentally defective malingerer at that! Such an aspersion was an insult to the medical profession. Mr. Swift proceeded to challenge my own testimony, on the ground that the wife had not been called to corroborate the prisoner's statements to me,

* Anyone familiar with our hospitals for the insane can tell us that there are a great many patients, undoubtedly insane, who have no delusions or hallucinations nor show suicidal or homicidal tendencies; and the experts who declared Spencer insane made no claim that he had showed suicidal tendencies for years past.

and he dwelt at some length upon the vagueness of the term "mental defective." Perhaps today we should be able to give a somewhat more definite classification than "mental defective" or "high grade imbecile" to such a case as Spencer's, but it is doubtful whether it would influence an average jury at a time of such popular clamor and indignation. Mental tests were not then in common use, but it is doubtful whether Spencer's mentality, under such psychological tests as were given the men who entered the Army in our late War, would have rated at more than ten to twelve years; and it is certain that he could not have passed the psychiatric examination given at Camp Devens. Mr. Swift's arguments were indeed ably presented, and they prevailed with the jury, not because they were sound but because the ableness with which they were presented disguised their weakness—at least to the lay mind. There is little doubt that the natural trend of the minds of the jurymen was in sympathy with the popular clamor.

Judge Crosby's charge to the jury was most able and scholarly—so scholarly in the choice of legal definitions offered that it would require a juryman of unusual education and mental ability to appreciate it. After explaining the meaning of "burglary," of "murder in the first degree," of "premeditation," and of "malice aforethought," he said:

> The Commonwealth contends in this case, as I understand it, that the prisoner is guilty upon two grounds mentioned in the statute, namely, first because the homicide was committed with deliberately premeditated malice aforethought; and secondly because it was committed while the prisoner was in the commission of, or in the attempt to commit, a crime punishable by imprisonment for life. If, therefore, the charge be proved to be upon both grounds or upon

either ground with the certainty required by law—that is, beyond a reasonable doubt, it would constitute murder in the first degree.

He then went on to explain that "beyond a reasonable doubt" referred not at all to the facts presented, but to facts necessary to establish the conclusion of guilt. He quoted in the language of "a former Chief Justice" in a charge which he made in a capital case:

> The prisoner's right to hold the Government to this strictness of proof is an absolute right. No consideration of public safety, no righteous indignation, at an atrocious crime which shocked the community, no zeal for the suppression of crime, can give the court or jury discretion to relax the rules of law, or to strain the evidence to any conclusion not warranted by its fair, convincing force. The government of this Commonwealth is a government of laws and not of men. . . .

He cited another charge, made by Chief Justice Gray, in regard to expert testimony, and concluding said:

> In this case it is for you . . . to say whether this defendant was of sound or unsound mind; that is to say, he was of unsound mind so far as this particular case is concerned. What you are dealing with here is the question of soundness or unsoundness as affects the defendant's responsibility for the homicide; not whether he might or might not be responsible in any other respect.

Among other points brought out in Judge Crosby's charge to the jury were the following:

> If you should find that the prisoner's mind was in such a diseased state that the fatal act must be regarded as an outbreak or paroxysm of a mind diseased, which for the time being overwhelmed his will and his reason so that there was an uncontrollable impulse, springing from disease, to do the act, then he is not to be considered as a responsible, accountable agent, though he may have been aware that the act which he was committing was wrong; that is to say, an irresistible homicidal impulse in an insane person, springing from a diseased mind, is a good defense, though such person knew that the act was wrong.

Referring to mental defectiveness, he said:

There is evidence to show that there are different classes or degrees of such mental defectiveness. Such a person I understand to be one who is not an idiot, but one who suffers from *want of mind* rather than from *derangement* or *delusion.* If such a person is charged with a criminal offense, his liability or responsibility therefor would depend upon the question whether the want of mind is such as to entitle him to acquittal on the ground of insanity. . . . Two questions, therefore, seem to present themselves to you upon this branch of the case: first, whether or not the prisoner was laboring under an irresistible, homicidal impulse at the time when the fatal shot was fired; and secondly, if he was not laboring under such an impulse, was there such a degree of mental disease or insanity as to make him unable to distinguish between right and wrong so as to exempt him from responsibility for his act.

Judge Crosby here quoted another "distinguished judge" in much the same vein:

And it is a general rule of law that, in order to be able to commit a crime, a person who is charged with its commission must have intelligence and capacity enough to have a criminal intent and purpose. At any rate, when the charge is of the commission of such a crime as this, if he were not capable of a criminal intent and purpose in what he did, then he can not have been guilty of a crime in doing what he did. If his reason and his mental powers were either so deficient that he had no will and no conscience, no controlling mental powers, or if, through the overwhelming power of mental disease his intellectual power was for the time obliterated, then he was not a responsible moral agent, and is not answerable for criminal acts . . . concluding, If his mind was from mental disease in such a state that he could not distinguish between right and wrong, or if he was a victim of an uncontrollable impulse to do wrong, though he knew it to be wrong, so that he could not refrain from it—if his will was overpowered and his conscience was overpowered, and what his hand did was not really his act, why then he is not to be held responsible for it. But if he did have that power and if he did act when he was able to control himself, so far as mental disease is concerned, why then he would be responsible.

If you should find the prisoner's mind was impaired, said Judge Crosby, although not impaired to an extent that you feel at liberty to hold that he is not responsible for his acts, still, if his mind was so far impaired that in consequence of such impairment you find that he was not capable of deliberate premeditation, you would properly find a verdict of murder in the second degree.

Unless you should find that he was accountable when he committed the murder, and committed it while in the commission of, or an attempt to commit, an offense punishable by imprisonment in the State's Prison for life,—if the evidence leads you to that conclusion, then he would be guilty of murder in the first degree, although committed without deliberate premeditation, provided, as I said before, you found he was responsible for his act.

If you should find that he committed the act, but are satisfied upon the evidence that he was insane at the time, then it would be your duty to return a verdict of "not guilty by reason of insanity."

In this case no suggestion has been made in the argument that there is any evidence to support a verdict of manslaughter, and so it will not be necessary to dwell upon that phase of the case.

If you are satisfied, according to the rules of law that have been laid down to you, that the prisoner, being an accountable person for his acts, committed the crime of murder in the first degree, it is your duty to find so upon your oaths.

If you are not satisfied that, at the time the homicide was committed, the prisoner acted with deliberate premeditation, and are not satisfied that he killed the deceased while in the commission of an offense punishable by imprisonment in the State Prison for life, but still consider him accountable when the homicide was committed, then it will be your duty to find him guilty of murder in the second degree. If you are not satisfied that he was of sound mind, it will be your duty to bring in a verdict of "not guilty by reason of insanity." Of course, gentlemen, it is within your province to acquit him altogether, but that is not suggested by his counsel, and as there seems to be no aspect of the case in which that can be presented, I shall say nothing to you about it. . . .

Mr. Stapleton excepted "to so much of the charge in regard to insanity as permits the jury to take into account the presumption of sanity, after evidence has been introduced of the defendant's insanity, arriving at a conclusion as to sanity or insanity."

The jury retired at 9.50 P. M., but returned at 1.55 A. M. for instructions on three questions:

1. If a man breaks and enters a house with burglarious intent and is caught and found guilty, is his crime punishable by life imprisonment?

2. Is it the privilege of this jury to bring in a verdict of guilty in the first degree, of guilty in the second degree, and of acquittal on the ground of insanity?

3. What is the testimony in regard to entering window?

The judge answered these questions at length, the first two in the affirmative within the limits of legal phraseology. The testimony in regard to the window was again read.

The jury again retired at 2.52 A. M., and at 3.08 A. M. rendered a verdict of murder in the first degree. The court adjourned at 3.11.

The trial cost the state between $25,000 and $30,000. The defense was obliged to raise money among relatives and friends of the prisoner, and at times the defendant's wife sat at a typewriter in Attorney Stapleton's office, copying manuscript for use at the trial, especially on the closing arguments on behalf of her husband.

Following the trial, efforts were made for commutation, also for a new trial. The chances for a new trial were very remote, for Mr. Stapleton said the only capital case he could recall in which a new trial had been granted was the Trefethan case, in 1892. The chances for commutation were lessened on account of the unusual conditions at that time: there were three cases up for commutation, the Phelps, the Richeson and the Spencer cases, and a member of the Governor's Council expressed the feeling that if they commuted one they should commute all three, "which," he said, "would practically abolish capital punishment."

The hearing on the motion for a new trial was held before the Hon. John C. Crosby, Justice, December 26th, 1911. In his argument, Mr. Stapleton said:

> I contend, may it please your Honor, that the courts of the State regard not the word which is used, whether it be "mentally defective" or "insane"; that the Commonwealth can not prevail over a defense of insanity by simply producing experts who will not use the word "insane," and will hide behind the words "mentally defective." . . .

Dr. Fuller, of the State Board of Insanity, an expert called in behalf of the State, said that any child of five years old knew right from wrong—that any child of four or five years old knew, to that extent that he would be punished, right from wrong; that to that extent he knew the consequences of his act. He said that the knowledge of right and wrong of a high grade imbecile was similar to that of a child.*

How could a jury say that this man, who six men employed by the State—not by the defense—who six men said was mentally defective —how could they say that he was fully responsible if they regarded this evidence? It is true that your Honor told the jury that the court instructed the jury that, as a matter of law, they might disregard expert testimony. . . . The jury technically were at liberty to disregard that evidence. They could not be compelled to accept it, but may it please your Honor, if the jury should go so far as to disregard the evidence of six experts employed by the state, reinforced by the testimony of three employed by the defense . . . the court, in its high discretion, could call a new jury in the case, who would give some consideration to the evidence in a matter involving life and death.

Mr. Stapleton then went on to point out the inaccuracies in the Attorney General's address to the jury:

And I think, may it please your Honor, that the court remarked that—and ruled that—it was not evidence that Spencer was faking when Dr. Hooker testified that he said to the defendant, "Spencer, you are faking."

The answer to Mr. Stapleton's argument by Mr. Callahan was brief, and brought out no new facts. The motion for a new trial was denied on January 3rd, 1911.

On March 12th, 1912, another hearing was granted on another motion for a new trial, before the Hon.

* Dr. Fuller testified that institutions for the insane might deal with individuals by refusing them certain privileges, such as being allowed to go out in the yard or being furnished with tobacco, if they did not behave themselves or were violent, and that in some cases such discipline helped in the government of the insane. He also testified that "mental defective" and "high grade imbecile" are synonymous terms, that is, that mental defectiveness includes the high grade imbecile. He said that there were a great many mental defectives at Bridgewater, and that part of his own duties consisted in the investigation of complaints and interviewing insane patients.

John C. Crosby, Justice,—this time on the ground of newly discovered evidence to prove that the State's Prison witness, St. John, alias Bell, had perjured himself, according to the evidence and affidavits of four of his companions in prison. Attorney Stapleton said in his argument that he offered the evidence of three witnesses that Bell had told them before and since the trial that he had an object in making the statements which he made, which was to accomplish his own liberation; that the testimony which he had given was not true, but was manufactured by him to accomplish that end; that he had also told them, in giving excuses for this act of his, of a personal motive in the nature of a grudge or personal dislike which he entertained for Spencer, and that he had said that the doctors of the institution held out an inducement to him, and that he would send his own mother to the chair to get out of State's Prison.

Mr. Callahan submitted an affidavit from St. John, alias Bell, denying, categorically, all the statements made about him by his mates at the State's Prison. The Warden of the Prison also deposed that the three men whose affidavits had been submitted by Mr. Stapleton had refused afterwards to be questioned by Mr. Callahan.

Judge Crosby denied the motion for a new trial. Bills of exception were filed and allowed, and were later argued in the Supreme Judicial Court, on May 23rd, and on June 22nd, 1912, a decision was rendered overruling the exceptions.

On July 2nd, 1912, Spencer was sentenced to death during the week beginning September 15th. He heard his fate, as the Springfield Republican said, "without quivering an eyelash," and betrayed no emotion whatever.

After the trial Mrs. Bertram G. Spencer, the wife, moved to Worcester, where she lived under her maiden name, Minnie Amberg. In an interview given to the Boston American in June, 1912, she said that Bert had always been a good husband to her and that she "loved him with all her heart"; that they had been "gloriously happy together." She said it had been a case of love at first sight. She was now twenty-two years old and had married him when only seventeen. There had been two children born to them; the second had died five days after the father's arrest. The older boy, three and a half years old at the time of the interview, had been named for his father. Mrs. Spencer said that she was then writing to her husband at least twice a week, and he to her as often.

The letters written by Bertram after his trial are significant of his naturally gentle, suggestible disposition, his extreme excitability and his instability. Under date of December 26th, 1911, he wrote from 79 York Street, Springfield, the York Street Jail, a letter of appreciation for what I had been able to do for him at the trial, saying:

> . . . I thought, Dr. Briggs, from my boyhood up I knew what sorrow was and untold suffering meant, but I was mistaken. Not till I was arrested for the awful crime that I had committed by taking a poor, innocent girl's life, shooting another woman and a motorman, assault on two women, stealing all my life and losing my home and loved ones, did I begin to realize what a terrible life I had been living. What can be the cause, Doctor, other than my early home life and environment? My ideals in life have aimed at the highest, but I was weak—oh, so weak! and why I can not understand. I never smoked, chewed, drank, used any drug—never went into but one

house of prostitution, and then only by a French fellow at about fourteen years of age—never since—never picked up any women on the street, never went in bad company, never gambled or spent my money foolishly, never read any dime novels or trashy literature in my life, and I honestly thought I was above the average, yet I am a disgrace to my country, my dear mother, wife, child, all my loved ones, and condemned to die a dishonorable death. What more can a man suffer than all these terrible things staring him in the face? The papers say I have no heart—I am cold and indifferent. It's a lie, Doctor. No one has ever heard me say but what I was a most sorry person ever lived, and if I could only die an honorable death I would gladly face a thousand guns or electric chairs—and if I die for this awful affair I am helpless of, I am a disgrace to all my loved ones and the world! May God and Man help me to rise above it! . . . I remain,

Your humble servant,
Bertram Gager Spencer.

On Thursday, January 11th, 1912, I received a letter very similar to those sent to six or seven other people, and which the officers of the jail thought to be the result of a fit of jealousy and anger against his wife, about whom some of the other men in the jail had been plaguing him because they found he was susceptible to teasing. Up to this time he had, apparently, been on the most excellent terms with his wife, sending her frequent messages of tender affection. I quote from this letter the following—a good deal of it is unprintable:

Doctor, lack of education, driven from home by my father's abusive treatment. . . . I never stole but two things in my life till I met my wife, and Doctor, since I met her, everything in my life's changed. A jack-knife in Lebanon was true, and a revolver in California—for I was always fond of shooting and it lay in the Armory in Oakland, where I was a member of Co. F., N.G. of Cal., and I asked the price and found I should have to pay $18, and knowing the Government furnished them to all the officers, I took it, fully intending to replace it before I came east, but I never gave it another thought till I was packing my trunk for the east, and it was too late to go then, so I kept it, and it was the one I shot poor, defenseless Miss Blackstone, Miss Dow and Mike Gilhooley. Dr., when

I met my wife I fell head over heels in love—why I can not say. . . . I was engaged to a wealthy young lady in Greenfield. . . .

He then describes his precipitate courtship and marriage and some of the events of his married life, in which he mentions intimate details and blames his wife for all his misdeeds since his marriage, even accusing her of stealing also. He says:

She sold all the household furnishings after my arrest, such as piano, beds, chairs, bureau, sideboard, pictures, two couches, dining table and center table—got $130, she says, for all. . . . I will suffer it all alone, Dr. Briggs, for in time her sins will find her out, and (she) will know how I am suffering, and will, long as I live, and when you sent me the best Christmas box of goodies I ever had in my life, I know, Dr., you were my true friend, guide and councillor hereafter. If I could only show you and Gov. Foss that I have plenty of good, pure blood in my veins, and with study and a little encouragement I will show the world that I am not what you all think I am—a heartless murderer and thief—no, by far, no—and if I was a free man tomorrow, not a single wrong would I commit. A woman has been my downfall, and thousands of others, I presume. . . . I made friends wherever I went with my musical talent, both vocal and instrumental, which I inherited. If I had of had an education, I know I should have been an honor to my country and loved ones, and if I am spared, I will show you and the World what's beneath my skull-cap. And, again referring to his wife, he says: . . . Not one cent, Dr., has she given me since my arrest—and earning $12 every week. She only came once to see me at Bridgewater, after the first day, when Mother and she came, and the last time I had to pay her fare both ways. When she comes to Springfield, she is allowed to come and see me any day, Sunday and all, and stay as long as she likes, as I now have an outside guard day and night. She came to Springfield the Saturday night before Christmas and stayed at her home till Monday night, and all the time she spent with me was four hours and six minutes, in three nights and two days, and my Christmas and New Year's presents consisted of two 25c. pairs of brown socks—not a love token of any kind, not even a card. . . . I made her, out of red ribbon, a pretty fringed book-mark, and printed in gold leaf from Bert to Minnie—Christmas 1911-1912; also an account book in red leather with her full maiden name on the fly-leaf. I printed her some appropriate verses inside and gave her twelve copies of the *Boston Sunday Post,* with a story, "The Money Moon" in it, which I have saved along a week at a time, as she likes to read such things; and I gave her a good-sized piece of everything you sent me and almost half of the chicken Mother sent me—and, if you believe me, she has not as much as thanked me—and I have sent her drawings that it took me just one and a half weeks to finish, and not a thank you. Does my heart ache. Well, Dr., I can hardly believe my own mind, sometimes, to think what a fool, what a fool. And she believes she is fooling me every day, and I am keeping it all to myself. Say, Dr., if my cousin in Cal. will send me $15, can I hire a detective for one week to give me further proof of what I would like to know?

He then branches off on a tirade about the light sentences of some men in jail, compared with the heavy sentences of others, and then speaks of how kind the officials are to him and what comfortable quarters he had, and winds up his letter with expressions of sorrow for his sister, who was apparently ill at the time he was writing.

On Jan. 4th, 1912, he wrote a long letter to his wife, of which he sent me a copy enclosed in a letter to me, in which he says:

You do not know how deeply repentant I am for taking a poor, innocent girl's life, or ever wronging a single soul on this beautiful earth. God has put so much beauty in both winter and summer for us all! No one will ever know how I am suffering for my wrong, wrong acts, and if truly penitent prayers offered to God will forgive my terrible acts, my prayers will and have been heard. Yesterday I asked Him to guide and direct my thoughts to write a last farewell letter to the woman I have and do so dearly love, and enclosed you will find a true copy of the letter I sent this morning to her. As a man, I have taken the step of helping her to be truthful instead of deceitful, and to be a free woman and do that which is upright and noble.

The enclosure is as follows:

My dear Wife:

Your loving letter of 721 words came Friday night, Jan. 12th, and it was certainly good of you to think enough of me after keeping me waiting a whole week with all your busy evenings to write such a lengthy letter, and though you did not answer all my questions, I suppose you will by another week, if not too busy. I know you consider me demonstrative, Minnie, but you and others know every word, every gift and sentence is from the depths of a heart and brain that only worshipped and idolized your every word, good or bad, and have always hungered after your words of love and cheer, longingly watched every mail for a true, loving, devoted wife's affections, either by letter or a postal or just a paper, or when you come here to see some signs of that affection that is bound to be demonstrative if there is one spark of true love burning in that heart of yours. Write what you will, say what you are amind to on paper, but actions speak louder than words by mouth or on paper. Minnie, I am no fool, and if you think I am blind or others are blind, you are wrong, way wrong, dear, and some day, some place, it will all come back to you like a moving picture. One doesn't have to live in jail or in palaces to find out who and what a true, loving and faithful wife means. I want you, Minnie, if you love any part of my feelings, to get a divorce, and you can by just the asking, as I am an outcast from society and home life, and what little time or long time, don't I pray, make it any harder for me to bear. I have thought and thought, as I am spending my last few months, I can not have this deceitfulness staring me in the face, and Minnie dear with (not one speck of hate) only true, manly love for the mother of my darling boy and you I wish to sever all loving ties from this day and forevermore, and from this day to the day I die never write or speak my name, and in the following mail or express you will receive everything that belongs to you or can recall our lives together. Now don't say I am mad, cranky or in any way hasty, dear, for I have been making up my mind ever since I heard of the "Spea" affair, and every day your heartless words and actions coming from you in various ways and nothing like it before I was arrested. From today on, as since my arrest, you are welcome to use your maiden name, go to concerts, theaters, parties, wherever and with whom you choose, early or late, and you will find pleasure in so doing as in the past. Do not come to Springfield to see me on any matters, or write or send anything by any one, or through the mail, for tomorrow morning I shall give orders to Mr. Wade and Sheriff Clark to remail all letters or articles hereafter coming from you in any form or to admit you if you come here to call. Your father and all your people have taken the (*let me alone side, too*) even when he came as far as the jail door he couldn't even come in, and say one word. When I sent for a coat by you, you sent me your father's old coat, so full of holes and dirty, for me to wear up into court. When outsiders notice and speak of these things, I surely ought to. I have been in confinement almost two years, and in all that time I have not received out of the $130 you received for my furniture you sold, with over $50 in the bank and $12 a week while at the Norton Co. in Worcester, a single penny or offer of such. Not a love token of any kind or a gift as such. The locket I have worn around my neck with your picture and my boy's I had to beg for. The rings you have you only wear when you come here to see me. Spend three nights and two days in Springfield over Christmas, and get down here late in the afternoon, and only spend from 3.40 to 6 P.M. one day, and the last day from 3.45 to 5.30, in all four hours and five minutes, and left me two pairs of woolen socks, which I also return for I really think and truly think they were begrudged me. I have given you all I could (and more than I did the dear loving mother who bore and will die for me) Christmas, yet not a flower I painted for her, as I did for you, has she forgot to love, cherish, and mention, and every picture, flower or gift I have ever sent her. Do you call that demonstrative dear? No, Minnie, it's true, true love. I have always longingly looked for from you and by you and whoever you get for a future partner I pray you to love him as a true, loving wife should do, and which I have hoped and longed for all in vain. It is most sad sad for me to part from you thus, but to keep on Minnie only causes me day after days fretting and worrying. I want to live right from this day henceforth, and I want you to do the same for God's and Baby's sake, if not for mine. We both have sinned, and I have asked God's full forgiveness and to forgive you and all your past sins and he has mine and I hope you place yourself in his care. I have asked his guidance this day in writing this letter, and if I have said one word that seems wrong, I ask your forgiveness in full. Wishing Minnie you God's speed in all your future undertakings and from this day to live an upright, law-abiding and God-fearing and loving mother, is the earnest prayer of your loving husband.

P. S. Please return the beaded belt to Mother, as I gave it to her when I came east, and also all my things that personally belonged to me, like watch, pins, chain, razor and outfit, etc.

Bertram Gager Spencer.

P. P. S. Minnie, as a last wish I beg you to leave Mother bring up and be guardian and teacher over our darling boy, as you are not in a position to do so, also to provide for him, in as much as you can till he is old enough to look after Bertram Herman.

Under date of January 28th, 1912, shortly after the motion for a new trial had been denied by Judge Crosby, Spencer wrote me:

Anything you place in my hands to study, I will leave not one stone unturned to accomplish that purpose. My ambition was never so great, and as Shakespeare says Take the instant way; for honor travels in a straight so narrow, where one but goes abreast; *keep then the path;* For emulation hath a thousand sons, That one by one pursue; if you give way or hedge aside from the direct forthright, Like to an entered tide, they all rush by and leave you hindmost. I do so appreciate your offer of a magazine now and then, which would be allowed me of course—anything of that kind always is—but there is no need of saying and I pray you will pardon any seeming lack of courteousness on my part when I request only the best you have, as I have never read fiction of any kind in my life and I will not today. . . . I am looking for an appropriate design to print, with flower emblem, for my dear mother's birthday, and though very old, I have decided on "Rock me to sleep" for one.

On Feb. 25th, 1912, he writes:

You of course do not know that my wife and my father were passing love letters back and forth unbeknown to me, until I was informed of it a short time ago, after it had been going on for six months or more.

There is an account of Spencer's having twice attempted suicide at the Hampden County Jail, first by putting his head through the glass window and attempting to cut his throat on the jagged edges of the window pane, and later by swallowing a spoonful of broken glass. On April 22nd, 1912, he writes:

I have been sick and utterly discouraged for three weeks, I will explain the best I can. You know I sent all my wife's things back to her and tried to forget her entirely, as I knew if I kept dwelling on my past five years with her and her actions, I should go mad, but I couldn't keep it from me, try as I would. The 18th of March was her 22nd birthday and we had been married just four years, so I sent her a painting in water colors of red and pink roses, with a verse in print and Loving Greetings, also a letter which Mr. Stapleton advised me to write, as she had been twice in Springfield and not come near me. . . . So I wrote her as long as she demanded an apology, I was perfectly willing to apologise to this extent—if I have said or written one word that was not the whole truth word for word, I would willingly on my knees ask before anyone her forgiveness. . . . Well, Dr., I got brooding over this and much more that I will not worry you about. My dear mother and darling boy near death's door, my sister and brother-in-law all down home—not a friend or kin to come and see me and to continually think of the awful crime

I committed two years ago the 31st of last March, and how weak I have been, and I had my crying spells right along and there was a week I could not retain anything on my stomach, and then and up to now I am eating nothing but milk and bread, which is of the best—and all these thoughts have been piling up, up, till I only thought of ending it all, so one week ago, Thursday, March 21st, I took a big tablespoonful of broken glass, fully expecting to be dead Friday. But Sunday came and I was still crying, and my troubles overcame me again, and I dove through the window, trying to cut my throat, but as usual I was unsuccessful and only slightly cut my head and ears, which is all healed now. Of course they put my hands in muffs for three days, which I suppose I deserved, and I stayed in bed five days. . . . Prison life is an awful life at its very best, and when I hear of men, boys and women coming back to such places, I think there is something decidedly wrong with their upper story.

April 30th, 1912:

I have had and am still having a hard siege of blues, and try as I may I can not fight it off. I am still taking bromide, and I am trying to sleep my troubles off, and it is especially such dreary weather—also drink three quarts of milk daily. And again referring to his wife he says, I do not have to have a door fall on me to know she has been deceiving me right and left. Did I write you she made a date with my own father to meet him at New Haven and go to Danbury Fair together while I was at Bridgewater? Don't you think she's pretty foxy? . . . I do not care to live any longer. Death in any form or shape will be most welcome for I am no longer a source of income to my family—not one bit of comfort to them or myself.

On May 27th, after thanking me for some books that I sent him, he wrote:

I shall never ask you but just one favor, which is a big one; knowing as I do of the decision that will be rendered in a few days or weeks, and the outcome of this farce, as I look at it, I can not prove in any way that my wife is not a capable person to have the bringing up of my darling boy, so I beg of you in some way to see that justice is done, if there is such a thing. There is much underhand work being going on these last six months, and I know if you hear from my lips what pen can not express or explain, you will begin to think. . . . You don't know how glad and happy I feel when I can do for some other poor unfortunate. I sent a dollar today to my wife's sister to buy a wreath of flowers and place on my wife's mother's grave for Minnie and I. Just think, there was never a tombstone or anything to mark the resting place of my wife's mother, so four years ago I set out a red rose bush, because I loved the mother of my wife, yet had never seen her. Minnie or her father never thought enough of her mother to even go there Decoration Day and place a few tokens of love for the one who had loved, suffered and died for them. As I sit here day after day, evening after evening, I can see through it all now, Dr., and I wonder why it was so. I have written my wife 8 or 9 letters and sent her an Easter card, and no reply to any of them except one card.

On June 14th I received a letter from Spencer's mother, of which the following is an extract:

I have just returned from Springfield, where I went last week on Friday with the little boy, who has not seen his father in a long time. I found Bertram very nervous, and *he is sure the officials are all conspiring against him, also his wife and Mr. Stapleton.* During the two and a half days I spent with him, there was scarce fifteen minutes but that the boy was raving over some fancied injury. . . .

About the end of May or the first of June some of his letters were written in a more or less tremulous hand, showing great emotion, especially when speaking of his wife. The change from irritability and extreme excitability at every noise and annoyance came only after he had embraced the Christian Science faith. This was brought about through the influence of one of his guards, who was strongly of that faith, and who not only brought books for Spencer to read which, with his susceptible nature, at once gave him comfort, but this guard interested a Christian Science reader, who visited Spencer immediately, comforting him and administering his doctrines to him up to the time of his death. It is a pity that suggestions of this nature were not brought into his life earlier, as his history shows that his actions were, to a great extent, the result of suggestion. Especially was this true when he changed from his occasional petty larcenies to house-breaking,

had gone through with for her
and I say (no) it would be
a cowards trick so I have
only told just a few so if
she tries to make trouble
for poor mother after I am gone
I pray you & Sheriff Clark. Mr
Wade & a few others to see
my boy is never, no never
in any way subjected to such
a life & temptations thrown
Is a lot and yet a here
I am. I sing I play my
mandolin I read & write
and yet I am always
always thinking [illegible] those
words my wife o[illegible] once
said. please excuse blots
my pen is not working
Goodbye Dr hope you have
a nice time
Lovingly Bert

Part of letter written by Spencer, May 28, 1912, showing effect of emotional thoughts when referring to his wife at this time.

on the suggestion given him through the report of the arrest of another Bertram Spencer for burglary, which the history of his life shows to have impressed him at this time very deeply. And again, in Bridgewater, it was evidently at the suggestion of the other inmates that he attempted to correct their wrongs, both real and fancied, especially the physical abuses which he had seen or of which he had seen the results.

The first letter in which I find any mention of Christian Science is dated June 26th, 1912, when he wrote:

Say, Dr., did you ever read "Science and Health" and compare it to the Bible? There are so many things in it that have already helped me to overcome, that I am already beginning to think it is only too true. Please do not evade this question like you do, Dr., in my other letters. Don't get provoked, now, for I only speak from a pure motive, and when I stop to think of it, of course you don't believe such a belief—but of course I am all the time thinking of my wife, my boy, my mother and crime, and I am at a loss to find just why everything came to pass as it has. God knows I hold no animosity toward a single soul in this world, neither did I before my arrest, except to my father, and today I forgive him. I have made oh! so many mistakes in my life, but none (leaving murder out altogether) like since I came to Springfield.

On July 6th, 1912, he makes his first reference to Mr. Perkins, the Christian Science reader, who stood by him to the end. It is a pleasure to recount this good man's devotion to a poor, condemned criminal, especially as later the papers were so full of mercenary transactions by people of his cult. Bertram writes:

I am making a thorough study of "Science and Health." All of these articles help me to get goodness out of life. Why is this not taken up more by Christian loving people, and those who care to be healed of all kinds of diseases? I have been taking bromide for my stomach trouble and I kept having those pains in my head and around my heart—could not sleep without the room being darkened, was so nervous at even the rattle of a paper, I would often want to scream, and last of all and most important is that my temper has left me like magic, and when I hold revenge toward those who have wronged others, my folks and myself, I can now forgive and pity them, for they know not what they do or say, and neither did I until Christian Science was read to me by one of my guards who is a Christian Scientist. There has been a practitioner here for over a week, almost every other day, bringing me beautiful flowers sent to me by his wife. They own a nice home in Longmeadow of ten acres, and he has got God's love, through hope, stamped upon his countenance.

I have spoken often to Mr. Perkins of you, telling him of your goodness. Do not think it strange if I do not speak of my sentence last Tuesday morning. I did so much want to say a few words of repentance and suffering for all of my sins and sickness, and to let people know I had tried to get permission from the time I was arrested till now to write a repentant letter to all those I have ever in any way wronged, and I have always been denied. . . . On June 27th I wrote a forgiving letter to my wife, telling her to cheer up and look for every good thing. Minnie received it on Friday, and she sat right down and answered it—a letter of 11 pages, but not one word did she mention of forgiveness or my case in any way. This being the only letter I had received from her since January 12th last, and she has not been here since Dec. 24th, 1911 . . . I am writing her every other day now, but I get no answers, and I can now overlook the whole affair, for I know she is weak, and I am trying to get her mind on facts instead of fiction. She writes she is reading now, more than ever, a story called "The Streets of Ascalon," by Robert W. Chambers. Of course it is a clean story, no doubt, but what or how can stories like that help to overcome all evil. As in the past, so shall I to the end try to get her mind to run in different channels. There is of course no use, Dr., of my trying to explain Mrs. Eddy's works to you, but her teachings are faith, hope and love.

On July 8th, 1912, he writes:

I received my sentence of mortal death last Tuesday morning at about ten o'clock by Judge Crosby, and since I understand "Science and Health" I keep my thoughts away from all thought or error of mortal man, and for this reason I did not mention it to you or my folks, except on the very morning I went up to court I wrote both my dear mother and wife to keep up good cheer, to think good and not to worry, for though mortals take my life in mortal sense, I still go into the great beyond forgiving each and all, just as Christ said "Father, forgive them, for they know not what they do." The love I hold for my wife today is so much different than four years ago—yes, four months ago—and my father, too. . . . I will enclose a cutting, Dr., regarding my last appearance in court. You will notice where it speaks of "cold as an iceberg"—Think not of it, Dr., for my heart within me was almost bursting with sorrow to think of my past weaknesses which had caused me to face mortal revenge. . . . I begged of my lawyer, Mr. Stapleton, to allow me to say a few repentant words and to say that I forgave fully and freely all those that had tried to injure me in any way in the eyes of the law, but he told me no—here at the jail and also again when I arrived at the court, so as you, mother and my brother advised me to do as Mr. Stapleton said and I complied all the way through and said nothing. . . . I am trying to live as St. Paul lived when in prison—I have learned that whatsoever state I am in, therewith to be content.

On July 17th, 1912, he writes:

If the soul of this universe understood God as Mrs. Eddy teaches, there would be no prisons, jails or asylums, and the medical fraternity of medicine would not be in existence, only as Christ left it to be, healing through divine principle. God be praised that such a healing power was left, and through it all my sins and belief in sickness are departed, for I was believing in unreality, which is evil—of matter and not of God. I feared God as I feared my earthly father, and kept revenge boiling within me day and night, believing that both were the cause of my downfall, but today I find all was an idea that was driving me insane, and it's not my father or Heavenly Father, mother, God, but my own belief in mortal error, that was all within everyone that does not understand. *My temper, moral weakness, hate, revenge, crying spells, stomach troubles and headaches I have had for years, left me after a second treatment by a C. S. practitioner, and today I never felt more happy and contented,* for I look upon everyone and everything with love, truth, life and understand that we in ourselves are simply nothing without understanding.

On August 5th, 1912, he wrote me immediately after a visit from his wife, during which he says she had admitted she had received "gentleman friends" in her room and had played for them; he again asks that a detective be employed to watch her and again accuses her of improper conduct with his father; and after stating a lot of things which to him mean deception on her part, he says:

I want to know if these facts had not ought to be brought before the Governor and Council—not to do her one bit of harm, but to show them how easy for men to be misled by what I supposed to be a true and loving wife. . . . I have no money, and in the mortal power of men who rank as Catholics, having no regard for the true state of affairs, just as I told Mr. Stapleton when he first took my case that I only wanted the truth in everything and my answer was, "They are not going to be fair." . . . I did do as he said, and what more could I have gotten—all my wife's folks, or her stepmother and her folks, and my wife's uncle's folks are strong Catholics. Mr. Stapleton and Callahan both attend the same Catholic Church. . . . Mr. Stapleton said, sarcastically, "Stick close to Christian Science if it does you any good," the last time he called. Yes, it has done me a world of good, but the Pope prays three times each day for the destruction of Christian Science believers. I understand, Dr., that you have showed some of my past letters to Mr. Stapleton. I request, Dr., you keep this to yourself.

Following the above letter came one dated August 6th:

Yesterday I sent you a letter putting forth my desires, but since I sent it I have had higher and better thoughts, and I say, "Let the dead bury their dead." Two wrongs can never make one right, and I do not want my wife's name defamed in or by one word. Yesterday I wanted to prove my statements, for the truth is always there, and by stirring up evil we can not expect to reap goodness. So again I say, Dr., I don't want you to do one thing towards my wife's being found out or her name in any way brought before the Council. I would gladly shoulder any and all blame, and leave it for God's infinite love and goodness to adjust all wrongs. As long as I live I am going to overcome all evil by high, sound, clean thoughts, and place before those I love no words or action that may be the first step backward instead of forward.

On August 10th, 1912, Spencer writes:

. . . As I look at it now, it matters not, and the sooner these people who are thirsting for my heart's blood are satisfied to see the law carried out by taking my life, let them have it. Life here is nothing, and in five minutes it is all over. Why, if I couldn't suffer five minutes in the electric chair, when Christ suffered for hours, I wouldn't be much of a man. I am more anxious to go than to stay, believe me, and after I have been lied about on every hand and deceived by everybody, there is no pleasure among my fellow men. . . . I have left good seed behind, and "if they seek they shall find." . . . Don't say, Dr. Briggs, I am not appreciative of what is done for me. Oh, yes, I am, and you'll never know how much. There was a time when I longed to live, but *"God"* says He that loveth life more than me shall lose it. I am ready and anxious to see the great beyond, for this kind of existence is only full of sorrow, and when everything goes wrong when I try to have right, I am far better off at rest. I do everything I know to bring cheer and comfort to my dear old mother, and I always said I hoped to die before she did because I loved her so. I send all the others cheer and comforting words and I "*hope*" some day they will understand.

On September 14th, the day before his execution, Spencer wrote me in a firm, even hand, without the underscorings so frequent in his previous letters:

God speed the day when Love, Truth and Life Eternal shall be justice to all mortal minds, then divine mind will be uppermost and error will have no place in the Christ-like consciousness which is in all mankind, but ofttimes so smothered that there only seems to be all evil.

We are the image and likeness of God, how? Spiritually, hence perfect, and with this knowledge that Mr. Perkins has taught me through Christian Science, I see why mortal mind sweeps all mankind off their feet without the higher understanding that God is Love, Truth and Life Eternal and sin, disease and death are all mortal beliefs hence powerless for God is of too pure eyes to behold evil which perishes with the flesh.

My wife I have not heard from or seen since she left me at York St. Jail Sept. 1st and my wishes have been turned over to my dear human God loving mother. God will bless her. No human mother could have done more for her child than she has done for me, all her life, and I praise God for such a mother. May she find peace and comfort and rest her weary mortal sense in God's loving care, for he is here now and everywhere.

God bless Gov. Foss and the Council. They have deprived me of mortal life and comfort to my family to the human sense, but they can not stop the continuance of God's Love and Truth and I would not exchange all worldly possessions for the knowledge of God gained through Christian Science, and it will continue for ever and ever, God be praised.

Will close with loving kindness to *you, yours,* and all mankind through Christ Jesus.

Bertram Gager Spencer.

The Christian Science Journal published an article shortly after Spencer's execution, telling of the work accomplished by Christian Scientists, saying that ninety-eight convicts in the New Jersey State Penitentiary were Christian Scientists, and speaking especially of the case of Spencer and another condemned criminal recently executed, who had died professing this faith. The Journal quoted a letter from Spencer's mother, as follows:

In corroboration of my son's testimony, I would like to state that if there ever was an example of regeneration and "new birth"—the shaking off this mortal coil and the putting on of a new garment—such was made manifest in the great change which completely transformed my boy, mentally and physically, during the last three months of his existence on earth.

Since early boyhood he had been afflicted at times with uncontrolled outbursts of temper, which on several occasions were of such a violent nature that they seemed more like epileptic fits. He possessed many sterling qualities of character, and to all outward appearances was living an exemplary life, as far as habits and choice of associates might indicate. His love for "mother" was almost divine, and his ever-thoughtfulness, unselfishness and great-hearted love for mother was touching and pathetic. All others with whom the boy came in contact sooner or later became aware of a "veiled stranger," and while at times loving and with a desire to please, if opposed in any way he would suddenly change in manner, and sometimes it would be two or three days before he would be himself again.

His mental condition seemed more aggravated after passing through the San Francisco earthquake, where for a month he was on duty as a member of the National Guard of California, and his desire for excitement was even greater than before. Between the ages of seventeen and nineteen, he attempted suicide on two different occasions, and all efforts to make him understand right and wrong in its truest sense were of no avail. After his arrest in April, 1909, his mental and physical condition became worse—frequent outbreaks, also bodily ailments—stomach trouble, also severe pains at times over kidneys and violent headaches. In May, 1910, while in the Bridgewater institution, he attempted suicide, but failed in the undertaking. Again during his incarceration in Springfield, Mass., and in May, 1912, he made two more attempts to end his life. It seemed to those in charge necessary to keep him under the influence of bromide given at frequent intervals, and as a light shining in his room at night could not be endured, a canopy was hung over the bed. The slightest noise annoyed him, and he imagined all the officials were his enemies, when in reality they were doing all in their power to please him and make him comfortable.

In this great distress of mind and bodily suffering, he was constantly reaching out and groping in the dark for some spiritual comfort, but nothing seemed to bring peace of mind. Several kind-hearted ministers of one or more denominations visited him, each with the desire of pointing out the right road of salvation, but all the efforts on the part of my son to follow the admonition to "look to a higher power for forgiveness and trust in God" did not give him the right understanding, and still left him unsatisfied with himself, as well as with God and man. In the early part of June, 1912, I visited him in Springfield, and found him more violent than I had ever seen him since his imprisonment, although there had been occasions previous to my visit when the combined strength of two men was required to hold him. One of the guards who had my son in charge was interested in Christian Science, and used to read him occasionally from "Science and Health" and other literature along this line. The attention of a Christian Science practitioner was brought to my son's need, and the great change and mental healing which came, gradual but sure, was a marvel to all who had him in charge. All bodily ailments disappeared, the bromide was discontinued, the canopy over the bed was removed, and no difficulty in sleeping was experienced, even though a bright light was streaming into his room.

Words can never express my deep gratitude, not only for the benefit Christian Science has been to my departed boy, but to myself as well, and I fully believe that a new era is dawning when there will be an awakening, and facts which are demonstrable will prove to the world that Love, Truth and right understanding of God and the teachings of the Bible will do more toward raising suffering humanity toward a higher plane of civilization than capital punishment and the electric chair.

The following letter was written by the prison guard:

Having been one of the guards of Bertram G. Spencer at the Hampden County Jail in Springfield, Mass., for over nine months, I had opportunity to observe his conduct both before and after he became interested in Christian Science; and I can truthfully say that the change wrought in him was very great indeed. He was benefited in all ways, the help he received and the interest in Christian Science enabling him to overcome many physical troubles. The change in disposition was also very marked. When I first became acquainted with him last November, he was in a very sad and despairing frame of mind, and continued in that condition until Christian Science was brought to his attention. . . .

CHAPTER VI

REMOVAL OF SPENCER TO CHARLESTOWN, SEPTEMBER 5TH, 1912. EFFORTS FOR COMMUTATION OF SENTENCE. EXECUTION, SEPTEMBER 17TH, 1912.

During Spencer's confinement in jail in Springfield I visited him, and just before his removal to Charlestown I spent quite a time with him, as he wished to show me what he was doing to prove to future generations that he was not really a criminal. His idea of proving this was to select from books and papers anything that he thought was beautiful or that seemed to him to show a high development of mind and character. He cut these extracts out or copied them most neatly, coloring the titles, and sometimes illustrating in colors the subjects of which they treated. His selections were such as a child of from eight to twelve years old would naturally make, and the whole procedure of pasting them in books and the rearrangement was what a child of that age would be capable of doing. He had asked for and obtained a trunk, and into this trunk he had put this large collection, saying he was going to lock and seal the trunk and leave it to his boy, to be opened when the boy was sixteen years of age; so that when they accused him of being the son of a murderer, he could show what a beautiful mind and what beautiful thoughts his father had. He had been given a small amount of money—I think only one dollar—and with it had purchased a second-hand hat from one of the jailers, and had also got from somewhere else some better clothing than that which he had when he entered the jail. When I arrived he was cleaning and "fixing up" his clothes, and he said, "I have got this nice hat and these nice clothes to wear when they take me to Charlestown, so that I shall make a good appearance." At that time efforts were being made to persuade the Governor to grant a commutation of sentence, and I told him that the Governor was very much worried over the situation. Spencer, who seemed very cheerful and happy over the childish work he was doing for his son, said, "Tell the Governor not to worry, but to cheer up. I am not worrying, so why should he?"

On August 25th, Spencer's attorney, Mr. R. P. Stapleton, personally presented a petition for the commutation of Spencer's death sentence to Governor Foss. Mr. Stapleton said that at the end of eleven days, not having heard anything from the Governor's office, he telephoned to the office but could not learn that any petition had been placed on record there.

On September 5th, 1912, Spencer was removed to the death cell in that part of the Charlestown State Prison known as Cherry Hill—and still no action of the Governor or Council on his petition. As I have before stated, Chester S. Jordan's petition for clemency was being considered at this time, and Clarence V. T. Richeson had been examined as to his sanity but a short time before. The crimes committed by these men had influenced the public mind, which had already been stirred by the long sensational reports in the papers of the Thaw trial and of the more recent case of the "gun men" in New York, whose trial was being held at about that time.

On September 9th, broken in heart and spirit, Mrs. Spencer, the mother of Bertram, made a final appeal to Gov. Foss. For more than an hour she pleaded with the Governor, and when she left him he said, "I will give the matter my most careful consideration, and make known my decision Wednesday." She also visited various members of the Council and put her case before them. Mr. Stapleton suggested to the Governor that a board of alienists be appointed by the Chief Executive to pass upon Spencer's mental condition, and asked for a respite of sixty days that he might present new evidence bearing upon Spencer's mental condition, in the form of several affidavits from persons who had had charge of him since his imprisonment, who deposed that Spencer was not sane. In the meantime, when his mother visited him, Spencer appeared to be in the best of spirits, and she said, "Instead of my visits cheering him, it seemed as though he was cheering me!"

Governor Foss failed to refer Spencer's petition that his death sentence be commuted to life imprisonment to the Council. It was the mother who took this news to her son, and his comment was, "I expected nothing different, Mother dear, and was prepared for the news you bring me. Don't worry about me, Mother dear; I am reconciled to my God and am ready to die." This was on September 11th. During the morning, Mr. Stapleton had called on the Governor and presented new evidence he had procured. The Governor listened attentively, but held out no hope. Mrs. Spencer was also in the Executive room early in the morning before the Council met at 10.30, and personally interviewed Councillors Goetting and MacGregor. She told them

Home-ward Bound...

Designed, drawn and printed by Bertram G. Spencer after passing under the influence of Christian Science.

she realized the hostility to her son in the western part of the state, but believed it to be due to the fact that the people did not understand his condition, and that if they knew, they would sympathize with him rather than hold resentment against him. She tried to see Governor Foss again, but he said that in view of the fact that he had already spoken with her about the case, he begged to be excused from giving her another audience.

But the devoted mother did not give up even now. On September 10th she visited President Taft's summer residence at Beverly. She was met there by Secret Service men to whom she told her story, and was referred by them to the executive offices which President Taft had in Beverly. Though not allowed to see the President, she was kindly treated and her story listened to in every detail for nearly an hour, when she was told that the President could do nothing to save her son—that the matter was beyond his jurisdiction. His secretary dictated a long letter to a Connecticut Senator, asking him to use his influence to stay proceedings, but it amounted to nothing.

Guy F. Perkins, the Christian Science reader at the church at Springfield, was first called to see Spencer by Frank Allen of the York Street Jail, who had immediate charge of Spencer for several months. Spencer's talent for drawing was developed after he became interested in Christian Science, without instruction and with no evidence of previous talent shown in this direction up to the time he embraced that faith.

The influence on Spencer of Christian Science teachings continued to the end. On the morning of his execution, he inquired on awakening, "What kind of a day is it?" and on being told it was rather rainy, he said, "I hope the sun will shine sometime today—it ought to shine on my last day."

In a letter dated the evening of September 16, 1912, Spencer writes to his mother, with a perfectly steady and natural hand two hours before his execution, a long, loving letter, in which he says:

> I am enclosing a lock of my human hair with a little ribbon tied thereto and rose leaves that expresses my most tender and loving regard for my dear mother. . . .
>
> It is my request, dear, that no one wear mourning for me.
>
> Love has provided me today with a check from Mr. Perkins sufficient to defray all expenses following tonight. No expense will remain to be defrayed by the State or anyone, thanks to Mr. and Mrs. Perkins.
>
> You understand, dear, this is a gift to me and is not as though you had to receive it as a charity or repay it as a loan.
>
> 10 P.M. Dr. Briggs has just left here with Warden Bridges after spending an hour with me. Through the kindness of Mr. Stebbins and Mr. Perkins I made out a request in writing to the Superior Court that Dr. Briggs be allowed to call upon me. Mr. Stebbins (the Prison Chaplain) took my request and it was granted.

He then expresses his wish to be cremated because he says he had been told it was "clean and hygienic" and continues:

> The Warden is a fine-looking and appearing man and the deputy warden and all the officers have been just lovely to me and my praise of them is in the highest human sense.
>
> Now, dear mother, child and folks, it is nearing the time when I must close this letter but in my most loving thoughts you all will abide forever.
>
> "Love is our refuge, Only
> With mine eye
> Can I behold the snare,
> The pit, the fall.
> His habitation high is
> Here and nigh.
> His arm encircles me
> And mine and all."
>
> Ever most lovingly,
> Bertram.
>
> 11 P.M., September 16, 1912.

On the afternoon of September 16th I was at my farm in Hancock, New Hampshire, when to my surprise I received an order from the Justice of the Superior Court to report to the Massachusetts State's Prison at once. On my arrival at about eight P. M. I was met by Warden Bridges, then in his 76th year, carrying a cane which he used to assist him, as he was enfeebled by age and rheumatism. He also used this cane to give signals for the current to be turned on at the different electrocutions. Spencer's electrocution was the fourth at which this cane fell to the pavement as a death signal during that year of 1912. He told me Spencer desired to see me and that it had been necessary for him to get an order from the Superior Court. He then took me through the dimly lighted passageways of "Cherry Hill" along "Murderers' Row" to Spencer's cell, which was brilliantly lighted. As we stopped at the cell door Spencer came to the bars and greeted us pleasantly. The prison guards had just finished preparing Spencer for the electric chair. With the clippers they had cut a wide swathe of hair, close to his head, to admit the close application of the head electrode, and the rest of his hair had been cut and arranged to his own satisfaction, the prisoner directing how he thought it would be most becoming. A slit had been made in the cloth of his left trouser leg for the other electrode. Spencer first spoke to me and then Warden Bridges introduced himself and explained that the reason he had not seen Spencer before was because he had been away on a vacation. Spencer's answer was, "I will see you later but now I would like to see Dr. Briggs alone." Although Warden Bridges was not supposed to leave a man condemned to die alone with a visitor he said he would trust me and ushered me into Spencer's cell and then withdrew to the end of the corridor, taking his guards with him, out of sight and out of hearing. Only once during the next hour or so did anyone disturb us and that was when Spencer at one time laughed so loud over something he was relating that Warden Bridges appeared to see if all was well and immediately retired again. Spencer's object in sending for me was to get my promise to see that his mother brought up his boy. He spoke in warm and affectionate terms of his boy and his mother and of her love for and devotion to him. He spoke of Christian Science and of what it had done for him and wished that everyone was as happy as he was that night, especially his mother and Governor Foss. At about ten o'clock he said, "Now, Doctor, I want you to go. You do not want to stay to see this affair—it would be unpleasant for you to see, but it is going to be a wonderful thing for me. It will be only that (snapping his fingers) and then I shall be in the next world with God and, oh, how happy I shall be ever after." I left him and he was smiling and cheerful and apparently happy, and I endeavored to show him the same spirit. Warden Bridges later told me that when the time came for Spencer to go to the chair, one of the "death watch" said, "Come on, Bert—what do you say? Are you ready?" Spencer answered, "I am ready," and slid from the bed on which he was lying, placed his feet in his slippers with a smile, and immediately began his walk to the chair, leading the way. The tap, tap of the Warden's cane, preceding the witnesses, was the only sound heard.

Spencer walked into the chamber unassisted, followed by the Warden and the death watch, and smiled as he entered, evidently not realizing the seriousness of the proceedings, as a normal man would have done. Being complimented upon his calmness, he planted his feet firmly together, clasped his hands before him and, standing before the chair, made his statement to the nine or ten witnesses present:

"I wish to say to the world and to the press that this is not nerve but the love of God that has sustained me."

He then looked about, and nodding to several of the witnesses, said "Good-night"; and, still smiling, he took his seat in the chair. The Warden's cane fell. Chief Engineer Currier, of the Massachusetts General Hospital, stood by the switch-board and turned on the current as the Warden's cane dropped at 12.16½ P. M. and Spencer was pronounced dead within a few seconds.

The body was removed to the North Grove Street Morgue, where an autopsy was performed by Medical Examiner McGrath, after which it was cremated, in compliance with Spencer's own wishes, and the ashes sent to his mother.

A history of the Spencer family subsequent to Bertram's execution would be of great scientific interest, but unfortunately for the scientist one is not free to publish intimate details of the personal lives of one's neighbors. I may say here that I have been more or less in touch with Mrs. Spencer, and have many letters from her written during the past six years. Both the sister and the brother of Bertram Spencer have had "nervous" breakdowns. It is interesting to note that in their cases these changes did not come in childhood as was the fact with Bertram, so as to be noticeable to their mother—but came on, in each case, at about the age of twenty-five, after Bertram's arrest. In the case of the sister, as with Bertram Spencer himself, her "nervous" symptoms gradually disappeared after she had embraced the faith of Christian Science.

The experts for the State and for the defence knew that Bertram G. Spencer was insane at the time of the homicide and at the time of the trial. They differed in that some thought that he was medically insane, but sane under the technical rule of law; while others thought that he was medically and legally insane. Recognizing the vital fact that Spencer was actually insane, all of the important experts believed that he should not be tried. They knew that the facts were undisputed and that they would not differ in their medical conclusions. Believing that the trial of an insane man would be an offence against humanity, an effort was made to stop the trial through a conference by the alienists of both the defence and the prosecution, but all parties not being willing to agree to such a conference the effort failed.

The whole legal machinery of the State had been put in motion to crush this defective and uphold the Majesty of the Law, and so it came about that Bertram G. Spencer, a defective from birth, with the mind of a child, was tried for his life and sentenced to death and was executed with a smile upon his lips.

PART II

CZOLGOSZ

INTRODUCTION TO THE CZOLGOSZ CASE

REASONS WHY INVESTIGATION WAS MADE. HISTORY AND INVESTIGATION OF THE CASE BY ALIENISTS AND AUTHORITIES IN BUFFALO. CONCLUSIONS AS TO HIS SANITY MADE MAINLY FROM STATEMENTS BY CZOLGOSZ HIMSELF

After the trial and execution of Czolgosz on October 29th, 1901, it appearing from the reports of the alienists, as published, that no thorough, scientific investigation or study had been made of his mental or physical condition previous to his arrest, Dr. Walter Channing, with whom I was then associated, suggested that we investigate his history and ascertain, if possible, his mental and physical condition for some years prior to the assassination of President McKinley. It was decided that I should make the investigation, Dr. Channing paying his part of the expense for a joint paper. On January 3, 1902, Dr. Channing wrote me as follows: "I depend on your going to Cleveland by next week, though I hate to have you take so much trouble, but I know you will succeed better than anyone else."

I thought it important to start my study at Auburn Prison, New York, where Czolgosz was electrocuted, and then to trace back his career, visiting all the places where he had lived, and the following history will show to what extent I carried out my purpose. Soon after I began my investigation, I realized it was important if Dr. Channing was to read the paper we were to write, that he should at least visit one of the cities where Czolgosz resided, and so urged. After I returned with the facts I had unearthed, as in substance appears in the following pages, he agreed, and on May 22, 1902, wrote me he had arranged to go to Cleveland the following Monday and said: "I should certainly not want to go out there without you. I am sure I should not accomplish as much as with you, and possibly we might get on the track of new things this time."

Little that was new was learned on the second trip. After this trip together, Dr. Channing wrote me the following letter:

Brookline, June 5, 1902.

My dear Dr. Briggs:

I much appreciate all the labor and pains you have taken in the Czolgosz case. You certainly have shown great ability and perseverance in following up clues. I also must heartily thank you for your considerate and unselfish efforts to make our recent journey to Cleveland pleasant and easy for myself. You succeeded in making an old maid comfortable.

Yours very truly,

(Signed) Walter Channing.

Dr. Channing left for New Brunswick while I was continuing my investigation, and in an answer to a letter from me, in which I described my visit to the Anarchists' meeting, he replied from Campobello Island, N. B., under date of August 15, 1902, as follows:

"I was very glad to get your letter of the 6th inst. The Anarchists' meeting was as extraordinary as interesting, and did give you a chance to study a strange sect at close range. I suppose the fact that they are allowed such entire freedom of action (within certain limits) is the reason they do no more harm. With restrictions the Government puts on or proposes to put on them, they may do more harm in the future. Certainly the more they are suppressed in Europe the worse they are. Suppression is a temporary remedy which does not cure the disease."

It was more than interesting to learn what was actually Czolgosz's mental condition for some years prior to his crime and how, instead of treating the crime as the act of a mentally ill man, the authorities and alienists accepted this deluded man's estimate of himself, even to his statement that he was an Anarchist, without corroborative evidence or a careful investigation into his antecedents or his life before this unnatural and purposeless crime. The alienists said: "We came to our conclusions from the history of his life as it came from him." The authorities said: "He claimed to be an Anarchist and a follower of Emma Goldman."

CHAPTER I

HISTORY OF CZOLGOSZ'S CRIME—THE ASSASSINATION OF PRESIDENT MCKINLEY, SEPTEMBER 6TH, 1901. EXAMINATIONS BY THE ALIENISTS

In the year 1901 the Pan-American Exposition was held in the city of Buffalo, New York. It attracted millions of strangers, and notwithstanding that on many occasions the population of the city was nearly doubled, there was less crime committed in the city during the six months of the Exposition than during the corresponding time of any previous year since the Department of Police of Buffalo was organized. This was primarily due to the precautions taken against an influx of criminals from all parts of the world. As the Exposition Company had a most excellent police force, under a veteran police officer, Col. John Byrne, the Buffalo police did not enter the grounds except on special occasions when requested.

President McKinley arrived in Buffalo on a special train of the Lake Shore & Michigan Southern Railway, which went direct to the Exposition Grounds, at 6 P. M., September 4th. At the railway gate of the Exposition, the President and his party were met by the Fourth Brigade, National Guards, Signal Corps, mounted, also twenty mounted police officers of the Buffalo department. In addition, there were four detectives who were especially instructed to keep near the President's person during his visit to Buffalo.

Thursday, September 5th, was the President's day at the Pan-American Exposition, and he was escorted to the Grounds by the same mounted escort that met him September 4th. The instructions of the mounted detail were to be in attendance upon the President during his stay within the city; but after the 5th, at the request of Mrs. McKinley, the detail of mounted police was reduced to eight men. On Friday, September 6th, the President again visited the Exposition Grounds, and also made a trip to Niagara Falls, returning to the Exposition on the afternoon of that day for the purpose of holding a public reception in the Temple of Music. It was while the President was holding this reception that, at seven minutes past four, a young man with one hand apparently done up in a handkerchief approached him and immediately fired two shots.

One bullet struck the President near the upper part of the sternum, the other in the left hypochondriac region. The man was immediately seized, his clothing torn, and he was beaten about the head and body by the crowd, but was rescued by Detectives and Police, who hustled him into a carriage and drove him directly to the Police Headquarters, Prison Department. The President was immediately conveyed to an emergency hospital on the Exposition Grounds in a motor ambulance driven by a medical student named Ellis, where he arrived at 4.18. Accompanying him in the ambulance were Dr. G. McK. Hall and E. C. Mann, a medical student of the house staff. On arriving at the hospital he was placed upon the operating table and undressed—one bullet falling out of his clothes. Dr.

Herman Mynter was the first surgeon to arrive, at 4.45. At that time Drs. Van Peyma and Fowler of Buffalo and E. W. Lee of St. Louis were present, and Dr. Mynter brought Dr. Eugene Wasdin, of the U. S. Marine Hospital Service. Dr. Mynter told the President it would be necessary to operate and preparations were at once made, as daylight was rapidly fading and internal hemorrhage was feared. Dr. Matthew D. Mann, who arrived at the hospital at 5.10, was selected to do the operation, which began at 5.29, ether being the anaesthetic used. Dr. P. M. Rixey, U. S. N., President McKinley's family physician, had been detailed by the President to accompany Mrs. McKinley to the home of John C. Milburn, where they were stopping, and did not arrive at the hospital until 5.30. He gave very sufficient service, first by guiding the rays of the sun to the seat of the operation by the aid of a hand mirror and later by arranging an electric light.

The President bore the operation, which took an hour and a half, very well, but the bullet which entered the body was not found. On Thursday morning, September 12, the seventh day, the President seemed at his best and a favorable diagnosis was given out, but on Friday the 13th his heart failed to respond to stimulation which had been kept up with varying degrees of intensity ever since the shooting, and in the evening he lost consciousness and died on the ninth day, Saturday, September 14, at 3.15 in the morning.*

* An incision was made from the edge of the ribs downwards, passing through the bullet wound. A piece of cloth was removed from the track of the bullet; the anterior wall of the stomach was found to have been perforated by the bullet, some of the liquid food escaping. This perforation was closed with a double row of fine black silk sutures using a straight round sewing needle, eight stitches being used in each row. With great difficulty the wound in the posterior wall of the stomach was reached and

After Czolgosz had been taken to Police Headquarters, he was brought before Assistant District Attorney Haller and the Superintendent of Police. He told them that his name was Fred Nieman and that he was born in Detroit, was 28 years old, that he was an anarchist, that he had killed the President and that he believed he had done his duty and was glad of it. Dur-

closed, it being somewhat larger than the anterior wound. All parts were carefully irrigated with hot salt solution. Dr. Mann introduced his arm so as to palpate carefully all the deep structures behind the stomach, but no trace of the bullet or of its further track could be found. The introduction of the hand in this way seemed to have a bad influence on the President's pulse, so a prolonged search for further injury done by the bullet or for the bullet itself was desisted from.

Before closing the abdominal wound, Dr. Mann asked each surgeon present whether he was entirely satisfied; each replied that he was. Dr. Mynter was in favor of a Mikulicz drain being placed down behind the stomach walls. Dr. Mann, with the concurrence of other surgeons, decided against this as being unnecessary. The tissues around the bullet track in the abdominal wall were then trimmed, in order to remove any tissue which might be infected. The abdominal wound was closed with seven through and through silk-worm gut sutures, the muscle being joined with buried cat-gut. Where the bullet had entered there was slight gaping of the tissues, but it was not thought advisable to close this tightly, as it might allow of some drainage.

The President bore the operation, which took an hour and thirty-one minutes, very well. At the beginning of the operation his pulse was 84; when the bandage was applied over the wound at 7:01, the pulse was 124, the respiration 36. Strychnine, brandy and morphine had been administered up to this time. Before recovering from the anæsthetic he was removed from the hospital to Mr. Milburn's house, where a hospital bed had been prepared for him. The difficulties of the operation were very great, owing partly to the want of retractors and to the failing light. Dr. Mann stated after the operation, "To have used the X-Ray simply to have satisfied our curiosity would not have been warrantable as it would have greatly disturbed and annoyed the patient, and would have subjected him also to a certain risk. My reason for not draining was there was nothing to drain."

After the President had been removed to Mr. Milburn's, Dr. Rixey, aided by Dr. Wasdin, was in constant charge of the sick-room, and Dr. Park helped to decide many difficult questions. The President rested fairly comfortably until 6:30 P. M. on Saturday, the next or second day, when he complained of intense pain in the pit of his stomach. His pulse was 130 and temperature 102.5. Morphia quieted him. During the day digitalis, morphia and saline solutions were given at regular intervals, and at 10:30 P. M. 5 gm. of somatose. On Sunday, the third day, September 8th, after a fairly good night, he had a day without much change, and his condition was considered satisfactory. He was given digitalis, strychnia and a nutritive enema, and a teaspoonful of water by mouth. His wound was dressed, the bullet track being syringed out with hydrogen dioxide. At 9 P. M. his pulse was 130, temperature 101.6, respiration 30. On the fourth, fifth and sixth days there was little change, excepting slightly for the better; a little slough was ing examination he was at all times cool and collected, showing no indication of remorse or sorrow for the crime he had committed.

On the evening of the first examination of the prisoner, Dr. Joseph Fowler, Surgeon of the Police, suggested to the District Attorney that investigation as to Czolgosz's sanity should be immediately begun, and

observed near the bullet track, covering a space nearly an inch wide, supposed to be caused by the infection of the wound from the bullet or a piece of clothing. The parts were washed with hydrogen dioxide and packed with gauze. The pulse went down to 116 and 120.

On Thursday, the seventh day, September 12th, the President in the morning seemed at his best and a favorable prognosis was given out. The time for peritonitis and sepsis had passed; the patient's tongue was clear, his appetite increasing and he was able to turn on his side easily; no pain nor tenderness in abdomen, spirits good, mind clear, temperature only 100, pulse strong. Toward noon the character of the pulse was not quite so good. Infusion of digitalis was ordered and strychnine. Dr. Charles G. Stockton was added to the medical staff.

On the eighth day, Friday, September 13th, his heart failed to respond properly to stimulation. As early as midnight strychnine and whiskey were given at frequent intervals, and hypodermics of camphorated oil. At 8:30 A. M., adrenalin was given hypodermically, and at 9:40 repeated. At 9, coffee, clam broth and liquid peptonoids were given; at 10 A. M. nearly two pints of normal salt solution were given under the skin, and a pint of the solution containing adrenalin at 6 P. M. Nitroglycerine and camphor were also injected at various times, together with brandy and strychnine. But at 3:30 P. M. the pulse was still growing weaker, and at 5 oxygen was resorted to. At 6:35 and 7:40 morphine was given, and at 10 P. M. oxygen was discontinued, the heart sounds being very feeble and consciousness lost. The President died on the ninth day, September 14th, at 3:15 A. M.

An autopsy was performed by Drs. Gaylord and Matzinger. It showed extensive necrosis of the substance of the pancreas; necrosis of the gastric wall in the neighborhood of both wounds; the left kidney showed that the ball had grazed the superior aspect; there was also evidence that the left adrenal gland was injured. The absence of bacteria from the tissues indicated that the wound was not infected at the time of the shooting. The extensive necrosis of the pancreas seemed an important factor in the cause of death; also the changes in the heart, including extensive brown atrophy, diffuse fatty degeneration of the muscle and especially the extent to which the pericardial fat had invaded the atrophic muscle fibres of the right ventricular wall, explaining the lack of response of this organ to stimulation. The injury of the pancreas was the result of the indirect rather than the direct action of the missile. Bacteriological examinations of the barrel of the weapon used, of the empty shells and loaded cartridges, made by Dr. Hill, a chemist, were negative. Dr. Matzinger closed his report with a statement as follows: "The absence of known pathogenic bacteria, particularly in the necrotic cavity, warrants the conclusion that bacterial infection was not a factor in the production of the conditions found at the autopsy."

each day thereafter Drs. Fowler, Putnam and Crego examined Czolgosz and the prison guards in charge of him carefully watched his conduct and made reports thereon. Their report, which is dated September 28th, 1901, reads as follows:

Hon. Thomas Penny,
District Attorney, Erie County, N. Y.
Sir,

Complying with your request to examine into the mental condition of Leon F. Czolgosz and report to you the result of our findings, we respectfully submit the following:

In conducting the examinations of the prisoner, we carefully eliminated all bias and personal revenge, which so revolting a crime might suggest, to reach a just conclusion as to his mental state.

The early opportunity afforded us to examine Czolgosz, the examinations beginning but a few hours after the commission of the crime, while he was still uninformed of the fate of his victim, or had time to meditate upon the enormity of his act, aided us materially in our work.

As will be seen from our report, the prisoner answered questions unhesitatingly during the first three examinations.

After this he became more cautious and less communicative when interrogated as to the crime. From September 10th until after his trial he never volunteered any information to the examiners, and answered only in monosyllables, except to his guards, to whom he talked freely. Leon F. Czolgosz is 34 years old, born of Polish parents at Detroit, Mich., single, 5 feet 7⅝ inches high, weighs 136 pounds, general appearance that of a person in good health, complexion fair, pulse and temperature normal, tongue clean, skin moist and in excellent condition. Pupils normal and react to light, reflexes normal, never had serious illness. He had a common school education, reads and writes well. Does not drink in excess, although drinks beer about every day, uses tobacco moderately, eats well, bowels regular. Shape of head normal, as shown by the diagram obtained by General Bull, Superintendent of Police, with a hatter's impress.

The face is symmetrical, one eyebrow was apparently asymmetrical, and elevated, as it had been cut some years ago by a wire while he was working in a wire factory. There was also a small scar on left cheek due to slight injury while at work.

At our first interview, held September 7th, he made the following statements during a lengthy examination by all three examiners: "I don't believe in the republican form of government and I don't

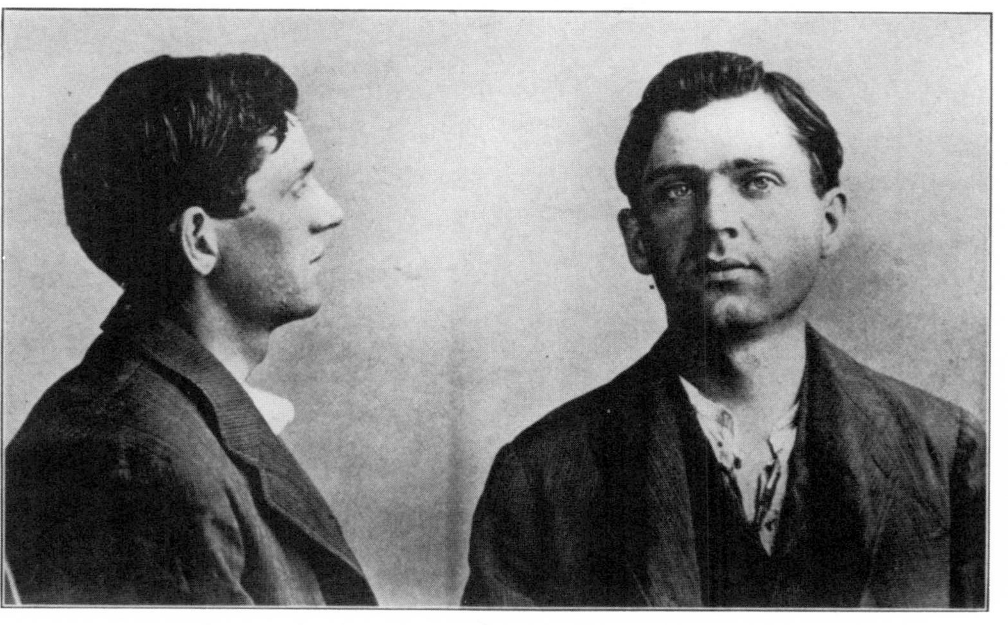

LEON F. CZOLGOSZ

The day after he shot President McKinley.
Correct age 28 years.

believe we should have any rulers. It is right to kill them. I had that idea when I shot the President, and that is why I was there. I planned killing the President three or four days ago, after I came to Buffalo. Something I read in the Free Society suggested the idea. I thought it would be a good thing for the country to kill the President. When I got to the grounds, I waited for the President to go into the Temple. I did not see him go in, but someone told me he had gone in. My gun was in my right pocket with a handkerchief over it. I put my hand in my pocket after I got in the door; took out my gun, and wrapped the handkerchief over my hand. I carried it that way in the row until I got to the President; no one saw me do it. I did not shake hands with him. When I shot him, I fully intended to kill him. I shot twice. I don't know if I would have shot again. I did not want to shoot him at the Falls; it was my plan from the beginning to shoot him in the Temple. I read in the paper that he would have a public reception. I know other men who believe what I do, that it would be a good thing to kill the President and to have no rulers. I have heard that at the meetings in public halls. I heard quite a lot of people talk like that. Emma Goldman was the last one I heard. She said she did not believe in government nor in rulers. She said a good deal more. I don't remember all she said. My family does not believe as I do. I paid $4.50 for my gun. After I shot twice they knocked me down and trampled on me. Somebody hit me in the face. I said to the officer that brought me down 'I done my duty.' I don't believe in voting, it is against my principles. I am an anarchist. I don't believe in marriage. I believe in free love. I fully understood what I was doing when I shot the President. I realized that I was sacrificing my life. I am willing to take the consequences. I have always been a good worker. I worked in a wire mill and could always do as much work as the next man. I saved three or four hundred dollars in five or six years. I know what will happen to me—if the President dies, I will be hung. I want to say to be published—'I killed President McKinley because I done my duty.' I don't believe in one man having so much service and another man having none."

On the second day's examination we covered about the same ground as on the previous day in order to test his memory and to compare his statements. We found his memory perfect, and his statements almost identical. On this examination we gained some further information, that for many months he had been an ardent student of the false doctrines of Anarchy; that he had attended many circles where these subjects were discussed. He related how a friend of his had broken away from the circle because he had changed his views and did not agree with him and the others in their radical ideas of government. He had heard Emma Goldman lecture, and had also heard lectures on free love by an exponent of that doctrine. He had left the Church five years ago, because, as he said, he "did not like their style." He had attended a meeting of anarchists about six week ago, and also in July. Had met a man in Chicago about ten days ago who was an Anarchist and had talked with him. The Friday before the commission of the crime, he had spent in Cleveland, leaving Buffalo, where he had been for two or three weeks, and going to Cleveland. Said he had no particular business in Cleveland. "Just went there to look around and buy a paper."

The circle he belonged to had no name. They called themselves Anarchists. At every meeting they elected a chairman, and usually it was one man (mentions name). "He was a sort of spokesman for the crowd. This friend of mine who left the circle I don't think much of. I don't like a man who changes around like he did. I like a man who has a fixed purpose, and one who sticks to his belief. At this circle we discussed Presidents and that they were no good." During this examination the prisoner was very indignant because his clothing was soiled at the time of his arrest, and he had not had an opportunity to care for his clothing and person as he wished. He refused to demonstrate again how he covered his weapon with a handkerchief, because his was soiled and bloody. When given a clean one he showed at once the method of concealing the weapon, and how he held it. His desire to keep himself tidy demonstrated that he was not careless in dress and appearance as most insane persons are. He requested clean clothing, and as he had a small amount of money a shirt and two handkerchiefs were purchased for him with it. When they were brought in the change was shown him. He instantl turned to the officer and said "How is that? Didn't I get more change?" The cost of the articles was told him, and he said, "Oh, that's all right then." Said he would have slept well last night but for the noise of people walking about. He had heard several drunken people brought into the station at night. Said he felt no remorse for the crime which he had committed. Said he supposed he would be punished, but every man had a chance on a trial; that perhaps he would not be punished so badly after all. His pulse on this occasion was 72; temperature normal; not nervous or excited.

On September 9th we observed a marked change in his readiness to answer questions. Many of the questions asked he refused to answer. He denied that he had killed the President or that he meant to kill him. Seemed more on his guard and refused to admit that he shot the President. He persisted in this course until nearly the close of the interview, and until we told him that it was too late for him to deny statements that he had made to us. He then said "I am glad I did it."

At all subsequent interviews he declined to discuss the crime in any of its details with us, but would talk about his general condition, his meals, his sleep and how much he walked in the corridor of the jail, or upon any other subject not relating to the crime. From the daily reports filed with us, we note that he talked freely; that his appetite was good; that he enjoyed his walks which he took in the corridor of the jail. He told his guards that he would not talk with his lawyers because he did not believe in them and did not want them.

In conclusion, as a result of the frequent examinations of Czolgosz, of the reports of his watchers during his confinement in the jail, of his behavior in court during the trial and at the time he received his sentence, we conclude that he was sane at the time he planned the murder, when he shot the President and when on trial. *We come to this conclusion from the history of his life as it came from him.* He had been sober, industrious and law-abiding until he was twenty-one years of age; he was, as others in his class, a believer in the government of this country and of the religion of his fathers. After he cast his first vote he made the acquaintance of Anarchistic leaders who invited him to their meetings. He was a good listener, and in a short time he adopted their theories. He was consistent in his adherence to anarchy. He did not believe in government, therefore he refused to vote. He did not believe in marriage, because he did not believe in law. He killed the President because he was a ruler, and Czolgosz believed, as he was taught, that all rulers were tyrants; that to kill a ruler would benefit the people. He refused a lawyer because he did not believe in law, lawyers or courts.

We come to the conclusion that in the holding of these views Czolgosz was sane, because these opinions were formed gradually under the influence of Anarchistic leaders and propagandists. In Czolgosz they found a willing and intelligent tool; one who had the courage of his convictions, regardless of personal consequences. We believe that his statement, "I killed the President because I done my duty," was not the expression of an insane delusion, for several reasons. The most careful questioning failed to discover any hallucinations of sight or hearing. He had received no special command; he did not believe he had been specially chosen to do the deed. He always spoke of his motive for the crime as duty; he always referred to the Anarchists' belief that the killing of rulers was a duty. He never claimed the idea of killing the President was original with him, but the method of accomplishing his purpose was his, and he did it alone. He is not a case of paranoia, because he has not systematized delusions reverting to self, and because he is in exceptionally good condition and has an unbroken record of good health. His capacity for labor had always been good and equal to that of his fellows. These facts all tend to prove that the man has an unimpaired mind. He has false beliefs, the result of false teaching and not the result of disease. He is not to be classed as a degenerate, because we do not find the stigmata of degeneration; his skull is symmetrical, his ears do not protrude, nor are they of abnormal size, and his palate not highly arched. Psychically he has not a history of cruelty, or of perverted tastes and habits. He is the product of Anarchy, sane and responsible.

Respectfully,
Joseph Fowler, M.D.
(Signed) Floyd S. Crego, M.D.
James W. Putnam, M.D.

While at Police Headquarters, Czolgosz was in solitary confinement, guarded day and night. He received the same food provided for other prisoners, except that upon the direction of the Police Surgeon after two or three days' confinement his diet was reduced. His breakfast consisted of potato, bread and butter and coffee; his dinner consisted of one kind of meat, one vegetable, bread and butter and coffee; and his supper was the same as breakfast. He had a very keen appetite. He was permitted to use a limited amount of tobacco daily.

On Friday morning, September 13th, at 11 o'clock, Czolgosz was secretly removed from Police Headquarters to the Erie County penitentiary, as the Jail was undergoing repairs. Here he was placed in the Woman's dungeon, and no one in the Penitentiary, with the exception of Mr. Sloan and one or two assistants, knew who was the prisoner confined in that dungeon. He was detained in the Penitentiary until five o'clock on the Monday afternoon following the removal of the President's remains from Buffalo, when he was brought to the Erie County Jail, and from thence conducted through the underground passage to the City and County Hall and arraigned before County Judge Emery. Czolgosz was indicted Monday morning, September 16th, by the Grand Jury then in session, charged with Murder in the First Degree. He was detained in the Erie County Jail until his conviction and then removed to the Auburn State Prison.

Dr. Carlos F. Macdonald of New York, at the request of Mr. Adelbert Moot, President of the Erie County Bar Association in Buffalo, arrived in that city on September 20th, 1901, for the purpose of making an inquiry into the mental condition of Czolgosz, "that he might be accorded every legal right, there being no desire to convict him if he were not mentally responsible." Dr. Macdonald invited Dr. Arthur W. Hurd to examine the prisoner jointly with him. In his report, Dr. Macdonald says:

After our examination of Czolgosz on Sunday, we reached the conclusion, independently of each other, that he was sane; and we so informed his counsel on Monday morning before the trial began. It should be said that, owing to the limited time—two days—at our disposal prior to the trial, and the fact that his family relatives resided in a different State and were not accessible for interrogation, we were unable to obtain a history of his heredity beyond what he himself gave us.

My last examination of Czolgosz was made jointly with Dr. Gerin, physician of Auburn Prison, the evening before his execution. This examination revealed nothing in either his mental or physical condition which tended to alter the opinion I gave his counsel at the time of his trial; namely, that he was sane—an opinion which was concurred in by all the official experts on either side: namely, Drs. Crego, Fowler and Putnam for the people and Dr. Hurd and myself for the defense, also by Dr. Gerin, the only other physician who examined him. Moreover, neither of the three careful personal examinations which I made of him—one alone, one with Dr. Hurd and one with Dr. Gerin—the measurements of his body by the Bertillon System, nor the post-mortem findings, disclosed the slightest evidence of mental disease, defect or degeneracy.

In conclusion, having viewed the case in all its aspects, with due regard to the bearings and significance of every fact and circumstance relative thereto that was *accessible to him,* Dr. McDonald records his opinion "unqualifiedly, that Leon Czolgosz, on September 6th, 1901, when he assassinated President McKinley, was in all respect a sane man, both legally and medically, and fully responsible for his act."

CHAPTER II

TRIAL AND EXECUTION OF CZOLGOSZ

Dr. Macdonald's description of the trial and of the execution is so concise that I will quote it verbatim:

The Trial.—The trial of Czolgosz, which took place in the city of Buffalo, N. Y., on September 23-24, 1901, Hon. Truman C. White, presiding justice, was neither attended by delay "nor harassed by the trivial technicalities of the law." The "machinery of justice" moved so smoothly and so rapidly that the jury was procured, the case tried, and a verdict of guilty rendered within a period of two court days with sessions from 10 to 12 o'clock in the forenoons and 2 to 4 o'clock in the afternoons, the time actually occupied being eight and a half hours in all. The proceedings were marked by no melodramatic or sensational episodes or unseemly wrangle among the counsel; while the fact that, under the extraordinary circumstances, the trial was not anticipated nor interrupted by any riotous demonstration against the prisoner—any attempt at mob or lynch law—when he appeared in public, affords striking proof of the respect for law and order which prevails in the community where the trial was held. Czolgosz was brought into court closely guarded by a double cordon of police and handcuffed to an officer on either side. He was neatly dressed and cleanly in appearance, his face clean shaven and hair neatly combed.

The preparation and trial of the case on the part of the people by the Hon. Thomas Penny, District Attorney, and his assistant, Mr. Haller, was well-nigh faultless. Shortly after his arrest, the District Attorney procured from Czolgosz a statement several pages in length, which was taken down in long-hand, narrative form, each page of which he signed after himself making corrections and revisions as to matters which he claimed the reporter had misapprehended. This statement gave in detail facts concerning his premeditations and preparations for the crime, also his movements for some time prior and up to the shooting. The District Attorney also, within a few hours after the crime was committed, proceeded to put the prisoner under the observation of local experts in mental disease, namely Drs. Joseph Fowler, Police-Surgeon Floyd S. Crego and James W. Putnam. These physicians had free access to him, down to and during the trial—covering a period of nearly three weeks, during which they examined him repeatedly and made a careful study of his case with reference to his mental condition. The District Attorney also permitted the experts on either side to confer together freely, and allowed those for the defense to have free access to all facts and information relative to the case in his possession—a proceeding which in effect was equivalent to the appointment of a commission of five experts, three for the prosecution and two for the defense, to determine the prisoner's mental condition. This course on the part of the District Attorney marks a new departure in the methods of getting expert evidence in criminal trials where the question of mental responsibility is involved, which is to be highly commended as a practical measure, tending to eliminate much superfluous testimony, and at the same time to minimize the danger of contradictory expert opinions.

In view of the great importance of the case, it is regrettable that no experts were called to testify on the trial as to the prisoner's mental condition in order that it might appear on the record of the trial that his mental state was inquired into and determined by competent authority. Had the experts on either side been given the opportunity of thus stating officially their unanimous conclusion, together with the grounds on which it was based and the methods by which it was reached, it would have left in the public mind no reasonable doubt as to its absolute correctness, and that it had been arrived at only by the rules of professional conduct governing the examination of such cases.

The attorneys assigned by the court to the defendant, at the request of the Bar Association of Erie County, were ex-judges Lorin L. Lewis and Robert C. Titus, both prominent lawyers and highly respected citizens of Buffalo. For obvious reasons these gentlemen were reluctant to undertake what they regarded as a most distasteful task, and consented to do so only from a high sense of duty to the public, at the urgent solicitation of the President, Hon. Adelbert Moot, and other prominent members of the Bar Association, on Saturday, September 21st, preceding the trial, which began on Monday, the 23rd.

Respecting the defense, it appears that substantially no preparation was made, beyond a fruitless effort of counsel to confer with the prisoner, and the examinations made of him at their request by Dr. Hurd and the writer, with reference to his mental condition, and a verbal statement by them to counsel of their conclusion that he was not insane. It also appears that no plea was entered by the attorneys for the defense; but Czolgosz, speaking for the first time in court, entered a plea of guilty to the indictment, which plea the court promptly rejected and directed that one of not guilty be entered on the record for the defendant.

Each juror, on qualifying, said in answer to the usual question, that he had formed an opinion as to the guilt of the prisoner, but that his opinion could be removed by reasonable evidence tending to show that the defendant was innocent. And yet, to one accustomed to being in court and observing jurors when qualifying, it was difficult to avoid the impression that each of the jurors in this case held a mental reservation to convict the prisoner. Had Czolgosz been on trial for the murder of a common citizen, instead of the President, it is safe to say that not one of the jury as completed would have been accepted by the defense; and instead of getting a jury in approximately one hour and a half, that feature of the trial alone would probably have occupied several days.

Having in view the nature and importance of the case, the fact that no testimony was offered on the defendant's behalf and that practically no defense was made, beyond a perfunctory examination of jurors and a mild cross-examination of some of the people's witnesses, which was limited to efforts to elicit information respecting the President's condition during his illness and of his body after death, and a summing up by one of the counsel—Judge Lewis—which consisted mainly of an apology for appearing as counsel for the defendant and a touching eulogy of his distinguished victim, renders the case, in this respect, a unique one in the annals of criminal jurisprudence.

The jury retired for deliberation about 4 P.M., and returned in less than half an hour with a verdict of murder in the first degree. Czolgosz heard the verdict of the jury standing, and without appreciable display of emotion. Several of the jurors were reported to have said after the trial, that the jury was in favor of conviction unanimously from the first, and could have rendered a verdict without leaving their seats, but deemed it best to make a pretense at deliberation "for appearance's sake." Czolgosz was remanded to jail for two days, and on Thursday, September 26th, was sentenced to be executed by electricity at Auburn Prison, in the week beginning October 28th, 1901.

When Czolgosz returned to his cell after his conviction he ate a hearty supper, and soon thereafter went to bed and slept continuously until midnight when the guard was changed, when he awoke for a few minutes, and then slept until 6 A.M., when he awoke and took a short walk in the cell corridor, after which he made a careful toilet, and at 7.30 partook of a hearty breakfast. He talked freely, as usual, on ordinary topics, but maintained his usual silence regarding his crime and would not talk of the trial or the verdict. On Thursday, September 26th, he was removed from the Buffalo jail to the State Prison at Auburn, N. Y., where he was confined in a "death cell" until his execution took place.

The Execution.—Czolgosz was executed by electricity on the morning of October 29th, 1901. The official witnesses, consisting of the Superintendent of State Prisons and other prominent New York State officials, several physicians, three representatives of the respective press associations, Mr. Spitzka and others, and the official physicians—Dr. John Gerin, prison physician, and myself—having been assembled in the execution room and having received the usual admonition from the Warden as to the maintenance of order during the execution, the prisoner was conducted to the room a few minutes after 7 A.M. Every precaution was taken by the Warden who had immediate charge of the execution to minimize the opportunity for notoriety or sensationalism on the part of the prisoner, as well as to insure that his taking off should be effected in an orderly and dignified manner.

As Czolgosz entered the room he appeared calm and self-possessed, his head was erect and his face bore an expression of defiant determination. The guards, one on either side, quietly and quickly aided him to the fatal chair, the binding straps were rapidly adjusted to his arms, legs and body, and the head and leg electrodes were quickly placed *in situ* and connected with the wire which was to transmit the lethal current through his body. These preliminaries occupied about one minute. Czolgosz offered no resistance whatever, but during the preparations addressed himself to the witnesses in a clear, distinct voice in the following significant language: "I killed the President because he was the enemy of the good people—the good working people. I am not sorry for my crime. I am sorry I could not see my father." At this moment, everything being in readiness, the Warden signalled the official electrician in charge of the switch, who immediately turned the lever which closed the circuit and shot the deadly current through the criminal's body, which was instantly thrown into a state of tonic spasm, involving, apparently, every fibre of the entire muscular system. At the same time, consciousness, sensation and motion were apparently absolutely abolished.

Two electrical contacts were made, occupying in all one minute and five seconds. In the first contact, the electro-motive pressure was maintained at 1800 volts for seven seconds, then reduced to 300 volts for twenty-three seconds, increased to 1800 volts for four seconds, and again reduced to 300 volts for 26 seconds—one minute in all—when the contact was broken. The second contact, which was made at the instance of the writer as a precautionary measure, but which was probably unnecessary, was maintained at 1800 volts for five seconds. That conscious life was absolutely destroyed the instant the first contact was made, was conceded by all of the medical witnesses present; also that organic life was abolished within a few seconds thereafter.

Czolgosz was pronounced dead by the attending physicians and several of the other physicians present, after personal examination in four minutes from the time he entered the room. One minute of this period, as already stated, was occupied in the preliminary preparations, one minute and five seconds in the electrical contacts, and the remainder of the time in the examinations by the physicians to determine the fact of death. The physicians present at the execution and at the autopsy were Drs. H. O. Ely of Binghamton, N. Y., W. A. Howe of Phelps, N. Y., G. R. Trowbridge of Buffalo, N. Y., W. D. Wolff of Rochester and C. R. Huntley of Buffalo.

Dr. Allan McLane Hamilton says in his Autobiography:

I was sent for by Ainsley Wilcox, the distinguished Buffalo lawyer at whose house the President finally died, and at the request of the District Attorney went to Buffalo on Sunday afternoon. On arriving I found that the three people's experts, and the two physicians retained by the Erie County Bar Association had made up their minds that the prisoner was *sane*. It seems that they were a long time reaching a conclusion, and had made their report only an hour before they heard I was coming to Buffalo. A secret meeting, to which I was not invited, was held that night by the experts with the attorneys of *both* sides, and it was decided to go on with the trial. It really would appear as if everyone had surrendered to the popular clamor for the life of Czolgosz, who was practically friendless and deserted. I was then told that no further examination was necessary, after I had been informed the night before that I was to see the prisoner at nine o'clock on Monday morning. I was, however, permitted to attend the trial, which I did. This was on September 23rd, 1901. I really do not think in all my experience that I have ever seen such a travesty of justice, nor have I heard of such a tribunal, except in the clever *Grand Guignol* little horror of *Les Trois Messieurs du Havre*.

The prisoner was brought into court accompanied by one of his brothers. He was a tall young man with good features, but bore the effects of his ill-usage, for a red scar ran across his face. His was a prepossessing personality, and there was none of the repulsive cunning or ugliness of Guiteau. *He was clearly demented,* though, and seemed to take little or no interest in the proceedings. When made to stand up, he evidently did not understand the nature of the indictment, which was read twice, and he had to be asked twice to plead. Finally, when his coat-tail was pulled by his brother and the hint given, he said in a low voice: "Guilty." This, however, was not received by the judge, who forced him to plead "not guilty" and the latter plea was entered on the records.

AUBURN PRISON (S) (M) (L) AUBURN, N. Y.

Height	1 m 71.4	Head lgth	18.6	L Foot	26.	Class	2	Age 28	Born in 1873
Stretch	1 m 81.	Head width	15.6	L Mid F	11.7	Areola	d m'ay	Apparent Age	id
Trunk	71.1	Cheek width	14.5	L Lit F	9.	Periph	ple ble	Nativity	Mich.
Curve		R Ear lgth	6.3	L Cubit	47.2	Pecul		Occupation	Laborer.

Remarks relative to Measurements

Inc. int	Bridge sec		Border int	Hair ch	Beard id
Hght. med	Base slt cl		Lobe ad. sep	Complexion pig san slt.	
Width. med	Height med	Projection grt	Breadth med	Teeth 5 ab.	Weight 141
Pecul			Chin slt. pro	Build med	

STATE OF NEW YORK.
Office of Superintendent of State Prisons,
BUREAU OF IDENTIFICATION.
Capitol, Albany.

Examined Sept. 29th 1901
By J. W. Ross at Auburn Prison
Re-examined
By at

LEON F. CZOLGOSZ

Just before his execution at Auburn, N. Y.

That this should be done, unless the learned Judge White himself had doubts of the prisoner's sanity, is inconceivable. Then this trial went on. The two superannuated and apparently self-satisfied ex-judges assigned for the defense apologized freely and humbly for *their appearance in behalf of this wretched man,* referred to "the dastardly murder of our martyred President," and really made nothing more than a formal perfunctory effort, if it could be called such. Long and fulsome perorations were indulged in by these remiss members of a great and dignified profession, and others who praised the dead President, and flattered each other, the District Attorney, the presiding Judge, the Medical Faculty of Buffalo and every one else they could think of.

The doctors and surgeons were called upon to tell what they had individually and collectively done for President McKinley, and after a great deal more of this sort of testimony the poor madman was sentenced to death. All through the trial he had appeared absolutely silent and indifferent, and in fact said little before his execution except to reiterate his insane claim that in killing McKinley he had acted only in the interests of the poor man and for the public good. Some of this was the reflex of the yellow journal—some the fruit of the months of insane brooding.

The postmortem examination of Czolgosz was performed by Edward A. Spitzka, under the supervision of Dr. Carlos F. Macdonald, an exhaustive account of which may be found in the New York Medical Record of January 4th, 1902. The results were summed up by saying that Czolgosz was in excellent health at the time of his death, and Spitzka says:

It is a probable fact that certain oft-mentioned aberrations from the normal standard of brain structure are commonly encountered in some criminal or degraded classes of society, and those who have attempted to found a school of degeneracy have attempted to explain crime and social wickedness as due to the "accidental persistence of lower types of human organization." But these structural anomalies, so far as they have been described in the brains of criminals, are too few and too insufficiently corroborated to warrant us in drawing conclusions from them. Various perversions or anomalies of mind may exist in this class without presenting a uniform criminal type, either from the sociologic or the anatomic aspect. Of course, it is far more difficult—and it is impossible in some cases—to establish sanity upon the results of an examination of the brain than it is to establish insanity. It is well known that *some forms of psychosis have absolutely no ascertainable anatomic basis;* and the assumption has been made that these psychoses depend rather upon circulatory and chemical disturbances. So far as this question touches upon the brain and body of Czolgosz, there have been found absolutely none of these conditions of the viscera that could have been at the bottom of any mental derangement. Taking all in all, the verdict must be "Socially diseased and perverted, but not mentally diseased."

CHAPTER III

CZOLGOSZ AT AUBURN, N. Y.—IMPRESSIONS OF THE OFFICERS IN CHARGE OF HIM

My investigation of the case began on January 7th, 1902. I arrived that morning in Auburn, New York, breakfasted at the Osborn House and immediately afterwards repaired to the office of the Chief of Police, Mr. McManus, who with eighteen others had been sent to Buffalo to convey Czolgosz to Auburn immediately after his conviction. He stated that the newspaper reports of the demonstration at the time of the removal were false; that they left Buffalo Jail at 10 P. M., and that no one knew of the move until they arrived at Auburn about three o'clock the following morning. Chief McManus told me that Czolgosz seemed ravenously hungry; that he ate a good supper before leaving Buffalo; that he ate or smoked during the whole trip to Auburn, and that he only stopped chewing or smoking long enough to answer the unimportant questions which were asked him. The jailer from Buffalo sat in the seat with him and he was provided with all the sandwiches and cigars he wanted. He was told by the Buffalo officers that he was a gormandizer, but he kept on eating all the same. The Chief also stated that Czolgosz's brother Waldek and his brother-in-law Frank Bandowski came to Auburn before the execution and stopped at 7 (or 9) Wall St., a boarding house kept by a Polish family with a curious name he could not remember, and that after the execution they all returned to Cleveland, the Overseers of the Poor paying their fares and helping them away. Dr. Gerin said that the night after the autopsy he was called by Waldek to see a man in a room dimly lighted by a kerosene lamp; that until he found the man actually had an injured foot, the surroundings were so suspicious he thought he might have fallen into a trap.

Leaving the office of the Chief of Police, I went to the prison. After I had introduced myself to Warden Mead, he tipped back in his chair and said, "I don't know who you are—how should I? My mouth is shut to you, sir." I then took the ground that what he said was what I had anticipated when I left Boston to make an investigation of Czolgosz's character, temperament and behavior as observed after his arrest, and to learn his history from his relatives and those who knew him before he was arrested; and that the only valuable information that I expected to obtain from many officials in this case would be such as I should be able to get after overcoming such rebuffs as he had given me. He told me that I had no idea "how many scientific men and cranks of all kinds" came to make measurements, take casts of thumbs, palms of hands, etc., of different criminals whom he had in charge, but about whom he could give no information. I talked with him for some time, but he remained obdurate.

During my conversation with him I found that he had not seen the Macdonald-Spitzka medical report, so I returned to my hotel for my copy, which I then showed him. He became interested, but denied having given any information contained therein, and said the

Superintendent must have given the information the physicians obtained, including the report of what Czolgosz had said. He claimed that the only words he had spoken to Macdonald or Spitzka had been to lay down the law to them and tell them what they could not do. He said that at the autopsy he had stationed his most trustworthy guard over them, with instructions to "run them out" if they attempted to secrete or carry away any atom of the remains of Czolgosz; that they both begged hard for the brain or a portion of it, but were disappointed and got nothing. He then showed me the photographic plates taken of Czolgosz shortly before execution, but not printed until afterwards—full face and profile. About this time the Warden told me that he would help me all he could, and gave out for the first time the story of Czolgosz at Auburn.

He told me that when Czolgosz was brought into prison, he shook or shivered, and trembled and went all to pieces; that after the prisoner had been placed in a cell the Warden interviewed him, Mr. Ross taking notes of the interview, which were later filed away at Mr. Ross' house, no copy having been made of them and no record existing at the prison. The Warden said he had made up his mind not to let any reporters or other outside people know Czolgosz had made these statements, and that only once afterwards did Czolgosz say a word which gave them any information about himself, other than to declare that he was an anarchist. This was one day when he asked the Warden when he was going to continue on his journey. The Warden told him that his journey was ended; Czolgosz answered, "I thought I had to go to Sing Sing—is it not

Sing Sing where they do all the electrocuting?" When told that they also electrocuted in Auburn he seemed surprised and said, "In Ohio they only electrocute in one place, Columbus." The Warden then read me a great many of the daily reports of the guards who were over Czolgosz. They were mostly repetitions: that "he rose about seven, walked, dressed, ate his breakfast with apparent relish, having a very large appetite, smoked, took exercise, ate a hearty dinner, smoked two pipes of tobacco, lay down on his cot, ate supper"—always enumerating what he ate—"smoked and retired, invariably maintaining a stolid silence."

Only once of many times when he was left alone with other prisoners to see if he would talk to them did he do so, and this conversation was about snow and other unimportant subjects. The Warden, the guards, the prison physician and others who had come in contact with him all told me that when he was asked any question, even the simplest, he *would not answer them for a long time, during which he was apparently* deep in thought. In answering a question the Warden asked him about his family the Warden said Czolgosz waited at his cell door half an hour before answering.*

* White says in his "Outlines of Psychiatry":

"The awkward and constrained attitude of these (dementia precox) patients makes us feel quite out of touch with them. They seem unnatural—their acts are unpsychological, to coin an expression."

According to Stransky, "there is a certain state of feeling which dominates all conditions of consciousness, a surprising stupidity and apathy, a certain poverty of affect, which is in strong contrast to the clearness which the patient may demonstrate. Cold and passive, without moving so much as an eyelash, without any spontaneous reaction, without expressing a wish, he is oriented as to time and place and person, is conversant with everything going on about him, shows good school knowledge, his memory is faultless, *shows up well in an examination of his intelligence,* and denies feeling sick. However, he shows no longing for freedom or feeling of sadness at his position; these all appear extinguished in him. This coldness produces an unnatural impression. One gets the impression of the dream state in epilepsy, the mental state of which has a certain symptomatic relationship with certain

Warden Mead said that when he asked Czolgosz why he took the name Nieman, the prisoner replied because it was his mother's name. Later he said his mother's name was Nebock, which in English is Nieman.* He said the reason he took an alias was because he had "struck" under his own name and he changed it that he might get work again. He said his mother died over fifteen years ago, and that he had a stepmother whom he could not stand. In 1892, he said, he had put about $400 in a farm of 55 acres that his family had then bought, in the township of Warrensville, four miles from the town itself, which is twelve miles southeast of Cleveland, Ohio. Since then he had drawn out most of his money. The Warden said Czolgosz appeared "way above the ordinary criminal" in many ways. He claimed to have gone to night school in Cleveland, but persisted that he could not write; and all the efforts of the physicians, guards and others to get him to write even his name while in Auburn failed. At one time he asked the guard to write a letter for him and dictated an unimportant dozen lines, addressed to Waldek Czolgosz at Warrensville, Ohio. After dictating these few lines he seemed much affected and did not want to dictate any more. He told the Warden that he had gone west for a time on July 1st, 1901, and

forms of dementia precox." White says cases of dementia precox "frequently complain that their thoughts leave them suddenly when they try to explain themselves, and we note in these cases, often in the midst of conversation, a sudden pause, and then a difficulty in resuming the train of thought. This *thought deprivation,* we have learned from association, is the result of strong emotional content—the flow of thought being inhibited by the presence of strong emotion. We have seen, for instance, how the reaction time is lengthened when an idea is struck with strong emotional coloring."

* This assumed name will be found spelled in various ways in these records, according to the ideas of the various persons interviewed: Nieman, Neiman, Nimen (as Czolgosz himself spelled it), and Niemand. Various accounts of its origin and of his reason for assuming it were also given me.

his brother Waldek also told the officers that Leon was travelling from place to place, that he sent for money at times, but also worked his way, being an expert thresher and skilled in repairing threshing machines. Waldek said that his brother would often disappear from home for five to ten days. The Warden said that Waldek insisted on having the body of his brother, but the Warden told him that he would be mobbed and that he would never be able to take it away from Auburn; when he became convinced of this fact, he signed a release of the body to the Warden.

During my interview of over three hours with Warden Mead, he sent for and introduced to me a number of officers who had had to do with Czolgosz. They were all unanimous as to Czolgosz's secretive attitude and their inability to draw him into conversation or to get him to answer questions, unless he so decided after mature deliberation. The officers thought that his brother-in-law, Frank Bandowski, was an avowed anarchist, and said they had heard him making up a lot of stories, which the reporters were eagerly jotting down. Father Hickey told me that Czolgosz sent for a priest after his arrival in Auburn, but before he could get to him Bandowski had visited him, and after that Czolgosz would not see a priest, but waved him away when he approached. He told the Warden and the guard that if the priest came to his execution he would swear at him, adding, "you see if I don't!" Warden Mead said that he told Czolgosz one day that he was going to send a priest to him, and Czolgosz replied, "If you send a priest down here, I'll smash his head." Mead replied, "I shall send a priest down, and you won't smash but just one head here." The next day the guards reported that he wanted to apologize to Warden Mead for saying he would smash anyone's head. The Warden sent Father Hickey, but Czolgosz would have nothing to say to him. He then sent the Rev. Father Fuchzniski, a Polish priest of Buffalo, who held some conversation with him, but Father Hickey said he never knew what passed between them. The Warden said the other murderers, quartered adjacent to Czolgosz, did not say what the papers reported they said, but they did seem down on him. He said that days passed with no remarks from the prisoner. Warden Mead referred me to Mr. John Nelson Ross, who took all measurements and descriptions of the prisoners at Auburn, and also worked with Davis, who had performed some sixty electrocutions, on the theory that possibly at certain hours of the day or under certain conditions and phases of the moon people die more easily, their resistance being less.

Mr. Ross I found to be a very intelligent young man of about 33, a student. At 12.30 I dined with him and his widowed mother, a typical New England woman, and his four brothers, all fine-looking fellows, industrious and successful. He had completed the measurements and descriptions of about 4,000 men and women, and was then working on Czolgosz's measurements as compared with different classes of criminals. He told me he was finding Czolgosz's measurements above the average and away ahead of any class he had found. He showed me the record of measurements, descriptions and record of scars, etc., he had made on September 27th. He said that for criminal investigations the left side was measured, as it changed less, being used less. His opinion after studying Czolgosz was that he had developed far above his family and surroundings; that he had got into the habit of brooding and had "soured on the whole world." Feeling that he was above his associates and having no other outlet, he had adopted anarchy as a way out of it all.

Mr. Ross and, later, Dr. Gerin, spoke of Czolgosz's fine and rather wavy hair, being the heaviest head of hair they had ever seen; also of the extreme heaviness of his eyes, the upper lid seeming to give a cold or dreamy look—Dr. Gerin said, "He *was* dreamy."

Soon Mr. Ross brought from his room the notes previously referred to, which he had made during Warden Mead's interview, and which, so far as is known, contain the only statement that Czolgosz made at Auburn concerning his history. The statement reads that:

He was born in Alpena, Michigan, in 1873, where he resided until he was five years of age, when he removed to Detroit, where he resided eleven years, when he went to Netrolia, Pennsylvania, near Pittsburg, where he worked in a diamond factory (he afterwards said glass factory) for one year and nine months, when he went to Warrenville, Ohio, where he invested his earnings with his family in a farm and worked on it for a time. It was afterwards sold, and he resided in Cleveland until July 1st, 1901, when he left there. He also spoke of being in Cleveland first and then going to Warrenville and returning to Cleveland. Of his family he said his own mother's name was "——— Nebock," his stepmother's name Catarina ———.

His father's name	Paul	age	59
" brother's "	Waldek	"	34, unmarried
" " "	Frank	"	32, "
" " "	Joseph	" abt.	30, "
Himself	Leon F.	"	28, "
His brother's name	John	"	— "
" " "	Jacob	"	23, married
" sister's "	Ceceli	"	— " Frank Bandowski, 7 yrs. ago.
" brother's "	Michael	"	21, unmarried
" sister's "	Victoria	"	18, "

The above by his own mother, Paul's first wife. He (Paul) had also by his second wife two children, Charles and Antoine.

Dr. John Gerin, of 68 North St., Auburn, N. Y., was prison physician to the 1,100 prisoners who were then confined in Auburn. He was also deeply interested in the study of defective children and had become convinced that in the prevention of crime we have got to begin by training the child. He spoke of his belief that Leon was far above his family in intelligence, judging from his brother Waldek and what he could learn from him of the rest of the family. He spoke of Leon's reticence and said he gleaned nothing from his visits to the prisoner except once, when Leon asked him to send a priest immediately. The Warden was out, but when he returned and sent a priest, Czolgosz would not see him, and *a smile played about his lips.* Dr. Gerin said he felt sure Czolgosz would have seen the priest if he had come at once. Warden Mead was quite provoked and told Czolgosz that the prison officials were not in the habit of running errands for prisoners.

Dr. Gerin said—and this was corroborated by Warden Mead and Mr. Ross—that, contrary to all published reports, Czolgosz went all to pieces at the hour of execution, and that his face was the picture of abject terror. Dr. Gerin said he was filled with fear and showed it. Warden Mead said the guards had virtually to carry him to the chair, he so nearly collapsed. The Warden said so many different reports had appeared—many emanating from those present at the execution—purporting to be what Czolgosz had said at the last moment, that he would ask Mr. Ross to give me verbatim what he took down in shorthand, which was absolutely correct. It seems Czolgosz had wanted to make a public anarchistic speech from the scaffold. The Warden said he had learned of this the night before, when at twelve o'clock, for some reason which he did not remember, he had gone to Czolgosz's cell. The prisoner then told him he had something to say; Mead replied that he would never have a better opportunity than at that time, and Czolgosz said he wanted to make his statement before all the people when he was going to the chair. The Warden replied that this would be impossible, and Czolgosz then resumed his sullen, ugly mood and refused to talk any more. Just as he reached the platform he started to make, as the Warden thought, his anarchistic speech, but was hurried to the chair and the straps were placed on his face and chin while he was yet talking, the last sentence being rather mumbled than spoken. This is just what he said, as reported by Mr. Ross:

"I shot the President because I thought it would help the working people and for the sake of the common people. I am not sorry for my crime." He was then seated in the chair and said "That is all I have to say." Just as the straps were being adjusted to his head and chin, he mumbled "I'm awfully sorry because I did not see my father."

Having exhausted the information obtainable at Auburn, I left for Buffalo. There I hired a carriage and interpreter and drove to the center of a district which is inhabited by many thousand Poles, living in small one-story or story-and-a-half houses, unpainted and disorderly inside and out. My object was to obtain an interview with the Polish priest, the Rev. Hyacinth Fudzinski, Rector of Corpus Christi Church, corner of Clark and Kent Streets. He was away in Syracuse; the two priests I found said they knew Father Fudzinski had interviewed Czolgosz, but that he had never told either of them anything about it. I subsequently wrote to Fr. Fudzinski, but received no reply to my letter.

CHAPTER IV

CZOLGOSZ IN BUFFALO, N. Y., PRISON—HIS LIFE AT WEST SENECA, N. Y., JUST BEFORE THE CRIME. A VISIT TO CZOLGOSZ'S BIRTHPLACE, DETROIT, MICHIGAN

The next morning after arriving in Buffalo I presented myself at Police Headquarters, where I met Superintendent William S. Bull, who gave me all the information he could in regard to Czolgosz, and did everything in his power to assist me in my investigation. He believed that Czolgosz was an anarchist and that he had been guided by others in all he did.

Chief Bull said that, after the arrest of Czolgosz, he was brought to Headquarters, arriving there just before five. He was covered with dirt and some blood from the rough usage he had received by being trampled on by the crowd. He was "grouty," and *not disposed to talk until he had been given something to eat. He ate all that was given him and then seemed more pleasant and willing to talk.* He talked freely, saying that he had killed the President and was glad that he had done it. He was told that the President was not dead at that time, but afterwards the condition of the President was kept from him, and he did not know the result of his shots for a long time. When asked if he knew the enormity of his crime and its results, he said that he did, but that he knew people sometimes escape being hung and that he might also escape.

Bull said that Czolgosz told him that he came to Buffalo on August 29th; that he was with the President at Niagara, and had an opportunity to kill him then and also at the Fair Grounds the day before he committed the crime, but that he had planned to kill the President on that day, so he carried out his plan. He held his head high and seemed rather haughty, *was much disturbed at his clothing being so soiled; one of the first things he asked was that he be allowed to wash up and change his clothes.* This request was denied him until later, when he was told that one of the guards would get him some fresh clothes if he would furnish the money, which he did. When the clothes were brought he disputed the change, but on being told the cost of each article he said "Oh, that's all right. Let it go." He spoke of Emma Goldman in rather a touching way, and Chief Bull said it was plain to anyone who heard him talk about Emma Goldman that he was in love with her. During this interview and at other times while being interviewed during his whole stay in Buffalo, he would take his handkerchief from his pocket and wind it around his hand as he had done when he concealed the revolver to shoot the President. He would fold the handkerchief over his hand when talking, in an absent-minded way, as if he did not know what he was doing but was doing it from force of habit. Also, while he was walking in the cell the guard would see him sometimes apparently thinking deeply and at the same time folding the handkerchief over his right hand. After his arrest he was asked by the Chief to illustrate how he used the handkerchief and he rather dramatically showed them what he had evidently practiced a long time.

The Assistant District Attorney, Mr. Haller, came at once to Headquarters and took down Czolgosz's so-called confession, which was a statement of why he killed the President, a very brief account of his movements prior to the deed and a still shorter account of his life. This, the Chief said, had never been seen by anyone outside and had been taken away by Mr. Haller; among other things the prisoner had said that he had once been in love with a girl who went back on him, since which time he had had nothing to do with women; that he had left home because his stepmother was very unkind to him; that on July 1st, 1901, he had left Cleveland for Chicago and that he had spent most of his time since then in Chicago and Buffalo; that on August 30th he had returned to Cleveland for a paper published by the anarchists; that he had boarded for a time in West Seneca, but that *he did not like the food nor the cooking* and had come to town for his meals. He said that he did not wish to see any of his relatives nor any lawyers, as he did not believe in courts—that he did not believe in rulers or judges; and he gave instructions to tell any callers who might come that he did not wish to see them. In this he was consistent; neither did he want to see any priest, absolutely refusing to do so, and he did not see any priest in Buffalo.

At nine o'clock he was taken to his cell, very indignant that *he was not allowed to wash up.* About ten, the District Attorney, who had hastened to the Fair Grounds on the report of the assassination, arrived at Police Headquarters with his assistant Mr. Haller, who had previously taken down Czolgosz's confession. The District Attorney, Mr. Penny, then read over the confession to him, asking him to sign each page. Czolgosz was very particular how it was worded, and made many corrections in a seemingly interested and absorbed manner. At one time he took a pencil, and drawing it through a line or more of the statement, said "I never said that." Indeed he denied a good deal of what had been written down by Mr. Haller in long hand. After the confession had been corrected to his satisfaction, he signed each page in a very fair hand, writing very quickly. Later he denied that he could write even his name and he would not write another word for anybody during his confinement in Buffalo. This interview lasted until about one o'clock.

When the prisoner wanted his clothes badly enough, he told where he had been living, which was at the hotel over the saloon run by John Nowak on Broadway, near Fillmore Street and opposite the Market, and it was found that his baggage consisted of a "telescope" with some clean clothes in it and two early pictures of himself. Chief Bull had forgotten where Czolgosz had lived in West Seneca and had no record of it, and the detective he had sent there was at that time away on another case. One of the photographs found with Czolgosz's clothing had been given by Chief Bull to a Mr. Quackenboss, a lawyer of Buffalo, and the other had been loaned to a New York paper which had never returned it. Czolgosz was *quite indignant to think that these had been taken from him.*

He talked freely for three days, after which he would not open his mouth on any subject connected with the assassination, although he talked freely with the guards on other subjects—such as Anarchy, little incidents of no moment which had occurred during his life, places where he had worked, the scar which he had got while working in a wire factory—and discussing other prisoners brought to Headquarters, etc. Chief Bull let me read some of the reports of the guards in charge of him; they were of no special importance, though the first two were rather interesting. These said that on September 9th he walked his cell most of the morning; after dinner he asked the guard to hang his coat and vest outside while he lay down on his cot; that evening at eleven o'clock it was reported that he had a nosebleed for about two minutes, when he lay down and it seemed better. The night of September 8th *he said the noise of the insane people over him kept him awake.*

It was denied that the third degree was given Czolgosz, or that he had been ill, with the exception of a cold. After being confined a few days he was secreted away in the jail, no one but the Chief and one or two detectives knowing where he was. Crowds were about Headquarters, sometimes numbering as many as 2000 persons. While in West Seneca, Czolgosz had received from Cleveland a $10 money order, under another name. The police of Cleveland were written to, and they also wrote to San Francisco, but without results in either case. The chief said the prisoner had received no letters nor telegrams of any consequence from either Battle Creek or Indianapolis, but that thousands of letters had come to him from all over the country containing advice, threats, etc. During Czolgosz's confinement, the Chief said, he had been *most immaculate about his dress and person, washing himself and "fixing" himself a good deal of the time;* he would eat all that was given him, and had a little beer each day. The prisoner was also allowed two or three cigars a day. They were never able to obtain from him any information which would prove where he had spent his time from July 1st, excepting such as was accounted for in Buffalo. They did not know what he had done nor where he had spent his time when away from his boarding places in Buffalo and West Seneca; it was at the time when thousands were visiting the city on account of the Fair, and it had been impossible to trace any one particular person with so many strangers about. No one saw him during his confinement in Buffalo, except the examining physicians, the District Attorney and his Assistant, and the prison physician; and his own counsel he saw only when virtually forced to do so. He did not want any counsel and said he did not believe in courts. His description and measurements, taken at the time, were as follows: "Age 28; height 5 ft. 7⅝ inches; weight 138 lbs.; build medium; hair brown; eyes blue; complexion medium; born Detroit, Mich.; occupation wire worker; scar on left cheek; arrested Sept. 6th, 1901." You will note that his weight taken at Auburn Prison was 141 lbs. on September 22nd, a gain of three pounds in two weeks. His measurements were "Outer arm 79.9; trunk 90.0; head length 18.7; head width 15.6; right ear length 6.4; left foot 26.1; left middle finger 11.7; left little finger 9.1; left forearm, measured from olecranon process to tip of middle finger, 47.3."

I interviewed District Attorney Penny who had taken down Czolgosz's confession, but who refused to show me his notes. He said that the prisoner's story was so conflicting that one could not be sure of anything in it, but that Czolgosz had told him that he had earned the money, on which he had been living since July 1st, and which he had previously invested in a farm, working in a wire factory in Cleveland; that he had been in West Seneca in July, and that he would not acknowledge having been west of Chicago; and that he stated why he had killed the President. He had barely recited the facts of his early life; he did not mention Netrolia nor say much about his family. Penny said that when his father, brother and sister came Czolgosz said he did not wish to see them, and that he, Penny, did not glean any information from them. Penny stated very plainly that he wished to say as little as possible—that he believed that any writing or talking on this matter only kept it before the public and that it had been his plan to suppress all that was possible, believing as he did that Czolgosz was sane and an anarchist without question. He said he had refused Dr. Macdonald permission to use the confession in his report.

I next interviewed Dr. Fowler, Prison physician, who resided at 131 Delaware Avenue, Buffalo. He said that he had been present when both examinations of Czolgosz had been made and when he made his confession. He gave me a printed report which he said contained almost every word of the confession, that is all of importance was embodied in this report; it contained all that Czolgosz had said to Dr. Fowler which had any bearing on the case, and had been made up by the three physicians, each pledging himself not to give any of its contents to the public until it came out officially signed by the three. He said Dr. Putnam had broken his promise and allowed himself to be interviewed, when the report was immediately put forth. Dr. Fowler implied that the reason why District Attorney Penny did not give the confession to Dr. Macdonald and therefore could not give it to anyone else was because Mr. Penny had requested that Dr. Fowler and one other expert should be invited to the electrocution. Fowler explained that, as he had been on the Grounds and had heard the shots, was at the Hospital before the President arrived there and had seen Czolgosz at least once a day during his confinement in Buffalo (excepting the five days when he had been in the jail, but when Fowler only knew he had been spirited away somewhere) he naturally wanted to see the case to a finish. Dr. Macdonald had promised to bring it about, but the evening before the electrocution—which took place at seven o'clock in the morning—he sent word to Fowler that he was sorry he could not do so. Dr. Fowler said: "As Macdonald had the power to place me on that jury and could have acceded to the District Attorney's request, why should the District Attorney give him any papers to look at?"

Fowler spoke of Czolgosz's *extreme cleanliness;* told how his hair was dishevelled for two or three days because he had no comb and brush and said that every time he visited Czolgosz the latter asked if he might not have these articles, and that he had promised them just before the prisoner was spirited away; and he said that the only thing he had heard that Czolgosz had said during those five days was that the guard had told him that Czolgosz had asked several times "Where is the brush and those cigars that Dr. Fowler promised me?" Dr. Fowler said he was *particular about his milk being clear, also the water he drank.* He spoke of his winding a handkerchief about his hand frequently while the doctor was talking with him. For the first three days Dr. Fowler said he had talked about his crime and how his stepmother worried him; but when the physicians came to examine him and first asked why he shot the President, he immediately assumed a different air and said "Did I shoot the President?" Later in the same interview he acknowledged the shooting and made statements which I have given in the report of the experts.

Having information that District Attorney Penny's office had Czolgosz's West Seneca address and that it could not be obtained elsewhere, I next interviewed Assistant District Attorney Haller, who had nothing new to tell me about Czolgosz, except his own opinion, which was that Czolgosz never read very much and that he believed he was a man who went to meetings and listened to what people said. After considerable search among the papers of the office, he found the address of Antoine Kazmarek, Ridge Road, West Seneca, which he said was the place where Czolgosz had stayed for a time.

With an interpreter, I drove to West Seneca. Leaving the city, we passed through a farming country, acres and acres of which were covered with stubble from which corn had been cut. We also passed through one or two villages or settlements, and arriving at Ridge Road, we located the house where Kazmarek had lived, but found that the Kazmarek family had moved still further away from the city; and we proceeded through a blinding snowstorm along Center Street, but were not able to reach their new residence except on foot. Crossing a ploughed field we found the Kazmareks soon after dusk in a new white house of four rooms, and dimly lighted by a kerosene lamp. On making known my errand, I was given a chair near the stove in the center of a room about ten feet

July 14. 1901

Dear Sir I am writing a few lines to you about me I am on the road to west. it is hard for me to tell you where will i be so i will write again

hoping this will find you well as it leaves me at present I remain yours.

Leon F Czolgosz

LEON F. CZOLGOSZ

Photograph taken in 1900 found among his effects at Buffalo. Letter written about the time he arrived in Buffalo.

square. In this room were three children climbing over each other on the floor, a mother nursing her baby, a young couple wooing in the corner, two strange men, and behind the stove, sitting on a trunk, were Antoine Kazmarek and a Polish friend. Near them was a bright boy of seven, the son of Antoine.

I found Antoine could speak English, and when I questioned him he said that one day about the 16th or 17th of July, when he and the Polish friend then sitting beside him were waiting for a street-car in Buffalo, a well-dressed young man stopped near them and passed the time of day and asked the Pole where he lived. The latter replied that he boarded out in the country with Kazmarek. The young man said that he *wanted to go out in the country where it was healthy*—that he did not like the city—and asked if he could get board at the same place. Kazmarek told him yes, if he had the money. The stranger then asked them to go with him to a saloon, where they had a glass of beer, after which they went home to West Seneca. On arriving at the house the stranger gave his name as Fred C. Neiman, and made arrangements with Mrs. Kazmarek to lodge him and do his washing for three dollars a month, providing he would sleep with the Polish friend. The Pole, evidently not understanding English, had retired to a corner soon after our conversation began, where he was sitting with his hands folded and his eyes shut as if about to go to sleep, when I requested Kazmarek to ask him if Neiman's sleep had seemed disturbed. He answered that he slept very well, occasionally getting up in the night, only to return immediately. The little boy spoke up and said that he had slept with Nieman and that

Nieman never disturbed him nights. Kazmarek said that Nieman boarded himself—that *he never would eat with them; that he lived on milk and crackers.* The house had been at one time used for a store; Nieman would send the little boy out for milk, which he would then take to the front room of the house, where he would eat by himself on the counter. He did not associate with the family, and when urged to join them, especially at meal times, he always refused—and one time he said he did *not wish to eat with "those fellows"* —referring to the other boarders. Kazmarek said Nieman usually rose before seven, *"washed very carefully, dressed neatly—would come downstairs, stand before the glass for a minute or two, looking at himself first on one side then on the other,"* rearrange his collar and necktie and brush any spots off his clothing.*

Kazmarek said that the days Czolgosz spent out there were generally passed as follows: He usually took a little walk in the morning; returning he would sit on the piazza with his chair tipped back, reading pamphlets and papers; early in the afternoon he hired the little boy to bring him a paper which he read very carefully; and he retired about ten each night. He kept

* Dr. William A. White, of the Government Hospital for the Insane, says in his "Outlines of Psychiatry," speaking of simple dementia:

". . . In addition, peculiarities of conduct and strange habits develop, the desire to be alone, some mannerism or slight evidences of muscular tension and simpler manifestations of negativism. . . . A study of this class shows quite frequently that the patient's resort to a hobo type of existence has been the result of his inability to adapt himself to the ordinarily complex conditions of social life—in other words, that he has slipped from under all responsibilities and all conditions which involved continuity of effort and industry. He goes from one position to another, unable to fulfill even the simplest duties because of his lack of continuity and interest. Such cases will show the history of a mild attack, with perhaps the development of a dilapidated and incoherent delusional system which subsides and remains dormant when the patient gets away from stress. Such patients, when they find themselves under conditions of stress that they can not escape from . . . quite frequently break down and have to be sent to a hospital."

by himself and away from the family as much as possible and never had any conversation with them unless obliged to do so. *He never ate once with them.* Three or four times a week he left quite early for Buffalo, returning at half-past nine to half-past ten at night. When asked why he went to the city so often, he said to attend some meetings. Antoine asked him how he got along without working, to which he replied that he worked in the winter and lived in the summer on what he had earned. Antoine said he always wore his Sunday clothes when he went to Buffalo, but on further questioning I found that Nieman had only one suit of clothes, and that Antoine meant that he dressed or tidied up more than usual. When Nieman had come to the house he had with him a little canvas trunk, as they called the "telescope," which contained his belongings. At the end of one month he paid three dollars. It was a little over two weeks later when Antoine, on coming downstairs one morning at seven o'clock, found Nieman arranging his collar, etc., before the glass, with his canvas bag packed and ready beside him. He told Antoine he was going to leave—Antoine thinks this was about August 29th. Instead of being as usual very quiet in deep thought or study, *he seemed in very good spirits,* and when asked where he was going said "Maybe Detroit, Toledo, Cleveland or Baltimore—maybe Pittsburg." When Mrs. Kazmarek asked for a settlement, Nieman said he could not pay the $1.75 then due, but finally left them a revolver which he had with him for settlement. This revolver Antoine said he had turned over to the police at their request, and had never received it back—nor the $1.75. Antoine said they looked upon Nieman as a rather strange young man, and wondered how he got along without working; that neither from his actions nor from anything he said had they suspected he was going to leave them; and they thought he seemed *too proud to carry his bag*—he paid the boy ten cents to carry it for him. Kazmarek added that he never saw Nieman take a drink, that he never swore and that he smoked only in moderation.

It is probable that Nieman left Kazmarek's on August 31st instead of the 29th, as on the former date he took a room at John Nowak's where his things were found by the police after his arrest when his desire for clean clothes induced him to give them his address. Dr. Fowler told me that he had asked Czolgosz if he wanted to see Nowak, and he had replied "No, he is nothing but an old pumpkin-head and does not know anything anyway."

Returning to Buffalo, I called on John Nowak and his wife at their saloon on Broadway. Nowak told me that a strange young man had come into his saloon on August 31st and said that he wanted to engage a room and to have his washing done. When asked, as was their custom, for recommendations, he said "Oh, Dalkowski of Toledo told me to come here—You know—he left last night." Nowak said this was true, and that he believed the man to be a friend of Dalkowski's, who was in the Post Office service in Toledo, and was in the habit of stopping with Nowak when he came to Buffalo to attend certain "singing conventions." The stranger gave his name as Fred Nieman. Nowak said that after the assassination he had written to Dalkowski, who replied that he had never heard of anyone by the name of Nieman or Czolgosz. Evidently Nieman was an enigma to John Nowak and his wife. Mrs. Nowak told me that they at one time decided he must be a waiter or a barber, *he dressed so neatly,* and at another time they decided he was a visitor at the Fair—only his hours seemed too regular—that he usually left at seven in the morning and returned about ten-thirty at night, retiring immediately; that she and her husband had often talked him over, and that she *thought him too proud to speak to them;* that if he did not go out he remained in his room, but *they never knew where he got his meals.* Only one night when he went out did he come home early, and this was the only time he sat down in the saloon. It was on a Sunday evening; a picnic was going on and a great many people were about. He sat at a table and listened. Finally one of the picnickers told Nowak he did not believe much in priests, and said "If you have got any money it is all right with them—if you haven't they have no use for you." After listening to this kind of talk for awhile, Nieman spoke up and said that he had been at St. Casimir's on Sunday morning, and *"all the priests talked about was money."* This ended his conversation, and Nowak said that Nieman only drank one or two beers with him and that he had been very proud to have a boarder—and so young a man—who was so temperate. After the assassination the police notified Nowak, he said, that they wanted Nieman's "telescope" and asked a great many questions which neither he nor his wife could answer.

As there was nothing more to be learned from John Nowak and his wife, I returned to my hotel and prepared to take my departure from Buffalo. I left by the 1.40 A. M. train for Detroit, Michigan, where I arrived about eight o'clock in the morning on January 9th.

After I had made a few inquiries, I proceeded to the village of Howlett in the town of Greenfield, south of Detroit. Here I called upon a Mr. J. T. Kerr, who lived in a nice little new house in the middle of a field about five miles from the city limits. He had just returned with his bride from Alpena, Michigan. Mrs. Kerr had lived within two blocks of the former home of the Czolgosz family. Kerr was a photographer, and he gave me views of the house in Detroit where Czolgosz was born and of another house in Sable St., Alpena, where the Czolgosz family had once resided. In response to my inquiries, he told me that Czolgosz had a brother Frank, now living in Metz township, Presqu' Isle County; that an aunt, Mary Czolgosz, was living with her husband, John Nowak, at 515 Lake Avenue, Alpena; that Andrew Kakubiak, a well-known Polish business man of Alpena, had told him that Paul Czolgosz, the father of Leon, was a law-abiding citizen. He said that Paul Czolgosz had a brother John, a blacksmith, who lived in Krakow, Presqu' Isle township; this John had said that Paul Czolgosz was born in the Province of Posen, Krais Schubin (or County) of Bromberg, village of Haido, near Barin. Kerr said that he had heard in Alpena a German priest had founded a settlement at Posen, Michigan, over which he had ruled with an iron hand, making people work under him like slaves. One day these people had rebelled and a party of them had raided and killed the priest; it was said that Paul Czolgosz had been of this party.

I took Mr. Kerr with me as guide to show me the

section of Detroit in which Czolgosz had been born and had lived. We went to their house at 141 Benton St., of which Kerr had taken a photograph. There had been very few houses in the Parish when the Czolgosz family lived there; theirs was one of the only two brick houses—a coal store had been built in front of it since they had left. They had occupied the first floor and a family named Smith the second. A Mrs. Mincel and her mother Mrs. Munro, who owned the house, had lived on the third floor. Mrs. Mincel had since moved to 344 Elliott St., and I interviewed her there.

She remembered the Czolgosz family perfectly well—a man and wife and four children, two of whom had been born there, one being the boy "Leo," born she thinks about 1874, which was the year she was married. The Czolgoszes were a law-abiding family; the man worked in the city sewers and his wife took in washing.

After unimportant interviews with Mrs. Mincel and others, I called on Jacob J. Lorkowski, at 894 Hastings St., who had lived opposite the Czolgosz family on Benton St. He came from Prussia, near the town of Zninn, the name of which he wrote out for me, saying that Paul Czolgosz had come from the same town. He thought that Paul had come to Detroit before the Chicago fire and had moved to Alpena when his first wife died; he had visited Detroit again for a month about fourteen years ago. Lorkowski described Paul Czolgosz as "foxy"—a good story-teller, who played cards and gambled a little, but did not drink much and was a hard-working laborer. He just remembered that there were children in the family. He said they belonged to the Parish of St. Alberta, and that Leon had been baptized under the name Czolcholski—but he seemed to have no authority for this statement. On inquiry I was informed that three priests had searched the Parish Records without success for three days and two nights to find any name which could be interpreted as belonging to a member of the Czolgosz family, and sisters who had been teaching in the Parochial School for thirty years said they had no memory of this family.

Through an interpreter I interviewed all the neighbors, scarcely one of whom spoke a word of English. It was a large settlement which had grown from a very small once since Czolgosz lived there. Returning to the town, I searched the public records and the directories for thirty years back, but without avail.

I then called upon the Superintendent of Police, Downey, whom I found very pleasant but of no help whatever in my search, as he scarcely knew that the Czolgoszes had ever lived in Detroit. He sent for the chief of the detective force, McDonnell, who said he believed the family had lived in Detroit at one time, but he did not know where, and he had no information to give me about them.

I interviewed Dr. G. H. Shelton, who lived on Rowland Street, between Grand River Avenue and State Street. He told me that he had practiced in Alpena from 1872 to 1885 and that he had attended the Czolgosz family in a house on the Lake Shore in Posen, which was afterwards burned, as well as on Sable Street in Alpena. They were a hard-working family, good wage earners, and paid him promptly. He thought he remembered the father playing cards in Alpena, but said he did not consider him a gambler as most Poles were card players; Czolgosz worked in the lumber yard and the Gilchrist Lumber Mill.

I returned to Chief McDonnell, who searched the police records for some years back, but was unable to give me any further information of the Czolgosz family. William McGregor, the County Clerk, said that he had searched the records again and again for any mention of them, but without success.

I left Detroit on the 8.40 P. M. train and arrived in Cleveland at 8.30 the next morning. This was the first of my two visits to Cleveland on this case, both of which are covered in the following chapter.

CHAPTER V

HISTORY OF CZOLGOSZ'S LIFE IN OHIO—HIS BREAKDOWN IN 1897 CAUSING HIM TO LEAVE HIS POSITION AT CLEVELAND. SICK BENEFIT RECEIVED. HIS LIFE ON THE FARM AT WARREN, OHIO. HIS SUDDEN DEPARTURE FROM HOME

A little after nine o'clock on the morning of my arrival in Cleveland, O., I presented my letter of introduction from Chief Watts of Boston to Superintendent of Police George E. Corner. *Superintendent Corner positively stated that he had been unable to connect Czolgosz with Anarchists.* When asked about Emil Schilling and Walter C. Behlen of the Liberty Association, to whom we shall refer later, he said he had some weeks previously broken up a meeting which had been organized and was being conducted by Behlen and that since that time Behlen had not wanted to have anything to do with him. Corner* said that he believed Czolgosz had been out of health; that he had gone west and was getting homesick, but did not want either to remain where he was or go back, after having left for his health, so he went to the Buffalo Exposition because the fares were cheap. After he got there, Corner thought he read in the newspapers that McKinley was coming, and wanting to do something to make himself *grand in the eyes of the world*—and perhaps before

* Corner was at one time Superintendent of a Hospital for the Insane.

the Anarchists—he had conceived the idea of assassinating the President. Corner said that the Golden Eagle Society, to which Czolgosz belonged, was a purely beneficial society and in no way anarchistic.

Through Superintendent Corner, I met members of the staff of the "Waechter Anzeiger," whose office was at 290 Seneca Street. They provided me with an interpreter, Dr. Ludwig Darmstadter. With him I then went to the Wiedenthal Photo Company, 204 Ontario Street, who on September 2nd, 1899, had taken the photographs found in Leon's bag, and I ordered copies of them after first having arranged to have the plates washed to eliminate the retouching, so that a truer likeness could be obtained from the negative.

We then visited the Polish settlement at Newburg, which is a suburb incorporated within the city and is the center of the Polish district. I first went to the residence of Leon's father, Paul Czolgosz, at 306 Fleet Street. On entering the house I found everything in confusion, the furniture piled up in the process of moving. The only members of the family at home were the daughter Victoria, and the two children of the stepmother who, I should judge, were about three and five years old, chubby, healthy-looking children, not showing the characteristics which I later observed in the children of the first wife, but rather those of their own mother.

Victoria said they were that day moving to 317 Kenyon Street, where her father had bought a house. She was a comely girl with light hair, fair skin, hazel eyes and a well-developed figure. The bridge of her somewhat retroussé nose was flattened and looked as if it might have been injured by an accident.

She was rather reserved in her answers at first, but finally told us that her father was now working in the city street department. He had applied for work on September 7th and had been told to come back on the following Monday morning. She said that at about this time he had heard of the act of his son; this was the first news he had had from Leon since the latter left home, with the exception of one letter which had come from Ft. Wayne, Indiana, a few days after his departure from Cleveland and which, if it still existed, she had not now in her possession. Victoria said she had been born in Alpena and was then eighteen years of age; John, aged 22, and Selia, aged 24, had also been born in Alpena; while Leon, who she thought would have been about twenty-five years old, had been born in Detroit; the family had left Detroit about twenty years ago and had lived in Posen, Michigan, for three or four years until her mother had died about sixteen years ago, when she (Victoria) was two years of age. She said her mother's maiden name was Mary Novak; after the mother's death they had moved to Alpena, where they had lived for three years; a year and a half after her mother's death her father had married Katren Metzfaltr; at that time he had been working on a boat.

Our conversation was here interrupted by the return of the team for the furniture, and Paul Czolgosz, his wife and his son Jacob came in. All seemed more or less confused and did not wish to discuss matters in any way. They did not stop their work, but continued loading furniture, paying little attention to the questions with which I was plying Victoria, except to try to get her to help them. While they were still busy, I got Victoria to ask her stepmother, a woman of medium size with a rather red face without much expression, some questions, from which I gleaned the following:

There had been no mills in Alpena when they were there; Leon had attended the parochial school, and the name of the priest was Sklizek; Leon had afterwards gone to the public school for a short time, but had been taken from school when they left Alpena for Netronia and after a little time had started to work there in the glass factory; after having lived a year and nine months in Netronia they had come to Cleveland.

Victoria described her brother as a nice boy (but rather lazy), of whom she had been very fond. She said *he would read and sleep a good deal of the time;* that *he would not eat with the rest of the family; that he was unable to work* on account of his health, but was fond of gunning. She told me that he could not get along with his stepmother; they were always nagging each other; he never swore, but he came pretty near it in talking to her. She also said he did not drink nor smoke very much and that *he did not like to be around with people—he preferred being alone.* Victoria had formerly been a waitress in a hotel in some other city but had come home when she heard the news about Leon. It is said that she had left home, as did Leon—simply went off. There were other members of the family also who had not been heard of for years, nor were their whereabouts known.

The father, Paul Czolgosz, was a rather rough-looking man. I saw but little of him at this time, but had a better opportunity to observe him the following day, and the result of my observation of him is as follows:

He had dark brown hair mixed with grey; moustache much the same, heavy on a prominent upper lip; heavy eyebrows that gave the eyes a sunken appearance, although they were really not so. The eyes were blue, pupils contracted. He had a habit of winking slowly, sitting perfectly immobile—while posing for his picture I think he did not move a hair's breadth in four or five minutes. His skin was rough and furrowed; his ears were heavy, developed backwards, and standing out from his head, with a great deal of hair on the tragus. The angle of his head was about 50 or 60 degrees, so that when he put his hat on it set well back on his head and down behind his ears. His lower jaw and that of his son Waldek show an arrest of development, the father's being weaker on the right side, producing an asymmetrical chin, flattened in front—almost drawn in. His nose (and that of every one of the children whom I saw later, by the first wife) had the effect of having sustained a blow on the bridge, flattening and deforming it at this point without arresting its growth,—rather showing a hypertrophy of the turbinated bones and septum; in some members of the family the nose shows more development on one side than on the other, making it appear deflected. There was an osseous deposit about the joints of Paul's fingers, which were short for a man of his size, though I could not get any definite history of rheumatism. He could not speak a word of English, but when asked by the interpreter about his health he said "Sometimes sick, but not very much—usually a cold, nothing more."

PAUL CZOLGOSZ
1902
Father of Leon.

With difficulty I elicited the following information: He had bought the farm of which Leon owned a share for $460. When interviewed he was working for the street department of the city, being employed in the parks. His son Frank, who lived in or near Alpena, had married a girl named Kuskiewicz. As to the family history—he said that he had been born in Gora, about half a mile from Rznin in Prussia; his first wife, Mary Nowak, was born in Pakoscy, about ten miles from Gora. They had been married in Prussia, and Waldek and two other children had been born there. Leon's paternal grandfather had died at the age of 40 of a severe cold, the paternal grandmother had died of old age at 72. The maternal grandmother had died when 30 years old of some "blood disease"; Paul did not know the cause of his wife's father's death, as it had occurred after he had come to this country. Leon's aunt, his mother's sister Ann, was "out of her head" for some time before she died. Paul said that this had occurred after he had left Prussia, but that the family had written him about it and he knew she was "crazy"; whether or no she had died insane he could not tell.

Paul said that he had preceded his family to America and had settled in Detroit, where his wife and family had joined him later. He had a brother in Michigan whose name was Woczich Czolgosz. He could give no dates—said he never could remember them, and had apparently lost track of time. Leon was born about a month after his mother had arrived in Detroit. She was thirty years old at that time. When the boy was about ten or twelve years old she was taken very ill at the birth of a child in Posen, Michigan, and her husband took her to his brother's house in Alpena, so as to be near doctors; but she gradually grew worse and died, about six weeks after childbirth. While she was very ill before her death, she would sometimes talk to herself—When asked to repeat some of the things she had said, Paul could only remember her saying "My children, the time will come when you will have greater understanding and be more learned." During her illness she would get up and walk about the floor. This was all the family history I could obtain from Paul Czolgosz.

Concerning Leon, he remembered that the priest who had baptized him was Father Gerick, who later went to the southwest and died there. *As a little child, Leon was always quiet and retiring and would not play with other children.* Except that it was hard for him to get acquainted with children, he was in most ways like an ordinary child. So far as the father could remember, he had never had convulsions nor fits nor any of the diseases of childhood—if he had ever been ill, the mother had looked after him, *but Paul did not think he had ever called a doctor to see Leon.* The boy was not quick-tempered and was fairly obedient. When punished for disobedience he would not say anything, but the father said that he could tell by his looks that he was thinking more than most children could say. He had times of not wanting to do as he was told, but perhaps not more frequently than other children. Altogether Leon had been to school for five and a half years, which included six months at evening school in Cleveland. As he grew older he was still very bashful—in fact he was *always bashful* and the father did not *understand how he could so suddenly have devel-*

oped a violent disposition if he was not insane. He did not think that Leon could have been responsible. He said his son had not been a very hard worker because he was ill, but he liked to read. He was a light eater. The father *remembered no chum or intimate acquaintance of either sex that Leon had ever had.** He never saw him in the company of any girl. When told that it seemed that Leon must have had some female associates and that he had said in Buffalo that the reason he did not like girls was because one had "gone back on him," Paul said that the year before Leon had often gone into the city from the farm, where they then lived, for several days at a time—from one to five days. They never knew why he went, but did not think it strange, because of his *secretive disposition.* Perhaps he had known some girl in town. He knew of no friends or acquaintances that Leon had ever had at Ft. Wayne, Battle Creek or Indianapolis, as reported. The *F* which appeared in Leon's name was without significance; he put it in because he liked the extra initial.

I persuaded Paul Czolgosz to accompany me to have

* Dr. White says: "In the subject of [dementia precox] the original impetus has been weak—only sufficient to carry him a short way, and when its force is spent development stops and the retrograde process is hastened or perhaps immediately initiated by some physical or mental stress occurring at the critical point of puberty and adolescent evolution. As the French have it, these patients are 'stranded on the rock of puberty'. . . . Jung, in his analysis (of cases of dementia precox) has specially called attention to the buried complexes with resulting symptoms, while Meyer considers the condition more from a biological standpoint as being the result of continued inability to adjust with the development of unhealthy biological reactions. Recent studies would indicate that these difficulties arise in people of peculiar character make-up—more particularly those who have what is termed a "shut-in" character. These persons do not meet difficulties openly and frankly, they are inclined to be seclusive, not to make friends, to have no one to whom they are close and with whom they can talk over things. They do not come into natural and free relation with the realities, are apt to be prudes, over-scrupulous, and exhibit a sentimental religiosity."

his picture taken by Charles Horton and Co., 121 Euclid Avenue. He dressed for the occasion in his best clothes with a small button-picture of Leon pinned through a black ribbon on the lapel of his coat. Mrs. Paul Czolgosz was visited, but was not inclined to talk, nor would Mrs. Bandowski vouchsafe any information.*

I saw Paul's brother, Michael Czolgosz and his wife. They were living at 112 Hosmer St. They could give me no further information as to Leon's early life. They said they had looked upon him as *a sort of "old woman," "a grandmother,"* and they seemed to have called him these names on account of *his habits of falling asleep and of being at times rather stupid.*

I next interviewed the principal of the Union Street School, where Leon and his brother Waldek had attended evening sessions—about 1897, the latter thought —but gained no information there, as no records had been kept of Polish pupils who came for a short time, and it was impossible to identify their teachers.

I then called on the wife of Leon's brother "Jake" Czolgosz. She seemed a rather intelligent and sensible young woman about 23 years of age. She said she had

* The Boston Daily Globe of Sept. 6th, 1912, says in an editorial:

"Paul Czolgosz of Cleveland, Ohio, father of the misguided young man who took the life of President McKinley, has since suffered without complaint from the shame and ignominy brought upon his family, but a few days ago he was taunted too much for his son's rash act by five unfeeling men, and in anger struck one of his tormentors. He was arrested on charge of assault and battery, but was acquitted when the circumstances of the case were made known. Judge Levine, who presided, rightly observed that the father was not responsible for the sins of his son. The Bible says that the iniquities of the father are visited upon the children of the third and fourth generation, but it does not hold a father responsible for his son's acts and of course it was cruel for the men to annoy Mr. Czolgosz. Judge Levine took a very practical view of the matter and in dismissing the prisoner said: 'You should have whipped the whole bunch.' That sentiment, although not found in the Bible, fits the case."

known the family for some time before her marriage to Jake on June 23rd, 1901. At that time she thought Leon was *odd and not like other boys,* and that he was *"acting very queerly."* He had *said that he was sick,* but she had been unable to see that he was and *"if you said anything to him about his sickness he would get mad."* He had told her that he wanted to sell out and go west for his health and she thought it would be a good thing for him to go away, as *he acted so queerly,* and so she had advanced him the money on his share of the farm. Later they sold the farm at a sacrifice, and if they had collected all the money $50 or $60 would still be due Leon. *For four or five years before leaving home Leon had been living on the farm and had not been doing anything but catching rabbits,* etc. He had a cough when she was there and would "spit out great chunks." She said that he was lazy and that instead of working *he would go out under a tree and lie down and sleep.* His stepmother had tried to "get him to work," but he would not. She did not believe him sick. Before he went away he had said he was going to Kansas and the stepmother had said it would be a good thing as he was always "making a fuss with her." He would call her names such as "old woman," etc., when he was angry with her. They always called Leon "Fred" on the farm. His sister-in-law also said that he played with the children, of whom he seemed very fond—providing he knew them. *He talked childish talk with them, but if anyone came he would turn around and talk differently.* He was always fixing wheels and boxes and tinkering around, but he never did any hard work on the farm. *His actions and the way he behaved with children made her say more than once that he must be crazy, because he would do such childish things.* He always took the milk from the barn to the cheese-house, and *never wanted anyone to go with him. For three or four months before he went away he would not eat anything at the table,* and lived on bread and milk, with sometimes a little cake. *He would take this up to his room and eat there.* He drank about two quarts of milk a day and sometimes more. She said her husband, Jake, had told her *Leon had never looked at a girl.* He never talked much and "did not like it if you talked to him too much"; *he liked to be let alone;* he retired early and slept a great deal. He was always called "cranky" at home. On the farm he did not "dress up well," but was "all ragged out." The day that she had given him $70 as his share of $260 *a change had come over him and he had seemed quite happy. That very day he left.* He went upstairs, dressed in his best clothes and went out, taking nothing with him but what he had on his back. He did not want the parents to know that he was going; he told his sister-in-law that he was going to Kansas, but to his sister he said that he was going to California for his health. After about four or five days he wrote to them from Ft. Wayne. This letter, which had been addressed to Victoria, she had torn up and burned, as there was nothing of importance in it and she expected to hear from him again. In it he had said that he was in good health and hoped they were—that he did not know where he was going but would write them later. The sister had been worrying for some time since receiving this letter, believing that he must be dead until the news came that he had killed the President.

This sister-in-law said that Bandowski, the husband

of Leon's sister Selia had gone off in the same manner as Leon, without saying good-bye. He and his wife had left the week before. He had lost his job because he had stayed away so long in Buffalo and Auburn, but she thought they had made that an excuse for discharging him. No one knew where he had gone. Victoria had been stopping with Bandowski and his wife, but when they went away she had returned to her parents, and Waldek was now occupying the rooms which the Bandowskis had had. She said that the family were all mad with her, because she had said that if Leon were her own brother she would tear him to pieces—Waldek, Selia and her husband had all taken the part of Leon. She said that Bandowski had been the secretary of the Socialist society for some time. Continuing her account of the family, she said that John was now farming in North Dakota, Frank in the lumber mills in Michigan; Michael had driven a baker's wagon for a time and had then joined the regular Army; but when last heard from he was in a factory at Barbenton, Ohio. Joseph was working in the packing department of the Cleveland Provision Company. Her husband, Jake, was loafing at the present time, but he used to work in the wire works.

The Jacob Czolgoszes lived in a very decent tenement on the first floor of a small house. The parlor was neatly furnished, pictures on the wall and the apartment clean. Jacob and his wife were clean and neat in dress, giving the impression of respectable, honest people.

Later I succeeded in getting an interview with Jacob Czolgosz, who was about five years younger than Leon. Jake was about the average in height, hollow chested with a flat abdomen, so that the body formed a curve from his chin to his feet. He was a large-boned, gawky-looking fellow, having the characteristic family nose already described. He had been married the previous summer and said he was not then working but lived on a pension of $30 a month which he was paid by the United States Government on account of the loss of one finger and the partial disablement of the hand and arm on the same side, incurred as the result of an explosion while he was in the service of the Ordnance Department at Sandy Hook. He had also served in the Heavy Artillery before being assigned to the Ordnance Department. He at first objected very seriously to having his picture taken, but later consented to have a photograph taken in his own house. Later he seemed willing to talk.

He said he had noticed a change in Leon after his illness—that he was more given to being by himself and less inclined to talk. He was the only member of the family who took his meals alone, which he always did when his stepmother was around. Jacob now thought this had been a strange thing for Leon to do. *He frequently dropped asleep in the daytime, without any explanation whatever; he never got excited;* "He was handy with tools." He once had taken to pieces a clock which would not go and put it together again so that it ran perfectly. Jake said he had not noticed any change in Leon's physical appearance after his illness. He had never known him to have anything to do with any girl nor with any Anarchists or Socialists. He was fond of reading and *the best educated member of the family.* Jake said that he himself had worked

JACOB CZOLGOSZ
1902
Brother of Leon.

for a year at the mill under the name of Crawley, because his own name was hard to pronounce.

My next interview was with Mr. and Mrs. A. Dryer, at 133 Hosmer Street. Mr. Dryer had bought out Paul Czolgosz's saloon on Third Avenue, and had run it until some six or seven years ago, when he had moved into his present quarters. Dryer seemed like an honest man, who might perhaps be too much inclined to drink beer. He had lost the sight of one eye. His wife was a big, stout, rough-looking woman. Both seemed honest in their endeavor to give truthful accounts of their observations, and their evidence was valuable as they had known Leon and his family for a good many years. He said that he and his wife had probably seen Leon more frequently than anyone else had seen him before he moved into the country. During the period that Leon had worked in the wire mill he spent most of his spare time and his "days off" loafing in their saloon. The only chum Mr. Dryer ever knew of Leon's ever having—if he could be called a chum—was a man named Jugnatz Lapka, who now lived in Fullerton Street. Dryer said that Lapka used to work in the same factory with Leon, and that they walked back and forth together—and he called this association more intimate than Leon was in the habit of having with anyone else.—I later made two unsuccessful attempts to call upon Lapka, but in any case he had not seen much of Leon for three or four years.—Dryer said that Leon used to come into the saloon after his work, wash up and sit down to read the paper, which he was always very anxious to get. *That he sat by himself in the corner and watched the others play cards, but would never play himself,* except when specially urged to make up a fourth hand; then he never played for much and if he lost anything he usually stopped playing. Neither Dryer nor his wife *had ever heard Leon swear or use profane language. They never saw him lose his temper, though he was plagued in and about the saloon about the girls to whom he never seemed to have the courage to speak.* He was looked upon there as an onanist, but no one had ever had proof of this. *If he came into the saloon with dirty shoes, he asked Mr. Dryer for a shoe brush and brushed his shoes before sitting down.* He often fell asleep in the saloon, then waked up and sat around until he perhaps fell asleep again. Mrs. Dryer said that it seemed strange to her that he could ever have perpetrated such a violent act as the assassination of the President, as *he would never kill a fly* in the saloon. He used to brush them off, or *perhaps catch them and let them go again,* but he never killed one. *He would not even step on a worm.* He was especially careful with his money, never spending more than was absolutely necessary, and *he never took more than one drink of any kind of liquor at a time.* Dryer said that sometimes they teased him about not spending his money, saying "Oh, come on! Blow yourself off!"—but he answered "No, I have use for my money." *He was never jolly.* Mr. Dryer described him as *"rather stupid and dull-like."* They said that he had come in one day about five years before and told them that he had left the wire works because he was sick, and that *certainly for five or six months he had always been taking medicine, carrying a bottle and a box of pills in his pocket. He never had much to say to anybody and never talked to* *strangers.* He never danced—said he did not care for dancing. When he was not working he sometimes sat all day in the saloon, "thinking-like," reading the paper and sleeping.*

Dryer said Czolgosz belonged to the social club of which his brother-in-law, Bandowski, was secretary, but he had never spoken in public in the club or taken any prominent part that they knew of. The club had finally split, part of it going to the Debs party and part to the Social Democrat Party, and was not in existence at that time—or if still in existence, had few members. Mr. Dryer said that the association to which Leon belonged when he wrote the letter which was printed in the German paper was purely a benefit association among the Poles—when any one member died the others all paid in so much money. The name of this benefit association was the Golden Eagle. There were several such associations to help the poor people with funeral expenses, etc., in case of a death in the family. Dryer said *Leon would never enter into any row or take sides with anyone who was in a row.* To illustrate, he told of once having seen the brother, Jake Czolgosz, across the street with a party returning from a dance, in the center of a crowd who were trying to knife him. Dryer called out to Leon "Aren't you going out to help your brother? He is in trouble." But Leon replied "No. If he will associate with those Polaks he will have to take the consequences," and turned and continued to read his paper. Dryer said that the Polish name

* White says, "The origin of simple dementia is insidious and it may be quite impossible to fix its date, largely because the beginning symptoms were not appreciated at their true value. . . . At first the patient begins to show a lack of interest in things, ceases going out and associates less and less with others. There is a general listless, apparently lazy and tired-out attitude toward life assumed."

of the section where Leon had formerly lived and in which he himself resided was "Warshau," and that it was in this section that Leon had gone to evening school while still at work five years before.

Mrs. Dryer said that *she had urged Leon many times to eat with them, but only once did he consent after much persuasion, and then he had sat at the table and eaten very little.* From what she knew of him she would say that "he was rather fond of cake, but not fond of meat or heavy things."

From the above and much more I learned, it would seem, that about 1897 Leon began to exhibit hypochondriacal symptoms, and that this condition made itself evident up to the time that he went to Buffalo.

On inquiry I found that Leon had consulted the following physicians: Dr. J. Sykora, 1453 Broadway, Newburg, Ohio; Dr. Koller, 1538 Broadway, Newburg; Dr. Parker of the Cleveland General Hospital, and Dr. Rosenwasser, Woodland Avenue near Forest Street, Cleveland. I spent some time with Dr. Sykora, who tried to identify Leon, but could not do so, and the other physicians were equally unsuccessful, with the exception of Dr. Rosenwasser. Dr. M. Rosenwasser gave me a copy of the following entry from his office case book:

April 28th, 1898.—Czolgosz, Leon, 23, Worker in wire mill—Res. 319 Cowan St.;—Sick two yrs.; short breath (catarrh)—palpitations—some wheezing at apices—emphysema (?).

R. Potass. Iodid ℥i, Tinct. Nux. vomic. ℥ fs av ℥iv.

Nov. 1st, 1898.—Has been better throughout summer—worse past two months—wheezing—aches all over—Pulse 64—respiration 25—Examination negative.

R. Strych sulph. 1/30 gr.

I next drove out to a little wooden house on Marcelline Street, behind a block of houses fronting on Broadway and, reaching the upper story by an outside staircase, found Leon's second brother, Waldek, and a rather rough-looking man with one eye in a small attic room which contained only a stove, three chairs and a table with a dirty red cover on it and a sort of bookshelf containing some books and pamphlets. Waldek was rather short in stature, but fairly stout, strong and thickset. He had the characteristic large mouth which I had observed in his father and in most of the children except Joseph; his face also was much the shape of his father's, except that his nose was very short showing, however, the flattened bridge. His eyes were gray, pupils dilated; his skin was smooth and his complexion florid; the hair light brown. His face showed an arrest of development of the lower jaw, giving an undue prominence to the upper lip, which was covered with a moustache, standing up like his father's, but reddish instead of brown. I should say that there had been an arrest of development of the bones of the nose, giving a very solid nose showing an upward tendency from the base to the point; and he had much the same heavy eye which, from the description, Leon also had. He looked rather sleepy at times while talking to me, as if it were hard for him to open his eyes wide. Waldek wore a button picture of his brother Leon in the lapel of his coat.

At first he wanted to know my business and said he had had enough of doctors; they had treated him badly in Buffalo and Auburn. Here I found the one-eyed man rather helpful, as he encouraged Waldek to talk.

Waldek corroborated the family history as already told by his father. He gave the date of his father's arrival in the United States as New Year's day, 1873, and said that his mother with her three children arrived in May of the same year. As he told the story, they remained in Detroit for about three years and then went to Rogers City, Michigan, about 40 miles from Alpena, where his father worked in the colony established by Mr. Molliter, who owned "all the country about." Molliter was killed, Waldek said, at the instigation of a rival in business—someone interested in the same sort of work at a nearby place. He claimed that his father was not in Rogers City when Molliter was killed, Waldek repeated substantially the same story already told of the removal to Alpena, where his father worked in the docks for a man named Fletcher, shipping lumber, for which he received from 25 to 30 cents an hour; and thence to the farm at Posen, where they had lived for five years, at the end of which time they sold it to a man named Rambuski and returned to Alpena, where his father had bought land and built the house on Sable Street. Leon was old enough to go to school at that time. Most of the time he went to a Polish parochial school, but was attending the public school at the time they left Alpena. The records of their births, etc., had all been burned some years previously, when a portion of Alpena was destroyed by fire, including, Waldek thought, the house in which they had first lived. He said that during the three or four years that Leon went to the public school *he was considered "the best scholar of them all."* They were in Michigan for sixteen years in all, finally leaving Alpena because the work was dull and going to Netronia, about twenty miles from

Pittsburg. Waldek said that they had no relations of the same name in Buffalo, but that his mother had a brother in Michigan, in or near Alpena. He was quite sure that Leon did not go to school in Netronia, but that he almost immediately got to work at the bottle works. There his duties consisted in carrying bottles red hot on forks to the different ovens, that they might cool off gradually. He did not remember that Leon had ever read very much there—the days were so long and they got pretty tired. Leon earned seventy-five cents a day until the last six months when he got a dollar a day. Their father had worked in the Philadelphia Diamond Chemical Works at the same time and place. About 1892 the family had first moved to Newburg where they now resided, and Paul had built a saloon on the corner of Third Avenue, which he ran for five months, after which he rented it to the Findlay Beer Company. When Leon worked in the Newburg Wire Mills, from 1892 to 1897, the work was so arranged that he worked ten hours a day for one or two weeks and then had twelve hours' night work for a similar period. He was paid $16 or $17 for the two weeks of his day work, and $22, then $24, for the two weeks of his night work. His first work was on galvanized fence wire, afterwards he was given more fancy work to do. During the time that he did day work he attended night school with his brother Waldek for about three months one winter.

About 1893 or 1894 Waldek said that Leon, with a great many others was laid off after a strike, and that at that time he changed—"got quiet and not so happy." *This gives the date of 1894 as the first time that Leon's illness was observed.* A list of the names of those who had struck was given to a new foreman, not the one under whom Leon had previously worked, so that after six months, when he applied for work again under the name of Fred C. Nieman, he had obtained employment. Waldek thought the foreman probably knew that some of the men who applied for work at that time were the same who had struck, but they were re-employed under their new names as the works were short of men. Waldek said that Leon would not drink nor swear, *"but would kick—kick like hell" if urged to drink.* Leon was cool—never got mad, he said, *but if plagued or provoked would not* talk. He was sure Leon *never had any girl* with whom he associated—he was quite sure that he, Waldek, would have known had Leon had any girl friend.

Up to about 1893 or 1894 when the strike came Waldek said he and his brother were strict attendants at the Catholic Church. Until then they had always believed what the priest taught them—that if they were in need or trouble and prayed their prayers would be answered. He said that at the time of the strike they both prayed very hard, but they got no answer. They then went to the priest and said that they wanted proof, and they were again told that they would be helped if they would pray. But no help came. So they, Leon and Waldek, bought a Polish Bible, and concluded after reading it over four or five times together that the priests had "told their own way," and had kept back most of what was in the book. He said that they had then made the acquaintance of one or two people who shared their opinions, and he remembered that Leon had once said to one of these men that he believed "the priest's trade was the same as the shoemaker's or any other." They then got other books and pamphlets about the Bible and on other subjects and studied them —and then, he said, they "knew how it was." They read these books regularly, buying them in Cleveland and sometimes sending to New York for them. One of the first books they had studied was a red book with a picture of a devil on the outside—he thought it was called "The Free-thinker," or that those words were used in the title somewhere. They had continued reading together until within a year and a half of Leon's death. Lately Leon had preferred to read alone and had read a great deal more than his brother. When Waldek was asked where some of these books were, he said that Leon had burned up almost everything in the way of letters or books before he left home, but added that he and Bandowski still had a few of his books, especially one of Edward Bellamy's which he said Leon had studied for seven or eight years. After hunting around for the books he found a little pile of them under the sloping roof. He had perhaps a dozen pamphlets, but did not seem to wish to part with them. Finally I purchased a few, which Waldek said were the identical books which Leon had studied up to a short time before he went away. I asked him about one of them, the "Peruna Almanac," and he said Leon had liked that because it always *told him his lucky days*. Waldek said that at the time they read together Leon did not believe that there was *no* God, but that the priests had deceived them. He thought that Leon had not read the Bible for about a year and a half before his death.

In 1897, Waldek said, Leon left work because he was ill. He went to several doctors (whom I have previously mentioned) who told him that he ought to stop work at once.

The family had then, 1897, moved to Orange township, four miles from Warrensville, where they had bought a farm of fifty-five acres, the boys paying in what money they had saved—Waldek said Leon had saved about $50 which he had deposited in the Stafford Bank on Broadway.

While on the farm Waldek said Leon *would go half a mile every afternoon for his paper and would read all the papers he could get in* English or Polish, being particularly interested in everything pertaining to working men, strikes, etc. Since he had been old enough to be independent, Leon had not obeyed his stepmother very well, but not until he had left work and gone to live on the farm with her did they get to calling each other names. The stepmother had never believed Leon to be ill and thought he ought to work like the others. Leon felt that she had no right to tell him what he ought or ought not to do. While on the farm Leon did not do heavy work; the first year he said he could not work, and the next year and thereafter he said he was all right, but refused to do heavy work unless obliged to do so—said he did not care for it, though he was not unwilling to take a hand when it was necessary. Most of his time was spent in repairing old machinery and wagons on the farm, and, as Waldek said, he *"fussed about with small things."* He also traded horses occasionally, and Waldek remembered that he had got badly "left" at least once. He did not even watch the others work, *but preferred to be away from them by himself, doing his little "odd jobs," or reading or sleeping.* Once during this time he applied for a conductor's job on the electric railroad of the Stanley Company, but was unsuccessful; and Waldek knew of no other attempt on Leon's part to get work since 1897.

According to Waldek Leon was a good hunter. He owned a breech-loading shotgun, and beginning early in the fall and up to as late in the winter as he could trap rabbits, he would start off almost every morning for rabbits and "big squirrels." He usually carried a shotgun, a revolver and a stick, and sometimes a bag. If the rabbit was some distance away he would shoot him with the shotgun; if he were nearer, Leon would use the revolver, with which he was quite skillful. The stick he used in this way:—he would take the sack and cover one end of a rabbit hole, then with the long stick he would drive the rabbit out from the other end into the bag. Sometimes he would build a fire at the other end to drive the rabbit into the bag, when he would kill it with the stick or a club. He would sometimes get a rabbit into a hole in a tree or wall and catch it with the sack in the same way. Waldek remembered his bringing home three live rabbits in the sack one day which he had caught in this manner.

Waldek said that *about three years before our interview Leon had felt so ill that he had advised him to go to the hospital,* but Leon had said *"There is no place in the hospital for poor people; if you have lots of money you will get well taken care of!"*

In March or April Waldek said Leon became quite restless and wanted to get his money out of the farm so that he could leave, and he kept up this talk about getting his money until July, at times getting quite put out that he could not realize on his share of the property. From that time he commenced his trips to the city—that is, it was thought he went to the city. At first he went one day a week; a little later he would go off for two or three days, and then he would go one week one day and the next week two or three days more regularly. When asked where he went, he said he went to attend meetings. They thought it was meetings of the Golden Eagle, but as he was *naturally secretive* they did not question him, beyond making a few inquiries. Several times in March and April Leon had said "If I can not have my money now, I want it this summer." He said he was going west in the summer. In July he said to Waldek, "I would like to have my money for my share on the farm—get me what you can." Waldek did not do much about it, and a little later Leon said *"I must have the money."* Waldek asked *"What can you want the money for?"—They were standing near a tree that was dying and Leon said "Look: it is just the same as a tree that commences dying—You can see it isn't going to live long."* Another day Waldek asked Leon how he could live if he went west, telling him that his share of the money would be so small it would not carry him far; Leon replied "I can get a conductor's job, or binding wheat or fixing machines, or something." Just before Leon went away *he told Waldek he had to go away and must have the money.* Waldek said, "To why you go away so far? What is the matter with you?" Leon answered *"I can't stand it any longer."* Waldek said that *when he went away he seemed changed—he had brightened up a good deal. He dressed upstairs, came down and walked right out of the house.* He had not told his stepmother anything about his movements for a good many years, and he did not tell things to his father, for the latter always told them to the stepmother. He left on July 11th, and on July 14th he wrote the letter from Ft. Wayne, of which I publish a copy, saying that he was going further west. On July 30th he wrote the letter which appeared in the German paper—I had the original, which was written in *red ink,* photographed by the same people who had taken Leon's picture.

After receiving the letter from Ft. Wayne they did not see nor hear from Leon again until after the assassination of the President, when Waldek went to Buffalo and later to Auburn to see him. Waldek said that he always talked to Leon in English when they were alone, and when he went down to the cell for the first time they shook hands and Leon said, "Is anybody else with you?" Waldek replied, "No"—but asked if he would like to see any of the family. Leon said yes, he would like to see his father if he came, but that if he did not it would be all right. The guard had told Waldek that on the previous Sunday Leon had told him to telegraph for his father, but Waldek said his father was not telegraphed for. Waldek said he asked Leon why he "did it"—meaning the assassination of McKinley, and that *Leon took some time to answer and then said, "I did it——" and then stopped and went off as if asleep, then "kind of woke up like" and finished "because I done my duty."* Waldek asked Leon if he wanted a priest, but Leon answered, "What can he do? He can't help me. If he comes down here I'll give him enough—he'll have enough—I'll smash his head!" When I asked Waldek if I understood correctly that they always spoke English when together, he said he meant that they did so in the prison, because the guards would not allow them to speak anything but English.

Waldek said he did not believe Leon had been buried. When asked his reason for this statement, he said it was because the doctors had lied to him so much —"I did not see it and I don't believe what I don't see." He said he had been told he might come and see the body immediately after the execution; he was then put off and told he might come and see what the doctors did with the body; then he was told he might come and see the remains disposed of. After returning to the prison several times and being put off with promises about seeing the remains of his brother, he said he was finally told that it was all over—that his brother's body had been buried. Waldek said he did not believe it. He wanted to take the remains to Buffalo to be cremated, but Warden Mead had persuaded him not to do so because he said there was a mob of men from New York City who had come to attack him if he did. Then Waldek said they telegraphed his father saying that Waldek would sign a release of the body to the authorities if his father would permit. At the same time they telegraphed him from Cleveland that his father would sign the release of the body if he, Waldek, would do so. Then, when Waldek saw his father again, he found that it was "all fixed up," as neither of them had agreed to the proposition until he believed he had heard from the other.

My impression of Waldek was that he was rather a useless member of the community. He seems to have been Leon's only confidant up to about a year and a half before the crime, when Leon apparently withdrew into himself. From Waldek's conversation I gathered that he felt he had influenced Leon a good deal during the early years in his change in religion. He described

Leon as quite pale, with a fine, soft skin like his own, but with less color.

Waldek himself was of an emotional character and might easily become excited. He seemed honest, but only fairly intelligent. He had a great deal to say about the troubles of 1892-3, and described himself as a Socialist. He denied that his brother Leon had ever associated with Anarchists or attended their meetings. He said that at the meetings of the Golden Eagle Leon had never spoken, so far as he knew, but would take a back seat and listen. *When I asked him whether he believed Leon would have become violent against his stepmother had he remained at the farm, Waldek said yes, he thought that might perhaps have been the reason Leon had felt he had to go away.* Waldek spoke of his sister, Mrs. Bandowski, as "uneducated" and said she did not understand things.

I obtained an interview with Joseph Czolgosz after much trouble and two applications at the office of the Cleveland Packing and Provision Company, where he was employed. They told me he had worked there since he was fourteen years old—he was then twenty-two—and that they had never had a better boy nor one with better habits; that he was correct in his deportment, faithful in his work and an all-around nice boy. They were so careful to protect him from the curiosity of prying visitors that they at first denied that he was in their employ. When I finally succeeded in getting permission to talk to him, one of the managers had him go to a remote corner of the works, that I might talk to him without subjecting him to the observation of his fellow workmen. Joseph appeared to be an intelligent boy, with rather a long face, blue eyes and a light complexion. He was of medium height and well-built. He said that he could not believe at first that Leon had killed the President; he never believed that he could do such a thing and did not know how to account for it. .

Joseph said that Leon was a nice boy; that *he always lived much by himself*—that *he did not like strangers;* that *he never talked to girls,* and that *when he met those he knew on the way from church or elsewhere, he would cross the street to avoid talking to them; he was always "awful bashful."* He said that he, Joseph, used to sleep with Leon, and that the latter *always slept on his right side—said that he could not sleep on his left; he slept well and slept a great deal of the time.* He would often go off hunting in the morning with his dog for squirrels and rabbits; he was a great mechanic—always "fixing up" boxes and wagons—once he had taken a sewing machine apart and put it together again; he mended the fences and could do anything in the way of "fixing up around." Joseph asked me if I had seen the pitcher which Leon had mended when I called at the house. He said this pitcher had been broken all to pieces, and that Leon had put some wires in it so that it was as good as new; it was tight and would hold milk—it was "a fine job."

He said that Leon had been sick about five years before. When I asked if he was really sick, Joseph said he had had a cough for a little while; he did not look sick, but was always taking medicine and had *sent a long way for an inhaling machine which he had used for about two months. Especially during the latter part of the time he was in the country he used to read and sleep all the time.* When asked what he meant by "all the time," he said, "a great deal—it seemed all the time." When Leon got his paper he used to sit in his chair reading it and Joseph would see him reading it and in a little while he would look and *Leon would have the paper on his breast and his hands folded over it and be fast asleep; then again in a little while he would wake up and continue reading the paper. He did not agree with his stepmother.* He ate but little at any time. That last winter *when his stepmother left the farm for the city, Leon stayed in the country and cooked for himself and the family, when they were there; but when the mother returned about March, he would never eat with them nor come into the house when she was there if he could help it; he used to take his milk each day from the milk cans after the cows were milked—about three quarts—and put it in the cellar. When he went in he used to go down and get it and take it to his room or out under a tree and drink it alone, with a little cake or some crackers. He seldom took anything else to eat unless his stepmother was away, when he would go into the pantry and eat some things.* There was a little pond near the house where *he caught small fish and he used to keep them until the stepmother went away from the house for a time, when he would run into the kitchen and fry and eat them by himself, but if she returned unexpectedly or if strangers came in, he would let the fish burn or throw them away.* Joseph did not know where Leon went in his excursions away from the farm, but he did not believe he associated with anarchists.

With Jacob as guide I drove to the Wire Mills, where we introduced ourselves to Mr. E. R. Putnam, the Superintendent. After we had overcome his objections, he sent for one of the foremen, Page, under whom Leon had worked for about seven years. Page stated that *Leon had been a steady worker; he never gave any trouble, never quarrelled nor got into any disputes with other workmen,* but was a quiet fellow. He carried his dinner to the mill as the other men did, but never had much to say—*sat around and kept to himself at the noon hour,* though he showed no desire to avoid the men. Page said that "Nimen" was as good a boy as he had ever had; and (referring to the assassination of the President) that he never could have done such a thing as that in his right mind. *Leon's occupation was that of a wire-winder, which required a fair amount of intelligence, and before he left the mill he was a sort of assistant superintendent of some of the machines.* The books in the mills show that "Fred Nimen" worked steadily without a break; and Page said that while the other men had a good many fines, Nimen had only a few, for such little things as letting the wire run slack, etc. He was engaged in 1891, and gave up his work on August 29th, 1898, as the books show. When he left, Page says he simply came up and said he was going to quit—that he was going out into the country for his health—*that he was not well.* It was a surprise to them all.

Page took us to the very men who had worked with Leon—Rathburn, Gunther and a young Pole. It seems that Leon had joined the Golden Eagle Society through these men, who were all members. Page had thought it very strange that Leon wanted to belong to that society, as the members were Americans and men socially above him; he thought *Leon had a desire to associate with those above his class.* Rathburn, Page

Orange Ohio August 11th 1899

To Forrest City Castle

#22 Knights of the Golden Eagle

Sir Knights and Brothers,

I am under Dr. L. Kuller. treatment and not able to work.

Brother Cull was visiting me this week.

Yours Truly.

Fred C. Niman

Orange Ohio.

P. O.

Warrensville Ohio

Letter written by
LEON F. CZOLGOSZ—FRED C. NIMAN
One year after he gave up work.

and Gunther were high-grade workmen of unusual intelligence. *They said that they had seen no reason in the seven years Leon had worked with them why he should not belong to their order.* They had seen him daily during this time. Rathburn said that when he joined the Golden Eagle Society the oath that he took was "like renouncing the authority of the Pope in the Catholic Church." *After Nimen left the mill he took a sick benefit for sixteen weeks and, according to the rules, he had furnished a physician's certificate once a month. This was signed by Dr. Koller.* Nimen attended few meetings, but came and paid his dues. Just before he left he had met Gunther on the street and paid him six months' dues in advance. At one time Leon had brought one of his fellow workmen a book, saying, "Here is a nice book to read; you will find it interesting." The man took it and found that it was the New Testament. Later he returned it to Leon, saying it was a very nice book, and Leon took it and placed it in his hip pocket without saying a word. They thought this rather strange.*

* In 1908 there was a report in a newspaper that a brother of Czolgosz had been arrested in Sharon, Penn.:

CZOLGOSZ'S BROTHER INSANE?

He is sent to the Workhouse in Sharon, Pa.

Sharon, Pa., Sept. 1st, (1908).—John Czolgosz, a brother of President McKinley's assassin, was today sentenced to the workhouse for three months. The police say Czolgosz is insane and his case will be investigated.

On inquiry a letter was received from the Chief of the South Sharon Police Department, saying that no one by the name of Czolgosz had been arrested there; that the story had started by the arrest of a man named Roskowich for vagrancy, who later created a great sensation by trying to break jail.

CHAPTER VI

CZOLGOSZ'S EFFORTS TO BECOME AN ANARCHIST—HIS INTEREST IN THE TEACHINGS OF EMMA GOLDMAN. ANARCHISTS CONSIDER HIM A SPY AND PUBLISH WARNING TO THEIR BRETHREN. CRITICISMS OF HIM IN THE ANARCHISTS' PAPERS

Emil Schilling was treasurer of an association of Anarchists known as the Liberty Club at 4 Elwell St., Cleveland. On the evening of June 2nd, 1902, I sent for him to come to see me in Cleveland, as he then lived twelve miles outside of the city on the edge of some thick woods, with his wife and three children.

He came and said that on May 19th, 1901, Nieman had come to him saying he had been sent by his friend Howser, of whom he had inquired where he could find an anarchist—or anarchists. Leon then talked about his own ideas. He said he had belonged to the Sila Club, but was not now a member of that or of the Social Labor Party, because they had quarrelled so the year before. He talked about capitalists and the laboring people in a way that Schilling called revolutionary. Schilling had given Leon a book to read about the Chicago martyrs and some other members of the Free Society, and he had also taken him home to dinner where he "sat down and ate the same as anyone, but kept very quiet at table. I thought he was all right this time when he called on me," Schilling said. "He did not talk German, but English—talked about his farm and said he lived in Bedford on a farm with his brother. He came to see me again in about three weeks and said he had read of Anarchists forming plots and of secret meetings. I said, 'We do not do any plotting.' He then asked if Anarchists did not organize to act; that is: 'If anybody do something against a king or officer and you was an Anarchist, would you say you was an Anarchist?' I told him yes, for everyone knew I was an Anarchist. When I answered him *he was always laughing at my answers, as if he either felt superior or had formed a plan and was putting out a feeler.* I thought that Nieman wanted to be smart enough to find out something as a secret detective, and I thought he was not smart enough to do what he wanted. I thought he was very ignorant. He asked his questions in a very quick way, such as, 'Say, have you any secret societies? I hear the Anarchists are plotting something like Breschi; the man was selected by the comrades to do the deed that was done.' I ask him, 'Where did you read that?' He answered, 'In some capitalist paper.' 'Well,' I said, 'you did not read it in any Anarchist paper.'

"During his second visit he came at a time I was eating my supper. He then handed me the book I gave him to read the first time he called. I asked him how he liked it. He said he did not read it—did not have time. This made me mad and I was suspicious of him. After supper we went out. *He refused beer when I invited him to drink,* but turned round and offered me a cigar. I told him to smoke it himself. He said he never smoked. On our way home I again asked him to have some beer and he said he did not care to drink.

Finally he consented to take a glass of pop and then he went home. After his second visit, I visited Howser and asked him about Nieman. He told me he was a good and active member of the Polish Socialist Society of the Labor Party, but that his name was not Fred Neiman and he had forgotten his real name. I then told him my suspicions, and Howser said to watch out if I thought so.

"Neiman came again about a week later and only remained with me about an hour. He talked with me and *said he was tired of life;* referred to his own affairs and said his stepmother abused him. When asked if his father would not protect him he said no, *his father had not his own will but was bound by the will of his stepmother.* I did not tell my suspicions. I wanted him to come once or twice more, when I would have settled with him—when I would have to tell him what I think and not to come again.

"The first two times he called he had on his every-day clothes, the last two times he had on his Sunday clothes. *He was awful particular about the care of his body—his clothes always nice and clean.* He had a red complexion—was healthy-looking—a round face. I see on his hands he did not work much.

"The third time he call *he ask me for a letter of introduction to Emma Goldman*, and then told me he had heard her speak in Cleveland in May. She was then in Chicago and I told him he could meet her himself, but I never introduce anyone by letter. I told him he could say to her, 'I have heard you speak in Cleveland,' etc. He said, 'I go to Chicago'—said he would like to see her where she is. He had heard her talk—her speech had influence him—please him. He talked much of her and wanted her acquaintance—wanted to meet her, but I could not introduce him. She was here only two days.

"The fourth and last time he came was in August. I was just reading a letter from Isaaks of Chicago asking about this man Neiman—he said he was a friend of mine—when a knock came on the door and in walked Neiman. I was then suspicious and thought the letter might have been opened in post. I put it in my pocket and told him to sit down. I asked him where he was all these months. He said he was working in Akron in a cheese-factory—*and then laughed.* I thought as I had catched him in a lie, I would give him a chance once or twice more. He took a walk with a neighbor, a good man and a friend of mine. Three of us walked along the road and the old man and me talked business and Neiman did not say anything at all. When we went back to the house he seemed tired and went home. I asked him where he was going. He said, 'Maybe Detroit, maybe Buffalo.'

"In Chicago he ask Isaaks the same questions he ask me and wanted money; said he would remain in Chicago two or three days if he had money, but that his family was poor and he could not remain without money. They told him they had no money but could give him something to eat. He seemed to be disgusted and left right away."

Several others spoke of a silly laugh which he had at times.*

* Dr. White, in describing dementia precox, hebephrenic form, says: "Among these symptoms is often noted a silly laugh, which is frequently

Schilling, continuing his narrative, said, "Two comrades wanted to take him home for the night and turn his pockets, taking any papers or other information they could get as to whether he was a spy or not. In Chicago he must have asked for Emma Goldman; he met her on the wharf as she was leaving on the boat. Isaaks and some other comrades were there to bid her goodbye. He introduced himself to Emma as a Socialist from Cleveland—he had heard her speak and was a friend of mine. Then Emma turned around and introduced him to Isaaks and asked him if he was an Anarchist. He said he was a Socialist—then he said he had not read any Anarchist literature but the 'Free Society.' They then walked toward the Hall and he asked his questions. All the comrades had their suspicions of him right away. Isaaks wrote to me asking about him and he would tell me more—saying to write him. I wrote him that I doubted Niemen's honesty. Isaaks then wrote me just what I thought, and I wrote back to him, 'If you think so you ought to give it to the public in the "Free Society," and he did, a week before McKinley was shot.

"Czolgosz seemed to be normal and sound as the average man. He might be excused as ignorant—not educated, or, as I had thought, a spy, a bad person. He was consistent in his tactics; he did not give himself away. He was not against the President, but against the party, as he said the last minutes, and we thought from his education he thought he could not leave the

developed while the patient is talking to himself, but which may occur at any time with absolutely no apparent cause. If the patient is asked for an explanation of why he laughed, he will reply in a characteristic manner, 'I don't know,' or else will give some shallow, wholly inadequate or manifestly false reason."

world without doing anything. After he done it, I assume he plan to do it some months before he done it, and only waited a good chance and hoped to get some help from friends."

Schilling said Niemen had told him things were getting worse and worse—more strikes and they were getting more brutal against the strikers, and that something must be done. "Then I did not think he had a plan—afterwards I did." *

That the Anarchists did not trust Czolgosz is proved by the notice which Isaaks put into the Anarchistic paper, "Free Society," formerly "The Firebrand," published in Chicago, Ill., under date of September 1st, 1901, which is as follows:

ATTENTION

The attention of the comrades is called to another spy. He is well-dressed, of medium height, rather narrow-shouldered, blond and about twenty-five years of age. Up to the present he has made his appearance in Chicago and Cleveland. In the former place he remained but a short time, while in Cleveland he disappeared when the comrades had confirmed themselves of his identity & were on the

* In the spring of 1902 Emma Goldman lectured in Boston at Paine Memorial Hall to an enthusiastic gathering of men and women on her ideas of modern phases of anarchy. The report of this lecture in the Boston Evening Record of May 12, 1902, says that there was no standing room left in the hal and that she began her address by saying that the lecture she was about to deliver was that which, according to the newspapers, excited Czolgosz to his attack on President McKinley. "Americans love their neighbor," she said, "for just as much as they can get out of him. As long as there are people willing to be made slaves there will be slaves. We must get the spirit out of the peoples. Revolutions have thrown down kings and kingdoms, but it will be harder to throw down prejudice in the minds of the people. Anarchy is a scientific problem and must undergo change with the progress of the years. With all their Statue of Liberty, their Constitution and their Declaration of Independence, the Americans have shown themselves greater beasts than the Russians. This was when they arose to figuratively tear Czolgosz to pieces, and the grief at the death of McKinley was not so great. A Chicago firm raised the price of black cloth when they knew it would be wanted to drape buildings in mourning. . . . I am held responsible for the deaths of King Humbert, Queen Elizabeth, President McKinley and I don't know how many more—but Anarchy has nothing to do with force."

point of exposing him. His demeanor is of the usual sort, pretending to be greatly interested in the cause, asking for names or soliciting aid for acts of contemplated violence. If this same individual makes his appearance elsewhere, the comrades are warned in advance and can act accordingly.

From other numbers of "Free Society," published after Czolgosz's death, I extract the following:

In the issue of Feb. 16, 1902, written by "Wat Tyler," we read:

> That the crime of Czolgosz was primarily of psychological interest rather than of political significance—the outcome of purely personal idiosyncrasy and not of any doctrine or propaganda, has just been positively demonstrated by the only impartial and scientific investigation (by Dr. Briggs) of the whole case that has yet been attempted. In printing this report, the Boston Herald, in an editorial, accepts the above view of the case. Indeed it goes farther and says that this was its own view, presented just after the occurrence at Buffalo. If these conclusions are correct, they show how uncalled-for was the attitude of some Anarchists in tacitly accepting Czolgosz at his own estimate, and treating the assassination as of political or sociological significance, which it clearly did not possess.

To show how much at sea the Anarchists were regarding Czolgosz, I quote from an article by Ross Winn in the same number:

> I do not think Czolgosz was insane. His act was not an insane act, neither was he a criminal. I can not bring myself to approve of his act—I do not believe in violence except in defense of human life and liberty, and I do not think the death of McKinley has served that purpose. We who denounce vengeance and retaliation when done in the name of the law can not consistently approve of this spirit when resorted to by individuals in the name of Anarchy. But I do not see that anyone can call Czolgosz a criminal. If his deed was a crime, the cause of it was tenfold more a crime.

Kate Austin, in "Free Society" of Feb. 14th, 1902, says:

> In regard to those "Anarchists who tacitly accepted Czolgosz at his own estimate" being mistaken in such acceptance, I heartily con-

cur with Comerade Tyler. A rebellious working man who deliberately gives his life in exchange for that of a worthless hulk of a ruler has such a very modest estimate of his own value that I, for one, would not dream of taking it. While I mourn for every noble life that has thus been given, I recognize and accept the act as the supreme protest of a brave and generous heart against the curse of government.

Abe Isaak, Jr., in the same issue, writes:

Notwithstanding Wat Tyler, I am not inclined to recede from the position I have taken in considering Leon Czolgosz's act of political significance. . . . One of the reasons for Czolgosz's insanity is stated as follows: "Moral chaos, e.g. He declared he did not believe in marriage nor in law, nor in government nor in God."—This probably puts Wat Tyler in the direct way of being declared a lunatic. Certainly all Anarchists come under this head. "Wat Tyler" bears a rather suggestive pseudonym to be engaged in the attempt to excommunicate Leon Czolgosz. I reject it utterly and entirely.

In the issue for April 27th, 1902, Walter C. Behlen, President, and Emil Schilling, Secretary of the Liberty Association of Cleveland, Ohio, came out with a signed statement addressed to their cult, headed, "Who was Leon Czolgosz? Was he a Governmentalist or a free man? Was he a State Socialist or an Anarchist?" In it they say that several German workmen, partly on account of Leon's radical views while a member of the Polish society and partly on account of the difficulty of pronouncing his name, nicknamed him "Niemand," a German word which means *Nobody*, and he finally assumed this name. They go on to say:

May 19th, 1901, Leon Czolgosz sought the acquaintance of several members of Liberty Association, after its session, introducing himself as Leon "Niemand." When asked about his political principles, he said that he was a Socialist and that he had affiliated with the Socialist Labor Party up to half a year ago; since then he had worked on his brother's farm in Bedford. When asked why he did not remain with his party, he replied that it was due to the split of the party into two hostile political organizations, and also that as a student seeking information he had become tired of mud-slinging and personal abuse. As to whether he had ever read any Anarchist literature, he answered no.

He was then given a book to read containing the speeches of the eight Chicago martyrs, as delivered in open court during their trial in Chicago, in 1886.

Czolgosz then asked us whether Cleveland Anarchists were secretly organized or held secret meetings. We told him no, and that all our meetings were public, because secrecy was no part of Anarchy. His questions and actions created a suspicion in the minds of his new acquaintances.

When he returned the book he said he had not read it for lack of time. Suspicion now grew stronger, and he was finally looked upon as a spy. Several weeks after this it was ascertained through a former party friend of his that Niemand was not his real name.

Several weeks before the assassination Czolgosz went to Chicago, where through similar behavior as here, he was also suspected as a spy. A week before the Buffalo tragedy "Free Society" published a pen picture concerning this man "Niemand," cautioning all comrades against him.

This is a true statement concerning Leon Czolgosz in his relation to the State Socialists on the one hand and the Anarchists on the other.

It can be proven by a quite a number in this city that he was a State Socialist and not an Anarchist, which shows that the blow struck at Buffalo was the deed of a governmentalist. Why then was Czolgosz classed as an Anarchist?

J. C. Barnes, of Hindsboro, Ill., in an article in the "Free Society" of April 27th, 1902, headed "What Constitutes an Anarchist," says:

A warm blooded being who can comprehend and understand human passions, which find vent occasionally in a violent, desperate deed, as did Breschi, may be an Anarchist. And a person who "philosophically sits back in a chair and demonstrates that human life is sacred and that a king has life which should be respected" may be an Anarchist. A person may rejoice at the acts of a Breschi, a Czolgosz, a Guiteau, a Booth, or any assassin, and be *an* Anarchist or *not* an Anarchist. A person may deplore and denounce their acts as brutal, dastardly or insane, and be an Anarchist or *not* an Anarchist.

Kate Austin, of Caplinger Mills, Mo., in the issue of August 17th, 1902, in an answer to a letter which she had received calling her attention to the fact that, bad as they were, the police protected Czolgosz from mob violence, published an article entitled "Who Are Trustworthy?", in which she says:

As for the form of protection extended Czolgosz by the police, the less said the better. The mob would have taken his life as an insane expression of sympathy for one whom they mistook for a victim. The officials saved Czolgosz from a speedy death in order that the beasts of authority might subject him to every species of mental anguish their diabolical cunning could inflict, and then led him forth and gave him the stroke of death. It is not a humane instinct that inspires the police to defeat the aim of the mob. This is especially true in the case of a regicide. The law must do its bloody deed to vindicate its awful majesty. The authorities not only prevent the mob from getting their lawful prey, but they also guard the prisoners condemned to death with great care, lest the poor wretches take their own lives.

It had now become time for the Anarchists to do just what the Government had given them the great opportunity to do, that is to make a martyr of Czolgosz, and in the issue of "Free Society" of Oct. 26th, 1902, Kate Austin, under the heading, "An Anniversary," says, in treating of Czolgosz as a sane person:

We, who are drawn together by a common ideal, can not permit the anniversary of Leon Czolgosz's death to pass in silence. Silence would shame the great cause, the first seeds of which were sown in the red blood of its advocates and martyrs. The movement against government means more than any reform movement of the past. It is not a struggle against one form of tyranny, but a struggle against tyranny in every form. Rebellion is thought in action. Thought that does not produce action is like a tree that bears blossoms but no fruit. . . .

Czolgosz saw that the State is merely a band of thieves, knaves and murderers; that the State was founded upon violence and existed by violence. He saw the parasites connected with it living in riotous waste and splendor off the products of slaves. He saw the political pimps of the money barons busy enacting new schemes and methods to rob the workers. Doubtless he had been taught in childhood that the starry banner floating over the housetops of his native city was the emblem of liberty and purity; perhaps the boyish heart thrilled with pride to think that he was an American born and therefore free. . . .

All hail the memory of Leon Czolgosz, sublime in his boyish candor and simplicity, magnificent in his high moral courage and iron will! With pride we lift our heads to greet the rebel who, on the threshold of death, uttered these sublime words: "I am not sorry I killed the President. I did it for the working people—the good working people."

To that class who murder by wholesale and always unite to torture liberty's martyrs, we say

"Go revel once more, ye cowardly knaves,
With the wantons your lusts have made!
Be drunken again on the blood of slaves
That are slain in your marts of trade."

But know this: the spirit that spoke at Buffalo is not dead. That spirit kindled new fires now smoldering in human minds. Government is doomed. On the far hills of our mental vision gleam the lights of social revolution. We do not weep for its dead; we only learn a lesson from their fortitude that drives more nails into the coffin of authority.

Liberty's martyrs are crowned with the flowers of hope—tyrants with despair, they are dead for all time. But our dead speak the language of the living, and are resurrected in each generation, to live in new beauty and strength.

Again to show the confusion among Anarchists as to whether Czolgosz belonged to their organization or not, I quote from an article by Helen Tufts in the "Free Society" of Dec. 21st, 1902, headed "Chicago Martyrs—and After," the following:

We have commemorated the brave death of five men, united in aim and hope, who accepted and were proud to bear the appellation which was meant to brand them with shame. We look back and see them standing together, their faces lighted with the same glow of revolt and self-sacrifice. . . . In the triumphant passing of these men was unfolded the significance of that era; in their martyrdom was at last translated the meaning of the terrible sequence of oppressive measures with which were ushered in the strikes, starvation and cold-blooded highway murders of the years previous to 1886. . . . It is with surprise and shame that I see this year's commemoration of their death inaugurated in "Free Society" with eulogies on the act of a lunatic, Leon Czolgosz. Whatever force the act eulogized might acquire had it been performed by a person in full possession of his faculties, it loses every vestige of significance before the well-established dementia and irresponsibility of the perpetrator.

But suppose it was true that Czolgosz was a "self-poised man," can the notion be for a moment entertained by any sane mind that his act was helpful to the cause of progress? McKinley was no bloody tyrant; he was a tool. Moreover, he was the representative of the majority in this country. It was for the interest of capital to bamboozle that majority into accepting him as their representative, but the fact remains that the great mass of the people of the United States regarded McKinley as their representative, and they supported the atrocious acts of his administration.

They were perfectly agreeable to the theft of the Philippines; ***they*** applauded the headlong rush of this country toward financial inflation; *they* viewed with pride the suicidal policy of the man they had elected. No matter that the people of this country were the mere puppets of a ring of capitalists, *they* are the ones with whom a Czolgosz must reckon, and it is folly to imagine that they will ever see any point in murder. As a matter of fact McKinley has become a saint, and in his dramatic death at the climax of his career, he exerts a more insidious influence than if he had been allowed to live and reap the harvest of his sowing. The forces of government have profited and have in every way recruited strength to oppress. I denounce every attempt to drag the Chicago martyrs into companionship with Czolgosz.

In "Free Society," of Dec. 28th, 1902, C. L. James says:

Fifteen months and more have passed since the bullet of Czolgosz avenged humanity for a series of acts about which only one opinion ought to exist among Anarchists, Socialist, believers in Republican institutions, in the American Constitution, the Monroe Doctrine or the Independence of the United States. The events of these months undoubtedly constitute the most formidable crisis through which Anarchism ever passed and the most brilliant victory it has ever achieved. On the night of McKinley's death—a night probably few American Anarchists are likely to forget—there seemed every probability that the history of our struggle against fraud and ignorance would be marked by a St. Bartholomew. In all the large cities most of us sufficiently known to attract personal interest had been, by way of preparation, imprisoned or put under surveillance of blue-bellied hang dogs. Half the Bible-bangers and all the bourgeoise pencil pushers in America had employed the previous week in inflaming the passions of the multitude against us. The millionaire thieves we, of course, knew to be the inspirers of the movement. The police and the militia might be counted on to assist the proposed massacre with a properly perfunctory attempt at its prevention. The ass who was becoming President had not yet brayed, as he did when Congress convened a few weeks later, but that he would do as his masters required was not within the limits of reasonable doubt. . . .

Czolgosz, however, was not an Anarchist. If there are comerades who still dislike hearing that said, I must remind them that an historian's first duty is to facts. The facts are that no one in Cleveland or elsewhere ever found Czolgosz out to be an Anarchist; that during his short visit to Chicago, where the comerades generally took him for a spy, he showed his ignorance of Anarchism by inquiring what he must do to be "initiated" into the "lodges" of our secret society, which does not exist; that the whole allegation of his Anarchism turned out at the trial to be an invention of the Buffalo police so ineffably clumsy that this silent, desperate enthusiast was made to skulk behind the skirts of a woman. Total failure to establish the affirmative of any proposition—such as that Czolgosz was an Anarchist—is all the proof that the negative requires or usually admits.

But, though not an Anarchist, Czolgosz evidently was a fanatic of some sort, and it becomes interesting, accordingly, to inquire of what kind. I have pointed out that there were parties who had much better reason to desire McKinley's assassination than the Anarchists. . . .

In the "Free Society" for January 11th, 1903, Abe Isaak, Jr., says:

Czolgosz's reticence proves nothing at all; and besides we do not know whether it was of his own choosing. Any number of cogent reasons may be advanced why a man in his position should decline to talk. So far as I can recollect, only one reporter (of the Associated Press) claims to have had an interview with him. The account of that interview states that he retired and turned his back when an attempt was made to implicate other persons. We know also that he especially requested to be allowed to make a statement on the morning of his execution, but this was positively refused. There is no reason, then, for the assertion that Czolgosz had nothing to say.

It is not true that the comerades in Chicago "generally" took Czolgosz for a spy. Very few of them had any knowledge of him at all, and among those who did the opinion that he was a spy was not unanimous. What finally determined the publication of the warning note was a letter from Cleveland. This letter, taken in the light of subsequent events, would not prove very damaging, but coming at the time, was decisive against a suspected man. It must also be remembered that several spies had been discovered in quick succession shortly previous to this time, which would naturally lead to suspicion more readily. . . .

I am not one of these "comerades who get mad" when it is stated that Czolgosz was not an Anarchist, and if he was merely a crank, as James has said, I am perfectly willing to have it known. But I am not willing to have facts twisted and distorted to make him out a lunatic or a fool as is done by those who are anxious to follow suit in a "repudiation craze" so prevalent since the Buffalo event. It makes no difference to me whether Czolgosz was an Anarchist or not, but his deed was one "about which only one opinion ought to exist among Anarchists, Socialists," etc. It was an act of protest and rebellion inspired by high motives and manly courage. In his own words he "killed the President because he was an enemy of the good people—the good working people." He was not sorry for his act. Let those who will make their calculations and protests; these facts remain.

Another writer in "Free Society," who desires to martyrize Czolgosz, writes in their issue of Jan. 18th, 1903, an article signed "B. Sachatoff," in which he says:

Listen to the voice of Czolgosz—to the last words before his death, and think for a moment of our brutal system, the basis of which is violence. Does Czolgosz then present himself to us as a fanatic Catholic? Oh, no. We see in him a man who took the sorrows and sufferings of the great mass of the working people to heart. He carried the burden silently until he could no longer endure it, and gave up his life. It was easier for him to die than to live in the midst of slaves and tyrants. Not being either, he stood alone in the world. Who can conceive of greater suffering?

Viroqua Daniels, in "Free Society" of Feb. 15th, 1903, writes an article under the title, "Much Fuss," from which I quote the following:

Was Czolgosz an Anarchist or a Catholic? What does it matter? If he was a conscious slave indulging in revolt against a master, the act gratifies me. His reported words signify that he knew what his position in society was.

And why such an ado by the slaves in all quarters about the death of a master? Do they not realize their condition? Why should the lives of our masters be of more importance to us than ours is to them? They kill us off with as little compunction as if we were flies. . . .

Every act done by a Catholic is for the "glory of God." The deed may be the taking of a life, either of a king or of a day laborer. It may be almsgiving or hospital service; but be it murder or what not, the object is the same always. They have ever acted without scruple, and there is no reason to doubt that they will continue to do so. Whomsoever or whatsoever stands in their way, they strike and strike to kill.

After my return home from investigating the life and the medical history of Czolgosz, I had a desire to attend one of the Anarchists' meetings, hear what they had to say and question them in regard to the belief among the Boston Anarchists as to Czolgosz being one of their cult. While in Cleveland I had learned that there were quite a number of Anarchists in and around Boston, and that they held meetings in a place called the "Woods of Liberty," on Buitta's Farm, Newton Upper Falls. I waited until I learned there was going to be a large gathering, so I should not be prominent among them, although I had become acquainted with several of them in Boston after my return. One of them told me that there was to be a "Solidarity Picnic" on Sunday, August 3rd, 1902, at Buitta's Farm, for the benefit of the victims of the Paterson, N. J., strike, and that there would be music by the Lynn comrades. It was to be an all day affair, beginning at nine o'clock and ending in the evening. On Sunday morning I took a Subway car to the Newton Boulevard, where I changed to a Norumbega car and asked for transfer to Newton Upper Falls. I left the car at Oak St., and walked down to the Pumping Station and turned to the right to Highland Avenue. It was rather a rough, wild country for a spot so near Boston—scrub oak and recently cut over woods as you approached the farm, but on the farm there was a very pleasant grove. Arriving at the farm about twelve o'clock, I found about one hundred men, women and children already there. Admission was 25 cents, children free. Refreshments were for sale on the grounds, and there were international songs and social games by groups here and there. I counted three red flags flying, but no American flags. The speeches were mainly along the lines of what one reads in their published paper. One could not help likening them to a lot of children, so enthusiastic were they over their games and music, which held their interest much more than the speech-making. I mingled with them all the afternoon and talked with many, but not one did I find who claimed Czolgosz as an Anarchist, and the feeling seemed to be pretty well disseminated among them that he was irresponsible.

CHAPTER VII

OPINIONS OF SPITKA, HAMILTON, CHRISTIESON, LYDSTON, HOLT AND HUGHES—SERVICE OF CZOLGOSZ'S BROTHERS IN THE WORLD WAR

The following quotations from Dr. William A. White, from whose "Outlines of Psychiatry" I have already quoted largely, as the authority today on mental diseases, would seem particularly suggestive in the Czolgosz case:

Mode of Onset.—The early manifestations of Dementia precox often go unrecognized for a long time and are diagnosed as other conditions. It must be realized that it may often be quite impossible to make a diagnosis by taking a cross section of the mental state at any time, particularly in the prodromal or initial stages. This is particularly true here as the early manifestations may be acute and transitory episodes, which clear up promptly. It is only by studying the life history of the individual that we come to realize that these episodes are but the early manifestations of a chronic process the tendency of which is toward deterioration.

These early manifestations may take the form of the various types of the manic-depressive psychoses, psychasthenia, neurasthenia, hysteria, hypochondria, acute confusion and paranoid states. In this class of cases, particularly if atypical, a search should be made for the fundamental symptoms as already described, particularly the emotional indifference and the attention disorders.

In describing the paranoid forms of dementia precox he says:

The fundamental fact is that in dementia precox cases presenting paranoid syndromes—delusions of persecution or grandeur—somewhat systematized—with perhaps hallucinations of hearing are found.

The difficulty of differentiating the conditions in their early stages is often very great, if not impossible. Since paranoia is no longer considered to be a purely intellectual disorder, its early stages are known to be marked by emotional depression. This same condition of emotional depression in the prodromal period of dementia precox is found. If then a boy of eighteen or twenty years old has a fairly well-organized delusional system and is somewhat depressed, showing little intellectual impairment, perhaps only a desire to seclude himself, with an apparent inability to apply his mind consistently to any end, it is difficult to know whether an incipient paranoia or a dementia precox is in the making.

Under the heading, "Courses and Progress of Mixed Forms," he says:

The simple and paranoid forms are the slowest of evolution and almost chronic in course, the paranoid forms often remaining in statu quo for two or three years. The hebephrenic and catatonic forms are more acute in onset and course, leading more rapidly to dementia in the majority of cases, although the catatonic form has rather the better prognosis.

Under "Prophylaxis," he says:

Preventive measures are dependent upon the ability to recognize in the child the possibilities of a future precox. The recent studies of character anomalies as found in the amnesias of precox patients, indicates the possibility of foreseeing this result in a considerable number of cases, particularly those presenting the shut-in type of personality.

No one recognized Czolgosz's early condition, else it might have been possible to avoid the tragedy which was the result of the development of his disease. Had Psychopathic Hospitals been more generally established, so that he could have gone to one for treatment when he first felt ill, or where one of the many physicians to whom he applied for relief could have referred him, the early symptoms of his disease would undoubtedly have been recognized, and the tragedy which resulted in the death of one of our Presidents and later in Czolgosz's own death would probably have been averted.

Mr. Spitzka, who performed the postmortem examination of Czolgosz, says at the end of his report, published in the New York Medical Record, Jan. 4th, 1902:

Of course it is far more difficult, and it is impossible in some cases, to establish sanity upon the results of an examination of the brain, than it is to prove insanity. It is well known that some forms of psychoses have little ascertainable anatomical basis, and the assumption has been made that these psychoses depend rather upon circulatory and chemical disturbances.

Nearly two years later Mr. Spitzka published, in Leslie's Weekly of Dec. 7th, 1903, an article entitled "Assassins Not Necessarily Insane." He states in his argument that assassins are not necessarily insane; that

Under exceptional circumstances assassinations may be a feasible means of bringing about reforms where other means fail—quoting many instances from history to bear out his argument—and he says that "misdirected patriotism impelled Booth and his associates to their concerted attacks at Washington." He gives other instances of what he calls misdirected patriotism:—

The fanatical hatred of a Huguenot killed Henry IV because his hatred took him to that deed as the culmination of a lifetime, and not as the ebullition of a momentary frenzy. It had been to alternately sharpen his dagger and break off the point, as the dominion of his project grew stronger or weaker. It led Czolgosz to dog the steps of the President most assiduously and it kept him firm, undeterred and unrelenting in his purpose. So little had impulse or momentary exaltation to do with it that Czolgosz could firmly resist any temptation to prematurely perpetrate the deed when its success was in the least degree questionable.

Those who claim "momentary insanity" should trace back the career to the point where it ceased, to possess any of the component elements of the regicide act. They would find that the moment of that "momentary insanity" was often a very long moment indeed. It lasted six years in Gerard's case, several years in Ravaillac's, two years in Clement's, a similar period with Felton, and several months with Booth, Bresci and Czolgosz. Witness Alibaud's shouting "Vive la Republique," Perri's singing the Marseillaise and Czolgosz's dying declarations. Lest it should be said that this is the consistency of dogged obstinacy, when it is remembered that the magnicide's pursuit of his object is very consistent with his previous course in life and that his act is the climax of his whole career, it must appear absurd to talk of "temporary insanity."

He writes as if someone had considered Czolgosz only momentarily insane, though I have seen no authority for such a conclusion in a most careful investigation and research into the literature on the subject of Czolgosz. Most of the men who have written about him have considered him, not *momentarily* insane, but insane, exceptions being those who examined him at the time of the trial and during his incarceration, and who made little or no attempt to investigate into his past history, and these men admit that he had false beliefs, one of them speaking of a "political delusion"; and the report of the experts says, "It should be said that, owing to the limited time—two days—at our disposal prior to the trial, and the fact that his family relatives resided in a distant state and were not accessible for interrogation, we were unable to obtain the history of his heredity beyond what he himself gave us."

This is not what one would consider a scientific investigation of the mental condition of Czolgosz, as any alienist would admit. Their opinion was evidently based upon the history given by the patient himself and their personal examination of him at a time when he was, we may say, at his best, the explosion which had been formulating for so many months having taken place and the protection of an institution having been afforded him, which temporarily relieved his symptoms. This is shown in other cases of dementia precox, who, after violent action, are taken to a hospital for the insane, where they immediately appear much better and remain almost normal for a time, as every superintendent of such hospitals can testify. This reaction from his delusional condition is further shown by the fact that for the first time in years he ate almost ravenously and of everything put before him, that he smoked to excess, and, for a short period, talked freely. Lombroso quotes Luccheni, who, he says, was what he calls a mattoid, or half-witted person, as saying in his confession:

> At first I was horrified at the idea of murder, but soon I found that a real inspiration had seized me. I felt inspired for a fortnight. I could not eat and could think of nothing but the assassination, but as soon as it was done sleep and appetite came back to me.

The trial for this man's life lasted eight and a half hours, with virtually no defense, and no evidence in his favor was brought forward; but the state of the public mind was such that probably no court or jury could have been found which would have opposed the will of the people. Dr. Allan McLane Hamilton says:

> The limit of tolerance was reached in the Guiteau case, but Czolgosz was hurried to death. The jury were in the room and heard the almost pharisaical protests of the two elderly judges assigned to the defense. It was just as much their duty to vigorously defend Czolgosz as it is a doctor's duty to succor a dying thief or a priest's to shrive a dying magdalen. Neither public opinion nor the personality of the victim should have influenced the lawyers. . . .
>
> The assassin was really a defective who had long been drifting to paranoia, and whose actual delusions of persecution and grandeur found soil in which to grow. As early as the spring of 1901 his family said he had "gone to pieces"; he neglected his trade and became a vagabond; he had delusions that he was being poisoned, for he bought and cooked his own food, and would not let even his mother prepare his meals. He talked a great deal about anarchy and murder, and eagerly read the accounts of the assassination of King Humbert; he likewise had religious and "exalted" delusions. His ordinary conduct before the commission of the crime had been orderly and gentle.

He was fond of children and simple things, and a week before his act had played with the little daughters of the people with whom he stayed. He was not notably vainglorious, and in the performance of the deed must have known that he was surely to sacrifice his life, and would probably be torn to pieces by the angry populace. He was undoubtedly of weak nature and absorbed the doctrines of anarchism in the same manner that certain morbid adolescents undergo a religious change which leads to a familiar kind of breaking down. Unlike the ordinary anarchist who, when he kills, takes means to save his neck and escape, this boy carried his fanatical recklessness to the extreme danger point with complete indifference to his fate.

In the electric chair his last words, I learn, were an expression of his delusions, which he consistently held to the last, and he died believing himself to be a martyr. The post-mortem examination showed nothing, but the young medical man who made it admitted very properly and fairly that "no indications of insanity can be found in many individuals who have been for a long period mentally disturbed."

If Czolgosz had been an Anarchist he must have had accomplices, but the prosecution never connected his act with anyone excepting himself. His desire to be an Anarchist was so great that he thought he was one, and that was probably one of his delusions, but even if he had been proven to be an anarchist, that would not have proven his sanity.*

* An editorial in the Rockland (Mass.) Independent, of February 21, 1902, refers to Czolgosz as "a poor ignorant creature who did not know the A. B. C. of Anarchy," and continues:

"Nor was there even evidence of his testimony that he ever was an anarchist—that was the testimony of only Policeman Bull. 'For years he not only refused to eat with others, but prepared his food for himself,' which is often the case with persons afflicted with hallucinations of persecution. He was 'rather stupid and dull-like' and 'had a kind of broken-down look.' He would never talk to strangers—'would sit all day thinking—like, reading a paper and sleeping'."

"The Government could have obtained this testimony as well as Dr. Briggs."

From an editorial in the Boston Herald of April 26, 1903, I quote the following paragraph:

"In the first place it has been made evident that the testimony given by Czolgosz, which these alienists accepted, but did not take the time to verify, was, in a large degree, misinformation. He did not give them the true number of the members of his family; he did not state what appears to be an indisputable fact, that for three years before the assassination he had

Dr. Sanderson Christieson, in this third edition of "Crimes and Criminals," published immediately after the assassination of President McKinley and after an investigation of Czolgosz's history, says:

At the age of 28 and after a life record of an exceptionally (abnormally) retiring and peaceful disposition, he suddenly appears as a great criminal. Had he been sane, this act would imply an infraction of the law of normal growth, which is logically conceivable.

Such a monstrous conception and impulse as the wanton murder of the President of the United States, arising in the mind of so insignificant a citizen, without his being either insane or degenerate could be nothing short of a miracle, for the reason that we require like causes to explain like results. To assume that he was sane, is to assume that he did a sane act, i. e., one based upon facts and for a rational purpose. . . .

Insane Egotism, e. g., his reason for killing the President was "I done my duty; I don't believe in one man having so much service and another having none."

Dr. Christieson brings out the following facts in Czolgosz's history as significant:

"(1) As a child he was markedly indisposed to associate with other children.

"(2) As a young man he studiously avoided the opposite sex and did not have a chum of any kind.

"(3) He was seldom distinctly ill, yet he was always complaining of ill-health and frequently took medicine.

"(4) He was notoriously prone to fall asleep in a chair at any hour of the day. . . .

"(6) At the age of 24 he quit work at the wire mill on account of his health, as he claimed to his relatives, and went to live on his father's farm, where he remained until about two months before his homicidal assault. Here he lived in comparative idleness. . . ." He continues:

"We thus see that his previous history reveals the development of a distinctly abnormal condition in his character and which could hardly be expected to continue much longer without a break or some peculiar overt manifestation, the precise form of which would depend upon the suggestions made to such a peculiar mind by passing events.

been a sick man; and it is further shown that while he had intercourse with the Anarchists in Cleveland and Chicago, the interviews that he had had were of a character to arouse general suspicion in the minds of these Anarchists that he was a spy."

"And yet he has been declared an Anarchist, sane and responsible, by the state's medical advisers."

Professor Regis of France says that

Regicides who survive almost invariably end in insanity and complete dementia; this confirms my opinion that they are unbalanced. As examples may be cited Sahla, Caleote, Passanante, Bernardi and Acciarito.

And yet, although sick, although delusional, although impulsive, they are almost always treated as responsible individuals, condemned to death both in order to punish them and in order to make examples of them. For my part, I think this method is both erroneous and unprofitable, and that society would be the gainer by treating these dangerous subjects, who so often cause upheavals of government, as insane patients.

Dr. Charles H. Hughes, in an article entitled "Medical Aspects of the Czolgosz Case," published in the "Alienist and Neurologist," January, 1902, says:

The too summary judgment and execution of the degraded assassin of one of the best intentioned Presidents since Washington or Lincoln, destroyed an excellent opportunity for studying thoroughly another psychological anomaly in the political history of our Republic, the third among the wretches who could deliberately murder an American President. . . . Czolgosz should have been kept alive under durance and scientific psychological surveillance, as the botanist would keep a newly-found exotic, until more might have been learned of his strange mental make-up, in order that our political future might profit by a better understanding of those anomalous integers and epochs of our anomalous present and recent past, when our Presidents have been slain by citizens.

The final record in this too hasty vengeance for the good of science, says that Czolgosz, the President's assassin, paid the penalty of the law for his crime at twelve and one half minutes after seven A. M. of October 29th ultimo, just forty-four days after the crime. . . . The autopsy was completed within four hours after death. The remains of the murderer were buried and destroyed by means of a carboy of commercial sulphuric acid poured upon the body in the lowered coffin. Thus ended the legal retribution in oblivion and extinction of every physical vestige of our President's destroyer, and even his clothing and effects were burned.

Lydston, in his essay on "Diseases of Society," says:

I do not believe that Czolgosz was an anarchist, although the matter of nomenclature is of little moment. I protest against obscuring true causes by a fallacious nomenclature. If all the anarchists in the world were slain, assassins of crowned heads and Presidents would still be at hand. The name by which each would be known would matter little, either to society at large or to our large army of degenerates. Czolgosz was considered an anarchist because he claimed to be one after the assassination. The same line of reasoning should settle the identity of John Alexander Dowie, who claimed to be John the Baptist. The assassin knew nothing of Anarchistic doctrines, and was repudiated by both the philosophic and destructivist branches of the cult. His claim was based upon the suggestion afforded by anarchistic literature and his egotism which impelled him to enlarge the importance of the deed.

Whether a fair study of Czolgosz was possible in the state of public excitement and resentment is open to question. A comparison of the rapidity with which this case was hurried through with the drag of ordinary murder trials is suggestive.

It is difficult in Massachusetts to find a lawyer of standing prepared, or even inclined, to take a criminal case. This is partly because criminal law is at a disadvantage, being almost entirely statute law. Instead of being made by judges, it has been made by legislatures composed of men of all sorts of pursuits, many of whom have had no training, but generally have prejudices as strong as their training is weak. Henry Holt, whose opinion I am quoting, says that criminal law is far behind the rest of the law and behind civilization and common sense. Punishment depends upon the result of the criminal's act; if a man intends murder he is punished for murder only in case the victim dies. Holt says:

The man commits his act, is arrested, and then the authorities wait, before trying him for a set of physiological processes in the victim, with which the criminal has no more to do than he has with the tides of Jupiter. . . . No wonder that under such conditions the question of the treatment of Anarchists has little more systematic attention than occasionally hanging one who kills somebody, . . . and the criminal law finds nothing more educative than the old-fashioned pains and penalties. . . . Czolgosz was found guilty of murder, despite the judge charging "If the defendant knew he was doing wrong at the time, the defendant was guilty of murder."—So far from knowing he was doing wrong, he believed he was doing right—a right for which he was willing to sacrifice his life, and from which he, in his grave, could gain no good. Nobody doubts this. The Associated Press report said that after the charge—

Lawyer Titus also asked the Court to charge the jury. "That if they were satisfied from the evidence that at the time of the committal of the assault the defendant was laboring under such a defect of reason as not to know the quality of the act, or that it was wrong, he was not responsible, and the jury must acquit."

"I so charge," answered the judge.

. . . But after Czolgosz was dead, the physicians were unable to find anything abnormal in his brain, and therefore he was not crazy and it was all right to kill him. Note the reasoning of the law: He had a good brain, and therefore should have been killed. . . . But the statement that he had a good brain assumes that the physicians could find all there was in the brain. . . . We do know the gross outlines of the brain, and sometimes can tell when a brain is grossly wrong, but then it is no news, for we knew it before seeing the brain at all. We know, regarding Czolgosz's brain that somewhere in it were tangles. . . . And yet the whole country is satisfied with the "moral responsibility," whatever that may mean, of Czolgosz, simply on the strength of what we do not know about his brain.

Holt goes on to say that if the world is angry the majority of doctors are angry, too, and the world kills the man and he is made a martyr for his whole crazy constituency, instead of becoming an object lesson. Suppose that, instead of making a martyr of Czolgosz, they had simply declared him the lunatic he was and immured him in a place which inspires only pity and aversion, how much greater would have been the educational result and the influence among other would-be assassins. A parent whips a child simply from being too ignorant or incompetent to impose a more rational punishment. The state acts in the same way when it kills, imprisons or fines for offences which have no more relation to killing, or to confinement, or to money than they have to the motions of the stars.

The most intelligent writers seem to be agreed that the principal cure for anarchism and allied cults must, after all, be educative.

Dr. Hughes says that Czolgosz's brain should have been given to science for more deliberate examination undamaged molecularly by his execution. Continuing, he says that the secular press of the country demanded that no more be said of the President's murderer and that he be speedily and silently disposed of and every vestige of him destroyed. The case is therefore ended and disposed of, and we are yet in darkness as to the real cause of this unnatural crime. . . . But what was the state of Czolgosz's mind? Legally sane, of course, for it would be contrary to sound public policy to extenuate such crimes on the plea of insanity in any but the most flagrantly insane. He was inspired by egotism not common to his station and the delusion of imaginary duty. "I killed the President," he said while in the chair about to be executed, "because he was the enemy of the good people. I am not sorry for my crime but I am awfully sorry I could not see my father." Stoic resignation, indifference and delusion in the face of certain death—courting rather than shunning the death consequences of his crime, as though it were a glorious martyrdom! No collusion, no instigation proved, but an abiding delusion of the President's responsibility for a condition which did not exist and which the President could not control if existing, and dominated by the egotistic delusion, the imperative conception, of his own mistaken duty to destroy the President. No hope of reward, death certain, no provision for nor attempt at escape, no shunning of consequences, no disturbance of mental equanimity, no regrets for detection, arrest or confinement, no compunction of conscience for the crime, no loss of sleep, of appetite, no motive but an imaginative and ordinarily uncompensating one of vicarious vengeance. A complacency and self-satisfaction abides with the fool after the crime and death, as one who, though execrated by the whole people for the most damnable of deeds, can calmly say "I am not sorry—I have done right. . . ."

Crank or crazed or criminal, these creatures are a menace to the welfare of the state. To summarily kill them in detail as crimes are committed, is no adequate remedy. Neither does electrocution enlighten us as to the engendering and evolving causes of the murderous breed. The thoughtful psychologist would find the nests and destroy the eggs of the abnormal neurones that make up these abnormal magnicides. . . . Carboys of vitriol obliterate the victim, but they do not solve the problem. . . . It is a pity that science should be crippled in her honest endeavors after truth by the too hasty executions of these mental anomalies among civilized mankind. It were better for the governments concerned, for science and for the world, that haste to execute vengeance should wait on scientific deliberation in these cases. They are morally and politically unique and out of harmony with liberal modern governments regulated by law and aiming at justice. . . . We are left sitting in the dark, still wondering how such a deed could have been done by a man in his sound and sober senses in fair and free America, and appalled at the possibility of a sane man murdering an American President.

It is interesting to note that three of Czolgosz's brothers served in the World War and one gave up his life for his country.

Joseph Czolgosz tried to join the United States Army but was not accepted because of his age, 49 years, so he joined the Canadian Expeditionary Force at Winnipeg on the 8th of May, 1918, under the name of Joe Peterson. He served in France and was discharged April 11, 1919; his War Service badge is No. 15,436.

Charles Czolgosz was anxious to join the Army at the beginning of the War, but his parents then being old persuaded him not to go until he was called. He was called in June, claimed no exemption and was placed in Class A1. He was sent to the University of Cincinnati Training School, transferred to Fort Sheridan, Illinois, and then with a detail of sixty boys was sent to Camp Mills to the Eighth Division for immediate service overseas. He was placed in Company D, Motor Supply Train, which was ready to sail when the Armistice was signed. He received an honorable discharge on the 7th of February, 1919.

Antoine Czolgosz, who was usually called "Tony,"

was Leon's youngest brother. He joined the Army at Los Angeles, California, and was transferred to Camp Lewis, Washington, where he was placed in Company K, 363d Infantry, 91st Division, American Expeditionary Force, and served with them in France. He was killed by a shell on the 4th day of the Argonne Drive.

THE AMERICAN RED CROSS
National Headquarters
Washington, D. C.

Jan. 31, 1919.
Private Tony Czolgosz,
Co. K, 363 Inf., Am. E. F.

Mr. Paul Czolgosz,
3557 East 59th St.,
Cleveland, Ohio.

My dear Mr. Czolgosz:

It is with deep regret that I am writing to confirm the death of your son, who died bravely fighting for his country and the glorious cause of freedom.

A grateful nation will never forget the debt it owes to all who have paid such a price for the cause, and as he lies in his soldier's grave he will be honored by the whole world, as one of the brave American soldiers who gave his life that the world might become a better and a safer place. I am enclosing a letter to you from the Chaplain of the 363rd Inf.

Please accept my very sincere sympathy for you in your great sorrow and believe me to be,

Faithfully yours,
(Signed) W. R. Castle, Jr.,
Director Bureau of Communication.

PART III

RICHESON

INTRODUCTION TO THE RICHESON CASE

THE CRIME OF REV. CLARENCE V. T. RICHESON ILLUSTRATING SEX DELINQUENCY. THE HISTORY OF THIS CASE IS UNIQUE IN THAT NO JURY WAS IMPANELLED AT THE TIME HE PLEADED GUILTY. HE WAS ELECTROCUTED WITHOUT TRIAL BY JUDGE OR JURY. AFFIDAVITS PRESENTED FOR THE FIRST TIME SETTING FORTH HIS MENTAL CONDITION WERE NOT CONSIDERED BY THE JUDGE WHO SENTENCED HIM AND WERE NEVER PASSED UPON JUDICIALLY. HIS PLEA FOR CLEMENCY WAS NEVER FORMALLY PRESENTED TO THE COUNCIL

The rest of this Volume, or Part III, is devoted to the case of Rev. Mr. Richeson, which is used to illustrate a certain type of sex delinquency and to show how Society neglects this class when given every opportunity to help them, and allows warning after warning to go unheeded until a crime is committed. Then Society which had shut its eyes and ears suddenly opens them to all the details of unpleasantness and horrors and kills the man it is responsible for. By not treating, helping or protecting him it left the community unprotected.

Should the layman chance to peruse this Volume, I must warn him not to read this case or especially

Chapter IV. His sensibilities might be shocked, as I have been obliged to frankly call a spade a spade.*

This History which must be a part of this Volume in order to illustrate the sex class with which we have to deal is written for medical men, scientific men, educators and those who have to do with this class; but I ask the reader who shrinks from sex problems especially as we find them in abnormal individuals to stop here for unless they feel their responsibility to Society they should not read the history of this man.

Richeson ought to have been kept alive and studied. He has been called an "inveterate liar." Certainly if amnesia does not explain his many contradictory statements he must be put down medically as a "pathological liar." A "dual personality" alone accounts for his conflicting characteristics.

After the newspaper sensationalism given this case the Rev. Father Hans Schmidt of New York killed Anna Annuller and in his confession he is said to have stated that Richeson and Thaw were "his inspiration." Such is the influence this class may exert if allowed to go on unguided, untreated and at large.

There is much that Richeson did in his life of which he was probably not conscious. Possibly his self mutilation was an act committed when he was in an unconscious state. It is quite apparent that Richeson's life, both conscious and unconscious, was dominated by the sex instinct. At times there was a bewilderment which is impossible for sane people to conceive of.

The State of Massachusetts should not wait for this class to commit some overt act, after a Commission appointed by the State has decided that they are irre-

* There is no evidence that Richeson was ever a sex pervert.

sponsible and should be cared for as soon as they are recognized.

If technical insanity cannot be established in these cases we must plead in the face of an angry justice and an unbelieving public their total irresponsibility, for a limited responsibility is both impracticable and impossible. They are not criminals but a class whom it is the clear duty of a civilized state to isolate from society and place under medical supervision.

The fact seems to be that we have not yet reached that stage of civilization where reckless immorality and persisting irregularity of conduct and temper are recognized as abnormal before some overt act is accomplished. Society is ready enough to condemn but not to pity and medical psychology has not advanced except sporadically to the recognition of the less apparent forms of mental aberration. It is a misfortune that so little has been accomplished by the medical profession to ameliorate the lot of these individuals. The existence of insanity if proven rightly exempts from punishment but it has always been the endeavor of the legal mind supported by a considerable section of public opinion to make light of medical evidence in all but the most obvious cases of insanity, for fear of encouraging too frequent resort to the pretext of irresponsibility. This erroneous idea is born of the old belief that morality and social order are entirely matters of police arrangement.

In a letter I received from Dr. John Macpherson, the High Commissioner for Insanity of Scotland, he wrote that "Hitherto at any rate the law has certainly erred on the side of severity, and has hanged ninety-nine irresponsible persons for one responsible person who has escaped on the plea of insanity. Although insanity exempts from punishment, society demands in its own interests the seclusion of the insane criminal, which seclusion is in itself of the nature of a very irksome kind of punishment, so that there is no question of the setting loose of the dangerous lunatic upon harmless society. The talk of the defeat sustained by justice in some cases is only a defeat of the old retaliative idea of punishment, which has had a fairly long reign over the insane in the past, and can now afford to relax its grim hold."

CHAPTER I

HISTORY OF THE CRIME. ARREST OF THE REV. CLARENCE VIRGIL THOMPSON RICHESON. HE PLEADS NOT GUILTY. ACTION OF THE CHURCH.

On Saturday evening, October 14, 1911, at 10 minutes after 7 P. M., Miss Avis Linnell who had just passed her nineteenth birthday was found dying in the bathroom of the Young Women's Christian Association on Warrenton Street, Boston. Groans emanating from the bathroom caused those who heard them to break down the door and Miss Linnell was found sitting in a chair attired in a nightdress and thin bathrobe with her feet in a tub of hot water. Soiled towels were near her and clean clothing was laid out ready to put on. Her head and body were thrown backward and she was unconscious. Dr. Mary Hobart was immediately summoned but Miss Linnell died at 7.35 without recovering consciousness. She had had supper and passed the evening with her companions with whom she was popular at the Association rooms. She appeared as cheerful as usual—she was naturally of a sunny disposition—and they had noticed nothing peculiar in her behavior. During the afternoon she is said to have had a long conversation with a "gentleman friend" and to have made an engagement with him which it is supposed she kept, as she left the rooms. When she returned she excused herself and retired early. Her friends knew that she had been engaged to Clarence V. T.

Richeson, at that time pastor of the Immanuel Baptist Church in Cambridge, and supposed that she had telephoned and been out with him. It was therefore natural that he was the first person with whom they tried to communicate, and a friend, Miss Inez Hanscom, succeeded in getting into communication with him about an hour after Miss Linnell's death of which she immediately informed him. He expressed surprise and said "Is that so? Are you sure that you are not mistaken? Why do you call me?" She replied "Because you were the only friend of Miss Linnell's near at hand and because we felt you should know of her death that you might come at once, and we feel that you are her fiancé." He then explained that he had baptized a Miss Linnell at Hyannis three years before and that she had a brother-in-law in Brockton who he suggested should be notified. Before ringing off Richeson asked "Did she say anything before she died?" Miss Hanscom replied "No, she didn't say anything before she died but she said something this afternoon." A few of her friends at the Association knew of her disappointment at the breaking off of the engagement with the minister and they at once attributed her death to suicide as Richeson's engagement to a Brookline girl had been announced in a Cambridge paper on October 11, three days before Miss Linnell's death, and invitations for the wedding on October 31 had already been issued.* The papers spoke of Miss Linnell as "a young girl from the country who had come to seek her fortune in

* About October 10 Richeson is said to have leased half of a double house next the Carters on Magazine St., Cambridge, at $35 a month, possession to be taken on the 1st of November. He is said to have told the agent he was to be married and wanted everything in readiness for his bride and was very particular to look after all the repairs and improvements himself, the furniture to be moved in the week following the lease.

Boston and was overcome by her disappointment at the loss of her fiancé with whom she was known to be deeply in love."

Medical Examiner Leary was notified as is required in all cases of suicide or violent death and after a thorough investigation he found that the conditions surrounding the death of Miss Linnell were not consistent with a suicide theory and ordered the body to the City Hospital Morgue for autopsy. His report of the autopsy was made on Sunday, October 15. It stated that Miss Linnell's death was caused by cyanide of potassium and that she was four months pregnant. On that same Sunday morning Richeson preached as usual in the Immanuel Baptist Church, his text being *"Blessed is he whose transgression is forgiven, whose sin is covered,"* and in the evening went to the home of his fiancée in Brookline. The young women at the Association were shocked by Mr. Richeson's apparent indifference and the fact that he did not come to see the body. Mr. McLean, the brother-in-law, who arrived early Sunday morning, strongly expressed his belief that Richeson was responsible for the tragedy, that his sister-in-law had taken the poison in the hope of relieving her physical condition and that she was ignorant of the deadly nature of the drug she had taken.

It was while preaching in Hyannis that Richeson became acquainted with Miss Linnell in June, 1908, meeting her first at the wedding of her older sister and Mr. W. J. McLean of Brockton, at which he officiated. Richeson was still a student in the Newton Theological Seminary from which he later graduated in 1909 but during the summer of 1908 he "supplied" in the pulpits of the Hyannis and South Yarmouth Baptist Churches.

Miss Linnell was the daughter of a well-to-do carpenter and builder and a student in the State Normal School. She joined the Baptist Church and became an active member. Her engagement to Richeson soon followed and on December 17, Richeson bought a gold ring at Hyannis and gave it to her on December 19, 1908, her 17th birthday. Miss Linnell's engagement to Richeson was announced at a small party given by her sister Mrs. McLean. Mrs. Linnell, the mother, said that she knew that after a time the engagement was broken but she firmly believed it was renewed and that Avis was engaged to him when she died. She stated that she loved Mr. Richeson as a son before he became formally engaged to Avis; that they were much worried by *attacks which he had at their house;* although the attacks did not appear to be serious they left him in a highly nervous state and he was often forced to leave the table because of them. He was worrying about them when he broke his engagement with Avis. The date for Richeson's marriage with Miss Linnell had been set for October, 1910, and Miss Ormsby of Hyannis was to be bridesmaid. Something happened to upset the plans and Miss Linnell left her home in Hyannisport in September, 1910, to study at the New England Conservatory of Music and took rooms at the Boston Young Women's Christian Association on Warrenton Street.

According to Mr. McLean she wore the engagement ring until Christmas, 1910, when she is said to have given it to Richeson to have it repaired, because a stone was loose and needed tightening. In April, 1910, Mr. Richeson resigned from his Hyannis pulpit after awakening considerable adverse feeling in the Church by his sensational manner and the subject matter of

CLARENCE V. T. RICHESON

A student at the Newton Theological Seminary, 1908.

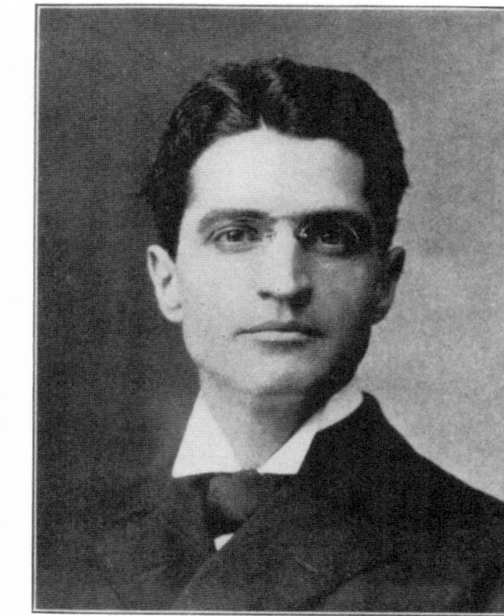

CLARENCE V. T. RICHESON

Pastor of the Immanuel Baptist Church, Cambridge, 1910.

his sermons. On May 20, the Immanuel Baptist Church of Cambridge voted to call him to the pulpit, where he began his duties as minister on June 1st, 1910. In August of the same year while visiting Miss Linnell at the home of her sister Mrs. McLean in Brockton he had one of *his nervous crises* followed by amnesia. While Miss Linnell was getting him a glass of water Richeson disappeared, turning up at his Cambridge lodgings late on the following day.

On March 13, 1911, the Barnstable *Patriot,* a newspaper published at Hyannis, printed the announcement of the engagement of Rev. C. V. T. Richeson and Miss —— of Brookline. About the same time Miss Linnell's mother received a letter from her daughter saying her engagement with Mr. Richeson was broken. On September 29, 1911, Miss Linnell after a summer at home returned to Boston for her second term at the Conservatory, again taking rooms at the Y. W. C. A.

During this same summer Richeson was granted a vacation of two months by his Church on account of a *"mental breakdown"* as one of his parishioners reported. He spent these two months in Hyannisport and again resumed his intimacy with Miss Linnell. The people there knew that the engagement had been broken and the only way they could reconcile this with the fact of his spending so much time with her was the belief that the engagement had been renewed, but this belief was destroyed when the announcement appeared in the paper of Richeson's engagement to another woman. Even after the invitations were out for Richeson's wedding on October 31 with Miss ——, Miss Linnell showed no sign of depression and possibly expected him to keep faith with her.

It was not strange considering the above history that the brother-in-law, together with the friends, the reporters and the police, began at once to try to ascertain where the poison had been purchased and by whom and to prove with whom she had lunched on the Saturday afternoon before her death. All indications pointed toward Richeson but actual proof of his guilt was at first lacking. Under this cloud of suspicion Richeson had many warm friends and defenders. He remained secluded at the ——'s home in Brookline for some days after the tragedy, only venturing out once in company with Mr. —— to do some business in Boston, driving all the way and closely muffled to avoid photographers. Miss Linnell's funeral was held in Hyannisport October 17. The crowd was so great that many were unable to enter the house but Richeson was not among them. On the same day the Immanuel Baptist Church of Cambridge refused to condemn their pastor until they had heard from him. In the meantime the police were working on the theory that the death was not the result of suicide and were making a systematic inquiry among drug stores. On October 18 Medical Examiner Leary issued a further report in which he said "The conditions surrounding the body are consistent with the belief she did not intend committing suicide. She came to her death from cyanide of potassium poisoning and lived 25 minutes after the drug was taken. The quantity she took was rather small and had been contained in an unmarked piece of white paper."

Miss Barkhouse, Miss Linnell's room mate, in writing to the mother said "A great many things happened that we dare not write but Mr. Richeson took Avis out to lunch yesterday. She returned at 4 P. M. apparently in good spirits and had supper with the girls in the dining-room."

The brother-in-law, Mr. McLean, held to the theory that Richeson was responsible for the death of Miss Linnell. He said that Richeson had a great fascination for women, that in conversation he charmed women and held them as if by magic. He had the "faculty of getting into difficulties which did not amount to much" and Mr. McLean could not understand the fact that he refused to help his sister when called by her friends at the Association to do so. He predicted that it would be found that Richeson was with his sister-in-law a few hours before her death and that it was he who gave her the powder.

While the police and others were working to fathom the mystery Richeson, as we have said before, preached in the morning at the Immanuel Baptist Church in Cambridge on Sunday, October 15. He then went to dinner with a friend on Oxford St. in Somerville. Here he was taken very ill and asked his hostess for camphor. At the evening service he referred to the death of a very dear friend and used a sermon he had written on the previous Thursday. After the service he went to the ——'s in Brookline and remained there. On October 19 he visited Boston and consulted a lawyer, Philip R. Dunbar.

The police investigation centered around Richeson but no evidence was found on which to arrest him until the evening of October 19 when William Hahn, a druggist on Union Street in Newton Centre, felt it his duty to make some statement of the fact that Richeson had bought poison of him. He consulted his lawyer, Rep. Elias R. Bishop, who telephoned to Deputy Watts that he thought he knew the man who had sold the poison and invited the Deputy to his house where he met William Hahn. Hahn's drug store had been a gathering place for the students of the Newton Theological Seminary and Mr. Hahn was intimately acquainted with Richeson who he said had come to his store on the evening of Tuesday, October 10th, apparently for a social call. After conversing for a time during which he spoke of his approaching wedding which was to take place on October 31 in the First Baptist Church at Newton Centre, he said just as he was about to leave that he had a dog at home that he wished to dispose of as she was messing his room and was whining and making a disturbance, and asked the druggist to give him something that would kill the animal.* Hahn advised him to use chloroform but Richeson declared that it left a disagreeable odor and would be troublesome to use. He asked for a poison that would act more quickly. Hahn then suggested arsenic but said that it might make the dog fat and then said that he would give him some cyanide of potassium. Enough of this compound to kill three dogs was placed in a wide-mouthed bottle. The druggist advised Richeson to be extremely careful in its use saying that even the bottle might be dangerous if thrown away. Richeson then asked more about the poison declaring that as long as the dog was about to have pups he wanted enough of the poison to kill the dog and the pups too, and Hahn weighed out an additional lump, the entire quantity being enough to kill ten people. No bottle or other

* Frank H. Carter with whom Richeson was boarding at that time said on October 21 "about ten days ago, Mr. Richeson told Mrs. Carter that he would kill our dog. The dog is a puppy and not thoroughly housebroken. Mr. Richeson was very much provoked and said he would kill the animal."

container nor any of the powder was found near Miss Linnell or on Richeson's person or in his room.—Before leaving the store to catch his car Richeson told Hahn to be sure to come to his wedding "on the 31st." He requested the druggist to maintain secrecy regarding the poison, adding that though it might seem mysterious his intended use of it was quite legitimate.

After hearing Hahn's story Deputy Superintendent Watts immediately called up Police Headquarters and with Chief Inspector Dugan, Inspector Mitchell and other police officials proceeded at once to the house in Brookline where Richeson was. It was now 1.30 A. M. and a score of reporters and photographers were already on the scene making efforts to gain admission but in vain. The officers demanded admittance in the name of the law but got no response. As they did not have a warrant to break in they took up positions outside, guarding all the means of exit. At 7 the next morning, October 20, when a maid came downstairs to prepare breakfast Sergeant Rutherford went to the rear door and told her he was an officer of the law and wished to confer with Mr. Richeson. The servant then told this to Mr. —— who said that he thought the people outside the house were all reporters. He declined at first to believe that the police had come to arrest Richeson; but after a telephone conversation with his attorney he led Deputy Watts to a room on the second floor which was occupied by the clergyman. They found Richeson in bed, awake and extremely nervous. When told he was under arrest he asked for a glass of hot milk and while it was being prepared he dressed with difficulty owing to his excited condition. He asked to see Miss ——, was accompanied to her room and bade her an affectionate farewell, then took leave of her parents and was taken to Police Headquarters in Pemberton Square, Boston, where he answered the questions of the officer, who booked him, in a clear, firm voice, giving his age as 31, and his address as 147 Magazine St., Cambridge. Outside the Headquarters were several hundred people who pressed so close that officers had to be sent out to clear the sidewalk. Before being taken into court Richeson was confronted with Hahn. When Hahn was brought into the room where Richeson was waiting, the clergyman left his seat and extended his hand with a word of greeting and it was noticed that of the two the druggist was the more perturbed. Hahn was seated facing the prisoner and repeated the story he had told Deputy Watts and through the recital of these details Richeson sat calmly looking in the face of the man who was helping to weave the net of evidence about him. After hearing Hahn through he declined to make any statement but asked for his breakfast which he ate with evident relish. At 11.55 the same morning a warrant having been signed by Judge Duff charging Richeson with first degree murder, he was taken before Judge Murray in the first session of the Municipal Court where Mr. Dunbar waived the reading of the complaint and asked for a continuance until October 21 which was granted, the prisoner being held without bail and then he was taken to the Charles St. Jail where he maintained a silence which was remarkable.

His loyal friends stood by him and financially helped him to secure the services of able lawyers. Philip R. Dunbar was the first lawyer to appear for Richeson after his arrest in Brookline. Judge Dunbar and Judge Robert O. Harris were retained as consultants.

Naturally Richeson's congregation in Cambridge were much concerned by his arrest. There were among them individuals of various shades of opinion in regard to his guilt but the Church as a whole as yet stood by him refraining from condemning him so long as there was the least possibility of his innocence. On October 24 Richeson wrote the following letter:

To the Immanuel Baptist Church,
Cambridge, Mass.
Dear Brethren:—

I appreciate the position in which the church is now placed, but I would ask its consideration until after the preliminary hearing, or, if the Grand Jury previously meets, until that time.

Most fraternally,
Clarence V. T. Richeson.

Boston, Oct. 24, 1911.

On October 27 Richeson's congregation met and considered his letter and sent him the following reply:

October 27, 1911.

Rev. Clarence V. T. Richeson,
Dear Sir:

Your communication of the 24th inst. was duly received and read before the church. We unanimously voted to await until such time as the grand jury makes its decision.

Praying that all things may turn out for the best,

Sincerely yours,
in behalf of the church,
Charles F. Cummings, Clerk.

In the meantime there were some persons in the town of his previous pastorate who were not as charitable and on October 31 an effigy of Richeson was found hanging on a tree in front of the Baptist Church in Hyannis. Placarded in big letters were words attacking the minister's character, also the reference "See Luke 17, 2." In addition, "This is no reflection on the Church. The offender will be burned in the ball field at 10.15 in the morning." Signed "Vigilance Committee." In contrast to this were the prayers offered up in the church at Hyannis on October 22 "for our sorrowing ones and for the minister now beset by so many troubles."

On October 26 a special session of the Grand Jury was called to consider his case and on October 31 the Municipal Court continued the case until November 7. In the meantime the Municipal Court lost its jurisdiction for on November 2 the Grand Jury brought an indictment and the district attorney nol prossed the case in the lower court. The indictment contained five counts, "that he gave," "that he sent and conveyed," "that he caused the poison to be taken and swallowed," "that he gave it pretending it was a medical preparation" and "that he did assault and poison with intent to murder by this giving and causing to be taken."

On November 2 he addressed his resignation to the clerk of the Immanuel Baptist Church as follows:

Charles Street Jail, Nov. 2, 1911.

Charles F. Cummings,
Clerk Immanuel Baptist Church,
15 Marlboro St., Belmont, Mass.
My dear Sir:

I beg to herewith tender my resignation as pastor of Immanuel Church.

Strong in the consciousness of my innocence and firmly persuaded that God in His own good time will lift this burden from me, I, nevertheless, feel that I should not permit the shadow thrown across my life to darken the religious welfare of my church and its people, whom I love.

I, therefore, deem it my duty to place the church in a position to select my successor.

With my heartfelt thanks for the many kindnesses shown me by each and all of the members of my church, I am

Sincerely yours,

Clarence V. T. Richeson.

After a meeting the congregation voted, 30 to 15, not to accept his resignation. On November 10 Richeson again urged them to accept his resignation in the following letter which was received by them on November 14:

Charles Street Jail, Nov. 10, 1911

To the Immanuel Baptist Church:

Dear Brethren:

I cannot express to you how deeply I am touched at your loyalty and manifestations of confidence in me, in this my great hour of trouble, and I thank you most sincerely.

I cannot but feel personally, however, that the welfare of the church might be prejudiced while its minister is placed in his present sad position, and I therefore feel, notwithstanding my grateful appreciation of your kindness, that the church should accept my resignation; of course leaving it entirely to you how and when the matter should be carried into effect.

Most fraternally,

Clarence V. T. Richeson.

On November 13 he was arraigned and pleaded "Not Guilty."

CHAPTER II

RICHESON'S RESIGNATION ACCEPTED. SUCCESSFUL SELF-MUTILATION. RETRACTS PLEA OF NOT GUILTY. PLEADS GUILTY TO MURDER IN FIRST DEGREE AND COUNSEL PRESENT CONFESSION. SENTENCED TO DEATH. ONLY CASE IN MASSACHUSETTS SENTENCED TO DEATH WITHOUT TRIAL BY EITHER JUDGE OR JURY. ALIENISTS FOR THE DEFENCE PRESENT THEIR REPORTS

On November 24 Richeson's original letter of resignation of his pastorate which had been laid on the table, together with the one written from his cell in Charles Street Jail and dated November 10 urging the acceptance of his resignation, were considered and the Church voted to accept, though with resolutions expressing faith in the minister. On December 14, 1911, Judge Sanderson was assigned by Chief Justice Aiken to try Richeson and the trial set for January 15.

On December 20 at 4 o'clock in the morning the quiet of the big stone jail on Charles Street was turned into feverish excitement by cries of agony from Richeson's cell. Three officers on duty rushed from the guard room, pressed on the lights and asked, "What is the matter in there?" "I am bleeding to death, I am dying," gasped Richeson, who was lying on the floor by the side of his cot. The door was thrown open and the officers rushed in and lifted him onto his cot. They found him bleeding profusely from a horrible mutilation by which he had endeavored to emasculate himself, which was partially successful. He had apparently used a piece of tin, jagged and sharp, the top of a marmalade jar. Dr. Sargent, the Jail Physician, was summoned, also Drs. Howard A. Lothrop, David D. Brough and John L. Ames, who rushed to the jail in automobiles. Richeson was hurried to the jail hospital unconscious on a stretcher, etherized and operated upon by Dr. Lothrop, who stated that while Richeson seemed conscious when he arrived he was very weak from the loss of blood. He closed the wound after completing the emasculation. Richeson was at the point of death for several days. He evidently tried to bring on a hemorrhage several days later, as Dr. Lothrop, in suing the County of Suffolk for his bill of over $500 the following year, stated that the operation was a delicate one and a major operation, and that several days after the operation he found the prisoner had loosened the bandages as if to remove them and pulled the stitches from the wound, after which the sheriff had Richeson pinned tightly in a blanket and a man left to guard him. Dr. Lothrop, continuing his testimony, said that he made 27 professional visits at the jail after the operation, all of which he considered necessary.

On December 27 three hundred veniremen were drawn from among whom to select the Richeson jury, but no jury was ever selected. On January 5 he retracted his plea of "Not Guilty" and plead guilty to murder in the first degree and his counsel presented the following confession:

January 5, 1912.

John L. Lee, Esq., William A. Morse, Esq.,
Philip R. Dunbar, Esq.

Gentlemen:

Deeply penitent for my sin and earnestly desiring, as far as in my power lies, to make atonement, I hereby confess that I am guilty of the offence of which I stand indicted.

I am moved to this course by no inducement of self-benefit or leniency.

Heinous as is my crime, God has not wholly abandoned me, and my conscience and manhood, however depraved and blighted, will not admit of my still further wronging by a public trial, her, whose pure young life I have destroyed.

Under the lashings of remorse I have suffered and am suffering the tortures of the damned. In this I find a measure of comfort.

In my mental anguish I recognize that there is still, by the mercy of the Master, some remnant of the divine spark of goodness still lingering with me.

I could wish to live only, because within some prison's walls I might, in some small measure, redeem my sinful past, help some other despairing soul and, at last, find favor with my God.

You are instructed to deliver this to the district attorney or the judge of the court.

Sincerely yours,
Clarence V. T. Richeson.

On January 9 Richeson plead "Guilty to murder in the First Degree" before Judge Sanderson in the Superior Court, and as there was only one penalty, only one course open for the Judge in first degree murder, Judge Sanderson sentenced Richeson to death during the week of May 19th. The following is a copy of the death warrant:

COMMONWEALTH OF MASSACHUSETTS.

Suffolk, *ss.*

To the Sheriff of our County of Suffolk, to such Deputy as he may name, and to the Warden of our State Prison at Boston in said Commonwealth.

WHEREAS, at a sitting of our Superior Court holden at Boston, within and for our said County of Suffolk, for the transaction of Criminal Business, on the ninth day of January in the year of our

Lord nineteen hundred and twelve, CLARENCE V. T. RICHESON of said Boston, pleaded guilty to the crime of murder in the first degree, and thereupon by our said Court the said Clarence V. T. Richeson was adjudged and sentenced for said crime to suffer the punishment of death by the passage of a current of electricity through his body within the week beginning on Sunday, the nineteenth day of May next, as to us appears of record, a copy of which record we have caused to be hereunto annexed, and whereas a certified copy of the whole record of said plea and sentence has been delivered to His Excellency the Governor, as required by law, execution of which sentence remains to be done:

We, therefore, command you, said Sheriff to confine him, said Clarence V. T. Richeson, in the jail in our said County of Suffolk, until within ten days of Sunday, the said nineteenth day of May next, being the first day of the week appointed for the execution of said sentence, and thereupon and within said ten days to convey him as secretly as may be to our said State Prison, and to deliver him with this our warrant and with a return of your doings hereon to the said Warden of said State Prison or to the officer performing the duties of said Warden.

And we command you, said Warden, that you receive him said Clarence V. T. Richeson and keep him in close custody, as provided by law, until the infliction of the punishment of death upon him, and that on some day to be by you selected within the week beginning on the said Sunday the nineteenth day of May next, and at an hour between midnight and sunrise, within the building provided for the purpose adjoining said State Prison, agreeable to the provisions of the statute in such case made and provided, you cause execution of the said sentence of our said Court in all respects to be done and performed upon him the said Clarence V. T. Richeson by causing to pass through his body a current of electricity of sufficient intensity to cause death and continuing the application of such current until he is dead; for all which this shall be your sufficient warrant.

Hereof fail not at your peril, and you said Warden are to make return of this warrant with your doings hereon into the office of the Clerk of our said Court within and for our said County of Suffolk as soon as may be after you shall have executed the same.

Witness John A. Aiken, Esquire, and the seal of our said Court, at said Boston, this twenty-second day of January in the year of our Lord nineteen hundred and twelve.

John P. Manning,
Clerk.

The Hon. William A. Morse says that to his knowledge Richeson is the only man in Massachusetts who ever pleaded guilty of murder in the first degree with confession and the only man he knows of who was executed without trial by judge or jury.

John L. Lee of Lynchburg, Va., one of the most successful criminal lawyers in the south, had been added to the counsel for the defence. Richeson's father, Thomas Varland Richeson, visited his son at the jail on October 25th.

After his sentence to death Richeson's attorneys raised the question of his sanity and employed Dr. Isador H. Coriat and Dr. Edward B. Lane to examine him and report their opinion.

On April 24, 1912, Dr. Lane made his report as follows:

April 24, 1912.

Hon. William A. Morse,
Equitable Building, Boston.
Dear Sir:

At your request, I have examined the affidavits prepared in the case of Clarence V. T. Richeson. Today, I interviewed Mr. Richeson at the Charles Street Jail. Since 1896, he has been subject to attacks lasting from several hours to two or three days, memory of which, he claims to have none. These attacks, in my opinion, are those of hysterical insanity or hysterical delirium. He tells me that, in addition to these, he has had several attacks of what is, in my opinion, hysterical amnesia. He has been subject, also to lesser losses of memory such as a temporary forgetfulness of his own name, or his address, etc. Such disorder is frequently associated with the attacks of hysterical delirium described by his intimate friends. This psychosis is a serious disorder, and in this case seems to be well established. Aside from the conspicuous attacks of amnesia and delirium, I should expect such a person at all times to have less will power and less judgment than the normal person. This being so, it follows, in my opinion, that such people have less responsibility than the normal individual. Mr. Richeson, in my opinion, is suffering from a mental disorder chronic and incurable in nature, the possessing of which implies impaired responsibility.

Very respectfully,
(Signed) Edward B. Lane, M. D.

On May 8, 1912, Dr. Coriat made his report as follows:

May 8, 1912.

On this day I examined Rev. Clarence V. T. Richeson at the Charles St. Jail and submit the following report concerning his mental condition.

There is a bad heredity in the form of a family history of insanity in various members of the family. When Mr. Richeson was ten years of age, he fell from a horse, striking on his head, was temporarily unconscious and since then he has suffered from periodic severe headaches. Since the age of seventeen, he has had a number of unconscious attacks and wandering spells, in which he would do peculiar things and wander from place to place. These attacks were followed by complete loss of memory for each attack which comprised hours and sometimes days. They would be repeated several times a year and usually followed mental or physical fatigue. They were always preceded by a dazed mental condition, of varying duration. On several occasions he has had sudden temporary lapses of consciousness with dizziness. For his auto-mutilation shortly after his arrest, he likewise has no memory. He was able to cite a number of instances of these attacks with subsequent loss of memory, for instance, on one occasion in 1910, after supping with friends in Brockton, his next recollection was two days later when he found himself in his own room in Cambridge, the intervening period being a complete mental blank. As a result of my examination, I am of the opinion that Rev. Clarence V. T. Richeson has, since the age of seventeen, suffered from hysteria, the disease manifesting itself in sudden attacks of losses of consciousness of varying duration. During these attacks he was irresponsible, while the repeated attacks themselves have rendered him more or less abnormal.

(Signed) Isador H. Coriat, M.D.

These reports were submitted to Governor Eugene N. Foss, who promised to consider the question of Richeson's commutation. Immediately there was a flood of letters and telegrams received at the State House and by others who were working on the case. Some threatened the lives of Governor Foss and of others if he did not grant a commutation of sentence; some threatened his life if he did. The following is a specimen of the many threatening letters he received:

May 9, 1912.

Governor Foss,
Boston, Mass.
Your Excellency:—

How would you feel if that beast in human form, named RICHARDSON, had murdered one of your beautiful twin daughters? Would there be anything bad enough for the creature then? Think this over and I am afraid that if you show any leniency to him, you may be punished in some unforseen way yourself.

Yours very respectfully,
CITIZEN.

The following is a copy of one of the letters pleading leniency:

Cleveland, O., May 7, 1912.

Governor Foss.
My dear Sir:

I am hoping that Rev. Mr. Richeson will be saved from the death penalty. I am an Eastern woman by birth, my only son a graduate of Harvard, and my late husband of Amherst College.

I do not believe in capital punishment, and great though his crime is, and pathetic as woman's trust is, we all know that blame is not confined to one sex, or to one person. I cannot see that the church or society would be helped by his death.

Sincerely,
Sarah K. Bolton.

One woman offered herself to go to the chair in his place. Such was the emotional excitement at the time. One man from Whitman, Mass., called upon the Governor offering his nine-year-old daughter to be electrocuted in the place of Richeson, saying that he had a vision that if he sacrificed his daughter in Richeson's place there would be no more capital punishment in Massachusetts. One woman called upon Mr. Morse and said, "The world has a claim on so handsome a man as Richeson and nobody has the right to rid the world of such a man." She left for the State House to plead with Governor Foss and then visited the State

Prison and informed Warden Bridges under pledge of secrecy that she wanted to exchange places with Richeson and allow him to walk from the prison a free man while she went to the chair herself. The above are not isolated examples, but scores of men and women besieged the office of Governor Foss and Lawyer Morse and many appealed to the alienists.

CHAPTER III

GOVERNOR FOSS ASKS DR. L. VERNON BRIGGS TO EXAMINE RICHESON AND REPORT HIS FINDINGS TO HIM. COMMISSION ALSO APPOINTED TO EXAMINE RICHESON FOR THE COUNCIL. HISTORY OF RICHESON'S HEREDITY AND EARLY LIFE. AFFIDAVITS OF PHYSICIANS ATTENDING HIM, ETC.

On April 29th I received a request from Governor Eugene N. Foss to examine Rev. Clarence Virgil Thompson Richeson at the Charles Street Jail to determine his mental condition. During my investigation and examinations, a member of the Council requested that a Commission be appointed for the same purpose. The Commission appointed by the Governor consisted of Drs. Henry R. Stedman, George T. Tuttle and Henry P. Frost. They examined him for two hours on a Saturday and seven hours on a Sunday. It was reported that on Sunday, after three hours' examination, the Commission could not agree, and at the end of four hours more there still was one member who did not agree with the others; not until after a long conference in the evening did they come to an agreement. After this examination, occupying virtually the whole of Sunday, Richeson returned to his cell and played a game of checkers with his companion, Butts, and smoked a cigar. The Commission first made an oral report to the Governor, who then issued a statement for the press as follows:

The substance of the detailed report of Drs. Stedman, Tuttle and Frost, the Commission appointed by the Governor to examine the mental condition of Clarence V. T. Richeson, is that although he is by nature emotionally unstable and subject to hysterical manifestations which occasionally have been pronounced, he was in no sense insane at the time of the commission of the crime for which he has been sentenced to death and is not insane now.

Later they rendered a written report substantially as above.

In my examination of Richeson I first considered his heredity, and for those who believe in heredity I give the ancestors, direct and collateral, of Richeson, in whom there seems to have been mental disease, according to the history given by his father and corroborated by affidavits from others who were in a position to know the facts. Following this history I give the instances in Richeson's early life bearing upon his future conduct and behavior.

The heredity of Clarence V. T. Richeson is as follows:

Thomas V. Richeson's mother was one of seven children:

1. Maggie Douglas, married and had four children—one has been deranged for some years, and *is now in a lunatic asylum.*

2. Sally Douglas had two children—*one is deranged,* but harmless.

3. Nancy Douglas had four children—*one was deranged;* and a daughter who married had a son who was *mentally deranged and so died.*

4. Mary, the grandmother of Clarence Richeson, had six children—one of the sons, an uncle of Clarence, *was insane* and *died in the Lunatic Asylum at Staunton, Va.*

5. Jennie Douglas married but had no children.

6. John Douglas, reported married, and it has been understood by the family *that he was insane.*

7. Fanny Douglas married many years ago and moved to a distant state, nothing having since been heard from her.

The great-uncle of Clarence, Samuel Richeson, on his father's side, had a son James, who is reported to be *now confined in an Insane Asylum in the State of Missouri.*

Clarence's Uncle Walter had two children, *one of whom is insane.*

Jennie, an aunt of Clarence, married, had five children; *two of them are insane.*

The following affidavits, corroborative of the above heredity, were properly executed and sworn to: First, the father of Clarence V. T. Richeson made affidavit on the 30th of December, 1911, at Lynchburg, Va., that he was 63 years of age; was born and has since resided in the County of Amherst, Va.; that he was married twice and that Clarence V. T. Richeson was his son by his first wife, Sallie Rucker; that his mother was Miss Mary Douglas and she was one of seven children, Maggie, Sallie, Nancy, Fanny, Jennie and John. Fanny married many years before and moved to a distant state. Maggie Douglas had four children, amongst them a son who had been deranged for some years. Sallie Douglas married John R. Maben, had two children, one of whom, William, is deranged. Nancy married James Richeson, who was his father's half-brother. They had four children; one a son, James, died deranged at sixteen; a daughter, Mary Catherine, married Samuel B. Rucker and had a son, Craighill

Rucker, about 30 years of age, who was mentally deranged. John, who has been understood to be insane, he could only remember having seen once and says that on this occasion his conduct was so violent that he felt no doubt as to his insanity. Samuel Richeson, his father's brother, had a son James, said to be confined in an asylum in the state of Missouri. Mary Douglas and Col. W. A. Richeson were his father and mother and had six children. One of their sons, his brother Douglas, became insane and died in an asylum in Staunton, Va. His sister, Jennie, Clarence's aunt, married William Rheil; they had five children; two are insane. A brother Walter, Clarence's uncle, married Miss Drummond; they have two children; one, a daughter, is insane.

Charles H. Richeson made affidavit that he was acquainted with Mrs. Jennie Rheil, an aunt of Clarence and sister of his father, that Mrs. Rheil is the mother of two children, both of whom are mentally afflicted or insane.

Samuel B. Rucker of Lynchburg, Vt., made affidavit that he had been acquainted with practically the "entire Richeson family for some generations back on both sides"; that T. V. Richeson married his sister, Sallie Rucker; that T. V. Richeson's mother was a Miss Mary Douglas; that she was one of seven children, of whom Maggie Douglas married a man by the name of Pyne; they had one son who was at the time of the affidavit a patient in a lunatic asylum. That Sallie Douglas married a man by the name of Maben and has one son, William Maben, mentally deranged but not being dangerous, resides with his sister at Stapleton, Vt. That Nancy Douglas married James Richeson and had a son

James who was mentally deranged and died at sixteen years of age. Jennie Douglas married a Mr. Matthews of Roanoke, Va., but had no children. John Douglas was reported to have been insane.

Douglas Richeson, an uncle of Clarence, was committed to the insane asylum at Staunton, Va., and died there. Jennie Richeson, an aunt of Clarence, married a man by the name of Rheil and had two children, both insane. Walter Richeson, an uncle of Clarence, married a Miss Drummond and had a daughter who was insane.

Dr. J. S. DeJarnette, Superintendent of the Western State Hospital at Staunton, Va., makes a sworn copy of the commitment papers and record of the history of J. Douglas Richeson while a patient at his hospital, in which he says that order for the commitment of J. Douglas Richeson on the complaint of Mrs. Mary Richeson was issued the 2nd day of October, 1883, the commitment papers being signed by John J. Robertson, M. D., and W. A. Richardson, M. D., in which they swore under oath that the patient's age was 38, born in Amherst County, Va., married, three children, occupation clerk in a lead factory, without property; has shown evidences of insanity for six months; general disposition to wander and nervous excitement with inclination to be violent; symptoms increasing; no period of exacerbations, no lucid intervals, loss of property and failure in business plus lead poisoning supposedly the cause; no former attacks; shows disposition to commit violence to others, not to himself; loss of flesh. Committed to the hospital October 4, 1883; deluded, incoherent of speech. In July, 1884, was removed to the violent wards because of his boisterous manner, becoming wild, noisy, restless and filthy. On November 8, 1884, fell to the floor suddenly but not in spasm and did not lose consciousness. On December 5 went into a comatose state during the night and until he died December 6 at 8 P. M.

Clarence V. T. Richeson's history is as follows:

Richeson was born on February 15, 1876, at Amherst, Va., coming from a family of devout Baptists; his father was a farmer, who is said to have been married three times, Clarence being son of the first wife. As a boy he was ambitious to leave the tobacco fields and wanted to be a clergyman. He dressed better than the other boys in the same town. He was a sort of Beau Brummel in his little town and very romantic at an early age. When 13 he left his home for Lynchburg, Va., where he worked in the field, in a mill and at other jobs. Little of interest has been learned of his early childhood. Clarence was ambitious and perhaps a "spore," for he seemed to aspire to a much higher social position than that occupied by his family and to that end he sought a better education than his surroundings would permit and determined to become a minister. He first prepared for college at Amherst Academy, Va. From this Academy he went in 1893 to Carrollton, Mo., where he worked for his cousin, W. J. Richeson, for three years while studying at the Academy at that place. He joined the Trotter Baptist Church of Carroll County.

He is said to have been unusually attractive to women and is variously described as a "tall, handsome giant with the classic face of a Gibson hero"; "handsome as a young God"; "touched with that mysticism which enfolds the pulpit"; "young and Apollo-like in appearance," and by other phrases. In his sacred calling he was brought into close contact with many attractive young women. In spite of his undoubted ability as a minister he seems to have succeeded in getting into difficulties wherever he went. When not over 18 he is reported to have become engaged to two young women in Carroll County, Mo., each of whom broke her engagement with him upon learning of a third affair in Kansas City. About 1896 he returned home, where he remained for three years.

While a student in Carroll County an episode occurred, an account of which says that while making a call at the house of a young woman Richeson was taken with some sort of an attack and lay upon a sofa, refusing to move or to go home; he was finally put out by two of her friends at two o'clock in the morning. The next day he returned to apologize, saying that he had had a fit, but the young woman refused to accept his apology, and closed the doors of her house to him thereafter. It is said that he had to be supported from the house to the sidewalk.

Barnett B. Hardy of the County of Kiowa, Oklahoma, makes affidavit that he met Clarence V. T. Richeson in St. Louis, Mo., in 1895, and grew to know him quite well; that Richeson was called to Virginia by the death of his mother and upon his return seemed to be grieved and depressed to an unusual degree, exhibiting many peculiarities which at first he supposed were caused by grief. The next year, 1896, he roomed with Richeson for two or three months when he more closely observed his peculiarities and his nervous temperament, and says he acted so strangely that he believed him to be *mentally unbalanced;* that his *strange acts, nervousness and mental condition were discussed among his acquaintances.* Hardy further says when he met Richeson at the Third Baptist Church in St. Louis he impressed him as being a very earnest and conscientious young man; after his mother died he seemed unable to restrain his grief; that when he shared his room with him in 1896 they did their own cooking; that he was fond of young ladies' company and devoted too much thought to them for a young man who was planning to enter college with the view of taking up the ministry and theological work. He chose refined young ladies. On one occasion he baked a cake and took it to the Third Baptist Church as a gift to one of the young ladies as well as a sample of his cooking. He was of a restless temperament and continually changed his occupation. He worked longest in the shoe business.

Once he invited Hardy and two other boys to take a ride in a surrey to Forest Park, where he asked them to kneel down and pray with him. A little later something was said about his mother and he began to cry and seemed unfriendly for the rest of the afternoon and *intimated at one time that it seemed as though his mother's death was the result of foul play.* He became desperately in love with two girls in Virginia. About the same time he claimed to be in bad health and took a vacation in southern Missouri where he met another girl to whom he became engaged, but the engagement was soon broken off. After he returned to St. Louis he was taken sick in the night, was delirious and talked about a girl all night. After this he was a nervous wreck and was taken to the Missouri Baptist Sanatorium where he was for weeks. *Through his peculiarities he often lost friends of long standing,* but

Hardy was always friendly and believed Richeson possessed noble principles.

May Townsend, a former resident of St. Louis and Potosi, Mo., made an affidavit and wrote a letter in which she said that Richeson visited her home in Missouri and showed "in a marked degree that he was *mentally unbalanced."* The doctor was sent for and remained with him throughout the night and told them that he was *"as crazy as he could be."* She further says that he is her first cousin. His illness began while he was in St. Louis when he became "very sick" and later came to her home in Potosi to recuperate. "He seemed to be very weak; one evening he retired about nine o'clock, but very shortly after he went to his room I heard him out on the porch maneuvering around and talking to himself. It was quite cold and I could not imagine what he was doing. It impressed me as being very strange. I told my father and mother, and on going out they *found him in his night clothes entirely out of his head and beyond control.* He talked only at random, but they supposed his sickness had caused this confused condition. They tried to get him to go back into the house but could do nothing with him. He went out on the farm still clad only in his night clothes and it was cold. It was only by great effort that he was gotten back to the house after one or two hours and to bed, where he talked at random all the time and did not know any of the family. A doctor was sent for and gave him some quieting medicine. The next morning he was in his right mind. When we told him not to get up, that he was very sick during the night, he did not seem to know it. *The physician advised us to take him back to the city just as soon as possible, and that afternoon I went with him to St. Louis and to the sanitarium."*

Dr. B. A. Wilkes of 4515 Washington Boulevard, St. Louis, made an affidavit in 1912 that he was Superintendent at the time that Richeson was a patient in the Missouri Baptist Sanitarium in 1896. Dr. Purington, Richeson's attending physician, has since died. Dr. Wilkes says: "He evidently had some kind of a *mental derangement*, but I never went into his case sufficiently to have a very clear or definite opinion as to what the trouble was."

Richeson's father made affidavit that his daughter Russell, a trained nurse living in Philadelphia, Pa., sent him a letter while Clarence was in St. Louis, written her by an *officer of the college* there in which he stated that *"Clarence had become deranged"* and was in such a condition they could no longer keep him as a student. A year after this Clarence came home for a visit to Virginia, and his father saw a very *decided change in the boy's manner and appearance.* He says he was *excitable and flighty,* which caused him grave anxiety, especially about his mental condition; he did not see him again until he visited him in the jail at Boston.

Mary Catherine Rucker, second cousin of Clarence and wife of Samuel B. Rucker, made affidavit that she saw Richeson when he made the above visit to Virginia; that he was *"so flighty and peculiar* and gave so many *evidences of being of unsound mind* in conduct and deportment it made me very much afraid of him. I felt a great relief when he left my house." Her daughter Lucy, the wife of Stephen Mundy, in an affidavit, corroborates her mother and says, "Every member of the family was impressed by his peculiar conduct and demeanor. He was flighty and at times incoherent and peculiar to such an extent that all of us felt uneasy during his visit."

At the time I made my examination of Richeson at the request of Governor Foss I received the following letter:

Kansas City, Mo., May 11, 1912.

Dr. L. Vernon Briggs,
Boston, Mass.
Dear Dr.:

I have been ill and confined to my bed and have been reading daily with much interest everything in connection with the conditions surrounding Mr. Richeson—and must confess have worried considerable about it—from the time of his confessed crime. And unless I am greatly mistaken, he came to me while attending the William-Jewell College at Liberty, Mo., saying he had no doubt I would pronounce him crazy when the real object of his visit was known to me.

He repeated again: "I know you will think I am crazy but I have come to you for an operation, and I want you to castrate me." I could not but help agreeing with him, and replied, "Yes, *I am sure you must be crazy,*" and told him that I positively refused to make such an operation. He said, "I am willing to pay you any amount you ask for." But told him he could not pile money enough on my table to tempt me to accept his case.

Then he sat and talked with me, telling me that he was studying for the Ministry and expected to devote his entire life to it. With his temperament and desires he felt he could not make his Pastoral visits and associate with women, without losing control of himself, that he wanted to remove every possible temptation from his path, which he felt the operation in question would do.

I firmly believe that his mind was unsettled then and no doubt, along these lines, must have been ever since.

I do not want to impress you for a moment that I am condoning his crime, quite to the contrary, but pity goes out to him just the same, knowing his eagerness to give up that part of nature that he might more fully live the life he was fitting and preparing himself for.

If I have given you anything to help you I am truly glad. When we as physicians are confined to our beds, we have more time to give individual patients more consideration, and for some reason my mind has rested with this young Pastor.

Very truly,
Philip C. Palmer, M.D.

In 1899 he entered the William-Jewell College at Liberty, Mo., and was ordained to the Baptist Ministry at the Third Baptist Church after matriculating at the Southern Baptist Seminary in Louisville, Ky. He supplied a mission church at Kansas City for some time. While still a student and residing at Liberty, Mo., he is said to have been engaged to a Miss ——, daughter of the Rev. ——, and it was generally thought he would marry her as soon as he completed his course in college. He was reported to have been suspended in 1905 for cheating in the final examination and to have been expelled the following year for repeating the performance. His engagement to the above young lady had not been broken at this time. Richeson is said to have brought suit against the college to compel it to give him a diploma, but to have withdrawn it after a conference with the faculty during which they are reported in addition to have charged him with unbecoming conduct with a young member of the Budd Park Baptist Church in Kansas City, where he was preaching during his student days. It was reported that while pastor of the Budd Park Baptist Church between 1901-4 he preached an eloquent sermon on "The Temptations of Young Girls in a City"; that after the service three girls approached him weeping, each claiming that he had asked her to marry him and asked him if he intended to fulfill his promise. He is said to have been calm and assured them there must be some mistake. The trustees are said to have written for his resignation and he left the church and went to Liberty, Mo.

After Richeson was expelled from college Miss —— resigned her position as teacher of Latin and Mathematics in the Liberty High School it was thought to marry him but he left hurriedly to accept a pulpit at Leadville, Col., and she later accepted a position in a school in Kansas City which she had to give up, it is said, because of failing health and grief over the defection of her lover, and went to reside with a sister. She is said to have loaned Richeson $750 after prominent ministers who had been assisting him refused to do so longer. The money without the interest was paid back within the year prior to Richeson's death.

He also preached during his student days at the Baptist Church in Stewartsville, Mississippi.

While in Liberty, Mo., he worked as a conductor on a street car line some time between 1901-4 and became involved in a strike in which he eloquently advocated the cause of the workers. He was made a member of the Union's Grievance Committee, which position he gave up when the strike was decided against the men.

Dr. G. M. Phillips of St. Louis, Mo., states in an affidavit signed and sworn to, that "in the latter part of November, 1901, a neighbor and shoe manufacturer of the city, a prominent member and officer of the Baptist Church, called upon him in reference to rendering a professional service to a young man named C. V. T. Richeson. He explained his interest in Richeson to Dr. Phillips by saying that he was one of those highly deserving and competent young men struggling without assistance to qualify himself for the ministry, that his wages as a shoe worker were very small, and as an encouragement to Richeson that he (Mr. Guyett) would be glad to remunerate him for his services." Dr. Phillips assured Mr. Guyett that it would give him pleasure to assume this responsibility and do what he could for the young man; that Richeson if able could remunerate him at some future time, otherwise there would be no obligation. On December 4, 1901, Mr. Guyett brought Richeson to him at his office and he made an examination with the following results: "Age 25; residence 2818 Washington Avenue; occupation shoe worker (factory); student at William-Jewell College. His family history presented no tuberculosis or other constitutional disease; several members, however, were nervous and hysterical. He claimed to have sustained no special injury, nor had he evidence of any serious disease. His history was entirely negative so far as all venereal disease was concerned. He complained of having three or four nocturnal seminal emissions each week; that he was nervous, wakeful and apprehensive. He complained of pains in his head, back, testes and limbs; that he was dizzy, *his memory was poor and he was unable to concentrate mentally,* and that this latter concerned him especially. He was a perfect and complete picture of 'neurasthenia sexualis in its most aggravated form.' " Dr. Phillips found that he had a rapid pulse (106) weak and irregular; temperature 99°; he was anemic in a pronounced degree. He had discovered the existence of a mild varicocele and had grown very attentive to this and ascribed his wretched physical and mental state to it. He despaired of ever being made well again and rather courted death. He was most melancholy.

An examination revealed a trifling varicocele; very

sensitive deep urethra; urine pale and of low specific gravity (1.002). The above are the main points recorded in Dr. Phillips' first examination. Dr. Phillips states that after the completion of this examination he counselled his treating the whole matter lightly and gave him every assurance of the curability of his disease and endeavored to impress him with his exaggerated estimate of its gravity. He assured him that he would be perfectly well, competent to pursue his studies and perform all functions to society. He saw him every few days. At first he seemed able and willing to accept his prognosis and made some progress both in a physical and mental direction. Very soon, however, he drifted into his former depressed state; his varicocele seemed uppermost in his mind and he insisted upon its removal. On January 8, 1902, Dr. Phillips operated upon him at St. John's Hospital, removing the varicocele, and continued his former treatment of him. His improvement now was very pronounced. He became hopeful, cheerful and displayed a high appreciation for the service Dr. Phillips had rendered him. Dr. Phillips suggested matrimony as the only positive cure for his other annoying condition, but Richeson assured him that this was entirely out of the question at that time. Then with proper apologies and explanations Dr. Phillips states that he suggested intercourse, which suggestion was flatly declined and he says "through this suggestion I lost his confidence and respect, for immediately following the suggestion he said, 'I had rather die than resort to such a cure.'"

Dr. Phillips continued to see him until January 23, 1902, when he had improved both physically and mentally and it was hoped he might overcome his fancied ailments. Dr. Phillips continues in his affidavit that in his opinion "at this time he was not responsible for his any act that was directly associated with his sexual organs; that such conditions as these, in my judgment, are competent to set in motion sexual manifestations to the end that all reason is overbalanced, and one's acts are beyond control."

It is interesting to note from payments by Richeson the frequency of his calls upon Dr. Phillips in one month: December 10-13-19-30, 1901; his last visit was March 31, 1902.

Dr. Phillips, in an interview later, said that Richeson's mind was fixed upon his sexual organs more in a psychic than in a physical way. The operation performed seemed to satisfy him for a time.

In 1907 Richeson resided in El Paso, Texas, for four months, from April to September, at the house of one Milton Estes, 1211 Wyoming St. Estes makes affidavit that while Richeson was an inmate of his house he was *afflicted with a mental disorder which for a considerable period rendered him insane;* that he had delusion that someone had done him a great injury and for a considerable period of time raved night and day of his supposed wrongs; one night he was so "bad" that Mr. Estes sent for Dr. Thompson W. Grace, who administered something to quiet the patient but that they both remained with him through the night. In a few days he recovered from this attack and was able to go about again.

Dr. Thompson W. Grace makes affidavit that he has practised medicine and surgery for over twenty years and was a resident of El Paso for more than five years; that in the month of July, 1907, he was called to see

Richeson, who was sick at the home of Milton Estes, and found him in a *cataleptic state.* When aroused *he raved against some men in El Paso who had been and were then among his best friends; and he seemed to imagine they were working against him and that some-one was seeking to do him an injury.* Dr. Grace prescribed for him, stayed with him all night, and in a few days he got better and was up and about. Later he had another similar attack, soon after which he left El Paso, and in August, 1907, went to Georgetown, Mass.

Asa S. Howe, in an affidavit, states that he first met Richeson about Christmas, 1906, when Richeson was visiting his home in Georgetown, Mass. He was then a student at the Newton Theological School and was an occasional guest at the Howe homestead until March 29, 1907, when he accepted a call to a church at El Paso, Texas. Several times while visiting Mr. Howe he appeared in a nervous state of mind and at times his exhausted condition led Mr. Howe to believe that he was applying himself too closely to his studies; that he returned from El Paso the latter part of August, 1907, and that it was very noticeable that his mental condition had not improved but on the contrary had grown worse; at times he was erratic and irritable, at other times morose and his faculties seemed benumbed.

One night early in September, 1907, Mr. Howe states that his family and their guest, Mr. Richeson, "retired to their rooms at the same time; within a few minutes after retiring all the members of the *family were aroused by the groanings and incoherent mutterings made by Mr. Richeson.* The *noises were very unnatural* and we at first thought that he had suddenly fallen asleep and was having a nightmare or bad dream, but as the noises continued and increased we became alarmed and went to his room. He was undressed and in bed; he was in a semi-conscious state and seemed to be suffering both physically and mentally. We tried to arouse him to consciousness, but he would not respond either by word or action but kept up meaningless mutterings." Mr. Howe then called Dr. Root of Georgetown, who treated him, and he became more calm but remained in bed the next day and part of the day following. After a few days he returned to his school in such a weakened condition that he appeared to be "very near a wreck." Continuing, Mr. Howe states that "he told us he had suffered at times in a like manner for a long time and *had similar attacks* while in El Paso and other places; that at one time while at Newton School he fell unconscious and remained so until nearly morning when he managed to get up and stagger to his room. During our acquaintance of over a year my continued attempt to better understand him was balked by his strange manner and our acquaintance ceased in March, 1908."

At the time of his illness in September, 1907, Mr. Howe wrote to Richeson's sister, Miss Katherine Richeson, who was then a student in Farmville, Va., and requested her to notify her father. "I considered him to be in a very serious condition and had grave fears that he might become worse and therefore *I deemed it my duty to notify his people.*"

While attending the Newton Theological Seminary in 1907 he was engaged to one and possibly two young women at the same time. He entered this Seminary in 1906, graduating in 1909, and returned in 1910 to take a post-graduate course in the Old Testament. A number of young women in Newton Center who knew him during his student days, in spite of their disagreements as to his other personal characteristics, all agreed that he possessed a remarkable fascination and was able to exercise an almost hypnotic influence over them. They say he never had much of a reputation as a student; but that he held their respect and they liked him. Some of his fellow-students in Newton described him as alternating "between suavity and fiery impetuosity" which turned some of them into his enemies. His work as a student was erratic and poor and he had "the politeness of a Southerner and the natural conceit of a handsome man." Descriptions of his character present a mass of contradictions; on the one side we have the eloquent preacher, the earnest worker, the struggling student, the revered pastor; on the other, the calculating self-seeker, the double dealer, the college cheat, the profane talker and the seducer of women. Men at large never liked him, but those in his church stood by him despite damning evidence produced against him. Women were attracted to him and he held them with a personality that seemed little short of magnetic. He is said to have had considerable friction with the church authorities at Hyannis which influenced him to resign and take charge of the church in Cambridge. A paper, in describing his last church service, says: "There is nothing more bitterly ironical in the whole case than the sermon of last Sunday morning in which he used the death of Avis Linnell almost as a text to draw a lesson on the fleeting and unstable happiness of life. Parishioners who heard that last discourse were so moved that they refused to believe that the man who so eloquently pointed the way could himself be one who had strayed so far from the path of righteousness."

The following is a copy of a letter that he wrote to a young lady to whom he was engaged and of whom he was very fond. It was written immediately after an attack such as has been described above and which lasted several days. This letter (similar to others written following attacks) is published because it shows his confused and irresponsible condition following one of these attacks.

Newton Center, Mass.,
Friday, 6 p. m., Sept. 20, 1907.

My darling * * * My Little Girl, I love you and you will know it, won't you. Your's written this morning just came, your's this morning come just now at 4.30. I am glad you are resting and hope you will get stout again. I am glad you had a nice time. I am not working so hard. I did not understand the Dr. to say that I should stop school? I had to attend five lectures today but I only have one tomorrow morning. Then I wish you were here to go for a ride. I am going to Higham this Sunday. I always dread going to a new church. But suppose I can stand it since I am not on trial. * * * will you please burn the letter I wrote that made you telegraph me and the one I wrote the night I came home this week. I kept copy. Why I wrote it I cannot tell. It should never have gone to you if I could have stopped it. But I went to the mail box in the Hall next morning too late to stop it. It had gone. Will you burn it and not think of it any more? I must go mail this now and come back and go to bed early, for this has been a hard day for me, so I must go to bed now and mail this now and so on and on. Hope you will keep well * * * and not work too much either. * * * will you go and see the Dr., not tell not tell him I sent you Dear, sent you. But just ask him but just ask him and tell him if he meant that I should not go to school Wednesday. When the train got into Boston I was asleep when the train got in I was asleep and they woke me to get up and to get off the train, and I dont know how long I had been there and I (for I do not know how long I had) could not for a long time tell (been there you know I could not tell where I was. And I could not tell my own name for I did not know my name name name nor think of you know I could not tell it where I wanted to go. But just walked around till I got to the South Station to go to the South Station supper then I walked and walked and around and around and saw the name around Newton and then I knew that I wanted to go here. And I came home and wrote and I wrote you two letters you two letters. I kept one this thing I never do and this I never do. I cannot tell why * * * I should never have written you. Because I should never have that way for it was not in my—for you know it could not be—heart ever to do such a thing. I had never thought of it, and when your letter came this evening, I felt as never before. For there was never such a girl as * * * any place in all the world. I know there was never a Dearer Woman living. You just did not say a word, just said not a word. * * * I cannot tell why I wrote as I did. I had never thought so. And I can manage things all O.K. And if I could not I should never say such things as I wrote to you. I do not even remember when I wrote it. Now I remember while I was in the city several people watched me and on the train too. And when I got off at Newton they looked at me so strange, they looked at me so strange. And I wonder that I am—now looking looking at me so strange—living at all when I think of all I have been through with no sleep Sat. night, none Sunday night nor Monday and not much Tuesday and you must come to see me some—(* * * you wont ever forsake me will you Darling) time when you come will you, just tell me once more you won't. And if I know myself I'll never wrote again less I know I am all right. I love you with all that I am.

Clarence.

This confused and irresponsible condition sometimes lasted for several days, and during these attacks and following them he was not responsible for his acts or conscious of what he did or said. These attacks came with more frequency as he grew older.

Dr. Richmond B. Root of Georgetown, Mass., makes oath that he was called to the house of A. S. Howe to see Mr. Richeson in September, 1907; that he found him *"lying in bed tossing about, apparently in a semi-dazed or unconscious condition and talking irrationally and incoherently* and I was unable to get a connected story from him as to the cause of his condition. He was tossing about after the fashion of a person suffering from hysteria. I prescribed for him. I saw him a day or two after and the effects of this attack seemed to have passed away."

In 1908 he took the pastorate of a church at Hyannis, Mass., and E. Isadora V. Hallett of Hyannis makes affidavit that Richeson came to room with her in June, 1908, when he entered upon his pastorate, and remained with her until June, 1909, when he moved to Mrs. Wyman's; that he again took a room at her house in November, 1909, which he occupied until April, 1910, when he resigned from the Hyannis Church to accept a call to the Immanuel Baptist Church in Cambridge. She states that she went to a prayer meeting one Wednesday evening in March, 1909. Mr. Richeson did not attend the prayer meeting and as soon as it was over she hastened to his room and found him lying in bed. She said, "Mr. Richeson, what is matter with you?" He did not reply nor open his eyes nor move a muscle. She telephoned to Dr. Binford, who came about nine o'clock. When the Doctor came down she asked him how Mr. Richeson was and the Doctor put his hand to his own head as much as to say that *it was his brain.* She goes on to state that when she got back from telephoning for the Doctor some of Mr. Richeson's parishioners were at the house, they having also noticed he was not at the meeting, and continues: "That night I heard him talking, but I could not understand what he said; he seemed to be *talking incoherently.* The condition continued until Friday noon when he came downstairs all right. Later there was another attack not so severe."

Dr. Ferdinand A. Binford of Hyannis made affidavit that he had been a practising physician and surgeon since 1898; that he knew Mr. Richeson personally all the time he was pastor of the Baptist Church in Hyannis and treated him professionally; that on the 24th of March, 1909, he opened and removed a calloused place on his right hand; that it was a painful operation but performed without administering any anæsthetic. At the end of the operation Richeson seemed to be more or less affected by the nervous strain he had gone through. The operation was performed at 1 P. M.; he says: "That same night about 9 o'clock I was called to see him at the residence of Mrs. Hallet, with whom he was boarding, and when I arrived I found there were with him two or three men whom I knew to be members of his church; he was acting violently and they were trying to control and quiet him both by words and by attempting to restrain him by physical force. He appeared at times to be partly conscious; then he would go into a state whereby he lost consciousness and was practically unconscious, apparently had no knowledge of what he was doing or saying. During this period of time he *talked irrationally, raved incoherently, and physically manifested an abnormal degree of strength;* in fact was so powerful while in this state that it took the combined efforts of three men, including myself, to restrain him from getting from his bed and out of the room; upon one occasion he was successful in so overpowering us that he really got to the door of his room before we again got control of him. I deemed it necessary to administer a strong injection of morphine which quieted him, and some of his parishioners remained with him all night. They said that he slept but little. The next morning I found him quiet and rational but physically quite weak. I had no doubt he was entirely abnormal and irresponsible during that attack when he was so violent and incoherent. I made five visits to him thereafter, my last being the 31st of March, 1909, when he was apparently as normal *as he ever was.* On June 12, 1909, I was called to him again and he had another attack of great mental excitability, but that was of short duration.

Betsy R. Wyman, in an affidavit, states that she had known Clarence V. T. Richeson since he arrived in Hyannis to take up his pastorate and until he left there; that during the period while he was there he took meals with her and lodged in her house; that about August, 1910, he came to her house at 11 o'clock one night much excited, face white, and said: *"I believe I am going crazy; I cannot stand the things that are being put upon me."* His whole manner and appearance were wild and excited and he remained in this strange condition for two hours or more, then became quiet and retired. During this "spell" he screamed violently. She remembers another occasion some two or three months later when he came home late one night and acted strangely, went to his room, was moving about and tossing on the bed, running his hands through his hair, and that his face was white and his eyes had a wild, strange look and he talked very excitedly. He said that he was compelled to undergo things that were completely upsetting him and wearing him out. She said: *"He screamed violently while in this spell which continued until four o'clock in the morning* when I became so alarmed that I called Dr. Binford, who came to the house and treated him. From time to time he had these 'spells,' as I should call them, and both my husband and myself said he was crazy. On some of these occasions he was more violent than others."

Dr. Charles H. Harwood of Hyannis in an affidavit says that he is 48 years of age and has been a practising physician for 20 years, graduating from Harvard University and Medical School; that he has given particular attention to the study of insanity and kindred subjects at the University and at the hospitals for the insane in Massachusetts. He states that he met Clarence V. T. Richeson in Hyannis in the summer of 1909 at the time he was preparing a thesis for his graduation. "I observed him and the peculiarity I noticed then was his apparent apathy regarding his work. He seemed to be abstracted in manner and not to have any interest or enthusiasm in the work at hand. The next time I saw him to talk with was *with reference to a robbery that he claimed had been committed* whereby certain property belonging to him—his monthly salary as a minister—had been stolen . . . about the first week in December, 1909. I had heard of this robbery, and on meeting Mr. Richeson on the train I talked with him to see what he had to say about it. I was familiar with the premises, and had prepared a sketch of the rooms in the house where he claimed the robbery had been committed. I showed him this diagram at the outset of the conversation and he became very much disturbed and excited and wanted to know how I had obtained it. He made an elaborate statement of the robbery and of the circumstances under which he claimed it was committed, including the condition in which he found his room when he returned to the house. As a student of criminology I had become interested in this case which, in the minds of the community, seemed to be a very singular one. State Police Officer Bradford had requested me to investigate it because of very curious circumstances surrounding it. I had made some investigation previous to the time of this conversation, and I knew that many of the circumstances he related to me were not true and were not borne out by the facts. What impressed me as a physician most was, that after his first excitement incident to my first allusion to the robbery had passed off, he seemed to evince no further interest in the robbery and no sense of personal loss; his sole concern appeared to be in what he said was an 'interruption of God's work.' He even intimated that there might have been no robbery, and that the money would appear later. He seemed to be not in the slightest impressed with the fact that the matter was being investigated by the proper authorities."

Dr. Harwood said "his whole state of mind appeared *insane* and this impression was confirmed by his talk about his clothes, his egotism; and in a subsequent interview he confirmed the appearance of a man *suffering from insanity*. He announced that he did not let his right hand know what his left hand did in good works and to me he clearly conveyed the impression that he was sole judge of the right or wrong of what he saw fit to do in 'doing God's work.' "

This robbery to which Dr. Harwood refers is described by Richeson's landlady as follows: Richeson came home one day and showed her his pay in an envelope which he then left on his bureau in her presence. Having occasion to go away from the house to preach or for some other purpose, he soon returned and called her, saying that the money had been stolen and his room was in apparent disorder. She notified the State Police and the above investigation followed without results so far as obtaining any clues were concerned; that later the money came back a few dollars or a dollar at a time in envelopes with the addresses printed instead of written. She noticed that these envelopes always came on Mondays following Mr. Richeson's absence while supplying some out of town pulpit and were postmarked from the town in which he had preached. On his return he would often find these letters awaiting him and showed them to her, expressing the belief that the person who took the money was sending it back because his conscience was troubling him. All or nearly all of the money was finally returned in this manner.

In April, 1911, Mr. Richeson *received a severe blow on the head* in getting out of an elevator at the Free Hospital for Women, Brookline, where he went to visit a member of his congregation, through a mistake of the elevator man in starting before he got out; his head was bruised and it was necessary to call a physician. He was in bed for three days and when he got up *dragged one of his legs when he walked.* Mrs. ——— makes affidavit that this difficulty became worse until he seemed to have *lost the use of both legs* and could not bear his weight on his feet.

Mrs. ——— of Brookline, made affidavit that on or about the 1st day of May, 1911, Rev. Clarence V. T. Richeson, with whom she was acquainted, called at her residence and she saw from his appearance that he was greatly agitated. Continuing, she says: "He told me he had just been to call upon a person suffering from pneumonia and that while there the person had died, and he asked for a glass of water. I went upstairs, but in a few moments (this was about 8 o'clock in the evening), I was called down and found him in a very strange state, sitting down, trembling violently all over and weeping. It alarmed me and I gave him a preparation of tincture of valerian, followed by a cup of hot malted milk. It was 11 o'clock that night before he quieted down to anything like a normal state, when he said he would go home. I did not think he was in a condition to go home. His appearance was strange and most distressing. On or about May 14, 1911, Mr. Richeson was again at my house and had another attack similar to the one described but not so severe in character and it did not last as long. About a week later he again came to my house in a very nervous condition and looked *very excited, very white, very dark under the eyes,* and as on all these occasions he *seemed to get very rigid and after the attacks had passed away he seemed to become perfectly limp and not to have a particle of strength,* as if completely broken down from nervous exhaustion. I know that he was ill in bed from about the 5th to the 10th of June, 1911, and was more or less in bed until the 28th of June. On Sunday evening, the 18th of June, I was called upon the telephone by Mr. Carter of Cambridge, who said Mr. Richeson was in a very excited condition and wanted to see me. About a half an hour later I was again called by a friend and acquaintance of Mr. Richeson, Rev. Mr. Smith, who said the doctor had arrived and wanted me to come to Mr. Richeson if I could. This was about 10.30 at night and I arrived at his house some time after 11. On my arrival I found a very excited group of persons,

One of them said to me that he thought Mr. Richeson was crazy. I said, 'Well, let me go up and see him,' and Mr. Smith called for me to come to Mr. Richeson's room. I went upstairs and found him lying on the bed, trembling, groaning and crying. He said, 'Mrs. ———, is that you?' and seized hold of my hand with a vise-like grasp, saying, 'Now, you will sit here with me, won't you?' There were three men in the room, Mr. Carter, Mr. Smith and a young man, and I said, 'If you men will go out of the room I will take care of Mr. Richeson.' They said, 'Oh, no'; that they could not leave me alone as he was violent. I said I was not afraid and the men went out of the room. I then said to him, 'I am going to stay and take care of you; you need not worry.' About this time he was trembling violently and said, 'Is there a man there?' pointing about the room. A little later his own physician, Dr. Gardner, gave him some medicine, saying it would put him to sleep. I sat by his bed all night, but he did not sleep. Every few minutes he would jump up with a start, very frightened, saying there was somebody in the room.

"As the night wore on he got somewhat over that and by morning seemed to be very quiet. While this Dr. Gardner was there he carried Mr. Richeson in his arms to the bath and back again as *he was unable to walk himself*. About the 1st of July, 1911, Mr. Richeson went to Hyannis. I was very much exercised about his going, as I did not think he was physically or mentally in a condition to take care of himself. Every day from the time of this illness until the 28th of June I went to his lodging house and stayed until evening. I thought he ought to have somebody with him. One Sunday evening the last of June, 1911, he got into another state of nervousness and talked irrationally and irresponsibly and *I said to my family we must try to persuade him to have a good nerve specialist; I feel very anxious that he is not right and needs examination. His physician, however, thought that perhaps he would be better if he had plenty of fresh air and sleep, so the matter was dropped.*

"On Monday afternoon, October 16, 1911, Mr. Richeson was seated in a morris chair in the library in our home at Brookline when he was taken violently ill. My attention was called to him when I *heard him groaning.* I immediately went to him and found him stretched out full length on the seat in the hall, writhing and groaning, and spoke to him, but he made no answer and *was apparently suffering great pain.* I shook him, attempting to arouse him, but could not; *his eyes were closed.* Others spoke to him, but he made no answer and seemed to be growing worse all the time. *His face was getting purple.* I sent for the doctor, who came immediately and took charge of him. The doctor said he did not think it was an epileptic fit, but was more in the nature of a nervous manifestation and seemed to be somewhat disturbed; he said *he thought Mr. Richeson's difficulty was a very serious one and that he ought to be examined by some expert physician as to these attacks.*"

Corroborative of Mrs. ——'s statement, Dr. Herman T. Baldwin of Chestnut Hill, Mass., made oath that about noon on October 17, 1911, he received a telephone call to go at once to the residence of ——— to see Clarence V. T. Richeson; that he found Mr. Richeson *lying on his side* on the window seat in the front hall, *breathing rapidly,* occasionally *twisting his body and contracting his arms and hands;* his eyes were *tightly closed* and he (Dr. Baldwin) *could not open them.* "At times he would lie quiet with muscles relaxed and breathing easily; he made no response when spoken to; there was no frothing at the mouth; at times he cried out. *I considered this an attack of hysteria and recommended a consultation later with a nerve specialist."*

The following is an account of what I believe to have been an hysterical attack associated with delirium and hallucinations which he had at Cambridge. The Rev. E. J. Smith writes from the Rochester Theological Seminary, Rochester, N. Y., that he knew Mr. Richeson, but left Cambridge before Richeson went to the Carter home to live; that his first knowledge of Richeson's illness happened while Richeson was rooming at a boarding-house on Bigelow St., kept by a Mrs. Gibbons.

"The breakdown came about the 15th of June, and began with a nervousness and inability to sleep; on Saturday, the 17th of June, George Richards, treasurer of the church, was accidentally drowned in the Charles River. When Richeson heard this news the next morning he was much stirred. He did not seem himself during the day and was completely unnerved by the time services were finished Sunday night. The funeral of Mr. Richards was held on Tuesday, Richeson conducting the services. After the services at the house Richeson said he felt so ill he thought it best he should not go to the grave, and I went in his place, returning directly to Richeson's room on Bigelow St. Hardly had I arrived when a telephone message came from Mr. Richeson saying he had gone directly to the home of Miss ——— in Brookline after the funeral and was about to leave there; that he was feeling very ill and wanted me to meet him at the corner of Boylston St. A few minutes after I arrived at the appointed place I saw him alighting from a car in a most depleted condition. Had I not known him well I should have certainly thought he was intoxicated; we were obliged to wait some ten minutes for the Cambridge car, during which time at short intervals Richeson was *taken with spells,* when *his entre body underwent nervous twitchings of a violent character and tears streamed from his eyes;* he seemed dazed and unstrung and was almost physically helpless by the time the car came. I had to almost lift him to the running board and lift him down at the other end of the route. I put him immediately to bed and called a doctor. Later in the evening I found him *moaning* and I went to his side and asked 'what the trouble was.' He replied, 'Smith, I want to go home to Jesus; don't want to live any longer. I have tried to do right, but I guess that I have failed.' Still later he told me he had gone to see the ——— of Brookline and that he had tried to break his engagement to the daughter. He remained in a very weakened condition for two days, or until Thursday, when at his request I called up the ——— and the young lady, Miss ———, and her mother came over and stayed with him part of the afternoon. Richeson's engagement to Miss ——— existed at the time of arrest and so far as known was never broken. Richeson did not appear to be improving and I preached for him on the following Sunday, June 25, both morning and evening. At Richeson's request I called up Mr. Carter, arranging for him to come over and stay with Richeson while I was at the evening service. When I left he seemed to be resting; upon my return the whole house was in a commotion; a doctor was there and Richeson was *crying like a baby.* I thought he recognized me at once and he began to complain that the *doctor and Carter were trying to kill him with poison.* He said he knew too much about drugs for them to try anything like that on him. Then he wanted me to call his own doctor and also the ——— and get them to come over, saying that the doctor would use him square and the ——— would see that he was well taken care of and not act like 'those damned lying hypocrites' in the room there. I tried to get the doctor but failed, pretended to call up the ———, then left for the doctor's office. On the way back to Richeson I called up the Brookline house and received word that Mrs. ——— would start immediately.

"When I returned to the room I made the report to Richeson which seemed to make him easier and assured him I would do all I could for him. After a little while he asked me to pray, which I started to do. Before I got very far with the prayer he interrupted with the words, 'Damn you, Smith; if you don't tell him the truth, if you don't tell him the truth, if you have been lying to me, I will pray to God to roast your soul in seven kinds of burning Hell. That is a nice way to treat a sick man; I will get up and go for the doctor myself. It is much better to tell the truth than to pray.' We had a hard time to keep him quiet, but soon the doctor came and after giving him some medicine he fell into a fitful sleep. I stayed with him for a day or two, when I had to leave."

Mrs. Margaret Gibbons of 16 Bigelow St., Cambridge, with whom Mr. Richeson boarded for three months prior to the latter part of June, is reported to have said that she did not want him longer because "I lost several roomers as a result of his peculiar habit of swearing. He swore violently when he had sick spells. He was very domineering, acted as if he owned the place. He had very peculiar spells. One day when he had friends to dine with him he suddenly left the room and was gone so long that I investigated and found him half reclining on the couch in his rooms; his eyes looked funny. I spoke to him; he did not answer. I shook him by the legs; he paid no attention. I shouted loudly and slapped his hand so hard the noise was heard downstairs. Still he paid no attention to me. While here he was treated by several physicians; when they gave him drugs he would hold them tightly in his hand and cry, 'I will not take them; they are trying to poison me.' At such times he would swear so loud that he was heard all over the neighborhood. On his dresser he kept pictures of Miss Linnell and Miss ———. The latter was a frequent visitor here, but she was always accompanied by either her mother or another member of the family. Miss Linnell spent a Saturday afternoon in May in his room. I saw her when she left the house with him. On his return he remarked to me, 'I had my lady friend with me in my room all the afternoon.'" Richeson is said to have had similar attacks when rooming with a Mrs. Crothers, 23 Bigelow St., and at Mrs. Tray's.

Dr. David C. Dow, a practising physician in Cambridge, made an affidavit that on Sunday evening, June 18, 1911, at about 8 P. M., he was called by Frank Carter to attend a friend of his who he said was unconscious; that he responded immediately and went to No. 16 Bigelow St. where he found Clarence V. T. Richeson and told Mr. Carter that he would sit beside him and observe him. Dr. Dow states "The patient was pale, active and restless, and as I entered the room he was screeching loudly. Mr. Carter introduced me but the patient stared at me giving no sign of recognition and was apparently unconscious of the attempted introduction. I seated myself on the side of the bed and attempted to gain his confidence. I examined him carefully; I found no evidence of organic disease. I stroked his hair with my hand in a soothing fashion and while I was doing so he screeched out in a loud tone constantly growing louder *'Carter, Carter, Carter, who is that man at the foot of the bed?'* at the same time looking and pointing in that direction. *As there was no person there* I saw at once that he was the victim of a hallucination. Mr. Carter attempted to quiet him in my presence and asked if he did not know that he was Mr. Carter, but Richeson made no response. I made an examination of his body and searched his room but saw no evidence of drugs or alcohol. I found his razor which I hid back of his bookcase. By sitting beside him and gently rubbing his scalp I somewhat quieted him. Up to 9.30 I gave him no medicine because I first wanted to know what his previous medical treatment had been. Rev. Mr. Smith arriving I sent him for some bromide and while he was gone Richeson *suddenly fell out of bed on the floor in a heap and with a groan.* His facial expression was like that of one suffering acute pain. He made no effort to arise and after allowing him to lie for a time Mr. Carter and I lifted him up on the bed. At the same time Mr. Smith returned with the medicine and

Richeson burst out violently screeching in language substantially as follows: 'Smith, those two damn fools have allowed me to fall from the bed to the floor and hurt myself and expose myself, and that is not swearing either.' He then had *another violent spell of talking irrationally and irresponsibly and screeching out* and still demanding to know who was at the foot of the bed. Mr. Smith knelt down beside the bed to pray; he prayed for a few minutes but Richeson reached over and seized him by the neck and said 'Damn you, Smith, stop your praying; I don't need your prayers; pray for some of my Hellish parishioners who need them more than I do, who have kept me on starvation wages and have taken $600 of my grandmother's money.' Mr. Smith was much agitated and both he and Mr. Carter were so shocked at such language from their pastor and friend that they apologized to me. I said to them at that time 'As a result of my observation I don't think you need to attempt to explain it, for in my opinion *Clarence Richeson's brain is gone.*'

"I attempted to give him the medicine but he absolutely refused to take it. I also attempted to give him nourishment, some beef tea the landlady had brought but during all this time *he was raving* on and was more or less profane. He was making such wild commotion that the landlady appealed to me to quiet him as he was disturbing the house and she would lose her boarders. I told her to be charitable as *in my judgment the minister was mentally irresponsible.* I stepped out of sight, but he still kept pointing at the foot of the bed demanding of Mr. Carter an explanation of the imaginary figure at the foot of the bed. Mr. Carter said 'Brother Richeson, do you mean Dr. Dow?' whereupon Richeson violently screamed 'That, that, that thing a doctor? He is not fit to treat mosquitoes in my back alley,' pointing all the time and looking intently at the foot of the bed where there was nobody.

"I attempted to get medicine into him without success. Beef tea was brought and Carter attempted to give it to him but sitting up in bed he held the cup of tea and in a most wild, agitated and violent way he said 'Carter, Carter, Carter, is there anything in that? If there is, Carter, I hope you will be burned in the seven fires of Hell.' All this time his eyes had a *wild, insane look;* they did not look right. For half an hour he sat with the cup of tea in his hands and asked and asked if there was anything in it. Finally, upon the most positive assurance from Mr. Carter, Mr. Smith and his landlady that there was nothing in the beef tea he took one or two teaspoons but no more. I remained with him almost till 1 o'clock in the morning, up to which time his *ravings, hallucinations* and excitement continued. Learning his regular physician was on the way to him I left as he was then in a condition in which I felt I could leave him in the hands of responsible people with whom he was acquainted, including Mrs. —— who had arrived at the house. I told Mrs. —— that in my judgment Richeson *was suffering from neurasthenia or nervous exhaustion; that it was not a case for drugs nor a general practitioner to handle. I said I thought that this man should not go back into his pulpit for six months or a year but should be committed to an institution not necessarily an insane hospital and I strongly advised her to put him under the care of men well versed in mental diseases. I think this is a mental disturbance and he ought to be placed under the care of men specializing in mental disease.* Mr. Carter left the house with me and before getting into my automobile I said with all the earnestness of which I was capable *'Carter, you ought not to let this man get by you; he needs no drugs nor medicine; he ought to have the care of one of the best alienists or neurologists. He ought not to go back into his pulpit for at least six months or a year for at the present time his brain is gone.' I said 'Carter, he is insane.' Carter replied 'Well, you ought to hear some of his sermons,' to which I answered 'Never mind his sermons; I am not interested in his sermons; that man is insane.'* At that moment Mr. Smith came up to my automobile and I said to him *'Smith, your friend Clarence Richeson is insane. You see to it that he has the best alienist look after him.'* I said this with all the earnestness of which I was capable because I so strongly felt that to be the actual fact and suggested that if his regular physician did not arrive they call Dr. Bryant who was an able and competent alienist. I returned after this five hours' visit completely worn out and exhausted."

CHAPTER IV

EXAMINATION AND REPORT OF DR. L. VERNON BRIGGS. RICHESON HAS AN HYSTERICAL ATTACK IN JAIL. PETITIONS GOVERNOR FOSS AND COUNCIL FOR CLEMENCY.

On April 30th, 1912, I made my first examination of Richeson. I found him seated alone in a large and sunny cell in the Charles Street Jail facing the Charles River; one might consider it a room, and leading from it was an inner cell in which was a colored man named Butts who was in the Jail charged with manslaughter. Sheriff Quinn said he felt it necessary to have a watch over Richeson and thought he would prefer to have a colored man born in Virginia and so placed Butts in the communicating cell as Richeson's valet and companion. Butts was later called Richeson's "Man Friday." Richeson was seated in a comfortable chair and was in a deep study. He greeted me without show of emotion or interest, his face being immobile. He put his hand out for me to shake but it was perfectly flaccid and there was no movement of his hand or fingers more than if they had been of wood. He asked me no questions but said that he did not usually see people without consulting his counsel. I explained to him I had come to examine him mentally and physically and asked him if he had objections. He said he had not and volunteered that Dr. Lane had made one short examination of him and that he thought he had seen one or two other doctors but was not quite sure whether they were doctors or not. I sat down and in starting my notes asked him the day and date. He looked at the calendar and said "Oh, I have not torn off this month's page," whereupon he proceeded to do so and said it was Wednesday, May 1st.

He said his full name was Clarence Virgil Thompson Richeson; age 35;* born February 15, 1876, in Rose Hill, Amherst, Va. Father temperate but nervous. (During examination patient kept cracking his finger joints.) First thing he remembered was when his colored nurse picked him up after a fall down the front steps. Did not remember what happened but there had been a "knubble" on the upper part of the back of his head ever since he was three years old. His family removed from Rose Hill when he was three. At about six he remembered he was struck in the forehead by his elder brother. His mother told him she sent for the doctor and when he arrived he (Richeson) was still asleep. The scar was located about 2½ inches above the meeting point of the eyebrows. When about seven he was riding on a horse sitting behind his uncle when the horse reared, and both slipped off and his head hit a rock. The hair never grew on that place again and it was so large, being about 3 inches in circumference, that when his father stood over him to teach him fractions he asked him what made him so bald. He had a headache and ringing in his head from the time of this accident until he was twelve years old. His mother told him that during this time he always imagined he was fighting a bear when he went to sleep. He was also hit by

* It is reported that he permitted his parishioners to celebrate his 29th birthday when he was living in Cambridge.

a rock in the hands of a colored boy who was stoning chickens and was unconscious for twenty-four hours or more after he was taken in a wagon to his home fifteen miles away. His people told him that if aroused he talked but he never remembered anything about it.

He said he had pneumonia at fourteen, at fifteen and at eighteen, and pleurisy at twenty-nine. Denied venereal diseases or self abuse. Had been troubled all his life with nocturnal emissions. After one of these at *seventeen years of age he went into an unconscious state* and was in bed for a day or two. At that time he saw a Dr. Cooper of Carrolton, Mo., who gave him something which made him "break out all over." Richeson said the doctor laughed at him and said it was a natural thing to happen. These had become less frequent. His first sex experience was at about twenty-three, when he was invited by a friend to visit two girls at what he said he thought was "some one's home parlor." He claimed the experience took place and was repeated while he was under the influence of whiskey which he drank while there. He remained until 3 A. M. In spite of the fact that he saw this same girl several times later in St. Louis he became very indignant in relating to me that after three years he found a letter written by her which reading as an acrostic made a suggestive request. He said "I was not long in destroying it, I tell you."

The following is another incident in the life of Richeson as related by him:

"When I was twenty-eight, a woman's husband was killed on a train. I was preaching at Kansas City and found crepe on the door and asked if I could do anything. To prove her case against the railroad she had to prove her residence, character, etc., and I made inquiries for her and told what I learned. I had a sex experience with her. After this I keeled over in the pulpit and they say I fell into the deacon's arms, Mark Thompson, of Independence Ave., Kansas City, who later moved to California. Mr. Baker, a deacon, of Budd Park Section, Kansas City, also saw it as did Mrs. —— of Colorado.* This woman came to the house to see how I was and sympathized with me and grabbed me as she went out of the door and insisted on my having intimate relations with her. I do not remember anything only I had two experiences at that time." He later went to tell her it must not occur again when he said "She got mad as the devil, and said I ought to marry her and I lost my head again. My next sex experience was at thirty-four with Avis Linnell in July, 1910." (In a later interview he said May, 1911.) "My engagement was broken July 4; I had been engaged since July 4, 1909. She did not want to announce it until she finished school; said she would get married if I would quit the ministry and go into business. September 1st I saw her again and I sent her home from the Barnstable Fair. In the middle of September I called on her and she gave me my engagement ring back. I wanted to get married then. She wanted me to put it off and to go into something else beside the ministry. In October, 1910, she came to Boston to study music. I saw her occasionally from November, 1910, until May, 1911, say seven or eight times."

* In relating his accounts of the frequent attacks from which he suffered Richeson made it very plain that almost invariably each attack was preceded by either nocturnal emissions or some sex experience. Unpleasant sights or experiences caused a few attacks. He also related many sex experiences and much unpleasant detail which I have omitted.

Richeson went to Hyannis the first of June, 1908, and remained until April 1, 1910, studying at the Theological Seminary in Newton in the meantime. He said he remembered he had one of his attacks June 12, 1909. In 1896 while in St. Louis, Mo., he had the first attack he remembered. He did not recall being out of doors in his night clothes at Potosi, Mo., though a cousin of his, May Townsend, told him that he ran about the barn at night in his night clothes.

He did not remember any attack in El Paso, but said he left there because of the high altitude; that he was nerved up all the time, being four months under a terrible nervous strain. He went to El Paso "to organize a church of persons who had split from the main body." He then thought he might have to give up preaching. Said he had an "attack" at the ——'s in Brookline at one time when he stayed there over night. In Dublin, N. H., in August, 1911, he feared he might do or say something and wandered off. People searched for him. He remembered an attack following the sight of a parishioner who died of tuberculosis; said he had been studying hard and he first saw the body at the funeral. Said he could "stand just so much and then I go to pieces." Early in June, from the 5th to the 10th, 1911, he was in bed most of the time; had many nocturnal emissions; he was tired out. He finished his work on a Saturday and was so tired mentally that he went to a circus, returned and worked until ten; slept until four; continued work and study on Sunday and again went to bed on Monday following a sex experience. He did not like to stay alone because "Sex dreams waked me so." Funerals had always "taken hold" of him; sometimes putting him to bed for days, even funerals of people he had never known. Afterwards it seemed as if everyone he met had been to a funeral. At one time Miss —— telephoned for him and he went to Brookline after a funeral and he "went to pieces again." Did not remember sending for Miss —— of Brookline while in Cambridge. At times he had felt he was "losing his mind." Remembers Dr. Phillips' operation at St. Louis and believes Dr. Phillips thought it was necessary. Did not associate the operation with self mutilation. Did not remember particular letter sent to Miss —— of Georgetown telling of finding himself in the South Station. Was engaged to Miss —— of Georgetown from the Spring until the Fall of the year he went to Texas. She broke the engagement because a "doctor told her he was insane." He minded very much breaking the engagement. Said he never saw or heard of Mrs. Brittain who claimed he was a Mormon Elder and that she had seen him at their meetings.*

In June or July, 1901, he had his first service; only missed seven Sundays in five years. Said he did three men's work while studying, attending country camp meetings and holding constant services "following summer school." Later he returned to the Seminary. July 21 was, he said, the last time he had intimate relations with Miss Linnell. Saw her the last of August when he was in Hyannis; thought he saw her only once that week. Saw her when she came to Boston to study music about the middle of September but had no intimate relations with her then or later. Next he saw her October 11th or 12th at the South Station with her mother whom she went to meet; met her at the station opposite

*There are conflicting stories regarding his association with the Mormons but I did not feel that anything was conclusively proved about this.

the telegraph office. Went from there to Arlington. Saw her the following Saturday, the day of her death.

He said "On Tuesday, the 10th of October, I bought cyanide; bought it to kill a dog and absolutely intended that. Did not buy chloroform because it would smell the house. Man did not charge me anything." Richeson said he never asked him if he could keep a secret or say that a dog was about to have pups. He said "I was with Miss Linnell on Commonwealth Avenue and we sat on a bench, then dined at the Oak Grove Restaurant on Boylston St. I do not recall the absolute details of giving the poison; I did not give a capsule but crystals. I think I threw the rest of the cyanide away on Saturday evening. I never knew who telephoned me. Miss —— of Brookline called me on the telephone. I do not remember what I thought when I heard the news. Miss Linnell had told me she would do something desperate if her condition was not relieved. I was not sure what really happened. I offered to marry her at the last interview; what weighed on me most was that she would rather die than be disgraced; suggested she go away where no one would know, but she refused."

He said "On January 3d or 4th the confession was made. Mr. Morse and Mr. Lee wrote confession and I copied it. I never associated poison with Miss Linnell when I bought it. On reading the confession I said I could not reconcile it with what actually happened.

"Avis Linnell gave me the ring back in September, 1910. I was settled and wanted to get married and she would not get married until I left the church as her sister's family were not church people and opposed her marrying a minister. I think I met Miss —— of Brookline before I met Miss Linnell. I did not go to Hyannis until June, 1908. I think I met Miss —— in 1907. A friend named Pierce asked me to take him to call on the —— girls in Brookline in the fall of 1910. I had met them both at receptions but I did not know one from the other. —— was the name of one (I did not know which one). I wrote to —— asking if I could call. I think I found out that —— was the name of the other, and I felt I could not ask to bring Pierce. I told him my heart failed me and I could not ask to bring him. I did not discover which was —— and which was ——. I received letters in two different handwritings signed either —— or ——, I cannot remember which. Yes, they were always signed ——, I remember now. They later said they thought they would have a little fun with me. I first called in October, 1910, and in November I took Pierce (Lawyer Dunbar has my letters and he can tell you the very dates). I then told Pierce that I had done him a social favor, that he could go all he wanted to but I did not believe in that courting business, that I was not going any more.

"In December I received a note from —— for Pierce and I to go to dinner with them. I did not know then which was —— and which was ——, and it was when sitting at dinner Mrs. —— called one —— in asking her to sit down and that was the first time I knew which was which. About the middle of February Pierce and I took them to the Symphony Concert and after we returned to the house was the first time I saw her to say a word no one else could hear. I told her I wanted to see her the next Tuesday and wanted to see her alone.

I then saw her once a week up to March when the engagement was announced.

"In July, Avis Linnell became pregnant. I had had relations with her since May. In May she threw her arms around me and said 'I do not care who you are going to marry. I am going to have you just the same,' and I remembered what a man in Kansas City said to me, 'A man will go to Hell for a girl if she looks at you that way.' I gritted my teeth and snapped my fingers and said I would not, and determined to come away but when leaving I just felt the devil had me. The next thing I remember was at daylight the next morning. I woke up with a terrible headache and I had had one of those experiences which always preceded an attack. I had no recollection of coming home or going to bed. I dreamed I was on the back of a car. I went to sleep again but woke up to find the same thing happened. The next day I felt so miserable I could not study or make calls so took a car to Revere Beach. I felt as I always did after these and did not want to see anyone or do anything. I was living in Cambridge and when I returned I found a note from Miss Linnell to ask if I got home all right; that she thought I was ill when I left." He said she told him he fell in a chair and seemed unconscious and she poured some cold water on him and he jumped, then took his glasses, put them in the case and threw them across the room and stumbled downstairs. "I know I had a feeling I must go home before I became unconscious or I would ruin her. She sat on the arm of my chair and I knew what I did but I could not stop. I then felt I must give up everything and marry her and give up Miss —— of Brookline who I had been engaged to since March. Miss Linnell knew of the engagement to Miss —— which had been announced in the papers."

He said relations persisted with Miss Linnell up until after July, 1911; on all occasions every precaution was taken to protect her. "Although I saw her frequently it was not until October that she told me that she was pregnant. She admitted at this time that she had been to a woman doctor, a friend of hers, in attempt to be relieved from her present difficulty, and at that time a solution of potash was recommended for a douche." Regarding the purchase of the drug, Richeson made the following statement: "I went to Hahn's drug store (the same day I met Mr. and Mrs. —— of Brookline and took supper with them) and asked for something to kill a dog that was messing up my room. He suggested chloroform. I said it would smell up the room too much. He then suggested arsenic but immediately said it would make the dog fat. He then suggested cyanide of potash. I said what and he said potash crystals. I told Miss Linnell I had these crystals to kill a dog. She said 'I have used those for a douche at the recommendation of a girl friend of mine on St. Botolph St., and I would not mind drinking some if they would make me all right.' This girl she said she met at a doctor's office on Tremont Street. I had a glass bottle with two pieces in it and I gave her one. I told her Hahn told me it was poison. She said 'Oh you are fooling.' I first offered to give up everything and go to New York or Ohio and marry her after making a clean breast of the whole thing to Miss ——. She refused as she said she would not have her mother know her condition. I then urged her to see my physician, Dr. Gardner. I left her at 2.30 and at 8 P. M. I was called on the telephone and asked if I was Miss Linnell's fiance. I said no. The person telephoning excused herself and said Miss Linnell had died suddenly. I never told Miss —— of Brookline anything about my conversation with Miss Linnell or about my relations with her. It is not natural for a man to." He denied any relations with Miss —— of Brookline and his statement was later substantiated. He said "They tell me I was taken up to court and copied and signed a confession but I do not remember it. Morse hypnotizes me. I just feel I shall die if I sit under him."

When he was questioned as to the reported self mutilation on Dec. 20, 1911, at the Charles St. Jail, he said: "I fixed my toe at 8 P. M. The knife was left with me. The guards gave me medicine to make me sleep. The next thing I remember a man was sitting on my chest, another at his feet and a light was thrown on the floor and one said 'there is what he did it with.'" In relating this he seemed amused and smiling. He said "I think the man sharpened the tin and put it there to protect himself" and that he heard one man whisper to another "Where is the knife?" With earnestness he said "I shall think to my dying day that two men came in and did it, the same men who sat on me."

I made six examinations of Clarence V. T. Richeson in April and May. He was tall and emaciated. His face was pale, asymmetrical, the left side showing a lack of development. Chin rather long. The head on the frontal occipital measurement was 209 m. m.; biparietal 154 m. m. This made the length, breadth index of the head 73. All indices below 78 are considered Dolichocephalic, 80 being the average. Back

CLARENCE V. T. RICHESON

Taken at Charles Street Jail, April, 1912.

of a vertical line drawn through the center of the ears the head was rather undeveloped being nearly flat. His upper jaw was under-developed drawing the alae of his nose in and up, giving the nose a very long appearance. The cheek bones were high and prominent, lower jaw prominent, chin long. Eyebrows heavy and irregularly arched. Eyes dark, and during the second examination reacted to light and accommodation. Small Darwin tubercle on each ear. Testing with steel points I found that there was anesthesia to pain on the entire left half of his body to the left of a line clearly drawn through the center of his forehead and face, chest and abdomen, complete hemi-anesthesia of the trunk and legs while on the arms anesthesia to pain was only found on an area on the outside of the right hand and arm from a line drawn between the second and third fingers to the elbow, front and back, which included the fourth and fifth or little finger. Punctures made with points violent enough to bring blood elicited no response from Richeson while within half an inch of the median line point pricks caused extreme pain. These tests were made in the presence of two people including Sheriff Quinn and it was not possible for the patient to have known what was being done when the tests were made for he was blindfolded and I was working from behind him much of the time.

The hearing and vision on the side of the anesthesia was also blunted, the distance he heard on the left being one-third less than on the right and his vision on test of a certain size type was 89 inches with his right eye and 69 with the left, but the knee jerks and other reflexes were normal. It was impossible for Richeson to meet the tests for coordination. Dermographia was very marked. Letters traced on his back and other portions of his body at the end of twenty minutes to half an hour were clear and like whipcords of bright red.

While I was testing his pupils which were contracted he said: "Oh Dr. McCoomb and another minister examined me a few days ago." His pulse was 93 and soft; his tongue rather beefy and on extension persistently deviated to the left of the median line. He had a tremendously heavy head of black hair, very coarse and wavy, parted on the side but difficult to keep in place. It grew well down to the outer eyebrows almost over the temple; in fact almost met the eyebrows; while the front of his forehead was rather high. His nose was pointed and asymmetrical and extended down in an irregular line; he denied that it was ever broken but said that it bled nearly every day. His teeth, regular and strong, the lower shutting somewhat over the upper and the surface of the upper and lower teeth much worn. The whites of his eyes showed below the pupils. When talking with him and as examination proceeded the pupils became very much dilated and did not then react. His arms were 34 inches long, hands heavy and fingers thick and stubby with extreme tremor on extension; in fact there was a constant tremor of hands and slightly of the head. His fingers were stained which he said was the result of smoking a few cigarettes each day at the Jail, before he came there he said he smoked only cigars or a pipe. Standing on his feet with his eyes shut did not disturb him but when asked to assume the Romberg position with one foot raised he found it impossible. His coordination was extremely poor; after several efforts he found it absolutely impossible to meet the tests for coordination. His knee jerks were normal. His answers showed retardation, his voice being slow and low. He was dressed neatly but frequently brushed the lapel of his coat with his hand as if brushing something off, and often during the examination he looked himself over apparently to see if his personal appearance was all right. I visited Richeson seven times and spent the greater part of six days in my examinations of him.

It was reported that Richeson had offered his jailers $100 at two different times to buy and bring poison to him. When I asked Sheriff Quinn if the report was true he answered "I had reason to suspect Richeson was preparing to commit suicide a few days ago (in May, 1912) and I removed everything from his cell and placed him in another cell by himself. After his removal he gave a blank stare at first and then went to pieces, became noisy and violent and had great difficulty in getting his breath." In describing this attack at the Jail, Sheriff Quinn interpreted it as being caused by his removal from one cell to another. Dr. Cilley was called and gave him "a good dose of morphine to bring him to himself and relieve him of his sufferings." Sheriff Quinn said that when Richeson came out of the attack he told him that there was a great ball starting in his stomach and rising to his throat. After a few hours he returned to his cell and to his "Man Friday," Butts. Sheriff Quinn had Richeson closely observed during his incarceration and said "I do not think he has faked fits once since he has been here and there has been no attempt to fake insanity."

I was permitted to make all of my examinations after my first in the large library of the Jail, alone excepting when accompanied by my stenographer or when I sent for officers to question them. After my final examination of Richeson I read my findings to him. He listened attentively and said "I do not want to be made out insane" and added that he thought I had "been fair" in my examinations and statements, and if the Governor did not commute his sentence on my report he was willing to die to protect others.

Not until April 25 did Richeson ask for a commutation of the death sentence when he sent the following letter:

Boston, Mass., April 25, 1912.

To his Excellency the Governor and
The Honorable Council

I respectfully request that the sentence of death pronounced against me by the Supreme Court for the County of Suffolk be commuted to imprisonment for life and I leave the presentation of this request and the reasons in support thereof to my counsel.

Clarence V. T. Richeson.

I presented my final report to Governor Foss on May 13, as follows:

64 Beacon St.,
Boston, Mass.. May 13, 1912.

Governor Eugene N. Foss,
State House, Boston, Mass.
Dear Sir:

In accordance with your request I have examined Clarence V. T. Richeson to ascertain whether he is sane or insane and if insane to designate the form of insanity from which he is suffering and to furnish you the data upon which I base my diagnosis. My opinion is based upon six examinations of Richeson, interviews with Sheriff Quinn in charge of the prisoner and with Mr. Morse his counsel and others in a position to observe him, and examination of all letters and affidavits relating to the case.

At my first examination, made on April 30, Richeson was reticent and in such mental and physical condition that the physical tests were not satisfactory. After my examinations of May 1 and May 2, it was very evident that he was suffering from Hysterical Insanity.

I then left at your office a preliminary report stating this was my opinion but that I wished to corroborate it by further physical tests and by examinaion of the affidavits in the case which up to this time I had never seen.

I therefore submit my final report and opinion which is that Clarence V. T. Richeson is unquestionably suffering from Hysterical Insanity; an incurable form of mental disease, being chronic and progressive, which runs a slow course and does not materially disturb the intellectual faculties until its termination in dementia. It is usually founded on a bad heredity, and fastens itself on individuals who have stigmata of degeneration. The basis of Hysterical Insanity is degeneration.

In Richeson's bad heredity, as clearly proved by numerous affidavits, and his stigmata of degeneration, Hysterical Insanity found just the soil necessary in which to develop. There is much in his history to show that he is mentally diseased, and at times irresponsible.

Affidavits from physicians who have attended Richeson for many years in different parts of the country describe attacks which are so characteristic of Hystero-Epilepsy that a mistake cannot be made. Just preceding the activity of those attacks, during the attacks and for a subsequent period covering twelve to twenty-four hours and sometimes even longer, Richeson would be irresponsible.

According to Bianchi, Paton, Dana and Church-Peterson, Hysterical Insanity is a chronic, functional disorder characterized by *nervous crises of an emotional, convulsive or other nature,* and by an interparoxysmal state in which certain marks or stigmata are present. It is essentially a psychosis.

The stigmata of hysterical insanity are sensory, motor and psychic.

In hysterical insanity the sensory disorders are anæsthesias and hyperæsthesias.

Anæsthesias may occur in three forms:—involving one-half the body, involving segments of the body or involving patches of the body.

A corresponding hyperæsthesia or morbid sensibility of the nerves is often found.

The subject is often incapable of performing several acts simultaneously. Voluntary, intentional acts are usually weakened. Movements are retarded and incoordinate. There is a *tendency to rigidities or contractures.* In hysterical patients local headaches, tremor and *temporary feelings of weakness in arm or leg are common.*

Psychic stigmata include: 1—Disturbances of the attention; 2—Anomalies of emotion; 3—General interference with normal, mental functions—particularly noticeable in disturbances of memory and in the vivid play of the imagination. Many patients *forget only facts connected with the train of thought, while retaining a logical and uninterrupted recollection of others.*

Impaired volition in the subjects reduces power of mental concentration and *renders them vacillating, impulsive and lacking in determination. Impressionability is often extremely developed and practically constitutes a mental stigma.*

Underlying the hysterical mental state there is a condition of *suggestibility* by means of which ideas and impressions easily become fixed and dominate the mind. Those unfortunate persons who are its victims are therefore creatures of impulse, *controlled by their feelings and not by reason.* In male hysterical insanity the tendencies are to morbid emotionalism, eroticism, exaggerated suggestibility, certain kinds of delusive suggestions, occasional threats, or apparent attempts at self injury or suicide.

Of the predisposing causes, heredity is the most important. In about 75 per cent there is history of some neuroses or psychoses in the parents.

Hallucinations are associated with marked emotional anomalies and are accompanied in many cases by *attacks of pain. Delirium* may be colored by marked sexual irritation.

The hysterical subject has an infantile mind,—but sexually is an adult. Hysterical insanity is *often accompanied by shameless sexual excesses* carried out in an impulsive manner. *Certainly the sexual instinct—precocious, perverted or repressed—furnishes preponderating importance of the sexual life in the genesis of hysterical insanity.*

The most common of the paroxysms of hysterical insanity are outbursts of laughing and *crying,* and after this, *motor disturbances* in the shape of convulsions of various types. The emotional crises are characterized by appearing *without* any good cause.

According to Church, there are four stages covering attacks of Hystero-Epilepsy. According to Dana, there are five stages as follows:

1st. The Prodromata consisting of irritability and depression which may last from several hours to a day.

2d. The Epileptoid stage, which ushers in the actual attack, during which patient *loses consciousness* and often *falls to the ground.*

3d. The phase of *contortions* or so-called grand movements when the subject suffers from tonic and clonic spasm and *writhes* as *if in severe pain.*

4th. The emotional phase where the patient experiences and often expresses intense feelings of *anger* or other *violent passion.*

5th. The last stage is one of delirium, during which there is a great deal of mental excitement of a *depressing* character which is usually followed by a great *physical weakness* and amnesia or *loss of memory,* which may extend over several hours and often several days. *Hallucinations* often occur together with religious ideas. Patients are frequently given to somnambulism.

We might quote several authorities to prove that an interest in religious matters is symptomatic. Some of the patients at large are for a time *active workers in church matters* or in public or private benevolences.

The symptoms of the inter-paroxysmal state are as follows: Between the crises the patient may have been in a fair condition of general health, but usually presents certain definite, chronic manifestations of the disease. The most characteristic are sensory symptoms, paralyses and contractures.

The somatic (physical) phenomena of hysterical subjects are therefore clearly psychic, and we must consider them as the expression of a psychic personality whose functions are performed defectively and abnormally. The predominant note is one of exaggerative excitability.

The *memory is halting, unreliable and sometimes confused.* An hysterical subject lacks the faculty to bring an event into relation with its circumstances of time, place and person.

Janet also regards Hysteria as a mental disease. Dr. W. A. Taylor, of the New Jersey State Hospital, claims that hysteria is connected with 10 per cent of all male admissions to that hospital.

Corroborative of the above, in addition to the heredity Richeson revealed on examination disturbances in sensibility which would not be accounted for by any organic lesion, the left half of his body being anesthetic, and the area being sharply defined by a median line drawn down the centre of his body. In addition to this hemianesthesia, there is a zone on his right hand and arm clearly defined on a line which separates the third from the fourth finger to the elbow. The fourth and fifth fingers, and above them, as is the case on the left side, where I made punctures in the skin deep enough to draw blood, elicited no response, while the areas opposite them, or outside of these lines, are so hypersensitive that he jumps at the slightest touch. These tests were without warning, from behind him, or in the front, with his eyes blindfolded.

*It is my opinion that Richeson is and always was able to distinguish between right and wrong, except during the four or five stages of his attacks of Hystero-Epilepsy.**

This case is unusual, in that the history and affidavits in Richeson's case have never been passed upon and his responsibility determined by a court or jury.

In forming my opinion I have considered the portions of the affidavits of physicians and others which I consider most important in determining Richeson's mental condition.†

L. Vernon Briggs.

* Although at the time of these examinations the term Hystero-Epilepsy was in common use to-day most authors writing on this subject would undoubtedly prefer the term Hysteria with Epileptoid manifestations complicating the picture.

† I here gave extracts from the said affidavits which I considered were diagnostic, but which would be only a repetition of what the reader has become acquainted with in Chapter III.

CHAPTER V

RICHESON'S REMOVAL TO MASSACHUSETTS STATE PRISON, MAY 14, 1912. GOVERNOR FOSS REFUSES COMMUTATION. RICHESON AGAIN HAS HYSTERICS WITH HALLUCINATIONS AND DELIRIUM. HIS EXECUTION, MAY 21, 1912

On May 14, 1912, Richeson was called from his cell and told that he was to be taken to Charlestown. His transfer from Charles St. Jail to the State Prison was made in eight minutes.

On arriving he was met by Warden Bridges and other officers to whom he was introduced after which he shook hands with the officers who brought him to the State Prison. The officers who accompanied him were serious and seemed sad at the parting and Sheriff Quinn as he was leaving said to Warden Bridges that he was so deeply moved he could hardly keep from crying. Leaving the group of officers Richeson did not utter a word until he arrived in the corridor of the "Death House" when still apparently unmoved he stooped, patted and spoke to Warden Bridges' French bull terrier "Jip."

On May 16, 1912, Governor Foss decided he would not refer Richeson's petition for clemency to his Council. He had talked with the different members and knew some of them were strongly opposed to commutation, one, it is said, having stated that even if Richeson was found insane he would vote against commutation.

Immediately following Governor Foss' decision he issued, through his secretary, Dudley M. Holman, the following statement for the press:

STATEMENT BY GOVERNOR FOSS

Executive clemency will not be extended in the case of Clarence V. T. Richeson. The prisoner was sentenced upon his own confession and without a trial for a crime which it appears impossible that any normal man could commit.

After his confession and sentence a plea of insanity was set up by his counsel and strongly supported by affidavits extending over his life. The character of these affidavits left no other course for the Governor than to submit these and the prisoner himself to an examination by our leading alienists, in order to protect the Commonwealth from the charge that the man was actually insane when the deed was committed as well as at the present time.

The evidence shows that Richeson's family is heavily afflicted with insanity, that he himself is neurotic, a somnambulist and a neurasthenic; that he is subject to extreme emotional disturbances, marked by loss of memory, which two alienists have diagnosed as hysterical insanity, one physician adding the alternative term of hysterical delirium, and the majority opinion indicating that these attacks are hysterical attacks marked by extreme emotional disturbances of brief duration, with loss of memory during the attack and for a varying period following it.

The evidence, however, while clearly revealing these attacks indicates that his crime was not committed by him during such an attack. Therefore, while there is some divergence of opinion among the alienists as to whether these attacks indicate actual insanity, there is sufficient ground for the conclusion that he is accountable for his crime, and that the exercise of Executive clemency in this instance would be contrary to the public good.

The affidavits and medical evidence as to Richeson's unfavorable heredity, his lapses of consciousness and his attacks of delirium, are too voluminous to include in this statement, and are not suited to publication.

The alienists referred to are: Dr. Edward B. Lane, and Dr. I. H. Coriat, acting for the defense; Dr. L. Vernon Briggs, acting at the personal request of the Governor; and Drs. Henry R. Stedman, George T. Tuttle and Henry P. Frost, acting as a commission for the Commonwealth.

Governor Foss' decision not to refer Richeson's petition or the alienists' report to his Council removed

Richeson's last chance and the next morning, May 17, at 9.30 A. M., his counsel Mr. Morse and the Rev. Herbert S. Johnson of the Warren Ave. Baptist Church visited him and broke the news to him. Mr. Morse said: "I have done all that lies in my power to save you from death but my efforts have been unavailing and the Governor has positively refused to refer your petition to the Council." "Richeson was standing when I broke the news to him," said Mr. Morse, "and aside from a slight dropping of his head and a dejected look there was absolutely nothing in his manner to indicate he was conscious of the fate that awaited him."

Rev. Mr. Johnson said: "Mr. Richeson received the communication from Mr. Morse with the same spirit of fortitude which he has exhibited from the beginning. He stated to me that his principal thought as he faced execution was not for himself but for the sorrow of his family and friends."

Four hours were then spent in discussing matters preparatory to the end and when his visitors left Mr. Morse is reported to have said "I would almost wish to change places with Richeson so hard was my errand."

Philip R. Dunbar, one of Richeson's counsel, is reported to have said "I consider that Governor Foss lost the point of the petition for commutation. Public sentiment has overtopped everything else in this issue. . . . Sentiment is not Justice. Justice is an abstract thing when weighed in the legal scales but when clemency is sought it becomes an issue involving the rights of the individual. . . . That he is irresponsible is my belief. . . . What harm would it have been for Gov. Foss to refer the matter to the Executive Council for that body to decide?"

CLARENCE V. T. RICHESON

One week before his execution.

The following night a death watch was assigned to Richeson. Rev. Herbert S. Johnson and the Prison Chaplain Herbert W. Stebbins volunteered and were accepted. One or both were with him from this time until he was electrocuted. The devotion of these men was splendid and they grew to know the minister and man and it was undoubtedly their influence and companionship that enabled him to go to the chair without a tremor.

Richeson at once began to make preparations for his death. He requested that his "body should not be dissected" but be sent to Virginia and be placed in a grave beside his mother's. His desires were communicated to his father who telegraphed Mr. Morse the next day:

Amherst, Va., May 18, 1912.

Tell Clarence if it is his wish he shall be buried at home. Give him my deepest love. Lee is writing you.

(Signed) T. V. Richeson.

Richeson said "If I could only see my old father before I go, I could die much easier. It might be asking too much to have him come here."

He gave Mr. Morse his watch and chain and Masonic charm to be sent to his father and his books to be distributed to his family and friends. His sister, Louise V. Richeson, again came on from Saranac Lake, N. Y., and visited him and plead with Governor Foss for his reprieve. She was described as tall, with a long chin and determined mouth, and pleasing personality. His brother, Douglas L. Richeson, came on for the fifth time from Chicago. He plead in vain with the Governor and then waited for the body of his brother.

The evening of May 17th Richeson had another attack of Hysteria with hallucinations and delusions. The

Prison Chaplain was talking quietly with him when his counsel, Mr. Morse, arrived. Almost immediately Richeson began to act queerly. The two guards became much alarmed. Mr. Morse who had seen Richeson in these attacks reassured them. In a few minutes Warden Bridges arrived and then Richeson was lying on his bed moaning and shrieking. He cried out that two men were watching him, constantly pursuing him, that two pairs of eyes were constantly focused upon him burning into his heart. He was in a semi-conscious state. Warden Bridges sent for Dr. Fred L. Lyons the Prison Physician who remained with Richeson until nearly midnight. He is reported to have said on leaving "Richeson does not appear to be rational or conscious. He is delirious and is talking about two men watching him and is moaning and crying. At first he was hysterical and screamed. He has not eaten anything since morning. I have administered some medicine." Richeson did not recover from this attack so as to be fully conscious until 11 o'clock the next morning, Saturday.

On Sunday morning, May 19, he was told by his watchers that he still had at least twenty-four hours to live. He replied "I am at peace with my Maker and ready to die. The sooner I go to the chair the better." He later asked Warden Bridges if he could not conduct the service in the Prison Chapel as it was his last Sunday on earth and that he would like to address the prisoners and tell them how to live properly. He was told that the rules of the Prison would not permit him to conduct the service or address the prisoners. He then asked if he could hold a service in his cell, which request was granted. With him were the Revs. Johnson and

Stebbins and the two prison guards. In a low voice he delivered the final sermon of his life. For his text he chose the 23rd Psalm, as follows:

The Lord is my Shepherd, I shall not want. He leadeth me beside the still waters.

He restoreth my soul. He leadeth me in the paths of righteousness for His name's sake.

Yea, though I walk through the valley of the shadow of death, I will fear no evil, for Thou art with me. Thy rod and Thy staff they comfort me.

Thou preparest a table before me in the presence of mine enemies. Thou anointest my head with oil. My cup runneth over.

Surely goodness and mercy shall follow me all the days of my life and I shall dwell in the House of the Lord for ever.

Immediately following the reading by his spiritual advisers of further quotations from the Bible, Richeson said:

This is Sunday my last on earth. If I had lived a righteous life I should today be delivering a sermon from the pulpit of my church in Cambridge instead of being caged here awaiting a felon's death.

But although I have sinned greatly, God is with me. For I have deeply repented.

I feel that it is fitting, indeed I feel that it is my duty to offer up a sermon before I die and this my last Sunday is the proper day.

He then entered on what Rev. Dr. Johnson declared was "a most beautiful exposition of the 23rd Psalm and brought in the scenes of his childhood." He said:

I again see the silvery brook that flows through the meadow near my old father's house. The stately pines whose whispers lulled me to sleep when I was enjoying blissful childhood.

Again he said in speaking of the shadow of death "I know that death is but a shadow for I have repented." He repeated many psalms at the service and during the day, including the 27th, 86th and 91st, and repeated from memory whole chapters from the Bible—Revelations XXII and many others.

Later in the day when Chaplain Stebbins was reading from the Scriptures "For now we see through a glass darkly; but then face to face," Richeson raised his voice and sang from memory in a clear. smooth full tone the following gospel hymn:

SOMETIME WE'LL UNDERSTAND.

Not now, but in the coming years
  It may be in the better land
We'll read the meaning of our tears,
  And there sometime, we'll understand.

Chorus:

Then trust in God thro' all the days;
  Fear not for He doth hold thy hand
Tho' dark thy way, still sing and praise;
  Sometime, sometime, we'll understand.

We'll catch the broken threads again,
  And finish what we here begun;
Heav'n will the mysteries explain
  And then, ah then, we'll understand.

We'll know why clouds instead of sun
  Were over many a cherish'd plan;
Why song has ceased when scarce begun;
  Tis there, sometime, we'll understand.

Why what we long for most of all
  Eludes so oft our eager hand;
Why hopes are crushed and castles fall,
  Up there, sometime, we'll understand.

God knows the way, He holds the key;
  He guides us with unerring hand;
Sometime with tearless eyes we'll see;
  Yes there, up there, we'll understand.

Just as he finished the first verse Warden Bridges, upon whom hitherto he had turned his back, entered and Richeson addressed him as follows: "O-o-ah, ah, Genl. Bridges, won't you join me in song?" Ignoring the invitation Warden Bridges asked "How are you feeling, Sir?" Richeson's answer was "I am ready to go whenever you say. I shall not make any trouble. You need have no further fear of any outbreak or collapse on my part. Since my attack on Friday night I have felt much better mentally and physically and I know that I will behave like a man. But I would that that time were soon." He then renewed his invitation to the Warden who declined saying his singing days were over. Richeson then sang the second and other verses alone. His listeners were moved to tears and could not join him. At the end of each verse he sang the chorus with all the strength and feeling he possessed. Warden Bridges said he had had numberless experiences but that he never had been so stirred as he was when Richeson sang this hymn. The wives and children of the Prison officials who liver near the walls of the Prison were gathered on the lawn within the Prison Yard enjoying the cool air for the sun had just set. They, too, heard the voice so clear and strong that they were able to distinguish the words, but little did they realize it was from the man who was so soon to pay the extreme penalty.

Among the many sermons preached on the last Sunday which referred to Richeson was one at Chipman Hall by Rev. F. H. Holt of Reading, in which he said:

> I ask for the mercy of God and that the loving kindness of humanity be shown toward him who is about to be put to death, inasmuch as he has repented and asked to be forgiven. I hope that the spirit of forgiveness will be manifested toward the erring brother.

Rev. F. A. Wiggin, who was described as the "psychic pastor" of Unity Church, Huntington Avenue, preached on "Richeson Electrocuted. Then What?"

During Sunday Richeson asked many times for water to wash his face and hands and a comb with which he frequently straightened out his hair and he also asked his guard to manicure his nails as he was not allowed to use anything pointed. Many hours of his last day on earth were spent in singing hymns and repeating quotations from the Bible. Among the hymns he sang are the following:

"My Faith Looks up to Thee."
"Nearer, My God, to Thee."
"Rock of Ages."
"What a Friend we have in Jesus."
"There is a Fountain Filled in Blood."

Rev. Mr. Johnson felt up to the end that Richeson was insane and Mrs. Linnell, Avis' mother, is reported as saying "I forgive Mr. Richeson of this dreadful thing. It is my belief he went to the electric chair an insane man and that he has been mentally irresponsible for some time past." Deacons of his church and many others who knew him well expressed the same belief.

On Monday morning, May 20, Warden Bridges entered Richeson's cell. Richeson inquired when the execution would take place and when told probably that night he asked if it could not be arranged sooner saying he was anxious "to have it over with as soon as possible." Later the Catholic Priest of the Prison, Rev. Father Michael J. Murphy for whom Richeson felt a strong attachment, called and he received the Father cordially.

At 6.45 P. M. he was prepared for the chair, a change of clothes, the shaving of a place on his head and a slit made in the left leg of the trousers. He calmly allowed these preparations to proceed. He had already written many notes of farewell to those nearest and dearest to him, one to Mrs. Linnell and one to his fiancée in Brookline. After the preparations were completed he resumed the singing of hymns and repeated many prayers. He also arranged for his funeral, how he wanted it conducted and where, and selected the hymns he wanted sung. Among the many letters he received on this his last day was one postmarked "Station N, New York City. May 19, 3 P. M." It contained no clue to the sender but only a powder enclosed in a small envelope marked "Headache powder." Analysis showed it to be cyanide of potassium, the same poison he gave to Miss Linnell.

At midnight following the evening of May 20, Richeson was standing with his hands resting on the bars of his cell his head thrown back singing "Safe in the Arms of Jesus," his face almost transfigured by the exaltation he felt while singing. Sitting directly in front of him huddled in a chair with a half lighted cigar clutched in his fingers was William A. Morse, his counsel, plainly laboring under a frightful mental strain. On the left with a Bible open in his outstretched hands, erect though plainly moved, was Richeson's spiritual adviser, the Rev. Herbert S. Johnson. To the right, the Prison Chaplain, a Bible clutched to his breast. Both were singing but Richeson's voice was strong above either of them. Guards approached but hesitated a moment until the last words—"For I know whate'er befall me Jesus doeth all things well"—were sung. When they approached, Richeson turned and looking Attorney Morse squarely in the eyes stretched out his hand and said "Goodbye." He then said goodbye to the two ministers.

Just past midnight, or at 12.08 A. M., Deputy Warden Allen appeared. The death warrant was read to Richeson and he was asked if he was ready. "I am ready" responded Richeson and with head erect looking straight ahead and with a firm tread he walked forward unassisted with a guard on either side. In his march to the chair the Prison Chaplain preceded the condemned man reading from the 51st Psalm in a deep, solemn voice which rang out through the chamber. "Have mercy upon me O God according to thy loving kindness; according unto the multitude of Thy tender mercies blot out my transgressions. Wash me thoroughly from mine iniquity and cleanse me from my sin for I acknowledge my transgressions and my sin is ever before me." Rev. Mr. Stebbins continuing read from II Timothy the 12th verse:

> I know whom I have believed and am persuaded that He is able to keep that which I have committed unto Him against that day.

Then turning to Hebrew he read:

> For he is able also to save them to the uttermost that come unto God by him seeing that he ever liveth to make intercession for them.

As the last quotation was being read Richeson reached the electric chair, turned half around, then settled himself slowly into it and the four guards strapped him in and Edwin B. Currier the official executioner who was also electrician or Chief Engineer of the Massachusetts General Hospital adjusted the face and head straps. Richeson is said to be the only man ever executed in Massachusetts who talked calmly and with a clear, steady voice after being strapped in the electric chair.

With the witnesses all gathered in the death chamber

and just as the last straps were being adjusted the Rev. Herbert S. Johnson stepped forward and asked Richeson the following questions which he answered in a clear voice:

"Would you like to confess Christ as your Savior before these witnesses?"

"I do confess Christ as my Savior."

"Have you the peace of God in your heart in this hour?"

"I have the peace of God in this hour."

"Does Christ give you the strength you need in this hour?"

"Christ gives me the strength I need."

"Do you repent of your sins?"

"I do."

"Have you the peace of God in your heart?"

"God will take care of my soul and I pray for all."

"Are you willing to die for Jesus' sake?"

"I am willing to die."

Just as he uttered the word "die," Warden Bridges tapped the stone floor with his gold headed black cane which had been used so many times as a signal to the executioner who switched on the electric current and at 12.17 Drs. McLaughlin, McGrath and Butler pronounced Richeson legally dead. The penalty exacted by the laws of Massachusetts had been paid and all hope of studying this abnormal man for the purpose of aborting criminal tendencies in others of his kind was wiped out in a few seconds. An autopsy of the body was performed and then his remains were taken by train to Lynchburg, Va., and to the Amherst Court House, thence in a springless farm wagon over a rough country road to its final resting place, where the brothers and near relatives acted as bearers and assisted in lowering the remains and filling the grave with earth. Could anything have been more destructive to this branch of science? Could Society have conceived any better plan to thwart the work of preventing the development of other men of this kind?

INDEX